Bible
Speaks
today

the message of

LEVITICUS

Series editors:
Alec Motyer (OT)
John Stott (NT)
Derek Tidball (Bible Themes)

T0340601

the message of

LEVITICUS

Free to be holy
Revised edition

Derek Tidball

INTER-VARSITY PRESS
36 Causton Street, London SW1P 4ST, England
Email: ivp@ivpbooks.com
Website: www.ivpbooks.com

First published 2005
Reprinted 2007, 2008, 2010, 2011
This edition published 2021

British Library Cataloguing-in-Publication Data
A catalogue record for this book is available from the British Library.

ISBN 978–1–78974–295–4
eBook ISBN 978–1–78359–630–0

Set in 9.5/13pt Karmina
Typeset in Great Britain by CRB Associates, Potterhanworth, Lincolnshire
Printed and bound in Great Britain by Ashford Colour Press Ltd, Gosport, Hampshire

Produced on paper from sustainable sources.

*Inter-Varsity Press publishes Christian books that are true to the Bible
and that communicate the gospel, develop discipleship and strengthen the church
for its mission in the world.*

*IVP originated within the Inter-Varsity Fellowship, now the Universities and Colleges
Christian Fellowship, a student movement connecting Christian Unions in universities
and colleges throughout Great Britain, and a member movement of the International
Fellowship of Evangelical Students. Website: www.uccf.org.uk. That historic association
is maintained, and all senior IVP staff and committee members subscribe
to the UCCF Basis of Faith.*

Contents

Bible Speaks Today

GENERAL PREFACE

The Bible Speaks Today describes three series of expositions, based on the books of the Old and New Testaments, and on Bible themes that run through the whole of Scripture. Each series is characterized by a threefold ideal:

- to expound the biblical text with accuracy
- to relate it to contemporary life, and
- to be readable.

These books are, therefore, not 'commentaries', for the commentary seeks rather to elucidate the text than to apply it, and tends to be a work rather of reference than of literature. Nor, on the other hand, do they contain the kinds of 'sermons' that attempt to be contemporary and readable without taking Scripture seriously enough. The contributors to The Bible Speaks Today series are all united in their convictions that God still speaks through what he has spoken, and that nothing is more necessary for the life, health and growth of Christians than that they should hear what the Spirit is saying to them through his ancient – yet ever modern – Word.

ALEC MOTYER
JOHN STOTT
DEREK TIDBALL
Series editors

Author's preface

Almost ten years ago I wrote a little commentary on Leviticus aimed for use by small groups for Crossway Bible Guides. It has been a pleasure to return to Leviticus and study it afresh in order to write this volume for the Bible Speaks Today series. I remain convinced that Leviticus is fundamental to our understanding of God and of the Christian faith. Without it, so much else in the Bible simply makes no sense. It is, therefore, essential that we encourage people to study it and hear its message. I am also convinced that Leviticus does not deserve its bad reputation and that if Christians could overcome their prejudices against it, they would soon find it yielding rich spiritual fruit. Paul's claim that 'all Scripture is God-breathed and is useful' certainly includes Leviticus. For these reasons I am also convinced that Leviticus is a book that can be preached, and needs to be, to congregations today.

A great deal of scholarly work has been done on Leviticus in recent years. It is not the purpose of this volume to engage in scholarly debates, but I have tried to acknowledge them in the notes, and those who wish to pursue matters can refer to the publications mentioned there. A textual critic will be able to discover a number of places where I have changed my mind since writing the Crossway Guide, but none of them are of crucial significance, and many, I hope, make for further clarification of the text and its meaning.

My thanks are due, as always, to a number of people who have helped in the writing of this volume. The book was written during a term's sabbatical leave from the London School of Theology and I deeply appreciate the extra burdens my colleagues shared during my absence, especially those on the College Executive and my personal assistant, Jenny Aston. Andrew Stobart read the earlier part of the manuscript and contributed many helpful comments. It has been a pleasure to work again with Phil Duce of IVP and to benefit from his detailed eye and personal support. And Alec Motyer, the Series Editor, has proved once more to be a great teacher, a wonderful encouragement, a perceptive critic and an exacting editor, for all of which I am deeply grateful. Thank you, too, to my wife and son who proved a great support during the writing of another book and who provided a wonderfully happy home environment in which to write. Not even the drums were able to destroy my concentration!

I have valued the BST Old and New Testament volumes so much in my own preaching ministry over the years that I found it a privilege to be asked to contribute this volume, even if it was one of the less easy books of the Old Testament on which to write! I dare to pray that, like the volumes from which I have profited, this one may be faithful to the text and help to unlock its message for God's people today. May it provoke, stimulate and motivate them to be free to be holy.

DEREK J. TIDBALL

Chief abbreviations

Bib Sac	*Bibliotheca Sacra*
DOTP	*Dictionary of the Old Testament: Pentateuch*, ed.
	T. D. Alexander and D. W. Baker (Downers Grove, IL,
	and Leicester: IVP, 2003)
EQ	*Evangelical Quarterly*
Int	*Interpretation*
JBL	*Journal of Biblical Literature*
JPS	Jewish Publication Society
JSOT	*Journal for the Study of the Old Testament*
NDCEPT	*New Dictionary of Christian Ethics and Pastoral Theology*,
	ed. D. J. Atkinson and D. H. Field (Leicester: IVP, 1995)
NICNT	New International Commentary on the New Testament
NICOT	New International Commentary on the Old Testament
NIDOTTE	*New International Dictionary of Old Testament Theology*
	and Exegesis, ed. W. A. VanGemeren, 5 vols. (Grand
	Rapids, MI: Zondervan, 1996; Carlisle: Paternoster, 1997)
NIGTC	New International Greek Testament Commentary
NIV	New International Version, 2011
NRSV	New Revised Standard Version, 1989–95
SBL	Society of Biblical Literature
SJT	*Scottish Journal of Theology*
ZAW	*Zeitschrift für die Alttestamentliche Wissenschaft*

Select bibliography

Works are cited in the text and footnotes by reference to authors' surnames and, if appropriate, short titles.

Commentaries

Bailey, L. R., *Leviticus*, Knox Preaching Guides (Atlanta, GA: John Knox, 1987).

Balentine, S. E., *Leviticus*, Interpretation (Louisville, KY: John Knox, 2002).

Bellinger, W. H., *Leviticus, Numbers*, New International Biblical Commentary (Peabody, MA: Hendrickson; Carlisle: Paternoster, 2001).

Bonar, A., *A Commentary on Leviticus* (1846; Edinburgh: Banner of Truth, 1996).

Budd, P. J., *Leviticus*, New Century Bible Commentary (London: Marshall Pickering, 1996).

Demarest, G. W., *Leviticus*, Communicator's Commentary (Dallas: Word, 1990).

Gerstenberger, E. S., *Leviticus: A Commentary*, Old Testament Library (Louisville, KY: Westminster John Knox, 1996).

Gorman, F. H., *Leviticus: Divine Presence and Community*, International Theological Commentary (Grand Rapids, MI: Eerdmans, 1997).

Grabbe, L. L., 'Leviticus', in *The Oxford Bible Commentary*, ed. J. Barton and J. Muddiman (Oxford: Oxford University Press, 2001), pp. 91–110.

Harris, R. L., 'Leviticus', in *The Expositor's Bible Commentary* 2, ed. F. E. Gaebelein (Grand Rapids, MI: Zondervan, 1990), pp. 499–654.

Harrison, R. K., *Leviticus*, Tyndale Old Testament Commentaries (Leicester: IVP, 1980).

Hartley, J. E., *Leviticus*, Word Biblical Commentary (Dallas: Word, 1992).

Kaiser, W. C., 'The Book of Leviticus', in *The New Interpreter's Bible* 1 (Nashville, TN: Abingdon, 1994), pp. 983–1191.

Kellogg, S. H., *The Book of Leviticus*, Expositor's Bible (London: Hodder & Stoughton, 1891).

Knight, G. A. F., *Leviticus*, Daily Study Bible (Philadelphia: Westminster, 1981).

Kroeger, C. C., and Evans, M. J. (eds.), *The IVP Women's Bible Commentary* (Downers Grove, IL: IVP, 2002).

Levine, B. A., *Leviticus*, JPS Torah Commentary (Philadelphia: Jewish Publication Society, 1989).

Lienhard, J. T. (ed.), *Exodus, Leviticus, Numbers, Deuteronomy*, Ancient Christian Commentary on Scripture: Old Testament 3 (Downers Grove, IL: IVP, 2001).

Mays, J. L., *Leviticus, Numbers*, Layman's Bible Commentaries (London: SCM, 1963).

Milgrom, J., *Leviticus 1 – 16*, Anchor Bible 3 (New York: Doubleday, 1991).

——, *Leviticus 17 – 22*, Anchor Bible 3A (New York: Doubleday, 2000).

——, *Leviticus 23 – 27*, Anchor Bible 3B (New York: Doubleday, 2001).

Noordtzij, A., *Leviticus*, Bible Student's Commentary (Grand Rapids, MI: Zondervan, 1982).

Noth, M., *Leviticus: A Commentary*, Old Testament Library (London: SCM, 1965).

Pigott, Susan M., 'Leviticus', in C. Clark Kroeger and M. J. Evans (eds.), *The IVP Women's Bible Commentary* (Downers Grove, IL: IVP, 2002), pp. 50–69.

Ross, A. P., *Holiness to the Lord: A Guide to the Exposition of the Book of Leviticus* (Grand Rapids, MI: Baker, 2002).

Wegner, J. R., 'Leviticus', in C. A. Newsom and S. H. Ringe (eds.), *The Women's Bible Commentary* (London: SPCK, 1992), pp. 36–44.

Wenham, G. J., *The Book of Leviticus*, New International Commentary on the Old Testament (London: Hodder & Stoughton, 1979).

Wright, C. J. H., 'Leviticus', in *The New Bible Commentary: Twenty-First Century Edition* (Leicester: IVP, 1994), pp. 121–157.

Other principal works cited

Bauckham, R., *The Bible in Politics: How to Read the Bible Politically* (London: SPCK, 1989).

Beckwith, R. T., and M. J. Selman (eds.), *Sacrifice in the Bible* (Carlisle: Paternoster; Grand Rapids, MI: Baker, 1995).

Brueggemann, W., *Finally Comes the Poet: Daring Speech for Proclamation* (Minneapolis, MN: Fortress, 1989).

——, *Theology of the Old Testament* (Minneapolis, MN: Augsburg, 1997).

Douglas, M., 'The Forbidden Animals in Leviticus', *JSOT* 59 (1993), pp. 3–23.

——, *Leviticus as Literature* (Oxford: Oxford University Press, 1999).

——, *Purity and Danger: An Analysis of the Concepts of Pollution and Taboo* (1966; London: Routledge & Kegan Paul, 1984).

Gammie, J. G., *Holiness in Israel*, Overtures in Biblical Theology (Minneapolis, MN: Fortress, 1989).

Grabbe, L. L., 'The Book of Leviticus', in *Currents in Research: Biblical Studies* 5 (Sheffield: Sheffield Academic Press, 1997), pp. 91–110.

——, *Leviticus*, Old Testament Guides (Sheffield: Sheffield Academic Press, 1993).

Hays, J. D., 'Applying the Old Testament Laws Today', *Bib Sac* 158 (2001), pp. 21–30.

Houston, W., *Purity and Monotheism: Clean and Unclean Animals in Biblical Law*, JSOT Supplement Series 140 (Sheffield: Sheffield Academic Press, 1993).

Jenson, P. P., *Graded Holiness: A Key to the Priestly Conception of the World*, JSOT Supplement Series 106 (Sheffield: Sheffield Academic Press, 1992).

Kiuchi, N., *The Purification Offering in the Priestly Literature*, JSOT Supplement Series 56 (Sheffield: Sheffield Academic Press, 1987).

——, 'Spirituality in Offering the Peace Offering', *Tyndale Bulletin* 50.1 (1999), pp. 23–31.

The Mishnah: A New Translation, trans. Jacob Neusner (New Haven and London: Yale University Press, 1988).

North, R., *Sociology of the Biblical Jubilee* (Rome: Pontifical Biblical Institute, 1954).

Rodd., C. S., *Glimpses of a Strange Land: Studies in Old Testament Ethics*, Old Testament Studies (Edinburgh: T&T Clark, 2001).

Sawyer, J. F. A. (ed.), *Reading Leviticus: A Conversation with Mary Douglas*, JSOT Supplement Series 227 (Sheffield: Sheffield Academic Press, 1996).

Wright, C. J. H., *God's People in God's Land: Family, Land and Property in the Old Testament* (Grand Rapids, MI: Eerdmans; Exeter: Paternoster, 1990).

——, *Old Testament Ethics for the People of God* (Leicester: IVP, 2004).

Wright, D. P., *The Disposal of Impurity*, SBL Dissertation Series 101 (Atlanta, GA: Scholars, 1987).

Introduction

Leviticus is good news. It is good news for sinners who seek pardon, for priests who need empowering, for women who are vulnerable, for the unclean who covet cleansing, for the poor who yearn for freedom, for the marginalized who seek dignity, for animals that demand protection, for families that require strengthening, for communities that want fortifying and for creation that stands in need of care. All these issues, and more, are addressed in a positive way in Leviticus.

Admittedly, this is not the usual impression people have of the book, which often suffers from a bad reputation. As far back as 1891, one evangelical commentator spoke of people's difficulties with it. A large number who wanted to own it as the word of God only did so, according to Samuel Kellogg, 'in a discouraged way'. Most, however, either chose to dismiss it as relevant only for the Mosaic age, or expressed discomfort at the extreme severity of its laws, or simply treated it with indifference and doubted whether it was the word of God.[1] The situation has not improved since then and, sadly, for most Christians today it is simply an unknown and unopened book.

Contemporary attitudes of indifference stand in contrast to earlier Jewish attitudes towards Leviticus, when it was valued so highly that it was made the first book of the Torah to which they introduced their children at school. It was the place they started when instilling the values and rules necessary for daily living.[2] Jesus would have known it well, along with the rest of the Pentateuch, and respected its authority.

---

[1] Kellogg, pp. 3–4.
[2] Caspari Centre Newsletter, December 1997; Douglas, *Literature*, p. 15.

The gospel, which presumes a knowledge of sacrifice and atonement, of law and grace, of sin and obedience, of defilement and cleansing, of priesthood and temple curtains, makes little sense without it. Leviticus serves as a preliminary sketch of the masterpiece that was to be unveiled in Christ. The fullest exposition of the relationship between Leviticus and the gospel, of course, is to be found in the letter to the Hebrews. Leviticus forms a foundation not only for the gospel but for Christian living. While the New Testament draws up new maps to guide the moral and spiritual life of the Christian, it does so by making use of the earlier charts of Leviticus. Particular applications may have changed, but the guiding ethical principles remain as firm as ever. Without Leviticus our Christian experience would be a house without a foundation.

1. Authorship and date

Fifty-six times Leviticus says, 'The Lord said to Moses', giving rise to Walter Kaiser's comment that 'Leviticus, more than any other Old Testament book, claims to be a divine word for humanity'.[3] But what of its human authorship and transmission? For obvious reasons, it was traditionally thought to have come from the hand of Moses, or at least to have been reduced to writing by scribes under his direction. Even though, therefore, Leviticus lacks a plain assertion that 'Moses wrote this book', it lays claim to Mosaic authority and influence throughout. When Jesus alluded to it, or to the other books in the Pentateuch, he saw no need to refer to it other than as the work of Moses.[4]

The modern scholarly consensus, however, has until recently given us a very different picture. The documentary hypothesis, which was classically expressed by Julius Wellhausen (1844–1918), theorized that, because various literary strands could be detected in the Pentateuch, the Pentateuch itself was the product of various schools in Israel, and so was neither from the pen of Moses, nor as early as it pretended. The first part of Leviticus, chapters 1–16, was said to come from a priestly source (P), while the whole book also incorporated a later holiness source (H), found in chapters 17–26. The central concern of P was the 'cult which makes possible interaction between holy God and his

---

[3] Kaiser, p. 987.

[4] Matt. 8:4; 19:7–8; Mark 1:44; 7:10; 10:3–5; Luke 5:14; 24:27, 44; John 5:46; 7:19–23.

people'.[5] Matters concerning the priesthood, cultic apparatus, correct rituals, and procedures for how to right things once they had gone wrong were uppermost in the minds of the writers. The role of Aaron was magnified in comparison with other parts of the Pentateuch. The worldview it assumed was orderly and disciplined. The purpose of cultic activity was closely tied in with creation's[6] own purposes of providing abundance; of promoting the well-being of God's people; and eradicating poverty, despair, barrenness and slavery. The cult restored the order of creation when it had been disturbed by sin or uncleanness. This explains why the Sabbath, as a mechanism for recreation, has a significant role in these writings.

Most scholars, until recently, have dated P to exilic or post-exilic times. They have seen Leviticus as a tract advocating a priestly stance on matters of contemporary importance (such as the re-establishing of the temple cult) by dressing them up in the garments of a much earlier age and setting out yesteryear as if it was the ideal to be recreated. It is suggested that, though elements of the book may go back to some primitive practices, most of it reflects the concerns of a generation who are either in exile or have recently experienced it.[7] As Mary Douglas has commented, this means that what 'hangs heavily over the interpretation' is 'the sceptical likelihood that the book is a beautiful fantasy, a vision of life that never was'.[8]

Most recently, however, confidence in this consensus has been eroded. Not only do some wish to date P much earlier than was customary, but others even doubt the existence of the separate sources the documentary hypothesis envisaged.[9] The most magisterial of recent scholars to date Leviticus early is Jacob Milgrom, who argues for a date shortly before the formation of the monarchy.[10] He does so on linguistic grounds, believing that its vocabulary is ancient and employs terms that were no longer in use by the time of the exile; that Deuteronomy is dependent on Leviticus,

---

[5] Walter Brueggemann and Hans Walter Wolff, *The Vitality of Old Testament Traditions*, 2nd edn (Atlanta, GA: John Knox, 1982), p. 102.

[6] Gen. 1:28 is central to the so-called Priestly view of the world.

[7] The suggested date varies, with the mid sixth century BC perhaps being the favourite. See Grabbe, *Leviticus*, p. 12.

[8] Douglas, *Literature*, p. 7.

[9] The details can be found in Grabbe, *Leviticus*, pp. 12–18, and Grabbe, *Currents*, pp. 93–96.

[10] See also Y. Kaufmann, *The Religion of Israel from Its Beginnings to the Babylonian Exile* (London: George, Allen and Unwin, 1961), pp. 175–211. Kaufmann shares Milgrom's arguments and adds that the rules of war outlined in P fit an earlier period. He dates it to the period of Judges or Samuel.

rather than the other way around; and that, rather than a nation in exile, its context is a small tribal people associated with Shiloh.[11] Those who doubt even the existence of P (and of H) take the view either that it is now impossible to separate out any distinct source documents that may have existed, or that, at most, P was an editorial perspective rather than a separate document.[12]

The present position has been summarized by Kaiser: 'It is now abundantly clear that there is no sole, higher critical position; rather, there are a number of quite diverse ways by means of which to understand the origins of the Pentateuch and, hence, Leviticus.'[13] All that recent scholarship can currently agree upon is that this well-structured book is the result of a long process of composition, editing and refinement. But, given that a number of respected scholars are now arguing for a much earlier date for Leviticus, it must be questioned why they consider the traditional Mosaic dating still to be unacceptable. The logic of their arguments allows that it may well be Mosaic. Those parts of the book that envisage life after settlement in Canaan are no obstacle to accepting a very early date, since it would have been easy enough for Moses to envisage the broad outlines of life in the Promised Land (such as dwelling in town houses and having to go up to a central shrine for pilgrimages) that Leviticus anticipates. With Kiuchi, I agree that,

> as regards the date of Leviticus, there seems to be no weighty evidence proving that the material of the book is later than the time of Moses . . . [and] if not by Moses, the book could well have been written by one of his contemporaries.[14]

2. Style of language and style of thought

Leviticus is a legal document and is broadly similar to other legal documents of the Ancient Near East in style, though not always in content, and not in the way it mixes civic, cultic, religious, moral, criminal, family

---

[11] Milgrom, *Leviticus 1 – 16*, pp. 3–35.

[12] See e.g. R. N. Whybray, *The Making of the Pentateuch: A Methodological Study*, JSOT Supplement Series 53 (Sheffield: Sheffield Academic Press, 1987), and R. Rendtorff, *The Problem of the Process of Transmission in the Pentateuch*, JSOT Supplement Series 89 (Sheffield: Sheffield Academic Press, 1990).

[13] Kaiser, p. 997.

[14] N. Kiuchi, 'Leviticus, Book of', in *DOTP*, p. 523.

and ritual law together.[15] Its concern with law gives it a measured tone and makes it less inspirational than, say, Deuteronomy. Even so, its style is not the mind-numbing, peremptory and litigious one that is popularly assumed. John Sawyer[16] has undertaken a linguistic analysis of Leviticus and shows that it possesses two 'striking characteristics'. It is marked, first, by the absence of imperatives and, second, by the infrequency of statements of facts. Direct commands are rare and negative commands not especially frequent. Most Old Testament books have three or four times as many imperatives (per 10,000 words) as Leviticus, and the Psalms ten times as many. Moreover, the number of commands does not increase in the so-called Holiness Code,[17] where this might be expected, with chapters 18 and 19 perhaps as the exception.

So, if commands and facts are relatively rare (and there are only two brief narratives), how does Leviticus address its readers? It encourages them to use their imagination and conceive of an ideal society where, because it is ideal, certain things are done and certain things are avoided. The tone is much more one of 'Of course, you will not steal', rather than 'Thou shalt not steal.' Furthermore, as Sawyer points out, the obsession with cleanness and matters of ritual purity is confined to a few chapters, whereas words such as 'freedom', 'liberty', 'atonement' and 'jubilee', some of which are unique to Leviticus, abound. The whole cast of the book is much less restrictive and much more uplifting and inspiring than its popular image suggests.

This interpretation of Leviticus is supported by the sense of the warming presence of God that pervades the book. In Exodus, God can be elevated in his majesty, and distant from his people. But in Leviticus, though awe-inspiring in holiness, he lives exactly where Exodus (40:34–35) places him – right among his people – and he constantly finds a way of removing all obstacles that might hinder their relationship so that they can enjoy each other's company.

Mary Douglas does not enthuse about the style of the book quite so easily as John Sawyer. She finds the writer of chapters 1–16 'unattractive, loftily abstract, impersonal, dry'. God, she says, never speaks to his people there directly, but only ever in the third person. But then, she concedes,

---

[15] Grabbe, *Leviticus*, p. 26.

[16] John Sawyer, 'The Language of Leviticus', in Sawyer, pp. 15–20.

[17] We shall refer throughout to the Holiness Code as a convenient shorthand for Lev. 17 – 26, without implying that it was once an independent document.

the writing changes and the writer becomes quite passionate; in his preaching of social justice he is 'like a modern Baptist, and like a good liberal', insisting 'on the equality of the stranger and citizen'.[18]

Understanding the approach Leviticus takes is aided when we place it in the context of wider discussions about two different patterns people adopt in their use of language. Basil Bernstein[19] introduced the concepts of elaborate and restricted language codes after researching working-class children in middle-class schools in the 1960s. An elaborate code is one in which a question is met with causal, even extended, explanation. A restricted code is one in which the reply to a question is couched in positional terms. The child asks, 'Why should I do this?' and the mother replies, 'Because I say so, and I'm your mother' – end of discussion. The restricted code, Douglas believes, is characteristic of Leviticus.[20] People know where they stand because God has spoken, and God is God. No further justification or explanation is needed. Leviticus does not wholly conform to the restricted language code because it frequently justifies God's aspirations for Israel on the basis of both his holy character and their experience of his mercy in their deliverance from Egypt (e.g. 19:2, 34; 11:45). Nonetheless, the theory is illuminating.

There are not only two forms of speech but two forms of thought. One is a rational-instrumental way of thinking, the other is analogical.[21] Analogical thinking works on the basis of an association of ideas, rather than on the basis of causal connections and explanations. One thing leads on to another and experience in one area becomes a pattern for under-standing experience in another. It is much more of a relational than a logical thought process and makes connections on the basis of social experience rather than empirical proof. Leviticus works on the basis of analogies, with experience of the daily practice of religious rituals serving as a microcosm for Israel's understanding of the larger picture of God's relationship to his creation. Impure animals, for example, remind them of the threat of chaos that could ruin God's creation and are associated with death that destroys the life God intends his people to enjoy. By

---

[18] Douglas, *Literature*, p. 34. Her allusion to Baptists draws on the American Baptist civil-rights tradition, rather than either British Baptists or American Southern Baptists, who have a tendency to conservatism in theology.

[19] Basil Bernstein, 'A Public Language: Some Sociological Implications of a Linguistic Form', *British Journal of Sociology* 10 (1959), pp. 311–326. The work is referred to in Douglas, *Literature*, pp. 36–42.

[20] Douglas, *Literature*, pp. 35–40.

[21] This is fully expounded in Douglas, *Literature*, pp. 13–26.

contrast, sacred objects and people serve to remind one of life and the wholeness God intended to be experienced by his people. Table 1, adapted from Gordon Wenham,[22] seeks to set out some of the connections. The various dimensions of life in the camp to which Leviticus refers serve as an analogy of life or death and can be plotted on a continuum between them.

Life → increasing disorder → *Death*				
Creation				Chaos
Normality				Disorder
Obedience				Disobedience
Sacred				Profane
God	Priests	Israelites	Gentiles and unclean	The dead
Most Holy Place	Holy Place	Camp	Outside	Sheol
Sacrificial animals	Sacrificial animals	Clean animals	Unclean animals	Dead animals
Food burnt	Most holy food	Holy food	Clean food	Unclean food

In interpreting the laws of Leviticus, then, we need to look beyond the immediate statements, not for rational explanation, but for the larger analogy that lies behind them. This approach, which has been championed by Mary Douglas and used extensively by Gordon Wenham, helps to unlock the meaning of many things that puzzle the rational thinker. The animals that are pronounced unclean are judged to be so because they do not fit with what might be considered normal for their type (11:1–47). They are comparable, therefore, to sick people, who are excluded from the camp and

---

[22] Wenham, p. 177 n. 34.

avoided because they symbolize disorder and chaos rather than order and life (13:1–45). Similarly, bodily discharges are judged unclean because they breach the walls of the body and may be taken as analogous to breaking down the walls of society and threatening it with disorder (15:1–33). Thus, they are also connected with death rather than life. These and other matters will be taken up in the relevant sections of the exposition.

3. Structure

A brief comment may be made here about structure. The book is certainly elegantly structured and carefully arranged. Until recently most scholars have assumed that it was composed of two earlier source documents: a priestly manual which comprised chapters 1–16 and the Holiness Code of chapters 17–26. Chapter 27 was considered a later appendix.

More recently, Mary Douglas has proposed a ring structure.[23] In her view the book comes full circle with chapter 19 as the turning point. The concerns of the opening chapters are matched by the concerns of the later chapters but in reverse order. So chapters 1–9 correspond to 25; 10 to 24; 11–15 to 21–22 (slightly out of order); 16 to 23; 18 to 20; and 19 to 26. This certainly has the advantage of ensuring that one part of the book is read in relation to the other, rather than being a series of disconnected documents. It especially overcomes the separation of the Holiness Code from the rest and preserves the essential unity of the book. One eminent scholar, at least, has warmly commended it as 'worth considering and even convincing'.[24] But on occasions the correspondences seem a little forced, and the centrality of chapter 19 rather than of chapter 16, which concerns the Day of Atonement, may be questioned.

The approach chosen in this book is more linear, as can be seen from the Contents pages. The division of the book into six 'manuals' is not intended to convey the belief that Leviticus is a composite work of six documents that all had a previous existence, which I do not hold. It is merely a device for making a long and complex book accessible and highlighting the central concern of each of its sections.

Concern for the internal structure of Leviticus should not eclipse the question of the overall structure of the Pentateuch, and of the place of

---

[23] Douglas, 'Forbidden Animals', pp. 8–12.

[24] Rolf Rendtorff, 'Is It Possible to Read Leviticus as a Separate Book?', in Sawyer, p. 32.

Leviticus within it. Rendtorff, to whom reference has just been made, asks the question: 'Is it possible to read Leviticus as a separate book?'[25] Leviticus makes little sense if wrenched from its wider context. Exodus is incomplete without it and Leviticus presupposes much of what is written there, including the exodus, the story of the wilderness, the giving of the law and the building of the tabernacle. So close, in fact, is the relationship with Exodus that the opening words of Leviticus offer no introduction or explanation but simply begin, 'And he called . . .' These words continue, almost without drawing breath, as it were, from the Lord's filling of the tabernacle with his glory at the end of Exodus. Graham Scroggie, a greatly respected Bible teacher of a former generation, explained that the message of Exodus was about God's approach to his people and their being brought near to him, whereas Leviticus was about the people's approach to God and their being kept near to him.

Scroggie also explained Leviticus's connection with Numbers. 'In Leviticus,' he wrote, 'the subject is about the believer's worship, but in Numbers it is the believer's walk. The one treats of purity, and the other of pilgrimage. The one speaks of spiritual position, and the other, of our spiritual progress.'[26] As for Genesis and Deuteronomy, while they are clearly separate books, the creation theology of Genesis and the legal concerns of Deuteronomy overlap considerably with Leviticus.

4. Direction-finders

Leviticus throws up several major issues to which some initial orientation might helpfully be given at this point.

a. The meaning of sacrifice

A great deal of discussion has taken place as to what people thought they were achieving when they offered sacrifices. Much of it has been driven by anthropologists who set aside any idea that the sacrifices of Israel could be unique and treat them as if they were like the sacrifices offered by others in the ancient world. These studies also sideline the rationale offered by the worshippers themselves in favour of some reductionist explanation. So, famously, W. Robertson Smith thought of them as a

---

[25] Sawyer, pp. 22–35.

[26] Graham Scroggie, *Know Your Bible* 1, 2nd edn (London and Glasgow: Pickering & Inglis, 1953), p. 34.

communion meal in which, following the sacrifice of a totemic victim, the worshippers strengthened their bond with their god by eating their victim.[27] Other views suggest that, through the sacrifices, worshippers were offering the deity a gift, or feeding him, as if the deity were dependent on the support of the devotees and would starve without them. Still others have conceived of them as a means of communicating between two worlds: the world of the sacred and the world of the ordinary, usually referred to as profane or mundane. The most popular scholarly explanations today make use of the analogical way of thinking referred to above and assume that rituals and regulations are tangible ways of expressing the values a group holds and the way they want to shape their community. Sacrifices, then, are 'a means of redressing equilibriums which have been upset' and restoring the unclean to a state of cleanness, the unholy to a state of holiness.[28]

Shades of several of these theories can be seen in Leviticus and help unlock the meaning of the instructions that are given. Some sacrifices were gifts of thanksgiving, though not because God was lacking in any way (Ps. 50:9–13). Others were an act of communion. Elements of consecration, especially in the burnt offering, are evident. But uppermost, in a way many wish to avoid, is the offering of blood to make atonement. The major purpose of some sacrifices was to secure forgiveness, provide cleansing and restore a broken relationship with God through the expiation of sin and propitiation of God's anger. All these nuances will be explored more fully as we look at the sacrifices individually.

b. The geography of holiness

Central to the teaching of Leviticus is the idea of holiness. Holiness is not perceived as a single, one-dimensional status but as a spectrum on which something may be more or less holy.[29] Philip Jenson has shown that in Leviticus we encounter 'grades of holiness'. For example, Israel thought about space as being divided into five zones: Zone 1: the Most Holy Place;

---

[27] W. Robertson Smith, *Lectures on the Religion of the Semites*, 3rd edn (London: A&C Black, 1927).

[28] There is extensive literature on this subject. In addition to the standard commentaries, special attention should be paid to R. E. Averback, 'Sacrifices and Offerings', in *DOTP*, pp. 706–733; D. Davies, 'An Interpretation of Sacrifice in Leviticus', *ZAW* 89 (1977), pp. 387–399; the various writings of Mary Douglas; R. E. Averbeck, 'Offerings and Sacrifices', in *NIDOTTE* 4, pp. 996–1022; J. Goldingay, 'Old Testament Sacrifice and the Death of Christ', in J. Goldingay (ed.), *Atonement Today* (London: SPCK, 1995), pp. 3–20; and G. Wenham, 'The Theology of Old Testament Sacrifice', in R. T. Beckwith and M. J. Selman (eds.), *Sacrifice in the Bible* (Grand Rapids, MI: Baker; Carlisle: Paternoster, 1995), pp. 75–87. The quotation is from Davies, p. 387.

[29] Jenson, *passim*.

Zone 2: the Holy Place; Zone 3: the courtyard; Zone 4: the camp; and Zone 5: outside the camp.[30] Where things take place matters. Only the events of the Day of Atonement take place in the Most Holy Place (16:11–17). Routine sacrifices take place in the Holy Place (16:18–25), and as matters partake less and less of holiness so they are removed further and further away from the sanctuary (16:20–22). So people who suffer a major uncleanness are exiled outside the camp, and the sins of the people are disposed of in the wilderness far beyond the boundary as well (e.g. 4:1–12; 13:46; 16:27).

The geography of holiness affects people, ceremonies and even the concept of time. This leads Jenson to produce a revised form of our earlier table (see Table 2).[31] The geography of holiness provided Israel with a graphic visual aid for their faith and enabled it to be expressed in concrete terms.

	I *Very holy*	II *Holy*	III *Clean*	IV *Unclean*	V *Very unclean*
Spatial	Most Holy Place	Holy Place	Court	Camp	Outside
Personal	High priest	Priests	Levites and clean Israelites	Minor impurities	Major impurities
Ritual	Sacrifices (not eaten)	Sacrifices (priests eat)	Sacrifices (non-priests eat)	Purification (1 day)	Purification (7 days)
Temporal	Day of Atonement	Festivals, Sabbath	Ordinary days		

c. Holy and common, clean and unclean

The terms 'holy' and 'common',[32] 'clean' and 'unclean' occur frequently in Leviticus. One of the major responsibilities of the priests was to distinguish between these categories (10:10). In the popular imagination

---

[30] Jenson, pp. 89–114.

[31] Jenson, p. 37.

[32] The word 'profane' is often used in scholarly literature, not in the sense of disrespect or being contemptuous, as when God's name is profaned, but in the sense of 'not holy', 'common' or 'ordinary'.

holiness is often equated with cleanness, and what is common with that which is unclean. But the words are not synonymous and their relationship is a little more complicated than that. Holiness is a status indicating that a person or object is dedicated to the service of God. Clean is the normal state of things (11:1–3, 9, 22). Uncleanness may be temporary, as in the case of a passing illness or minor act of defilement (11:24–25, 31–32, 34; 12:1–8; 13:1–59), or permanent, as in the case of certain species of animals (11:4–8, 9–20, 23–31). 'Common' is what Gordon Wenham describes as 'a category between the two extremes of holiness and uncleanness'; he surmises that this may be why it is mentioned only once in the whole book (10:10).[33]

There is a certain fluidity to the categories. Something that is clean may be holy or common. Clean things can be made holy, usually through sacrifice but sometimes through some other act of dedication (e.g. 27:9, 14). Clean things or people can become unclean, if they are defiled by disease or by contact with something that is already unclean. Even something that is holy can be made unclean, if it is defiled (e.g. 21:1–4, 10–12). But great care was exercised to ensure that the holy and the defiled did not come into contact with each other.

To give some examples of how all this affects the priestly understanding of the world: only priests are holy, while other people may be clean; priests, however, as well as ordinary people, may become unclean if they are in contact with something that is already impure. Clean animals may be eaten, but they become holy if offered in sacrifice. Common property can become holy if it is clean and consecrated to God. Clean people, who are not priests, can never become holy although they can be consecrated to God. Unclean people need to be cleansed by washing or atoned for by sacrifice to restore them to a state of normality. Leviticus is permeated with this type of thinking (especially in chapters 11–15), and these four overlapping categories of holy, common, clean and unclean are major factors informing the whole book and its approach to being holy.

d. Understanding the law

Another major question that Leviticus throws up is how we are to understand and apply its laws today. People have customarily distinguished between the civic, ceremonial and moral laws of Moses, and argued that

---

the first applied to Israel as an ancient theocracy and have no continuing significance today; the second were fulfilled and therefore abolished by Christ; and the third continue to have authority over us today. But there are several difficulties with this approach. While it may be an intelligible interpretation of law from a New Testament perspective, no such distinctions are explicitly made in Scripture. The ancient laws themselves certainly do not make any such distinction and in Leviticus all three strands are woven together in such a way as to make it hard to separate them. It often proves difficult in practice to decide which category a law belongs to, and so the approach tends to end up being arbitrary.[34] If the laws can be categorized at all, they should probably be categorized along the lines of criminal, case, family, cultic and compassionate law, rather than the traditional threefold structure.[35] In any case, Christopher Wright has correctly argued that the desire to unearth enduring moral laws with a view to ditching the rest is fundamentally misguided. Instead, we should be studying the laws in their original social context with a view to understanding the moral principles behind them all rather than assuming that only some continue to be relevant today.[36] But how precisely are we to do this?

Richard Bauckham[37] and J. Daniel Hays advocate discovering the principles that are enshrined in the laws. Bauckham's approach is explained more fully, and adopted, in chapter 16 below. So here we refer to the outline of the approach as laid out by Hays. While aware of the danger that this procedure may oversimplify complex issues, he nevertheless identifies five steps that must be taken in order to distil timeless ethical guidance from the specific laws. They are:

1. identify what the particular law meant to the initial audience;
2. determine the differences between the initial audience and believers today;
3. develop universal principles from the text;
4. correlate the principle with New Testament teaching; and
5. apply the modified universal principle to life today.[38]

---

[34] For a critique see Hays, pp. 21–30.
[35] For this categorization see C. J. H. Wright, *Ethics*, pp. 288–301.
[36] Ibid., pp. 288–289.
[37] Richard Bauckham, *The Bible in Politics* (London: SPCK, 1989), pp. 20–40.
[38] Hays, pp. 30–35.

Christopher Wright nuances this approach in his various and stimulating writings in this area. Wright prefers to speak, not of principles that can be derived from the law, but of Israel as a paradigm; that is, a model or pattern for other cases where a basic principle is fixed – which enables one both to critique other claims and to reapply the principle to other contexts.[39] Paradigms, he explains, are meant to be applied rather than slavishly copied. He hopes this approach will lead interpreters to avoid the extremes of, on the one hand, thinking that Israel's law is to be literally imitated today and, on the other hand, dismissing it as irrelevant. The paradigm he then constructs is impressive. It gives due weight to the theological angle of God's choosing, redeeming and then covenanting with Israel, the social angle of Israel structuring its community and family relationships around the covenant, and the economic angle of the land as a promise, gift and responsibility.[40] Each 'angle' in the framework interacts with the other two, giving a comprehensive vision of the life of Israel that can serve as a model for today. Wright's perspective has a number of advantages. It avoids the rather fragmentary and superficial understanding of Israel's laws that can result from adopting the approach of *principlism* (represented by Bauckham and Hays) and it yields some fruitful insights. C. S. Rodd has criticized Wright, saying that 'although the idea of a paradigm is extremely suggestive, it is doubtful whether it actually takes us much further than Bauckham'.[41] But Wright correctly counters that, while a paradigmatic approach '*includes* the isolation and articulation of principles', it cannot be reduced to that alone, and ensures that the particular historical reality of which the Bible speaks is not lost sight of, as can easily happen if we are in too much of a hurry to look for principles.[42]

Rodd himself dissents from the search for principles or paradigms as a matter of principle! He believes that they all 'contain the danger of introducing our own ethical values and ideas' into our interpretation of the text instead of letting the text speak for itself in all its strangeness.[43] So, for example, he is critical of feminist approaches that try to make Leviticus fit contemporary attitudes concerning the equality of women. He calls for 'something completely different' by way of approach, which

---

[39] C. J. H. Wright, *Ethics*, pp. 62–74.

[40] The paradigm is expounded in ibid., pp. 23–99.

[41] Rodd, p. 318.

[42] C. J. H. Wright, *Ethics*, pp. 70–71.

[43] Rodd, p. 327.

involves abandoning the idea that God communicates to his people through making statements of truth, and belief in 'the Bible as an external authority'.[44] In place of this we should leave 'the Old Testament where it is, in its own world – or rather worlds', and we should visit it as we visit a strange land to get glimpses of its very different life without desiring to hide the strangeness or lessen the difference between us.[45] He fears that too many ethical approaches to the Old Testament try to make it fit our own modern culture too much. The value of gazing at a strange land lies, not in providing us with rules or applications for today, but in opening 'our eyes to completely different assumptions and presuppositions, motives and aims' that cause us to question our own.[46] In this way, Rodd believes, we shall be helped, less directly but more securely, to solve many of the puzzling issues we face today.

The value of Rodd's approach lies in preventing us from erecting a bridge between the culture of the Mosaic era and that of our own too easily. He is right in wanting us to enter the culture of the time for its own sake, rather than as tourists on a package holiday, who want to take their own culture with them. He is right to be cautious about claims that Leviticus, or any other part of Old Testament law, may yield trite answers to complex problems. Yet the ethical structure he builds is based on a weak foundation of biblical authority, which renders his whole enterprise problematic.[47] And, consistent with much in the postmodern era, his approach plays up diversity and ambiguity, revels in complexities and questions, but yields very few answers and gives very few directions. On this basis the Bible is left trapped in its own culture, and it is not easy to see how it speaks today. Providing we exercise appropriate caution, the search for principles and paradigms is the most credible way to interpret Leviticus and gives due weight to it as divine revelation and historical document and as having contemporary relevance.

5. The message of Leviticus

The message of holiness pervades the book of Leviticus. Its intricate, complex, yet unmistakable theme runs through the entire book. At its

---

[44] Ibid., p. 327.
[45] Ibid., pp. 327–328.
[46] Ibid., p. 329.
[47] See the various criticisms by C. J. H. Wright in *Ethics, passim*, esp. pp. 32, 439–440, 465–467.

core, holiness is separation.[48] It describes that which is *set apart from* the ordinary, the mundane, the fallen and the pagan, and that which is *set apart to* a person or *set apart for* a purpose. Three major currents of holiness flow back and forth, together and apart, in Leviticus. The first current is a statement, the second a promise and the third a command.

The statement: God is holy. To speak of God as holy is to 'touch on what constitutes the deepest and innermost nature of the God of the Old Testament'.[49] In his being, God is altogether different from the people he has made and so separate from them. He alone is immortal in nature, all-powerful in majesty, all-knowing in wisdom, all-present in creation and, without exception or qualification, morally pure. God's revelation of himself in the words 'I am holy' is the fundamental premise on which Leviticus is built (11:44–45; 19:2; 20:26; 21:8). He displays his holiness in awesome power to his people, yet no longer, as in Exodus, from a mountaintop, but now from within the sanctuary at the centre of their camp (10:3). Everything that is employed in offering him worship – whether priests, sacrificial animals, altars or pots and pans – has to be set apart for his exclusive use and must partake of his holy character. His holiness must never be breached, compromised or trivialized. When his holiness is affronted, the offence must be quickly repaired through the offering of sacrifice. If not, the offender may be consumed in judgment. His holiness is both dramatically portrayed in the worship of Israel and ethically portrayed in the laws given to Israel. It is in observing the one and obeying the other that his people will manifest his holiness to the world.

The command: 'Be holy because I, the LORD your God, am holy.'[50] The very statements that assert the holiness of God usually command the people themselves to live holy lives.

The command, though, is premised on grace. The formative event in Israel's experience was that the Lord delivered them from the bondage of Egypt.[51] As a result they have become bound to him by unique ties of gratitude and obligation. They are now his servants, set apart from other nations not only to obey his will but also to display his character in the world (20:26). They are to live in imitation of him. They have been set free

---

[48] See Gammie, pp. 9–44.
[49] Ernst Sellin, quoted in Gammie, p. 3.
[50] Lev. 19:2; 11:44–45; 20:7, 26.
[51] Lev. 11:45; 19:36; 22:33; 23:43; 25:38, 42, 55; 26:13, 45.

to be holy. Consequently, they are given instructions as to how they are to separate themselves from the pagan nations and what distinctive patterns of worship and behaviour they should adopt.

Though the greatest concentration of holiness language may occur in the so-called Holiness Code of chapters 17–26, replete as it is with ethical vision and instruction, holiness is more than ethics. The call to be holy makes its first appearance only in 11:44–45, but it is implicit throughout the earlier chapters, which dealt with worship and priesthood. The need for atonement arises because of a failure to reach the exacting standards of holiness that the service of God requires. The chapters that concern issues of purity (11–15) teach the importance of holiness from a different perspective, as they discuss food, illness and bodily discharges. The claims of holiness affect what one eats and how one deals with the physical, and even sordid, matters of life. Holiness is comprehensive; no area of life is untouched by it. If we wish to be God's holy people today, we must acknowledge the wide-ranging claims of holiness more than we sometimes do. As Leviticus illustrates, they affect our life as members in a family, as citizens in a society, as workers in a marketplace, and as consumers in a global economy, as much as they affect us as worshippers in a church.

The promise: 'I am the Lord, who makes you holy.'[52] The responsibility of holiness is awesome, but made lighter by the promise of God. The goal of holiness is not to be reached unaided. The one who set Israel free and conferred on them the status of being his special people is the one who would continue to refashion them by transforming grace so that they could increasingly become in reality what they were already in fact – a holy people. The promise of God's transforming power, through the Holy Spirit, continues to inspire his people to undergo change so that they manifest his likeness in the world more and more.

Holiness, then, is a statement about God, a command to his people, and a promise concerning his Sprit. The summons of Leviticus leaps across the yawning cultural divide and the intervening centuries to call us once again to holy living. Christian believers, no less than Israel, are called to be holy (1 Pet. 1:15–16) and to pursue holiness in every dimension of their lives. Like Israel, we too have been set free, by Christ, but not so that we might continue to live in sin or with indifference to God; rather, we have been set free to be holy.

---

[52] Lev. 20:8; 21:8; 22:9, 16, 32.

A. The manual of sacrifice: enjoying God's presence (1:1 – 7:38)

Leviticus 1:1–17

1. Consecration to God: the burnt offering

Human beings instinctively sacrifice. There is something deep within their nature that compels them to do so. In the recent mindset of the Western world, to sacrifice has come to mean surrendering something of value for the benefit of another person or perhaps even of one's country, as when parents live frugally to pay for their child's education, or when a soldier dies in battle. But for most of history, to sacrifice was to make an offering, usually a costly one, to a deity or a king. It still carries this meaning today in many regions beyond the Western world. In such places it needs little justifying or explaining. And so it was with Israel. Leviticus begins with no explanation, no justification – just an assumption, and the command that 'when anyone among you brings an offering', here is how it should be done.

However, initial appearances can be deceptive. The absence of any justification for sacrifice is partly explained by the fact that Leviticus does not stand alone but is part of the unfolding story of the children of Israel as related in the Pentateuch. More particularly, it is a continuation of the events recounted in Exodus, which tells of the deliverance of the children of Israel from Egypt, the forming of the covenant at Sinai, and the designing and building of the tabernacle, or Tent of Meeting. The last verses of Exodus found Moses standing outside the Tent, which had been engulfed by the glory of God (Exod. 40:34–38). The first verse of Leviticus finds him standing there still, only now he is addressed by God from within the Tent where God has taken up residence among his people.

These events point to the saving grace of God and his extraordinary loving-kindness in choosing to make Israel his special people and dwell among them. Since God had just delivered the nation from oppression, revealed himself to them in majesty and shown his presence among them, the need to justify the giving of a sacrifice may be deemed superfluous. Saving grace, majestic holiness and awesome nearness are reason enough. That is why God says, 'When' – not 'if' – 'anyone among you brings an offering . . .'

And yet, just any sacrifice would not do. It was because sacrifice was so common in the ancient world that the God of Israel gave specific instructions to the people who were covenanted to him. They were to be different: a holy people, set apart for him, and bound exclusively to him alone. They were to be free from the spiritual poison that fatally infected the sacrifices of surrounding cultures. Unlike those sacrifices, designed to twist the arm of a reluctant deity, the sacrifices of Israel were provisions of God's grace to bestow grace. So they were not cheap imitations of their neighbours' offerings. Their sacrifices were divinely prescribed and personally revealed, and, therefore, were to be carefully performed. Even while doing what came naturally, the people were playing with the fire of God's holiness and so needed to approach him, not as they chose, but as he required.

1. 'The Lord called' (1:1)

We should not pass lightly over the opening words, as if they were merely a necessary bridge to open up the subject. They speak of *the summons God issues* and *the desire God has*. This was the third time that Moses had been called by God. God had called Moses from a burning bush in a desert to commission him to lead Israel out of Egypt (Exod. 3:4). He had called him from the summit of Mount Sinai to announce his covenant with Israel (Exod. 19:3). Now God called him to reveal more fully how Israel should live, in the ordinariness and totality of their daily lives, in order to enjoy continuing fellowship with him.

The key message of Leviticus, summed up in 19:2, is that the children of Israel were to 'be holy because I, the Lord your God, am holy'. Holiness was a large concept that affected every area of life: the kitchen, the bedroom, the boardroom and the courtroom, no less than the sanctuary room. It covered matters of life and death, of times and seasons, of the country and the city. It had to do with approaching God with worship that would please him, with stewarding his creation in ways that would respect it, and, with loving his people by living with integrity and compassion. The key to holiness lay in the notions of separation and purity.[1] The Israelites in their lifestyle were to be distinct from those around them: in how they worshipped, what they ate, how they loved and in their dealings with one another. They were to be governed by ideas of purity. At the very heart of their understanding of holiness was the call to reflect the character of their God in their lives.

The vision of being a holy people was demanding to the extreme. So God, in his grace, provided them with careful guidance as to how it was to be achieved. He did not leave them without direction to guess his will, or to speculate in the dark. He spoke. Thirty-five times, at least, we read that 'the LORD said to Moses'.[2] These instructions were not the product of Moses' over-fertile imagination, still less the invention of later scholars; here is a revelation from God.[3] Consequently, they are to be read carefully, studied conscientiously, interpreted and applied prudently, and obeyed joyfully.

Behind the summons lies *the desire God has* for fellowship with his people. He longed to reside at the centre of their community, and to enjoy continuing companionship with them. Leviticus, rightly understood, is primarily about relationship, rather than regulation. It speaks of how people may be kept near to God.

Inevitably, the people of Israel failed to live faithfully before God and fell short of the vision of holiness he had set before them. Impurities, sins and faults crept in and became facts of life – facts that needed to be dealt with and overcome, if God's presence among his people was to be maintained. A means of forgiveness and restitution was required so that harmony, both with God and within the community, might be restored when necessary, and so that the disorder they had brought into the world – a disorder that threatened to return creation to chaos – might be replaced with life-enhancing order.[4]

The opening words of Leviticus tell us that, as before, when they were in Egypt, the continuing well-being of Israel still lies with an initiative of

---

[1] Gammie, p. 43.

[2] Lev. 1:1; 4:1; 5:14; 6:1, 8, 19, 24; 7:22, 28; 8:1; 11:1; 12:1; 13:1; 14:1, 33; 15:1; 16:2; 17:1; 18:1; 19:1; 20:1; 21:1, 16; 22:1, 17, 26; 23:1, 9, 23, 26, 33; 24:1, 13; 25:1; 27:1. Once all variations are included, Kaiser makes the number fifty-six. Seventeen of the twenty-seven chapters start in this way. Kaiser, p. 987.

[3] Kellogg, p. 5. For a discussion of the contemporary views of authorship and composition see the Introduction above, pp. 2–4.

[4] The same theme runs throughout the Bible; see 1 John 1:7.

their gracious God. He breaks the silence, giving instructions as to how their friendship is to be nurtured and how restoration is possible should they fail.

2. 'When anyone among you brings an offering . . .' (1:2)

The first seven chapters of Leviticus are preoccupied with the sacrifices Israel was to bring to God. Five offerings are mentioned in detail. The first three are the whole burnt offering (1:1–17), the grain offering (sometimes known as the cereal offering) (2:1–16) and an offering that is variously named, but often spoken of as the peace, fellowship or well-being offering (3:1–17). These are voluntary offerings, sometimes even presented spontaneously, which, when burned on the altar, make *an aroma pleasing to the LORD* (1:9, 13, 17).[5] There is no 'must' about them: they flow freely from grateful hearts.[6] The last two offerings, detailed in chapters 4:1 – 6:7, are atonement offerings, which deal with the commission of sin and the incurring of guilt. These offerings were obligatory in certain situations. Once all the offerings have been introduced from the laypersons' standpoint, the ground is gone over again in 6:8 – 7:38, with further insights provided from the perspective of the priests. Though these chapters cover most of the sacrifices of Israel, others are subsequently mentioned. For example, there are offerings made in connection with cleansing (14:1–7, 48–53) and with a vow (27:1–33); and the annual Day of Atonement, recounted in chapter 16, made use of both these offerings and also introduced the further, unique, rite of the scapegoat (16:20–22).

The order in which Leviticus first introduces the sacrifices differs from that used when the priests are addressed. Later chapters reveal that when the sacrificial system came into practice the order in which they were offered was different again. The changes made to the order have spiritual significance, as we shall see.

Even though each offering had a different purpose and involved different sacrificial materials, leading to some necessary variation of practice, the dramatic rituals can be seen to follow the same overall shape. An offering was selected and presented; hands were laid on it; the victim

---

[5] Cf. Lev. 2:2, 9; 3:5; 6:15, 21; 23:18.

[6] Kaiser, pp. 1009, 1014.

was slaughtered; its blood was sprinkled; at least part of it was burned; and, where appropriate, the portion saved from the fire was disposed of or eaten. Each element of the ritual is significant, and the variations between them are highly meaningful. Every particular, as Jacob Milgrom has said, 'is pregnant with meaning'.[7] God used the performance of these symbolic, sacred actions to teach Israel spiritual truth. It is for this reason that Samuel Balentine has commented that 'the readers of Leviticus will find God in the details'.[8]

3. 'If the offering is a burnt offering . . .' (1:3–17)

The burnt offering was the most frequently offered sacrifice, routinely offered at the start and twilight of each day (6:8–13; cf. Exod. 29:38–43; Num. 28:3–6). It was a basic, all-purpose offering that conveyed the message that God desired a people who were wholly devoted to him, which probably explains why the Lord made a priority of this offering in giving his instructions to Moses. It is the only offering that is laid wholly on the altar and is totally consumed by fire.

a. The worshippers God invites

The burnt offering could be offered by anyone, male or female, as the use of the word 'ādām, translated you, makes clear (2). All were invited to draw near (the root meaning of qorbān, which occurs in one form or another four times here, is 'coming near' but is translated offering) and present an offering to God irrespective of their gender, or, as becomes clear, their economic status and social standing. The majestic God of the exodus and of Sinai coveted the close friendship of his people. Yet they were not to take this privilege lightly. Walter Brueggemann has pointed out that what goes on in the tabernacle 'evokes a sense of dramatic participation, so that active verbs of making and doing, bringing and offering require Israelites to be actively, physically engaged' in availing themselves of the blessing of the presence of God among them.[9] Even with the important role played by the priests, worship required active participation rather than passive observation and could not be undertaken vicariously. People were to

---

[7] Milgrom, *Leviticus 1 – 16*, p. 42.

[8] Balentine, p. 20.

[9] Brueggemann, *Theology*, p. 668.

present the offering in person at the Tent of Meeting (3), then kill, skin, clean and cut up the animal (5–9, 11–13). It was not for others to do this for them. They were to be spared none of the violence and mess of offering a sacrifice, but were to experience it personally.

The element of personal involvement is emphasized further in the instructions given to the worshipper *to lay your hand on the head of the burnt offering* (4). The significance of this act (literally of leaning heavily on the victim) has been much debated. Those who object to the theology of substitutionary atonement see within it no more than a means of identifying the victim, or of indicating its ownership, or, at most, of consecrating the victim to God in the same way in which hands were laid on the Levites to consecrate them (Num. 8:10). But this is extraordinarily shallow. Those who believe that atonement is gained by a substitute dying for sin in place of the worshipper rightly have a deeper understanding and see this act as involving a transference of the worshipper's sin on to the victim. The victim stands in the place that the worshipper should rightly occupy and serves as a proxy. The most obvious interpretation of verse 4, which says that the offering *will be accepted on your behalf*, is a substitutionary one. Kaiser rightly asks why, if its purpose is merely to indicate ownership, the laying on of hands occurred only with blood sacrifices.[10] Furthermore, Leviticus 16:21 is explicit, and would seem to weigh decisively in favour of the idea that the laying on of hands involves a transference of sin from the worshipper to the victim, even though both hands were involved on that occasion.[11] The worshipper has the closest involvement with the offering that is made.

b. The victims God accepts

The victim may come from the herd (3–9) or the flock (10–13), or may even be a bird (14–17). Because this is a voluntary offering, God is concerned to ensure than none are prevented from offering the burnt offering, if they desire to do so, on the grounds of being unable to afford it. Nothing tells us that the rich had to bring a bull, the relatively well-off a sheep or goat, while the poor might trap and bring one of the plentiful pigeons that were to be

---

[10] Kaiser, p. 1011.

[11] See discussion in Budd, p. 47, who follows Milgrom and Levine. While agreeing that some idea of transference is hard to avoid, he argues that a distinction should be made between a one-handed rite, as in the burnt offering, and a two-handed rite, as in Lev. 16:21. Single-handed actions, he concludes, indicate identification, and only two-handed actions involve transference in any meaningful sense. But there seems to be no real basis for this conclusion.

found everywhere – though that is implied. In practice, it was sheep that were most frequently offered. Even so, as a voluntary offering, people could presumably determine themselves what they brought. Yet the unmistakable message is that God wishes to exclude no-one from enjoying his presence on the grounds of cost. 'God does not expect ordinary Israelites to give what they could not afford.'[12] His grace is inclusive and his welcome wide.

That 'wideness in God's mercy'[13] was in tension, however, with the command that, if a young bull, sheep or goat be brought, it should be *a male without defect* (3, 10). The animal needed to be *acceptable to the LORD* (3), and for this to be so it had to be chosen from the best of the species. The burnt offering was not a convenient way of disposing of maimed or deformed animals whose absence would not be particularly detrimental to the financial well-being of the family. Nor was any dead animal that happened to be lying around acceptable. God was not to be passed off with second best. He deserved nothing but the best.[14] To this extent the sacrifice was to be costly to the giver. Later, when David had sinned by conducting a census of Israel to fuel his own pride and Araunah offered him a cheap option by which to make atonement, his anguished heart cried, 'I will not sacrifice to the LORD my God burnt offerings that cost me nothing' (2 Sam. 24:24). Worship that costs nothing means nothing. Worship that is cheap leads to a cheap, superficial and diminished experience of the living God.

Why was a *male* required? Traditional interpretations tend to speak of the strength or superiority of the male, or of the higher value placed on the male in ancient society.[15] More convincingly, it has been pointed out that the male might actually have been more dispensable in Israelite society because of the female's value in producing milk and offspring.[16] Though it is difficult to judge categorically between the arguments, it should be noted that female victims were perfectly acceptable in both the fellowship and the sin offerings (3:1, 6; 4:28, 32; 5:6). This would suggest that the idea is something particular to the burnt offering rather than being a general rule. It may well favour the idea that the male was the more

---

[12] Knight, p. 17.

[13] From the hymn 'Souls of Men! Why Will Ye Scatter?' by F. W. Faber (1814–63).

[14] Exceptions to this are mentioned in Lev. 22:23 and 27:9–10, where deformed and unclean animals are accepted as freewill offerings resulting from vows, but not as sacrifices.

[15] Bonar, who overdoses on typology, says it must be a male to represent the second Adam, p. 13.

[16] E.g. Milgrom, *Leviticus 1 – 16*, p. 147, and Demarest, p. 37, contra Hartley, p. 18.

expendable, and therefore acceptable in the burnt offering, which was only a voluntary sacrifice.

c. The rituals God commands

The worshipper's task is to slaughter the animal – except in the case of the birds, which are too small to be handled by several people and so are handled only by the priests (15). After slaughtering the sacrifice, the worshipper is then required to skin it, cut it up and *wash the internal organs and the legs with water* (9, 13). The importance of this is that nothing unclean from the intestines and no muck picked up by the legs should touch the altar of the Lord. For a similar reason the priest is to remove the bird's *crop with its contents* (16, NIV mg.), which would contain food that was dirty.

The priests' task was to take the blood *and splash it against the sides of the altar at the entrance to the tent of meeting* (5, 11), or, in the case of a bird, to drain its blood out *on the side of the altar* (15). Leviticus 17:11 makes it clear why blood figures so prominently in the sacrifices. Blood is the seat of life, and when blood was shed it meant that a life had been laid down and offered to God, in place of the worshipper's own life, as a means of expiating sin. The priests' handling of blood was to assume an even more notable role in other sacrifices, but is still part of the ritual here.

Then the priests took the pieces to the bronze altar near the entrance to the Tent (Exod. 27:1–8). This altar was the designated one for burning the voluntary sacrifices of laypeople. Though within the precincts of the tabernacle, it was lower on the scale of sacredness than other altars, as measured by its distance from the Most Holy Place. The pieces of the victim were arranged on the wood that was already burning there. The offering was burned in its entirety, with nothing left for any human to reclaim; the total offering belonged to the Lord. The particular vocabulary used suggests not so much a gentle grilling as a total incineration: the offering is 'transformed into smoke, sublimated, etherealised'.[17] The transformed sacrifice ascends as *an aroma pleasing to the Lord*.

d. The devotion God receives

The burnt offering seems to have been used in a wide variety of contexts and for various reasons, but the underlying purpose stated in the

---

[17] Douglas, *Literature*, p. 69, and Milgrom, *Leviticus 1 – 16*, p. 161, quoting F. C. N. Hicks, *The Fulness of Sacrifice* (London: SPCK, 1953), p. 13.

regulations was that it would *make atonement* for the worshipper (4); that is, it would restore harmony with God.[18] Such an explicit statement cannot be set aside lightly in favour of other explanations, as some wish to do. It is true that the note of sin is not as dominant as in the sin and guilt offerings, which were mandatory when particular sins had been committed. Nonetheless, the burnt offering was a blood sacrifice akin to the other atonement sacrifices, and so reminds us, as Kellogg suggests, 'of the necessity of atonement, not so much for what we fail to do, as for what we are', that is, sinners by nature and disposition as well as by practice.[19] Whatever other purposes the sacrifice may have fulfilled, it was – and is – impossible for anyone to approach God without being conscious of sin and having this barrier removed before other business may be conducted.

The many references to this sacrifice elsewhere show us something of the comprehensive nature of the burnt offering. Noah offered it in worship when the floodwaters abated and the earth enjoyed its recreation (Gen. 8:20–21). Many used it as a gift to God – an offering given freely, not because God had need of it, still less to bribe or manipulate him, but simply to express thanksgiving or dedication to him (Lev. 22:18). Job offered it as part of his regular devotional discipline. David offered it to accompany his confession of sin. Solomon offered it three times a year, and Hezekiah offered it in thanksgiving for the completion of the cleansing of the temple from paganism.[20] Speaking of temple worship, God said burnt offerings were 'ever before me', fulfilling the role of the main sacrifice both morning and evening.[21]

All these uses demonstrate that the thrust of the sacrifice lay in a desire to cause God pleasure by offering him a gift out of fully devoted and thankful hearts. Given this, it is obvious that it was impossible to offer an acceptable sacrifice merely by performing the outward rite. The inner disposition of the worshipper was just as important. Unless the sacrifice expressed 'a broken spirit . . . a broken and contrite heart' (Ps. 51:17), it would cause God pain rather than pleasure.

The essential meaning of this sacrifice is explicitly and powerfully captured in the ritual itself. The distinguishing feature of this sacrifice,

---

18 The meaning of atonement will be discussed further in chapter 4 below.
19 Kellogg, p. 109.
20 Job 1:5; 2 Sam. 24:25; 1 Kgs 9:25; 2 Chr. 29:20–28.
21 Exod. 29:38–42; Ps. 50:8. See also Pss 20:3; 40:6; 51:16, 19; 66:13.

as opposed to others, was that the whole of it was burnt up on the altar. It speaks of total surrender, entire consecration and complete dedication to God. None of it is held back. It is offered without reserve. No less than an unqualified and unreserved giving of oneself, as represented by the substituted victim, was – or is – an adequate response to the saving grace and covenant love of God.[22]

4. 'An aroma pleasing to the LORD'

Burnt offerings later became devalued through their frequent repetition, often without the accompanying inner brokenness of spirit and devotion to the Lord that they were designed to express. Yet the sacrifice continued to speak to believers in Christ in the days of the early church and still continues to do so today.

a. It points to the sacrifice of Christ

Time and again the New Testament alludes to the sacrifice of Christ – the sacrifice of his flawless life as well as his voluntary death – as the perfect burnt offering. The Gospel writers recount Jesus' total surrender of his life, voiced in his prayer in the Garden of Gethsemane.[23] Paul sees Jesus' death on the cross through the lens of the burnt offering when he says, 'Christ loved us and gave himself up for us *as a fragrant offering* and sacrifice to God' (Eph. 5:2). And he sounds the note of total surrender involved in the burnt offering when he speaks of the way Jesus became 'obedient to death – even death on a cross!'[24] Peter similarly uses the model of the burnt offering to draw attention to Jesus Christ as 'a lamb without blemish or defect' (1 Pet. 1:19).

But the typical significance of the burnt offering is most fully developed in Hebrews. Hebrews 10:5–7 quotes the Septuagint version of Psalm 40:6–8:

Sacrifice and offering you did not desire,
   but a body you prepared for me;

---

[22] This is all evident in Gen. 22, where Abraham is commanded to offer Isaac as a burnt offering (2), where the idea of a substitute is already well established (13), and where God affirms his blessing on Abraham's life because 'you . . . have not withheld your son, your only son' (16).

[23] Matt. 26:39, 42; Mark 14:36; Luke 22:42; John 17:19.

[24] Phil. 2:8. Hartley, p. 25, sees the same truth in Rom. 8:32, but the subject there would seem to be the Father rather than the Son, even though the effect is the same in that the Son is given up for us all.

with burnt offerings and sin offerings
  you were not pleased.
Then I said, 'Here I am – it is written about me in the scroll –
  I have come to do your will, my God.'

Applying this to Jesus Christ, Hebrews continues in verse 10 with the statement that 'we have been made holy through the sacrifice of the body of Jesus Christ once for all'. Jesus was the consummate and flawless whole burnt sacrifice, who offered himself in total obedience and most perfect consecration to the Lord. His sacrifice is superior to any that had been offered before, and any that could yet be offered in the future. No other sacrifice is needed.

b. It points to the service of believers

It speaks of our need as believers to approach the Lord in our worship with care rather than presuming on our right to draw near to him, full of our own inventiveness and self-importance. It speaks of the need for daily confession and cleansing from our continued sin (a reality recognized in 1 John 1:7–9), even though we already have the assurance that his blood has wiped the slate clean and we can be confident of our acceptance in Christ. It encourages us to 'continually offer to God a sacrifice of praise – the fruit of lips that openly profess his name' (Heb. 13:15). If those God delivered from Egypt expressed their delight at his salvation, how much more should we, who look back to the greater salvation available through Christ, express our appreciation to him from hearts that overflow with gratitude – not because we must, but because we may?

Above all, it speaks of the total dedication of life that is required of all believers – male or female, rich or poor, lay or ordained – if their lives are to be an aroma pleasing to the Lord rather than an offence to his nostrils. The burnt sacrifices once offered in the Tent of Meeting in the wilderness need to be offered daily in the lives of those who follow Jesus in the desert places of the modern world. The burnt offering captures in dramatic form what Jesus called for when he invited us to love God with all our hearts, understanding and strength (Mark 12:33; cf. Deut. 6:5), and with the totality of our abilities to will, think, feel and do. It was the image of the burnt offering that Paul drew upon when he urged the Roman Christians, 'in view of God's mercy, to offer your bodies as a living sacrifice, holy and pleasing to God – this is your true and proper worship' (Rom. 12:1).

'Just one life,' Michael Griffiths once wrote after being lost in the highlands of Malaysia.

> This is all any of us has to offer. How can it be used for the greatest glory of God and the greatest blessing of men? How can we be as useful as possible and as effective as possible as Christians?[25]

The burnt offering gives us the reply. This one life must be laid on the altar and totally consecrated to God.

Believers who truly appreciate the wonder of God's grace have no life of their own, nor do they desire one. For nothing pleases them more than being an aroma that is acceptable to God; an offering, composed of the totality of their beings, that he accepts.

---

[25] Michael Griffiths, *Give Up Your Small Ambitions* (London: IVP, 1970), p. 10.

Leviticus 2:1–16

2. A gift for God: the grain offering

The grain offering seems the poor relation among the sacrifices of Israel. Its brief introduction is sandwiched between instructions about the burnt offering and the peace offering, appropriately enough, since it usually accompanied one of these rather than standing alone. Unlike the other offerings, although fire is involved, no meat is offered and no blood is shed. This marks it out as distinctive. So, too, does the absence of any reference to atonement.

The rabbis believed that the grain offering was a poor man's burnt offering.[1] Several factors lend weight to the suggestion that it was an offering for the impoverished. Those who were too poor to afford the usual animals for sin offerings, even if they were only a couple of doves or pigeons, were permitted to substitute something akin to the grain offering and still make atonement (5:11–13). And when the grain offering was presented together with the burnt offering as part of the routine of daily worship, only a tenth of an ephah (6:20) was involved (just over 2 litres in contemporary terms), and even then only half of it was offered in the morning, the other half being offered in the evening (see also Num. 28:3–8). But however true these insights are, they are only part of the whole truth, and must not be allowed to distort the rich and varied role played by this small but important offering.

---

[1] Milgrom, *Leviticus 1 – 16*, p. 195.

1. Understanding the instructions[2]

Although a different word is used (*nepeš*, not *'ādām*), the same inclusive invitation is issued to the children of Israel as was issued for the burnt offering. Any individual or group, regardless of gender or status, is invited to bring the gift of a grain offering to the Lord and to participate fully in the ensuing ritual as an equal.

Søren Kierkegaard compared worship to a theatre in a way that is particularly apt for the sacrificial rituals of Israel, especially when we grasp the point he was making. Theatres are places where dramas are performed by actors in front of an audience. In the worship of Israel, the worshippers were the players, not the audience, and they were assigned an active role. It was God who was the audience for whose benefit the drama was presented, and God who was to be satisfied. For that reason, the rituals were carefully prescribed and observed. How different from much present-day worship that turns the congregation into an audience of passive onlookers whose feelings need massaging and whose every taste and whim need satisfying! It is a foolish reversal of roles that places God on the stage as an actor who is required to entertain his people.[3]

a. The variety God permits

Right from the start we are told that the grain offering could be offered in a number of ways, the flexibility of approach mirroring its flexibility of purpose. Three types of offering are outlined here. First (1–3), a worshipper could simply bring uncooked *finest flour*, but if so the worshipper was *to pour olive oil on it* and *put incense on it*. The priest would then take it, burn a proportion of it on the altar of burnt offering and set aside the rest for consumption by the priests. The fine flour was made from semolina, 'the choice part of the wheat taken from the inner kernels'.[4] Again, nothing but the best is good enough for God.

Second (4–13), a worshipper could bring a baked offering, which might have been cooked *in an oven* (4), *on a griddle* (5) or *in a pan* (7). The variety of ways in which the offering could be prepared reflects no more than the different methods of cooking of the day. An oven was made of mud or clay

---

[2] Further instructions, addressed to the priests, are found in 6:14–23.

[3] I owe this point to Marva Dawn, who develops it in *Reaching Out without Dumbing Down: A Theology of Worship for the Turn of the Century* (Grand Rapids, MI: Eerdmans, 1995), p. 82.

[4] Levine, p. 9.

with an opening at the top and was often partially embedded in the earth. The griddle was a flat implement, again usually made of clay, whereas the pan would have been a deeper pottery vessel with a lid and would have been used for deep frying. If this cooked offering was brought, oil was still used but no incense was added, and yeast and honey were forbidden (4, 5, 11). All the offerings were also seasoned with salt (13). Part of this offering was burned, and part given to the priests (9–10).

Third (11–16), special reference is made to the grain offering which consisted of *firstfruits* brought *to the* Lord. This would seem to refer to special offerings presented voluntarily on any number of occasions, rather than those spoken of in 23:15–22, which were offered during harvest time in thanksgiving for God's bountiful provision for Israel and in recognition of his prior claim on all that they produced. Even though the occasion may have been different, however, the motivation would have been the same. The distinctive feature of these offerings was that *oil and incense* were added to the *crushed heads of new grain roasted in the fire* (14–15). As before, only a proportion was burned on the altar, and the rest was set aside for the benefit of the priests.

b. The ingredients God specifies

Oil (1, 2, 4, 5, 6, 7, 15–16), salt (13) and, in two out of three types, incense (1, 2, 15) were the required ingredients for this offering. In some respects the use of the oil may appear obvious. Olive oil was the omnipresent medium for cooking in Israel whether it was poured over, mixed in, spread on top, or simply what the food was fried in, all of which are mentioned here. Yet, bearing in mind that these rituals were dramatic, symbolic acts that represented spiritual truths, we would be stopping short of understanding God's intention if we did not look beyond the obvious. Oil is associated with the work of the Holy Spirit (1 Sam. 10:1–11; most notably in Zech. 4:1–6), as well as with gladness (Ps. 45:7; Isa. 61:3). It reminds us that whatever we offer to the Lord as a gift in worship we owe to the Spirit's inner working in us, and not to talents we naturally possess. It also points to his powerful ministry of taking what is merely human and transforming it into something worthy of God.[5]

The grain offering, like the other voluntary offerings, is intended to be an *aroma pleasing to the* Lord (2, 9, 12). This accounts for the use of

---

5 Kaiser, p. 107.

incense. Baruch Levine, arguing that fumigation was widely used in the Ancient Near East, follows Maimonides in giving us the pedestrian, if pragmatic, explanation that the scent was intended to cover up the stench of the blood sacrifices.[6] R. K. Harrison writes of its function as 'that of a fumigant and deodorant, cloaking or removing some of the less pleasant smells of the sacrificial ritual, and thereby contributing to the physical effect of making the offering "a pleasing odour to the Lord"'.[7] This would explain why incense was not required of the cooked offerings, since the aroma of the baking itself would prove attractive enough. True though this may be, this threadbare, utilitarian explanation draws attention away from the delight caused, speaking anthropomorphically, to God's nostrils, which is where the emphasis of the text lies. Like a delightful fragrance worn by a woman, the perfumed odour given off by the grain offering was attractive and pleasurable to God.

The aroma symbolizes the quality of life that should characterize every true worshipper of God. When, long after the tabernacle had become but a memory, Mary anointed the feet of Jesus, John commented that 'the house was filled with the fragrance of the perfume' (John 12:3). And Paul saw his life, as he was led captive yet triumphant in Christ, as an aroma, spreading 'the aroma of the knowledge of him everywhere' (2 Cor. 2:14–16). It is no longer the liturgical rituals of the tabernacle but our acts of devotion and obedient service in proclaiming Christ that need to waft heavenwards as *an aroma pleasing to the* LORD.

The third common ingredient was *salt*. *Season all your grain offerings with salt. Do not leave the salt of the covenant of your God out of your grain offerings; add salt to all your offerings* (13). Salt was not only the chief means of preserving food in the ancient world (thus 'render[ing] the offering fit'[8]) but also a key component in the offering of hospitality and sealing of covenants, and therefore seems to have indicated friendship, bonding and unity.[9] Numbers 18:19 speaks of 'an everlasting covenant of salt before the LORD'. The worshippers came not haphazardly, nor to express an intermittent need for God, but in true binding friendship

---

[6] Levine, p. 8.

[7] Harrison, p. 49.

[8] Hartley, p. 32.

[9] Noth, p. 29, records that the idea is still present among Arabs, who, he writes, believe that 'eating salt together establishes a mutual community bond'. The Old Testament nowhere makes the meaning of salt clear, but it is used by Elisha to reverse the curse on Jericho and to reintroduce the blessings of the covenant, 2 Kgs 2:19–22.

as those who belonged to an eternal covenant of grace that would never be broken (cf. 2 Chr. 13:5). When Jesus told his disciples that they were 'the salt of the earth' (Matt. 5:13), he was doing more than telling them they had a mission to stave off moral corruption in society. He was telling them they were the true people of God, bound to him by a new covenant, and, consequently, called upon to fulfil the mission that Israel had abandoned.

These three necessary ingredients were balanced by two ingredients that were prohibited: *yeast* and *honey* (4, 5, 11). Yeast was not always forbidden in offerings, and it plays a part in the wave offering that was presented during the Feast of Weeks (23:17). Some argue that the unleavened nature of the offering is designed to provoke memories of the Passover meal (Exod. 12:8). But this connection is never explicitly made. The most obvious and common explanation for its unacceptability here is that yeast causes corruption, and it is excluded for the very reason that salt is included. Mary Douglas points out, however, that this explains neither why it is sometimes permitted, nor why it is allied to a prohibition of honey.[10] Douglas's view brackets yeast and honey and says both are forbidden because, in the ancient world, both were kept in dough, rather than separate from it, and would have inevitably activated the old dough, causing it to swell and grow until it erupted and disintegrated. For her, this is an example of 'teeming life'; an example of the natural and human process of generation that stands in contrast to the divine generation of life.[11] With curt simplicity Gordon Wenham says something similar that, while it refers to yeast, also applies to honey: 'yeast is a living organism and only dead things could be burned on the altar in sacrifice'.[12] The plain fact is that we do not know what these ingredients symbolize, but the simpler explanation has much to commend it. Furthermore, it is consistent with the fact that honey was in widespread use in pagan rites, and holiness required separation. Here was a call for Israel to be distinct from their neighbours rather than imitating them in the way they worshipped their God.

---

[10] The honey in question probably refers to the nectar of dates and figs as much as to any honey produced by bees. Levine, p. 12.

[11] Douglas, *Literature*, pp. 164–166. Hartley comments that 'since no reason for the restriction . . . is given all suggestions are speculative', p. 33.

[12] Wenham, p. 71.

c. The ritual God initiates

The performance of this rite is straightforward enough, but still highly suggestive. Only a portion of the gift is laid on the fire and burned. This is called a *memorial portion* (2, 9, 16). This portion belongs to God and, in a way we shall discuss further below, serves as a reminder to him of the covenant.

The memorial portion is only a token of the whole offering: the rest *belongs to Aaron and his sons* (3, 10). Their part, somewhat surprisingly, is called *a most holy part of the food offerings presented to the* LORD (3, 10). In Leviticus there are gradations of holiness that map sacredness, with the holiest of all referring to the Most Holy Place, where God himself has his footstool.[13] The designation of the remainder of the food as *most holy* is a signal that the food could be eaten only by 'holy' people, that is, the priests. Lay folk were able to eat the peace offering, which was about communion with God and one another. But the peace offering is not given the status of 'most holy'. The grain offering was a voluntary offering of one's labour to God and so was reserved for his near servants to eat. In addition, the grain offering could be eaten only within a 'holy' place, that is, within the precincts of the tabernacle. To eat it elsewhere would risk contamination and render the offering unclean.[14]

Here was a way, one among several, by which the needs of the servants of the Lord could be met. Throughout the instructions concerning tabernacle worship, God showed a compassionate awareness of the need for priests and Levites to be supported by the community they served, since they were unable to engage in ordinary work and economic activity and, consequently, unable to provide for themselves. It was in language borrowed from this offering, among others – the language of a 'fragrant offering' – that Paul later thanked the Philippians for their gift (Phil. 4:18). The continuing responsibility to support those engaged in particular ways in the Lord's work was reiterated both by Jesus himself and by the apostle Paul (Luke 10:7; 1 Cor. 9:13–14; 1 Tim. 5:17). We pay for what we value. It is perhaps a sad reflection that many Christians today fulfil neither the letter nor the spirit of biblical teaching in this area. Nor, apparently, do they value the services of spiritual leaders as much as they value the service of others whom a secular society has conditioned them to rate more highly.

---

[13] See the Introduction above, pp. 10–11, and Jenson, ad loc., for a full exposition of this theme.

[14] Budd, pp. 58–59.

2. Understanding the significance

The Hebrew name for the grain offering is quite general. *Minḥâ* simply means 'a gift'. But in Leviticus it is used exclusively of the grain offering. It seems to encompass a variety of purposes and is used, in Harrison's words, 'as an expression of reverence (Judg. 6:19; 1 Sam. 10:27), gratitude (Ps. 96:8), homage (Gen. 43:11, 15, 25) or allegiance (2 Sam. 8:2, 6)'.[15] An altogether different use is made of it in Numbers 5:15, where it is described as 'a grain offering for jealousy' and is part of the ritual for discerning whether a wife had been unfaithful to her husband. Can we be more specific? Can its nature be defined more precisely?

a. It is a tribute to a sovereign Lord

One way in which the word *minḥâ* was used was in the context of a tribute paid by a subject people to their superior. It was sometimes an act of appeasement, calculated to set aside displeasure and to ensure goodwill. For example, at the end of his fugitive years Jacob sought to curry Esau's favour by sending several gifts ahead of him before they met in person (Gen. 32:13–21). When the Moabites had subdued the children of Israel, Eglon, the king of Moab, was presented with a tribute (*minḥâ*) by Ehud, the judge. Ironically, in this case, far from being a sign of subservient submission, it was the means by which Ehud gained access to Eglon in order to assassinate him and liberate Israel. The tables were turned and Moab became subject to Israel (Judg. 3:12–30). When the Moabites and the Arameans became subservient to King David, they brought him a *minḥâ*, a tribute (2 Sam. 8:2, 6).

The grain offering is a tribute in recognition of the sovereignty of God over the lives of those who offered it. But, in contrast to occasions when other tributes were offered, his authority is not imposed and this payment is not obligatory. It was a gift, voluntarily offered to God to acknowledge his 'supreme authority, and as an expression of desire for his favour and blessing'.[16] It was an expression of loyalty to the one who was not only their saviour but also their Lord and king. The bringing of an ordinary gift of flour or bread symbolized God's jurisdiction over the totality of life. Relationship with him was not kept in a compartment labelled 'spiritual'.

---

[15] Harrison, p. 49.
[16] Kellogg, pp. 63–64.

The routine labours of every day were brought into his presence and surrendered in an act of worship because he was Lord over all.

This aspect of the grain offering comes into particularly sharp focus when the offering is an offering of firstfruits (23:17, 20).[17] In presenting these to the Lord, worshippers were recognizing that the harvest was a result of God's blessing, not their own unaided work. They were returning to God the best of what they had first received from his hand. The harvest, no less than the benefit derived from daily labour, was a gift, not a right. Presenting the offering declared this in an intentional way and prevented the children of Israel from sliding into a 'taking things for granted' syndrome or a 'rights' mentality. The sovereign Lord was a bountiful giver.

b. It is a reminder to a covenant God

Three times (2, 9, 16) this chapter speaks of the part that was burned on the altar as being a *memorial portion*.[18] The meaning of the phrase is disputed, but obviously significant if we are to understand the purpose of the grain offering. The token on the altar acts, in some way, as a reminder. But to whom? And a reminder of what? The thought that God needed reminding of anything suggests that he could be forgetful. Understandably, therefore, some people have shied away from saying that it is God who was being reminded. So, they conclude, it is the worshipper who is being reminded, either that the whole of the offering rightly belongs to God, even though he is prepared to accept just a part of it,[19] or that he or she needs to serve the Lord loyally in every area of life.[20] If this is the case, it was a way of reviving one's active appreciation of the covenant and renewing one's commitment to it. Without such occasions of conscious recommitment, our relationship with God can too easily settle into dull monotony and go into steady decline, until it ceases to matter at all.

But it could well be that the phrase does refer to bringing something to God's remembrance. It is not that God is forgetful, like an elderly person suffering from one of those 'senior moments'. Rather, it is a very human way of speaking about God, just as we, following the path forged for us by the Bible, constantly resort to using anthropomorphisms when speaking

---

[17] See also Exod. 23:16, 19; 34:22, 26; Num. 18:12–13.

[18] The phrase is also used of the poor person's sin offering in 5:12, of the grain offering in 6:15, and of the incense placed on the table of the bread of the Presence in 24:7.

[19] Wenham, p. 68 n. 2.

[20] Kaiser, p. 1020.

of him. In Hartley's view, which is persuasive, it means that the offering caused God to remember the worshipper in covenant faithfulness. He adds, 'When God remembered he blessed.'[21] Nehemiah frequently spoke in these terms, reminding God first of his promise to Moses, but then asking God to remember the work of reconstruction he had undertaken in Jerusalem, so that God would look on him in mercy and with favour.[22] The aroma of the burnt portion of grain ascended to heaven like the prayers and petitions of the saints mentioned in Revelation 5:8, keeping the worshipper's need and situation before the Lord and reminding him to fulfil his promises with diligence.

c. It is a response to a generous Creator

i. Our work and our worship

Significantly, the recognition that God is the provider of the harvest is held in tension with the fact that what is being offered on the altar is the result of human labour. The fine flour was prepared by grinding grain in the millstones. It was a daily chore. The baked bread was the result of kneading the flour, water, oil and salt together, and of the toil of cooking. The firstfruits were the result of sowing and reaping; or of pruning, tending and picking. Even if God was the originator of it all, human effort was involved in bringing the offering to the altar. Given this, it is fair to view this offering as symbolizing the consecration of our daily labour to the Lord. The gifts that we utilize in the routine of our daily employment can be brought to the Lord as a gift and can find acceptance with him.

Biblically speaking, work is not a necessary evil but an act of worship: it is service rendered in the presence and to the glory of the Lord. Though, ever since the disobedience of Adam and Eve, the curse (Gen. 3:17–19) has tainted our experience of it, work remains a positive part of our Creator's purpose for us. What the children of Israel vaguely understood through this sacrifice, Christian believers can grasp with transparent clarity because the New Testament teaches that all our work is done to serve the Lord and to be pleasing to him. Even the slaves in the Colossian church were led to appreciate this by Paul. Believers work neither for earthly recognition nor for reward but, with all their hearts, for the Lord (Col. 3:17, 22–25).

---

[21] Hartley, p. 32.

[22] Neh. 1:8; 5:19; 13:14, 22, 31. He also asks God to remember those who had sought to frustrate his work and to judge them accordingly (6:14; 13:29).

ii. Our work and our atonement

The role of the grain offering in relation to atonement needs clarifying. The grain offering was obviously welcomed by God, but it was, in part, a gift that resulted from their own labour. Does this mean that we are accepted by God on the basis of our works? Furthermore, we need to ask the related question of how the positive evaluation of the grain offering here fits with the negative reception given to Cain's offering of the fruit of the soil in Genesis 4:2–5. Traditionally, the rejection of his offering in contrast to the acceptance of Abel's offering has been explained by reference to the difference between the offerings. Abel's offering was considered superior because it was an animal, blood sacrifice, which secured atonement, unlike Cain's, which was an offering of natural products that required no blood to be spilt and that boasted of human achievement. The fact is that there were bigger issues involved in God's rejection of Cain's offering. It was not a question of God preferring meat to fruit, or cowboys to farmers, as Walter Brueggemann expressively puts it.[23] The issues in Genesis concerned not the nature of the offering, nor essentially the question of atonement, but the nature of the offerers, and their respective characters and destinies, as the rest of the story suggests – and, of course, the abiding truth is that it is for the Lord to declare sovereignly how he is to be approached and worshipped, and for us (unlike Cain) humbly to accept and conform.

Even so, the apparent contrast between the rejection of Cain's offering and the favourable commendation of the grain offering still provokes us to examine further why the grain offering was apparently encouraged and accepted so easily. Does it indicate that God accepts our works, and therefore us on the basis of them? The fact is that these instructions never explicitly connect the grain offering with atonement. But this silence should not be taken as implying consent; that is, as agreeing that if we come to him with what we have – the labours of our own hands – he will accept us, forgive our sin and be reconciled to us.

No. Two features of the offering suggest otherwise. First, the grain offering was rarely offered alone, and the supposition is made that it will be offered in conjunction with one of the other offerings that were the channels of atonement for sinners. Our works, however valuable, are

---

[23] W. Brueggemann, *Genesis*, Interpretation (Atlanta, GA: John Knox, 1982), p. 56. See also David Atkinson, *The Message of Genesis 1 – 11*, The Bible Speaks Today (London: IVP, 2021), pp. 87–105.

never enough to gain us forgiveness from God. Only one man's perfect works could ever do that – those of our Lord Jesus Christ, the perfect man. Second, this is underlined when we note that the individual worshipper was not permitted to lay the gift on the altar personally. The gift was presented to a priest, who laid it there and sacrificed the memorial portion to God. A mediator was necessary. Our gifts to God can be presented only through the mediation of our great High Priest, whose perfect consecration and unblemished work alone are able to atone for sin and make us acceptable in his presence (Heb. 2:17; 5:1; 8:3; 9:11–12). Atonement, then, is not central to this offering but is brought into play by the manner in which the ritual of the grain offering was celebrated. It confirms the truth of A. M. Toplady's words:

> Not the labours of my hands
> Can fulfil thy law's demands;
> Could my zeal no respite know,
> Could my tears for ever flow,
> All for sin could not atone:
> Thou must save, and thou alone.[24]

iii. Our work and our goals

We should note that this offering encourages us not to make work an end in itself but to bring our work and 'lay it on the altar' so that, through it, we are serving not ourselves but the Lord.[25] Many in contemporary society find that work has become a tyrant, enslaving them at the cost of family well-being, community good and even physical and mental health. Consciously bringing it to God would help us to keep it in a healthier perspective.

This is not just an issue for those in so-called secular employment, but for those in Christian service as well. Ironically, it is easy unintentionally to forget the Lord, or even half-consciously exclude him from our lives, in the busyness of service for him. The Chinese Christian leader Brother Yun confessed that at one point in his life, 'ministry became an idol. Working for God had taken the place of loving God.' He hid his condition from others 'and carried on in [his] own strength, until God decided to intervene

---

[24] A. M. Toplady (1740–78), 'Rock of Ages, Cleft for Me'.
[25] I owe the point to Kellogg, pp. 66–67.

in his mercy and love'. God's intervention led to a second spell in prison, which he describes disarmingly in these terms: 'The Lord saw I was exhausted in the ministry, so he graciously allowed me to rest in him behind bars for a while and learn about inner spiritual life.' He urges the Lord's servants not to fall into the same error, warning them that 'if we ever put anything before our relationship with Jesus – even our work for Jesus – then we will be ensnared'.[26]

The grain offering, unimportant though it seems to be, is eloquent with spiritual encouragement and truth. Whereas the burnt offering speaks of the dedication of ourselves, the grain offering speaks of the dedication of our work. It highlights the sovereign rights of God, while at the same time pointing to his generous provision for his people. It tells us that God enjoys what we offer to him, while calling on us not to ape the cultures around us as we make our offerings. It affirms God's bounty in creation and encourages the enjoyment of what the earth supplies, while preventing us from idolizing it. It tells us that true fulfilment in work will be found only if that work is consecrated to the Lord. It is about pleasing the Lord, while looking after the needs of his servants. Above all, it points forward to Jesus Christ, the great High Priest, in whose obedient life and through whose perfect work alone we see a more excellent sacrifice laid on the altar – one that covers all our deficiencies and shortcomings. As S. H. Kellogg wrote,

> How exceedingly comforting this view of Christ! For that which, at the best we do so imperfectly and interruptedly, he does in our behalf, and with never failing constancy; this at once perfectly glorifying the Father, and also, through the virtue of the boundless merit of this consecration, constantly procuring for us daily grace unto life eternal.[27]

---

[26] Brother Yun and Paul Hattaway, *The Heavenly Man* (London: Monarch, 2002), pp. 198–199.

[27] Kellogg, p. 81.

Leviticus 3:1–17

3. Fellowship with God: the peace offering

'There, in the presence of the LORD your God, you and your families shall eat and shall rejoice in everything you have put your hand to, because the LORD your God has blessed you.' Here, in a sentence, Deuteronomy 12:7 reveals the heart of the third voluntary offering that the Lord invites his people to present to him. Uniquely, once a portion of it had been burned before the Lord, this offering led to the worshippers enjoying a feast of the parts that remained as an act of celebration for God's goodness.

It is difficult to know what to call this offering. Frequently named 'a peace offering', it is also called 'a fellowship offering',[1] 'a communion offering', 'a shared offering', 'a sacred offering of greeting' or 'an offering of well-being', each of which picks up an aspect of the offering.[2] The key word in the Hebrew title is *šĕlāmîm*, which comes from the same root as the word *šālôm*, meaning 'peace'. Consequently, 'peace offering' is the translation that has generally commended itself, and it certainly captures one of the principal features of the sacrifice, namely, enjoying peace with and from God. In our day 'peace' has come to be a fairly shallow word meaning the absence of conflict, rather than having the wonderfully rich overtones of positive well-being and of a wholesome way of life meant by *šālôm*. Some, therefore, wishing to avoid superficiality, opt for the more rounded title of 'well-being'.

---

[1] This is the preferred translation of the NIV. I have chosen to use 'peace offering' as the best general translation of its title.

[2] Details can be found in Hartley, pp. 37–39; Levine, pp. 14–15; and Milgrom, *Leviticus 1 – 16*, pp. 220–221.

1. The procedures it follows

As with all the offerings, God carefully sets out the procedures to be followed, first in the initial statement made in Leviticus 3 and then in supplementary guidance given in 7:11–21.

a. What Leviticus 3 reveals

The offering may consist of a cow or bull (1–5), a sheep (6–11) or a goat (12–16). Although this variation is permitted, however, no further divergence is allowed from the prescribed ritual. These animals would have made this a costly sacrifice, but there is no scope for reducing the cost by offering birds instead. The reason for their omission is threefold. As a voluntary offering, the purpose of which was not explicitly atoning, no-one was compelled to bring the sacrifice and so there was no need for an exception for those who were poor. More significantly, birds would have been unable to fulfil the role assigned to these sacrifices, as is made clear by the unfolding ritual, which focuses on the sprinkling of blood and burning of fat. The insufficient amount of blood and suet they would yield would make such offerings 'an embarrassment'.[3] Finally, birds would not have been large enough to yield excess meat for a family celebration, but would have been wholly burned on the altar. This makes them inappropriate as a peace offering.

Unlike most other sacrifices, the victim to be offered may be either male or female (1, 6). Milgrom surmises that both sexes are allowed to ensure that the ample supply of meat needed for this sacrifice was available.[4] Others assume females are included to give the person wishing to bring a voluntary offering greater choice. But, whichever sex the animal was, it had to be *without defect* (6).[5] With only one minor exception – that of the freewill offering mentioned in Leviticus 22:23 – nothing less than perfection is adequate for sacrifices that are offered to God. He requires the best.

The chosen animal was presented *at the entrance to the tent of meeting* by the presenter, who laid a hand on its head (2, 8, 13). This was not only,

---

[3] Milgrom, *Leviticus 1 – 16*, p. 222.

[4] Ibid., p. 204.

[5] The instructions regarding a goat sacrifice (12–16) omit reference either to the sex or to the unblemished nature of the goat; however, the very close identity between all three forms of this offering makes it legitimate to presume that both factors apply for the goat too.

as we have argued before, by way of identifying ownership, but also a sign that the animal was a substitute for the worshipper. Having done this, however, the presenter was not free to withdraw and become a mere spectator. As always, the worshipper was then required to slaughter the animal personally before handing the dead body over to the priests (2, 8, 13). True worship can never be done by proxy.

The next act in the ritual drama sees the priests taking centre stage because it concerned blood, the most sacred element of the slaughtered victim, which spoke of its life being laid down (17:11). The priests catch the blood in a bowl (Exod. 27:3; 38:3), and then *splash the blood against the sides of the altar* (2, 8, 13) by swinging the bowl back and forth around the altar, dramatically representing the pouring out of the animal's life to God.[6] No mean quantity of blood was involved.

Certain parts of the animal were then selected for burning *on top of the burnt offering . . . it is a food offering, an aroma pleasing to the* LORD (5, 11, 16). From our perspective the choice of which parts were to be burned is curious. The parts chosen for burning from the cattle were *the internal organs and all the fat that is connected to them, both kidneys with the fat on them near the loins, and the long lobe of the liver, which you will remove with the kidneys* (3–4). The same instructions were issued for sheep and goats (9–10, 14–15), but, in the case of sheep, there was the additional requirement to burn *the entire fat tail cut off close to the backbone* (9). A breed of broad-tailed sheep is known to have existed in the Middle East, their tails, consisting mainly of fat, weighing on average about 7 kilograms. They are known to have been so heavy that shepherds would sometimes construct a primitive trolley to enable the sheep to be mobile. These were probably the sheep in mind here.[7]

The portions of the animals that were offered to God as choice cuts are the very portions most Westerners today despise. Why were fat and kidneys so special? We must disabuse ourselves of thinking about this matter from a dietary viewpoint. God is not hungry and in need of 'fattening up' with a good meal. These items were chosen for their cultic value rather than their nutritional merit. Though Milgrom thinks the explanation is 'shrouded in mystery',[8] it is not unreasonable to venture some rationale for the choice.

---

[6] Noordtzij, p. 35.

[7] Demarest, p. 51; Milgrom, *Leviticus 1 – 16*, p. 212.

[8] Milgrom, *Leviticus 1 – 16*, p. 207.

The suet around the entrails and organs was a hard waxy fat that symbolized strength and prosperity. Fatness spoke of abundance and was not culturally despised, as it is by many today. True, the Israelites could recognize the spiritual liabilities of prosperity (e.g. Deut. 32:15; Jer. 5:28), but they more often spoke of it as a positive symbol of blessing. When, for example, Isaac blessed Jacob, he prayed that God would give him 'the fatness of the earth' (Gen. 27:28, NRSV). The blessing of God was measured by the fatness of lambs as well as by the plumpness of the grain and the grapes (Deut. 32:14). All this suggests that it was the richest part of the animal that was being reserved for God. Liver and kidneys, similarly, have symbolic significance. Both were considered delicacies because they were thought to be the seat of a person's deep emotions and innermost thoughts.[9]

In offering these parts of the anatomy to God, then, those who drew near with a peace offering were not only offering God the best, but also offering up their greatest strengths and deepest emotions of gratitude to the Lord in submissive worship.[10]

A final observation about the ritual calls for our attention. Verse 5 says that the priests are *to burn it on the altar on top*[11] *of the burnt offering*. The peace offering was not an atonement sacrifice; it could fulfil its part in enabling people to celebrate God's goodness only in conjunction with the atonement already made by the burnt offering. Without atonement, people were not in a position to draw near to God and offer this sacrifice, which would not have been acceptable had they done so.

b. What Leviticus 3 omits

For all the details mentioned when the offering is first introduced, we have to look elsewhere for a fuller picture, especially to the instructions given to the priests in Leviticus 7:11–21. This fuller picture may have been held back deliberately so that the worshipper did not rush too quickly to the communal-meal element of the sacrifice and so perform the sacrificial aspect before the Lord in a perfunctory manner. The worshippers were to give attention to the Lord first, and only then to one another.[12]

---

[9] Pss 16:7, 9; 73:21; Jer. 11:20; 17:10; Lam. 2:11. Hartley, p. 40, points out the relationship between these and the heart.

[10] Kiuchi argues that in Lev. 3 neither inner emotion nor the outward expression of ritual was sufficient on its own, but each needed the other. 'Spirituality', p. 30.

[11] The Hebrew may be 'with' rather than 'on top of', but the significance of the comment remains the same. Levine, p. 16.

[12] See Kiuchi, 'Spirituality', pp. 26–27.

The meat that was not burned on the altar was used to provide a celebratory meal for the worshipper's family and others from the community, not forgetting the priests. It was a communal activity, intended to strengthen the bonds of fellowship both with God and with the neighbours, friends and relatives who were invited to it (hence the name 'fellowship offering' that some give to it). Eating meat was a luxury in ancient Israel and these celebrations would have been occasional rather than regular. The menu consisted not only of meat but also of both leavened and unleavened bread (7:12–14). Both kinds of bread were to be made available; the providers could not opt for their favourite.

A couple of instructions gave guidance on how the meal was to be conducted; however, these did not interfere with its character as a joyful feast. Neither fat nor blood was ever to be eaten, for reasons we have seen, in line with the general restriction on eating blood (3:17; 17:10–12). The meal was eaten in or near the precincts of the Tent of Meeting. Unlike the grain offering (2:3, 10), it was not among the 'most holy' sacrifices and, therefore, did not necessarily have to be eaten within the precincts of the sanctuary, nor need it be consumed by priests alone, although they did join in the celebration. Only those family members or friends who were ritually unclean were prevented from coming to the table (7:20); otherwise, the welcome was as wide as the celebrants desired to make it. Among the guests invited, there would almost certainly have been some who were too poor to be able to afford the sacrifice for themselves.

If the purpose of the offering was to express thanksgiving to the Lord, the meat had to be eaten on the day it was offered (7:15). If its purpose was to seal a vow or was otherwise a freewill offering, the eating could extend for a further day. A variety of reasons have been suggested for these different restrictions. They may have been meant to moderate the flow of offerings, by demanding that the meat be eaten fairly immediately, and prevent a queue building up.[13] If the food could not be stored, it would encourage daily dependence on God's provision.[14] The restrictions may have been motivated by health concerns, given the hot temperatures in their climate. After three days the food would almost certainly have been contaminated. More convincingly, it would encourage the celebrants to share their meal widely and include the poor among the

---

[13] Bellinger, p. 48.

[14] Wenham, p. 124.

guests, rather than waste the food.[15] But, chiefly, we should remember these are cultic restrictions, designed to express the ritual concerns of purity and impurity, rather than seeking to rationalize them with modern explanations.

2. The purposes it served

Peace offerings were widely deployed on public as well as private occasions and figured in some of the highest and lowest points of Israel's history.[16] Three specific and usually more personal purposes are mentioned in Leviticus, within the context of one overall aim.

a. To express one's thankfulness

The instructions given to the priests speak of it first as 'an expression of thankfulness' (7:12), and this reason seems uppermost. Worshippers were celebrating the way God had blessed them by giving something back to him in gratitude. The dominant note was that of joy, as Deuteronomy 12:7 makes clear. The giving of a gift was then, as it remains now, a natural way to express appreciation; this is what the children of Israel were doing to their generous and gracious God.

Gordon Wenham has queried whether the word *tôdâ*, which he says is usually translated as 'thanksgiving', is not better rendered as 'confession'.[17] Confession, he argues, is not only a legitimate translation but a broader concept, involving both the confession of sin and the confession of faith. While this may have some merit, it is still evident that thankfulness is the major theme of this particular sacrifice.

Israel was frequently invited to 'enter his gates with thanksgiving and his courts with praise; [to] give thanks to him and praise his name' because 'the LORD is good and his love endures for ever'.[18] In presenting the peace offering Israel was doing just that – not with words[19] or music, but by symbolic action.

---

[15] Harris, p. 557; Kaiser, p. 1051.

[16] E.g. Judg. 20:26; 1 Sam. 9:12–13; 10:8; 2 Sam. 6:17–18; 24:25; 1 Kgs 8:62–64; 2 Chr. 29:31–35; 30:22–27. They seem particularly associated with times of covenant renewal.

[17] Wenham, p. 78 n. 11.

[18] Ps. 100:4–5. See also, e.g., Pss 105:1; 106:1; 107:1.

[19] Leviticus is curiously silent with regard to any words spoken during its liturgies and concentrates exclusively on actions.

b. To confirm one's vow

Another purpose of the peace offering was to seal a vow (7:16). Vows were common in Israel, and diverse. The final chapter of Leviticus gives one example of the way some people were vowed to God's service (27:2), just as Hannah promised that any son God blessed her with would be devoted to him (1 Sam. 1:11). Nazirites entered a vow committing themselves to a particular lifestyle in their service of God (Num. 6:2, 21). David vowed that he would not sleep until he had found a dwelling-place for God (Ps. 132:2–5).

Women and men, it seems frequently resorted to pledges of one kind or another (Num. 30:1–5), so much so that perhaps the integrity of those promises was liable to be devalued. The wise teacher thundered against the folly of rashly making a vow before God and then delaying or excusing its execution (Eccl. 5:4–6). Accompanying a vow with a sacrifice was a way of stressing the solemnity of giving one's word in a vow. Whereas thoughts can be fleeting and words cheap, a solemn ritual action is a conscious activity that can have a restraining impact on those tempted to promise something too casually.

c. To profess one's love

Psalm 116:12 asks, 'What shall I return to the Lord for all his goodness to me?' One answer to that question was to offer him a peace offering, a sacrifice freely given with no strings attached. Such is the 'freewill offering' mentioned in 7:16. It may have been given to celebrate a particular answer to prayer or experience of deliverance (Pss 22:25–26; 54:1–7), but it was not given as exact payment, or to win God's favour, or to manipulate him for the worshipper's own ends. It was purely a spontaneous expression of love.

d. To strengthen one's communion with God

Whatever the specific reason that occasioned any particular sacrifice, in general this offering was a meal celebrated with others in the presence of God and had the effect of strengthening the bonds of friendship, not only with one another, but also with the Lord. It is easy to see why some prefer to call it the fellowship offering.

Modern anthropologists often interpret sacrificial worship primarily as a communion meal that unites a people with their deity, and that construction is frequently laid on the sacrifices of Israel. There is a large element of truth in it, but, while accepting its thrust, caution must be exercised to prevent the rise of any distorted understanding about Israel's worship. Though the meal is a celebratory one offered and enjoyed by family and friends, the host at this meal is God himself. The Lord is not even just the chief and honoured guest, but the one who invites his people to come, ultimately provides the necessary food, arranges the details of the feast and hosts it near to his dwelling-place. Those who enjoy the fare owe the occasion to his favour.

In pagan cultures, the worshippers thought of themselves as providing sustenance to their gods, who were consequently reduced in their eyes by their dependence on their providers. But the God who hosted Israel's peace offering had no such need. In the words of Psalm 50:9–12:

> I have no need of a bull from your stall
>> or of goats from your pens,
> for every animal of the forest is mine,
>> and the cattle on a thousand hills.
> I know every bird in the mountains,
>> and the insects in the fields are mine.
> If I were hungry I would not tell you,
>> for the world is mine, and all that is in it.

The idea of the fellowship meal must not be used to diminish Israel's God, for he was great beyond compare. 'God desires the sacrifices of His worshippers not because He requires sustenance but because He desires their devotion and their fellowship.'[20]

Other sacrificial meals were deemed to strengthen the bonds of union between a people and their deity through some sensuous experience or magical technique. But these forms of spirituality are foreign to the ethical and atoning spirituality of Israel. This meal is not eaten, in some mystical way, 'with' the Lord but 'in the presence of the LORD'.[21] Such feasting does not, as the latter part of Leviticus will remind us, exempt us from the need for obedience to God's word. The enjoyment of his presence is enhanced both through spending deliberate and worshipful time in his presence *and* through faithful and obedient living in his world.

The meal speaks of the assurance Israel feels in the presence of the God of the covenant, and tells of the bounty they have received from his hand.

---

[20] Levine, p. 17.
[21] Deut. 12:7. Milgrom, *Leviticus 1 – 16*, p. 221, and Kaiser, p. 1024.

It was a happy, beneficial and settled relationship, as long as Israel kept their obligations under the covenant.

3. The meaning it conveys

The peace offering has continuing significance for Christian believers, as we can see from the way it is referred to and reapplied within the New Testament.

a. It speaks to our life in community

The peace offering gives us a picture of the children of Israel living in harmony with one another, celebrating the goodness of God together and providing for the needs of the poor among them, through communal feasting on a luxurious meal. This may be an idealized picture of well-being, but it is one they experienced in reality on occasions.

John Hartley helpfully suggests that the picture Luke sketched of the early church in Acts 2:44–47 'fulfils the design of the offering of well-being'.[22] The life of the early Christian community, no less than the peace offering, was characterized by providing for the poor ('They sold property and possessions to give to anyone who had need'); gathering together in the house of God ('Every day they continued to meet together in the temple courts'); eating a shared meal ('They broke bread in their homes and ate together'); and expressing thanks and praise to God ('with glad and sincere hearts, praising God').

Here, then, is a model of the community life of the church. It is far from the stiff, formal reality that is often encountered within the church. It speaks of a community whose fellowship is characterized by genuine care that finds expression in practical action on behalf of the needy, not by a superficial camaraderie. It is marked equally by a God-centred spirituality that overflows in joyful worship in his presence.

b. It speaks to our practice of communion

Paul makes use of the model of the peace offering when he writes to the Corinthians about the Lord's Supper.[23] His words in 1 Corinthians 11:17–34

---

[22] Hartley, p. 42.

[23] Bailey's claim, p. 28, that Christian communion derives historically from the Passover rather than the peace offering, though correct, forces an unnecessary choice between them. Shades of both are evident in the New Testament.

conspicuously echo this Levitical offering. Both meals celebrate a covenant with God. The peace offering celebrates God's covenant with Israel forged on Mount Sinai; the Lord's Supper celebrates the glory of his new covenant[24] forged on the hill of Golgotha. The former required people to be in a state of ritual purity before they participated in the meal; the new covenant requires people to be in a state of personal purity before they participate in the supper (1 Cor. 11:27–32). The former forbade the drinking of the blood of the sacrificial victim;[25] by contrast, the latter requires the drinking of the blood of the sacrificial victim. Indeed, Paul quotes Jesus' explanation that the cup of wine signified his shed blood and was the cup of 'the new covenant in my blood'.[26]

As we have seen, there was a very real social dimension to the peace offering, which, in addition to binding friends and family closer together and to the Lord, may well have been an occasion when those unable to afford such a luxurious item as meat were invited to join those who could. In this respect the Corinthian experience of the Lord's Supper had proved the very antithesis of the peace offering with its emphasis on social holiness and community bonding. Paul rebukes the Corinthian Christians for falling below the standard set in ancient Israel. It seems the rich selfishly fattened themselves on plentiful food and became intoxicated with drink while remaining indifferent to the needs of the hungry and thirsty who sat alongside them (1 Cor. 11:17–22). Rather than building community, the way the Corinthian Christians behaved at the Lord's Supper destroyed it. The communion meal had degenerated into a game of one-upmanship. Natural social divisions were being not only tolerated but exacerbated, thus betraying the very gospel they claimed to believe. Many churches still fail to experience a genuine communion with God as they sit around the Lord's Table, not because their doctrinal statement is defective, or because their liturgy is faulty, but because they, like the Corinthians, have disconnected what they believe from how they treat those who are less advantaged among them.

Paul's damning verdict was that whatever the meal they were eating in this divisive manner was, it was not the Lord's Supper. So he instructs them more perfectly about the Lord's Table, with a view to leading them

---

[24] 2 Cor. 3:1–18; Heb. 8:6–13; also John 6:53–58.

[25] Lev. 3:17 applies this prohibition particularly to the peace offering and insists on it as 'a lasting ordinance'.

[26] 1 Cor. 11:25; Matt. 26:28; Mark 14:24; Luke 22:20.

to repentance and to developing a true communion meal over which the Lord himself would be pleased to preside. Such a meal would build genuine bonds of friendship with him and between each of them.

c. It speaks to our motivation in worship

A further echo of the peace offering is found in Hebrews 13:15–16:

> Through Jesus . . . let us continually offer to God a sacrifice of praise – the fruit of lips that openly profess his name. And do not forget to do good and to share with others, for with such sacrifices God is pleased.

It, too, combines the upward dimension of praise to God with the outward dimension of service to others. Praise, it reminds us, should be continual rather than occasional, and service sacrificial rather than casual. Here, rather than in the endless round of meetings and the perpetual singing of songs, is true worship.

d. It speaks to our hope for the future

The peace offering was presented not only as an act of thanksgiving for God's blessing in the past but also as an expression of hope for God's blessing in the future. The picture of God's people sitting down at a banquet in his presence is one that fuelled Israel's hope. Isaiah used the image to look beyond the dark days of Israel's defeat and failure to the age of the Messiah. 'On this mountain', he prophesied, 'the LORD Almighty will prepare a feast of rich food for all peoples, a banquet of aged wine – the best of meats and the finest of wines' (Isa. 25:6).

Jesus adopted the same imagery in his teaching about the coming kingdom of God. Picking up the note of celebration inherent in the peace offering, he recast the imagery of the feast to come as a wedding feast (Matt. 22:1–14). But he did more than merely adapt the image. He revolutionized it. Leviticus made it clear that participants at the table of a peace offering were required to be ritually pure, and the Pharisees had stoutly maintained this perspective in their thinking about who would be invited to the messianic banquet. But Jesus says that his banquet would be different. Those who were invited to sit at the feast of the Messiah would be those most considered to be unclean. They were to be the Gentiles, the poor, the crippled, the lame and the blind – the very folk whom respectable religious leaders would have barred from their table. But Jesus' sacrifice would make them clean and qualify them for a seat at the feast (Luke 13:29; 14:12–24). This hope still remains to be fulfilled in the future. Believers still look forward with keen anticipation to the wedding supper of the Lamb (Rev. 19:1–9).

When the sacrificial system came into full operation the peace offering was the last offering to be performed.[27] It brought the other offerings to a climax. For that reason it has been called 'the completion offering'.[28] Having secured atonement through the sin offering, provided reparation through the guilt offering, expressed consecration in the burnt offering and dedicated their work to the Lord in the grain offering, it was possible for worshippers in Israel to enjoy God's presence and bask in his goodness through the peace offering. Without any shade of arrogance, it sounded a note of assurance about their present relationship with God and a note of confidence about the future provision he would make for them.

As the Christian believer might put it:

Perfect submission, all is at rest,
I in my Saviour am happy and blest;
Watching and waiting, looking above,
Filled with his goodness, lost in his love.

This is my story, this is my song,
Praising my Saviour all the day long.[29]

---

[27] Alec Motyer has insightfully suggested to me that the order of the sacrifices in 1:1 – 6:7 expresses the Lord's desire that worship begin with full consecration and move to the full enjoyment of fellowship with God and others, with the sin and guilt offerings coming at the end of the list to deal with occasional lapses in commitment, whereas the order in 6:8 – 7:38 expresses the order of priestly duty. My own understanding differs slightly, as is evident in my exposition of the relevant passages, but neither of us can be certain.

[28] P. Jenson, 'The Levitical Sacrificial System', in Beckwith and Selman, p. 31.

[29] From 'Blessed Assurance, Jesus Is Mine', by Fanny J. Crosby (1820–1915).

Leviticus 4:1 – 5:13

4. Forgiveness from God: the sin offering

From offerings freely offered to the Lord in worship, Leviticus turns to obligatory acts of atonement, resolutely required by the Lord. Two such sacrifices are introduced: the sin (or purification) offering in 4:1 – 5:13 and the guilt (or reparation) offering in 5:14 – 6:7. Both reflect a deep concern about sin and the impurity that ensues from it.

Sin is taken seriously because it is a personal attack against God, a repudiation of his grace and a rejection of his loving will for Israel. It results in people being alienated from him, and in the pollution of the world, which causes it to be out of harmony with its Creator. Given the seriousness of the problem, it is essential that there should be a way of restoring people's relationship with God and of bringing balance back to his world. Indeed, there is such a way. For ancient Israel the sin offering is the means of repairing the harm caused by sin. It is a remedy that God himself graciously provides, even though he is the offended party.

The details of the sin offering are given in two sections. They are first set out in general terms in 4:1–35, then developed somewhat differently in 5:1–13, which itemizes the sacrifices required according to what a penitent sinner could afford. For this reason, this second presentation of the offering is sometimes referred to as 'the graduated sin offering'.[1]

---

[1] Hartley, pp. 51 and 54, and Milgrom, *Leviticus 1 – 16*, p. 307.

1. When was the offering presented?

God's initial words to Moses about the sin offering say that it should be offered *when anyone sins unintentionally and does what is forbidden* (4:1). This obviously catches a fair range of sin in its net, though not all. From what follows, it is clear that one major concern is failure in the performance of religious duty, through either negligence or ignorance. But this offering also embraces failure to observe God's ethical law. This initial statement is not elaborated further in chapter 4, but the opening verses of chapter 5 present a number of specific examples that are intended, presumably, to illustrate the general principle. Both the general and the specific statements require further exploration.

a. When sin was unintentional (4:2, 13, 22, 27; 5:15, 18)

The only help given in clarifying what it means to 'sin unintentionally' is that it is about doing *what is forbidden*. It raises a lot of questions. What does the word 'unintentional' mean? If one sins 'unintentionally', which must mean sinning without being conscious of the implications of what one is doing, how does a sinner become aware of the forbidden act and so be brought to a place where he or she wants to remedy it? Does it mean that there is no possibility of forgiveness for deliberate, intentional sins? Are we condemned to bear the consequences of those for ever?

The translation of *bišgāgâ* as 'unintentional' or 'inadvertent' may put a slightly misleading spin on the word, although opinion is divided. Some say that it means just what it says. The Jewish scholar Baruch Levine, for example, explains that it is perfectly possible to sin unintentionally through being either ignorant of the law or ignorant about the offensive nature of an act one commits.[2] Since most commentators attribute these sins to ignorance, 'inadvertent' is certainly a better translation than 'unintentional', which wrongly focuses on the subjective will of the sinner. The point being made, then, is that ignorance of God's law is no excuse: sins have consequences that need remedying whether their perpetrator is aware of them or not, and guilt is a real condition that needs atoning for whether the sinner feels guilty or not.

In this case, anyone who has committed sin inadvertently may become aware of it in a number of ways. Others might point it out to him or her.

---

[2] Levine, p. 19.

Fresh knowledge of the law might be gained. Conscience might smite. Prophetic or other supernatural communication might reveal it, perhaps through the use of the Urim and Thummim.[3] The dawning of an awareness of sin is not uncommon in the experience of recent converts to Christ who, having been blithely ignorant of their wrongdoing until their conversion, now discover how truly objectionable to God their previous way of living was. Once they realize their guilt, they wish to confess their sin and seek forgiveness. And that is the situation here.

But if expiation is provided only for unintentional sins, does that mean there is no hope for those who, overcome by its power, sin deliberately and in full knowledge of the wrongness of their actions? Israel's hope for remedying such sin would seem to lie in the ritual of the Day of Atonement, which atones for all sin. But, as some would point out, it does not do so by exempting a deliberate sinner from experiencing punishment for the offence, by first being 'cut off'.[4]

Other commentators,[5] however, point out that the root meaning of the word (šāgag) is simply 'to wander' or 'to err' and so is best translated 'to go astray in sin' or 'to do wrong' rather than 'to sin unintentionally'. It covers situations where, although God's people have an intention to be obedient to him, they lapse on occasions. This leads Harris to conclude that 'the usual sins we fall into are covered by the sin offering'. Harrison puts it even more strongly, saying that the word refers to all 'conscious acts of disobedience and offences committed as a result of human weakness and frailty'.[6] Therefore, those with a tender conscience need not fear that they will be unable to secure forgiveness for sins they knew were wrong but were unable to prevent themselves from committing, or which were done through carelessness (5:4). Ignorance may be one cause of sin, weakness another.

Support for this more inclusive view of sin is gained from Numbers 15:22–31. It contrasts the person who sins unintentionally with the person who sins defiantly, that is, with a deliberate and rebellious intent to subvert God's law and to ridicule his name. It is these sins 'of a high hand', akin to Jesus' reference to 'blasphemy against the Spirit',[7] for which the

---

[3] Exod. 28:30; Lev. 8:8. Wenham, p. 99; Kaiser, p. 1035.

[4] The phrase 'cut off' first appears in 7:20 and on many occasions subsequently. Its meaning will be discussed in chapter 6 below. This position is maintained by e.g. Milgrom, *Leviticus 1 – 16*, p. 228.

[5] Harris, p. 547. He is supported by Kaiser, p. 1033.

[6] Harrison, p. 60.

[7] Matt. 12:31–32. Jesus speaks of this sin in the context of stressing that 'every kind of sin and slander can be forgiven' except blasphemy against the Spirit.

sin offering cannot provide a remedy because they involve the sustained and considered rejection of God. The more inclusive translation still holds out no hope for the flagrant sinner who mocks God.

While the broader view is a more reassuring interpretation, it still means that somehow the sinner has to become aware of sin, face up to it and have a desire to seek atonement – an atonement that the sin offering can provide.

b. When sins were casual (5:1–4)

Leviticus moves from the general to the particular. Chapter 5 verses 1–4 lists three specific sins that require the remedy of the sin offering. The common error that links them is that of a casual attitude towards social and spiritual responsibilities.

The first sin (verse 1) betrays a casual attitude towards one's responsibility to the community, especially in matters of justice. Biblical law leaves us in no doubt that every member of the community had a duty to see justice done, which involved not only speaking the truth rather than speaking falsely, but also speaking up rather than remaining silent. Long before it was said that 'The only thing necessary for the triumph of evil is for good men to do nothing',[8] the Bible was warning that the good and integrity of the community could soon be undermined if people failed to speak up against wrong and injustice. Silence was not an option for the Israelite in the face of evil, especially if it concerned the rights of those who were poor and needy (Prov. 31:8–9).

There is a real concern today that the growth of a self-absorbed individualism is eroding what is fashionably called 'social capital' – the moral inheritance that binds a society together and makes it wholesome.[9] Many have retreated into their own concerns and do not want to get involved in building an improved society that is more honourable, just and full of integrity than the one we currently inhabit. To do so would necessitate being involved in the ugly worlds of politics, law and the media, and this putting oneself on the line may well attract opprobrium. But the faults specified in reference to the offering here clearly label such indifference to the needs of the wider community as sin.

---

[8] These words are often attributed to Edmund Burke (1729–97), but their exact source is unknown.

[9] See further discussion in chapter 16 below.

The social philosopher David Selbourne listed eleven reasons why people engage in moral evasion today.[10] They protest that (1) there's nothing we can do about it; (2) it's never been any different; (3) there's no quick fix; (4) it's the price of a free society; (5) you must move with the tide; (6) you can't turn back the clock; (7) the problem is more complex than you think; (8) it's beyond the reach of the law; (9) you're focusing on the wrong issue; (10) who are you to talk?; and (11) everyone's doing it so who are you to object? None of these excuses would have been acceptable in Israel. People were not permitted to take refuge behind casual pretexts, and so were unable to avoid responsibility, as verse 1 stresses in its assertion that *they will be held responsible*. As a people bound together by covenant they had obligations to one another; their whole identity was based on their relationships. Sin, though personal, was never a private matter. All sin was sin against society, and members of that society were charged with the responsibility both to guard against sin and to do what they could to correct it.

The second sin (2–3) betrays a casual attitude towards issues of ceremonial purity and relates to touching something that is unclean, be it in the animal or the human world. Uncleanness was viewed as contagious and so anyone who came into contact with it was considered ceremonially impure. Impurity had serious consequences and could be removed only by an act of cleansing. This issue was of such importance that detailed explanations of what falls into the category of 'unclean' and of what a person was to do about any impurity that might have been contracted occupy a good deal of Leviticus.[11] Here a 'taster' is given, which stipulates that touching the carcass of a dead animal, or coming into contact with a ceremonially unclean human being, renders people impure whether they were aware of the contact or not. The resulting defilement could be cleansed through confession and by the presentation of a sin offering (5–6).

The third sin (4) betrays a casual attitude to personal integrity and highlights the sin of making rash promises, especially those that involve the swearing of an oath. If the first charge was about being too slow to speak up, this charge is about being too quick to speak out. Leviticus taught positively the importance of taking vows seriously when it

---

[10] David Selbourne, *Moral Evasion* (London: Centre for Policy Studies, 1999).

[11] Particularly 11:1 – 15:33; 17:15–16; 21:1 – 22:16.

commanded that they should be accompanied by a grain offering (7:16). Here, the same point is made from a negative perspective. Making promises without being aware of the import of what was being vowed would do more than reflect badly on the rash speaker: it involved sin before God, for which atonement was necessary.[12]

2. Whom did the sin offering ransom?

Unlike other offerings, which were, generally speaking, of a 'one size fits all' variety, the sin offering is remarkable for the way in which its instructions are applied differently to various groups and individuals in Israel. The community of Israel is included as a whole, as well as the full range of individual members within it. The list begins with the high priest (4:3–12), moves through the community seen as an entity (4:13–21), and on to the community leaders individually (4:22–26), before concluding with the individual citizen (4:27–35). The organization of the list in this way is no accident, nor are the differing requirements laid upon those within it.

The list begins with the high priest (4:3–12), who is called by his alternative title of *anointed priest* (6:22).[13] His sins would involve failure to perform the ceremonies of Israel correctly, perhaps through negligence or some contamination of his ritual purity. Considering that the cost of it would fall on his shoulders alone, he was required to offer the most expensive sacrifice of all. He was to offer *a young bull without defect* (3). The high priest was the essential intermediary who stood between God and his people, acting as their teacher and representative. If, for whatever reason, he was found in a state of impurity, the people would 'have no one to lead them to God'.[14] That would be a grave situation for a community covenanted to the Lord to face, and one that would require urgent repair. The sins of the high priest were no private matter and had repercussions for all, as the failure of those in any public Christian leadership positions still has today. The failure of earthly priests and leaders points to both the necessity and the wonder of God's provision of Jesus as our great High Priest, whose life and service manifested unblemished purity (Heb. 4:15).

---

[12] See pp. 315–316. The topic is mentioned again in Lev. 27:1–25.

[13] The high priest alone was anointed (Lev. 8:12). Note the close connection between the high priest and his anointing in Lev. 16:32; 21:10; Num. 35:25.

[14] Hartley, p. 59. This, rather than the failure to lead by example, mentioned by Kaiser, p. 1034, is probably the primary reason for the priority given to the high priest.

Attention then turns to the people of Israel as a whole (4:13–21). When they fell into collective sin, they also were required to offer a young bull in sacrifice (14), with the elders of Israel acting as their corporate representatives in the purifying rite (15). How could they sin 'inadvertently' en masse, especially in view of their profession, as expressed through the burnt offerings, to obey the Lord? One suggestion might be that they had observed one of the festivals on the wrong day because of a miscalculation of the calendar.[15] A more probable illustration is found in Joshua 9, where Israel entered a treaty with Gibeon without consulting the Lord.[16] In the ancient world, it was much more common for people to think collectively – to think of themselves as a corporate personality rather than as individual beings – and so the inclusion of *the whole Israelite community* as a single unit responsible to God is entirely understandable. In areas where individualism has triumphed over the collective, people still need reminding that 'Righteousness exalts a nation, but sin condemns any people' (Prov. 14:34).

Next in line (4:22–26) comes any of the leaders of Israel who had fallen into error through negligence or ignorance. The clan chiefs or tribal leaders of Israel are dealt with separately from ordinary citizens because of the responsible positions they held and the impact their sin could have on others. The offering they are required to make is less valuable than that required from the high priest or the nation as a whole. Furthermore, its blood is dealt with at the altar of burnt offering, situated in the outer court of the tabernacle, rather than at the altar of incense, which was deemed to be more sacred because it was located in the Holy Place.

Finally come the other members of the community (4:27–35). Their sin was still serious and atonement was still necessary. But, given that it was the sin of an ordinary citizen, it was not thought to attract as great a penalty as the sin of the one whose position was more influential. They could, therefore, bring a female goat (4:28) or a ewe lamb (4:32), and if even that was beyond their means then common doves or pigeons (5:7–10), or even a small quantity of flour – *a tenth of an ephah*[17] – unadulterated by oil or incense (5:11) would prove sufficient. God's intention was that forgiveness should be readily available to all, and not beyond the reach of

---

[15] The festival calendar is set out in Lev. 23. The suggestion is Milgrom's, *Leviticus 1 – 16*, p. 242.

[16] Hartley, p. 62.

[17] A tenth of an ephah is approximately 2.2 litres.

even the poorest member of the community. G. A. F. Knight expresses the wonder of it: 'How gracious, understanding and merciful this God is whom we meet here. Just a mere cupful of flour for the sin of your soul! *And he shall be forgiven* ([5:]13). What a God this is.'[18]

3. How was the offering performed?

The basic pattern of these sacrifices was the same, but there were significant differences to tailor the sacrifice to the person bringing it. The sacrificial victim was presented *at the entrance to the tent of meeting* (4:4, 14). Even the high priest had to take his sacrifice there to start with. He had no fast track or special privilege just because he was the high priest. Where sin was involved, he stood where others stood – distant from the presence of God until the matter was resolved. The entrance to the Tent is specified because it was as far from the Most Holy Place as it was possible to be and yet still be at the Tent.

For the main animal sacrifices, those presenting the offering would lay their hands on the victim's head and slaughter the animal (4:4, 15, 24, 29, 33). Priests would then take the blood and dispense it in the prescribed manner. It is here that the chief differences in the ritual emerge. In the high priest's case, he himself takes the blood into the Tent and is instructed to

> *dip his finger into the blood and sprinkle some of it seven times* [symbolizing fullness, thoroughness] *before the LORD, in front of the curtain of the sanctuary. The priest shall then put some of the blood on the horns of the altar of fragrant incense that is before the LORD in the tent of meeting. The rest of the bull's blood he shall pour out at the base of the altar of burnt offering at the entrance to the tent of meeting.* (6–7)

An identical ritual was carried out when the sin offering was made on behalf of the entire community (16–18). But if the sacrifice was offered on behalf of an individual leader, the blood was not sprinkled seven times in front of the sacred curtain, or daubed on the horns of the altar of incense, but rather simply painted on the horns of the altar of burnt offering, which was in the outer court, with the surplus poured at its base (25). The same procedures

---

[18] Knight, p. 34.

and location were involved if the offering was presented by ordinary members of the Israelite community (30, 34). The differences are explained in terms of sacred geography. The high priest was a holy person, and the nation was a holy nation. Sprinkling the blood on the curtain that divided the Holy Place from the Most Holy Place – the very centre of God's presence on earth – and anointing the horns of the inside altar indicated, therefore, that their sins were taken and dealt with more seriously than those of ordinary people, whose sins were dealt with outside the Tent itself.

The final act in the ritual was the burning of the fat, liver and kidneys of the sacrificial victim on the altar of burnt offering (4:8–10, 19–20, 26, 31, 35). The reasons for choosing these particular bits of the carcass are the same as in the peace offering. Then, instead of eating the meat in a celebration meal, as they would have done in the peace offering, the priests have to take it *outside the camp to a place ceremonially clean, where the ashes are thrown, and burn it there in a wood fire on the ash heap* (12; cf. 21). The reason for the difference at this point is obvious. No-one can be seen to profit from sin. God will not reward wrongdoing, even if it has been done in ignorance or because of a slip in memory. Therefore, nothing was to be left, not even the hide, that could have been of profit. Everything was to be turned into smoke.[19]

This instruction, in fact, is given only in relation to the high priest's offering and that for the whole community. Leviticus is silent about the disposal of the leftover meat in the case of individual leaders and ordinary citizens. It is likely, on the basis that we are told what is to happen to the surplus in the case of the poorest offering (5:13), that the surplus meat would be used for the support of the priesthood; but we cannot be sure.

4. What does the offering achieve?

The purpose of the sin offering seems abundantly clear. Five times the instructions are brought to a conclusion with the wonderful words: *In this way the priest will make atonement for the community, and they will be forgiven* (4:20; cf. 26, 31, 35; 5:13).[20] The purpose is the removal of sin, together with all its consequences, and the restoration of the sinner's

---

[19] Hartley, p. 61.

[20] There are two slight variations in wording, neither of which alters the meaning: *make atonement for the leader's sin* (4:26) and *make atonement for them for any of these sins they have committed* (5:13).

relationship with God. 'God, we see,' writes George Knight, 'has now stooped to win. He has placed in man's hands the means whereby he will forgive man's sins, if only man wants to use those means.'[21] So each sacrifice is completed with the pronouncement of forgiveness.

However, a careful examination of the rite, and of the occasions on which it was used, has led some to believe that the purpose of the offering is better expressed in terms of purification rather than, as traditionally, of expiation. For that reason, some prefer to call it 'the purification offering', rather than 'the sin offering'. We examine both ideas in turn, starting with the emphasis on purification.

a. Purification

God commanded the sin offering to be presented on a number of occasions in addition to those we have been considering. A woman who had given birth was required to offer it, along with a burnt offering, as part of the process of her reincorporation into the active worshipping life of Israel (12:6–8). While it is still said that the offering would secure her atonement, this is amplified by the words 'and she will be clean' (12:8). A similar situation arises in the case of someone re-entering the community following leprosy. Among the offerings required was the sin offering, and again it is said that the priest would 'make atonement for them, and they will be clean' (14:19–20).

The third example where a sin offering is connected with impurity comes in chapter 15, which concerns bodily discharges. A new factor is added to our understanding, for it states there that the Israelites must be kept from things that would defile them so that 'they will not die in their uncleanness for defiling my dwelling-place, which is among them' (15:31). Sin, evidently, not only defiles the sinner but also pollutes the tabernacle where God dwells, driving him from his home among them. 'The God of Israel will not abide in a polluted sanctuary',[22] and without its cleansing the death of those who are responsible for the pollution would follow, as the tragic story of Nadab and Abihu illustrates (10:1–5). Once the rituals of the Day of Atonement are taken into account, those who advocate this interpretation argue that the essential purpose of the sin offering was to

---

[21] Knight, p. 32.

[22] Milgrom, *Leviticus 1 – 16*, p. 258. Milgrom is the chief proponent of the 'purification' view, but is followed by many others, including Wenham, pp. 88, 93–96.

cleanse the polluted sanctuary – not the polluted person – so that God might dwell securely among his people.[23]

If the principal purpose of this offering was to purify God's dwelling-place, several things follow. Blood is the cleansing agent that acts as the detergent that 'de-sins'[24] the sanctuary. This explains why key places within the tabernacle – the curtain and the altars – are sprinkled with blood, but the sinner was not. It explains the difference between the place where blood was sprinkled for the high priest and the whole community of Israel and the place where it was sprinkled for lay members of Israel. The high priest worked in the sanctuary and represented the whole community of Israel there. He, therefore, had opportunity to cause pollution within it by his sin, unlike the laypeople, who were not permitted to enter the Holy Place. What was being cleansed, then, was not the sinner but the tabernacle, and the act of atonement was an act, not of expiating sin, but of purging impurity. *Kipper*, the word for 'to atone', can certainly carry the meaning of 'to purge', as well as 'to expiate'.[25]

Clearly sin does defile, and its pollution causes offence to God, who needs to be reconciled to his people. Without question, blood is the cleansing agent. To that extent, this interpretation gives a wonderful insight into the grace of God in providing a way for purification. But this view is not wholly adequate if it is held to the exclusion of the more traditional one, to which we shall turn shortly. While it helpfully explains some of the unique aspects of the ritual – principally, where the blood is placed – it gives little consideration to other aspects. Wenham says we need not give attention to these, because they form the 'common core to all the sacrifices'.[26] But the laying on of hands, the killing of the victim, the burning of select parts of it and the subsequent removal of its body outside the camp (in two cases, 4:12, 21) still cry out for interpretation. Furthermore, if it is the sanctuary that is being cleansed, then the poor sinner is still left in a state of impurity, notwithstanding Milgrom's attempt to explain their cleansing as unnecessary.[27] The traditional interpretation addresses some of these questions far more adequately.

---

[23] Milgrom argues that the offering 'never purifies its offerer' and has no need to do so because the very fact that 'he feels guilt . . . means that he has undergone inner purification', *Leviticus 1 – 16*, p. 254.

[24] Hartley, p. 55.

[25] Further consideration to the meaning of *kipper* will be given in chapter 13 below.

[26] Wenham, p. 94.

[27] See note 22 above.

b. Atonement

The traditional position may be stated briefly. Sin does indeed pollute and demands the shedding of blood in order for atonement to be made. Having discovered their sin, offenders draw near with the required sacrifice to deal with their guilt, transferring their sin to the victim, which then forfeits its life as a substitute for them. Its blood is borne by the priest and sprinkled as a symbol of life being offered to God. Part of the animal is burned in an offering to God. This atones for the sin by offering up a life in place of the sinner's life, which, because of the commission of sin, merited death; and thus it propitiates the wrath of a holy God. Then, in the first two cases, the rest is taken *outside the camp to a place ceremonially clean, where the ashes are thrown,* and it is burned *in a wood fire on the ash heap* (4:12), as a symbol that the sin of the offender has been totally removed and dealt with. The sinner is therefore reconciled to God and his or her sin atoned for, just as the announcement of absolution by the priest says (4:20, 26, 31, 35; 5:13).

This position elucidates the role of the priest, the blood and the burning of the sacrifice before God in the sin offering, although it does not particularly explain why blood is used in a special way – indeed, in some cases, uniquely brought into the sanctuary. But it does better explain the offering as a whole. Kaiser suggests that those who advocate the purification theory are in danger of reading back specific things from later chapters, especially from the Day of Atonement,[28] and imposing them on the sin offering, which has a different and broader remit.[29]

In a thorough study of the issue, N. Kiuchi points out that the pronouncements of forgiveness are quite explicit. They say that when the priest has made atonement it is the person who is forgiven. It is personal language, the language of 'he', 'she' and 'they'. The priests do not say, 'the sin shall be forgiven', still less that the sanctuary will be purged, but that the offender is forgiven.[30] Violating God's commands, Kiuchi underlines, incurs a real guilt on the part of the sinner, not just a subjective feeling of guilt, as Milgrom surmises. The sin offering is designed to restore the sinner, remove the guilt and deal with all the consequences of sin, not just its pollution of the sanctuary. Only the traditional interpretation makes

---

[28] See especially 16:15–20.

[29] Kaiser, p. 1033.

[30] Kiuchi, *Purification*, p. 37.

adequate sense of the rituals of the sin offering and offers the sinner the forgiveness needed.

5. Why does the offering matter?

The sin offering continues to be of value for Christians both through its dramatic portrayal of a number of spiritual truths and supremely in the way it points to Christ as the ultimate offering who secures our forgiveness.

a. The loathsome nature of sin

The understanding of sin this offering contains is far richer than the rather superficial understanding many believers have of it as a private matter that unfortunately involves the breaking of a few commandments. Sin is a loathsome offence to God, which seriously disrupts our relationship with him and with the world he has made. Sin defiles us when we commit it and places us in need of cleansing deep inside our being. It pollutes our lives, as smog once polluted the streets of London, causing us to be lost in the world that was designed to be our home. Sin is never an individual matter, the consequences of which affect only the person who commits it. It is a social matter and has a detrimental impact on others who are members of the same community, as is taught both by the seriousness with which the leaders' sin is treated and also by the way in which Leviticus speaks of the sin of non-involvement (5:1). Leaders cannot separate their public responsibilities from their private lives. They carry responsibility for others and, having received the great privileges of leadership, will be judged with greater strictness than others, as both Jesus (Luke 12:48) and James (3:1) reaffirmed. Sin may well sometimes be the result of carelessness or negligence rather than malice or forethought, but it is still sin. Sin has consequences, whether we are aware of them or not. As soon as we are aware of it, we need to confess and deal with it, not leave it to fester and pollute further. Yet forgiveness is possible – even for the poorest person, who can offer a cup of flour. None need stay mired in sin.

b. The wonderful grace of Christ

Cleansing from sin takes place through the offering of blood, which acts as a spiritual detergent. Hebrews 9:22 points out that 'the law requires that nearly everything[31] be cleansed with blood, and without the shedding of blood there is no forgiveness'. The principle crosses over from one covenant age to the other, as Hebrews 9:14 explains, because it is now the blood of Jesus Christ that cleanses us. If the old sacrifices made those who were ceremonially defiled clean, 'How much more, then,' it cries, 'will the blood of Christ, who through the eternal Spirit offered himself unblemished to God, cleanse our consciences from acts that lead to death, so that we may serve the living God!' Jesus Christ not only acts as our great High Priest who offers the sacrifice to God on our behalf, but also voluntarily surrenders himself as the perfect offering whose blood is shed and body sacrificed in our place. His flawless offering purifies us outside and in, and restores our broken relationship with God.[32]

Hebrews 13:11–12 picks up one further connection between the work of Christ and the sin offering. 'The high priest', it says,

> carries the blood of animals into the Most Holy Place as a sin offering, but the bodies are burned outside the camp. And so Jesus also suffered outside the city gate to make the people holy through his own blood.

Its purpose in saying this is to encourage Christian believers to accept willingly the contempt they receive because of their faith in Christ. But equally true is the assurance that Christ's sacrifice removes our sin from us completely, just as the ashes of the bull were removed outside the camp.

In Henry Francis Lyte's words:

> Ransomed, healed, restored, forgiven,
> Who like thee his praise should sing?[33]

c. The continuing possibility of offence

Even though they are the temple of the Holy Spirit, believers can still live in such a way as to grieve the Spirit of God by persistent disobedience, and so drive him away (Eph. 4:30), just as in Israel sin distanced God from his people. Believers need to 'keep in step with the Spirit' (Gal. 5:25) and be

---

[31] A reference to the sin offerings of flour from the poor, which did not involve blood.

[32] In spite of Wenham's favourable attitude towards the purification interpretation of the sin offering, he concedes (p. 101) that 'whereas in the Leviticus laws it was the place of worship that was purified, under the new dispensation it is the worshipper himself'.

[33] From 'Praise, My Soul, the King of Heaven', by Henry Francis Lyte (1793–1847).

continually filled with him (Eph. 5:18) in order continually to enjoy his presence.

When fellowship between a believer and God is interrupted by sin, the way back remains the same in principle as it was for Israel. Confession should certainly be made to God, but perhaps on occasions there is wisdom in making it to others also, as the ancient Israelites did to the priest, and as James seems to recommend for the church (Jas 5:16). The remedy still lies in an offering of blood, although for Christian believers the offering has been sacrificed once and needs no repetition (Heb. 9:28). Nevertheless, we need to apply the atoning work of Christ's cross to our lives afresh and, having done so, find again the assurance of forgiveness. The words of pardon with which the priest brought the sin offering to a climax are words that the apostle John applies to believers: 'If we confess our sins, he is faithful and just and will forgive us our sins and purify us from all unrighteousness' (1 John 1:9).

The sin offering made atonement for the people of ancient Israel and yet was only a sketch of the fuller work of Jesus Christ. With hindsight we see that all the blood of beasts slain on Jewish altars could never wash away sin, make sinners clean and draw them back to God, apart from the single offering of Jesus, the Lamb of God.

Leviticus 5:14 – 6:7

5. Amendment before God: the guilt offering

Grace is dangerous. The marvel of God's unconditional love is that it makes forgiveness so freely available that it risks being reduced in our thinking to cheap grace. Dietrich Bonhoeffer, the German pastor who was executed by Hitler's regime in the dying days of the Second World War, warned of the damage done to our Christian discipleship when we make grace too cheap. He wrote:

> Costly grace is the gospel which must be *sought* again and again, the gift which must be *asked for*, the door at which a man must *knock*.
>
> Such grace is costly because it calls us to follow, and it is grace because it calls us to follow Jesus Christ. It is costly because it costs a man his life, and it is grace because it gives a man the only true life. It is costly because it condemns sin, and grace because it justifies the sinner. Above all, it is costly because it cost God the life of His Son: 'ye were bought with a price', and what has cost God much cannot be cheap for us. Above all, it is grace because God did not reckon His Son too dear a price to pay for our life, but delivered Him up for us.[1]

The guilt offering – the fifth offering God commands his people to present – guards the Israelites from falling into the error of believing that grace is cheap. Like the sin offering it was a blood sacrifice that obtained pardon for sinners, but it differed from the sin offering in that it was concerned

---

[1] Dietrich Bonhoeffer, *The Cost of Discipleship* (1948; London: SCM, 1959), p. 37.

with specific sins and included a unique element of reparation as part of the ritual.

Traditionally, the offering has been called a 'guilt offering' because its Hebrew name, 'āšām, has the meaning of legal culpability. Those who presented the offering, it has been believed, were in a state of guilt. Milgrom has questioned this interpretation and concluded that the word 'āšām refers to a subjective feeling of guilt rather than an objective state of guilt. On this basis, those who brought the offering were seeking to silence their disturbed consciences by compensating for any damage caused by their actions rather than by appeasing an offended God. Milgrom thinks, therefore, that the name 'reparation offering' is preferable to 'guilt offering'.[2] True, the focus is certainly on the element of restitution but, even so, the guilt incurred is an objective one, not merely a subjective feeling that is dependent on the variable conscience of the Israelite worshipper. The twin elements of real guilt and tangible reparation are closely bound together in this offering.

1. The particular concerns of the guilt offering

This offering deals with three classes of sin, each introduced by the phrase *If anyone sins* (5:15, 17; 6:2).[3] The first and third groups relate to a breach of trust. The second category is of a more general nature and leaves some uncertainty as to how it may be distinguished clearly from the wrongs that are atoned for by the sin offering.

a. The sin of sacrilege (5:14–16)

The primary purpose of this offering is to atone for the unintentional misuse or misappropriation of *any of the LORD's holy things* (15). An example of the sacrilege that might transpire is given in Leviticus 22:14, where the priests are warned to make sure that 'laypeople' do not eat meat that has been set aside as 'a sacred offering' for consumption by the priests and their families alone. People might equally have been remiss in using some of the utensils or furniture from the tabernacle for their own ends, without realizing the sacredness that was attached to them. It would appear that a broad range of sacred objects is in view.[4]

---

[2] Milgrom, *Leviticus 1 – 16*, pp. 327, 339–345.

[3] The NIV translates the first, *When anyone is unfaithful . . . by sinning.*

[4] Milgrom, *Leviticus 1 – 16*, pp. 320–325.

On this occasion, the offering does seem to have *unintentional* violations in view.[5] The guilt offering offered no 'quick fix' for those who had wrongly appropriated sacred things in full awareness of what they were doing. When Achan, for example, took and hid the spoils of war with an intention to use them for himself, even though they had been devoted to God, he and his household bore the unmitigated punishment for his sin without any possibility of gaining acquittal through the offering of a sacrifice (Josh. 7:1–26). The things that have been consecrated to God are never to be treated casually or used for ordinary purposes. Sacred things are ring-fenced to prevent them from being contaminated by contact with the secular world.[6] As soon as people became aware that they had unwittingly trespassed in this regard, they needed to put the matter right and receive the pardon God graciously provided.

b. The sin of disobedience (5:17–19)

The second category of sin relates to people who did *what is forbidden in any of the LORD's commands* (17). This category seems to be a wide one, embracing disobedience to God's ethical law as much as the infringement of any regulations concerning sacred things. If this were so, it is hard to see the distinction between this offering and the sin offering.[7] It is more likely that things connected to the tabernacle are still in view; that is certainly how later Jewish interpreters understood it. Given this, one must ask how the sins of this category differ from those covered in verses 14–16. Some say that it is a shift from a violation that was known to one that was unknown, and that as soon as the infringement was discovered, a ram was to be offered in sacrifice.

However, the probability is that these verses refer to cases where individuals suspect they have transgressed in regard to sacred things but cannot be certain. Whenever such tender consciences smote, it was recommended that the offering was presented as a precautionary measure.[8] In this way relief from both the uncertainty and the fear of guilt was obtained when the priest pronounced acquittal. Since the exact nature of the sin was questionable, no reparation was prescribed.

---

[5] See pp. 56–58 above.

[6] Gerstenberger, p. 68.

[7] For a summary of the various attempts that have been made to distinguish them see N. Kiuchi, 'Sacrifices and Offerings', in *DOTP*, p. 720.

[8] Levine, p. 31, and Wenham, p. 108.

c. The sin of unfaithfulness (6:1–7)

The remarkable thing about the third category of sin is the way in which it is introduced. It concerns anyone who sins *and is unfaithful to the LORD by deceiving a neighbour* (2). When the Israelites entered a covenant with God they were simultaneously entering a covenant with one another. They were bonded together as God's special people and had responsibilities towards one another that required all their relationships to be marked by love and integrity. To break faith with one's neighbour, therefore, was to break faith with God; to sin against one's neighbour was to sin against God.

The thread that connects the various misdemeanours listed here is a breach of faith – the sort that occurs in the ordinary business of life, especially in relation to money and property. Sadly, a couple of the examples given are all too familiar in our own day. The first offence concerns the failure to look after someone else's property when asked to care for it, and then the refusal to assume responsibility for its loss or damage (2). The second offence involves stealing (2) or the gaining of any acquisition by false means, perhaps through extortion (2, 4). The third example is the practice of deceit (3). Anything less than transparent honesty misses the mark. The fourth offence happened when someone worked on the basis of 'finders keepers' (3). The law was explicit that when people found something that did not belong to them it was their duty to seek out the owner and give the item back (see Exod. 22:9; 23:4; Deut. 22:1–3). The fifth offence concerned the swearing of false oaths (3, 5), either deliberately in the making of a vow or consciously in a court of law. Complete integrity was required at all times in one's dealings with one's neighbours. Anything less than that resulted in the need for payment of compensation and for an offering to be sacrificed to God.

All three classes of sin display an impressive concern on the part of the children of Israel to protect what they held sacred and to prevent sin from undermining or destroying it. So concerned were they that it seems they even offered sacrifices 'just in case' sin had occurred. As in the story of Job (1:5), so here, the Israelites left nothing to chance and refused to regard as trivial any sin that might lead to what was sacred being turned into something secular.

2. The unique provisions of the guilt offering

'The neglected Book of Leviticus is a long study', writes Walter Brueggemann, 'on the good news that God has indeed provided ways through the paralysis of guilt.'[9] Whether guilt was actually merited or whether it was simply feared, there was a remedy close to hand. It came in two halves, making the guilt offering unique among the sacrifices of Israel. First to be mentioned was the payment of *a penalty* consisting of *a ram from the flock* (5:15, 18; 6:6). Second was the payment of another kind: a fine for the purpose of reparation.

a. The sacrifice it involved

Little detail is to be found in these verses about the sacrificial ram and what happened to it, except that it was to be a domestic animal rather than a wild one and was to be *without defect* (5:15, 18; 6:6). Only later, in 7:1–10, when instructions are given to the priests, do we learn that the procedures that followed the presentation of the ram were similar to those for the sin offering. The ram was killed and its blood 'splashed against the sides of the altar' (7:2). The suet and kidneys were then burned on the altar as an offering to God.

The stipulations for this offering are then complicated by the addition of the requirement that the ram must be *of the proper value in silver, according to the sanctuary shekel* (5:15, 18; 6:6). What could this mean? The surface meaning is that the ram had to be of a certain value, which, since it is unspecified, would be left to the priests to determine, perhaps according to the seriousness with which the sacred had been infringed. The value of it was to be calculated not in ordinary currency but in the currency of the tabernacle, which was heavier than the currency in ordinary circulation. This currency was still in use in Jesus' day, and its strict use (or abuse) was, in part, what provoked him to clear the temple of those who traded in sacrifices and engaged in money-changing.[10]

There are, however, other ways to understand these words. Since there is no reference to the ram being slaughtered in the initial regulations, some think that even though a ram was presented, it was not killed, but rather converted into a monetary value that was given to the priests as a

---

[9] Brueggemann, *Finally*, p. 23.

[10] Matt. 21:12–17; Mark 11:15–19; Luke 19:45–48; John 2:13–22.

guilt offering. God had been robbed, so God should be repaid.[11] This, however, is exceedingly unlikely, since the subsequent regulations make clear that the ram was sacrificed, exactly in the way one would expect of an atoning sacrifice.[12] Others believe that the regulation means that a suitable sum of money should be brought to the priest, who would then purchase a ram on the offender's behalf.[13] Still others argue that it provided the guilty person with a choice: he or she could bring either a ram or its equivalent value in money.[14] One way or another, a ram of a certain value was required and slaughtered.

b. The restitution it required

Little more is said about the fate of the ram because interest focuses on the second, unique, aspect of the guilt offering; namely, reparation. When either God or a neighbour had been deprived, for whatever reason, of what belonged to them, the law required that the guilty person should *make restitution in full, add a fifth of the value to it and give it all to the owner on the day they present their guilt offering* (6:5). In other words, not only should the property be restored in full but also a 20% fine should be added to its value to compensate the owner for the inconvenience caused.[15] This would serve as an effective deterrent and prove a suitable form of justice in a community that was still small enough to involve face-to-face relationships. The 'fine' was not going to be swallowed up by the cost of administering justice by the state, as it would be today.

It is important to note that restitution had to be made before the sacrifice was offered (6:5). Putting matters right with one's neighbours was as essential as putting matters right with God. Indeed, the debt that sin had incurred before God would not be removed until the debt to the neighbour had been paid in full. Yet offenders were not forgiven their guilt simply by making amends with their neighbours. On its own, making things right with one's neighbours was not sufficient, because to sin against them was also to sin against God, and so the matter needed to be cleared with him.

---

[11] Noth, p. 47; Milgrom, *Leviticus 1 – 16*, p. 327. The guilt offering referred to in 1 Sam. 6:1–18 was an offering of gold figures rather than a ram.

[12] Noordtzij, p. 71.

[13] Wenham, p. 107.

[14] Levine, p. 31.

[15] Hartley, p. 84, notes that the 'one-fifth' addition is lower than that required elsewhere (e.g. Exod. 22:1–9), but may be designed to encourage voluntary confession of sin and restitution rather than resorting to legal proceedings.

Furthermore, only by securing atonement from God through sacrifice could the 'weighty residue of ache'[16] that sin brings in its train be dispelled. The Godward and the human dimensions of spirituality are inseparable.

The act of reparation would have the value not only of making amends to the victim of the crime, but also of testing the genuineness of the offender's confession and remorse. Words could be cheap and the blood of sacrifices made to flow too easily. Neither of these revealed the true state of the guilty person's heart. But the restoring of filched or damaged property to its owner with the added 20% bonus would soon reveal how seriously the offender wanted to put the matter right. It was, says Milgrom, an early portent of the doctrine of repentance, which would 'flower into full bloom with Israel's prophets'.[17]

3. The continuing relevance of the guilt offering

The guilt offering receives only occasional attention in the rest of the Old Testament and does not figure among the great sacrifices of Israel (see 1 Sam. 6:1–18; Ezra 10:19; Ezek. 46:20). The most significant reference to it, as we shall see, occurs in Isaiah 53. Furthermore, there are no direct references to it in the New Testament, although there are a number of allusions. For all the puzzles about this offering, though, it continues to point to important spiritual truths.

a. The claims of God

Our society has long lost virtually all consciousness of the sacred. Almost nothing seems sacrosanct and nothing inviolable. Practically everything is open to cynical probing and secularized abuse. Very little seems to be held sacred other than an individual's right to live how he or she likes, the right of children to know protection, and the right to freedom of speech, at least on the part of the press. The principle of 'human rights' is the value that drives both contemporary politics and law. But Israel was concerned about 'God's rights'. He claimed certain rights – including those over sacred property – and no excuse of ignorance, negligence or unintentionality could exempt his people from a binding obligation to respect his possessions and his will.[18]

---

[16] Brueggemann, *Finally*, p. 26.

[17] Milgrom, *Leviticus 1 – 16*, p. 345.

[18] Kaiser, p. 1042.

Malachi took up this theme when he charged Israel with unfaithfulness, not least in robbing God of tithes and offerings (Mal. 3:8–10). But, he claimed, they showed contempt for his sacred name in other ways too, such as by presenting him with maimed sacrifices and failing to keep their commitment to their marriage partners (Mal. 1:13–14; 2:10–16). As with the guilt offering, no hierarchy of sins is involved; one act of unfaithfulness is not more heinous than another. Breaching faith with God and breaching faith with one's partner amounted to the same thing – sin!

The same emphasis on God's rights over our lives is found in Paul's writing. Galatians, for example, echoes Malachi's admonition when, having spoken about integrity in both relationships and finances (Gal. 6:1–6), Paul concludes, 'Do not be deceived: God cannot be mocked. A man reaps what he sows. Whoever sows to please their flesh, from the flesh will reap destruction; whoever sows to please the Spirit, from the Spirit will reap eternal life' (Gal. 6:7–8). His instructions to the Corinthians had run along not unrelated lines. Although they were in the age of the new covenant and not subject to the legalistic paying of a tithe, their financial giving to God's work should be regular, considered, joyful and generous.[19] Only so would they reap a rich reward in eternity and only so could they express tangible thanks for 'his indescribable gift'.

God still has a claim on our lives. It is a claim that includes our money and our time. Failure to give God his due, even if we just unconsciously crowd him out in the busyness of our lives or short-change him in the midst of financial pressures rather than consciously exclude him, puts us at odds with him and in need of reconciliation and restitution.

b. The debt of sin

If the sin offering pictures sin as dirt that needs cleansing, the guilt offering pictures sin as a debt that needs paying. It is a debt we accrue either by not honouring God or by breaking faith with our neighbour. To see sin as a debt seems a natural thing to do. Jesus certainly saw it like this. Twice he used the analogy in his parables. In Luke 7, having been anointed by a disreputable woman in the home of a prudish Pharisee, Jesus explained that those who had had many debts forgiven were bound to love him more than those whose debts were few (Luke 7:36–50). In Matthew 18 the same analogy is used with a different emphasis. Telling the story of

---

[19] 1 Cor. 16:1–2; 2 Cor. 8:1 – 9:15. See further chapter 23 below.

an unmerciful servant, Jesus warns that those who will not release others from their debts will not receive release themselves from God (Matt. 18:21–35). In line with this, when Jesus taught his disciples to pray, he taught them to ask God to 'forgive us our debts, as we also have forgiven our debtors' (Matt. 6:12; Luke 11:4).

This understanding of sin is taken up by Paul, who makes use of it to explain both the consequences of our failure to keep God's law and God's wonderful way of remedying our failure. The Israelites had entered into a covenant to keep God's law, and when they failed to do so the penalty clauses were invoked, putting them in God's debt. Gentiles did not have the benefit of the covenant, but their position was no more advantageous than that of the Jews, since, in their case, their conscience led them to keep God's law and so to be indebted to him when they did not do so (Rom. 1:18 – 3:31). Neither Jew nor Gentile was capable of meeting the cost of the penalty incurred. But Jesus took 'the certificate of indebtedness' and discharged it for us, by nailing it to his cross.[20] Through his crucifixion the debt of our sin has been paid in full.

We must be careful not to reduce this wonderful solution to an impersonal financial transaction, as if the quantity of our sins were balanced in the scales against the quantity of Christ's blood shed on the cross. This devalues it to what Edward Irving called 'stock exchange divinity'.[21] The debt of sin is found not on an impersonal balance sheet but in the profoundly personal effect it has in disrupting our relationship with the living God and, indeed, with our neighbour. It is in the giving of himself, through his Son, that the relationship is restored and the barrier of debt removed.

c. The blessing of substitution

Isaiah 53 speaks of the suffering of the servant as a guilt offering (Isa. 53:10). The servant, who was despised by his fellow humans and crushed by God, was, in reality, bearing the consequences of the sins of others, including our own. Taking our infirmities and carrying our sorrows, 'he was pierced for our transgressions' (Isa. 53:5) so that, through the offering of his life as a substitute for ours, we might be 'ransomed, healed, restored,

---

[20] Cf. Col. 2:13–14. The paragraph follows P. T. O'Brien, *Colossians, Philemon*, Word Biblical Commentary (Waco: Word, 1982), p. 125.

[21] C. Gunton, *The Actuality of Atonement* (Edinburgh: T&T Clark, 1988), pp. 129–131.

forgiven'.[22] Whomever else the suffering servant might have portrayed, the early Christians saw Jesus as the ultimate fulfilment of Isaiah's prophecy. They alluded to Isaiah 53 again and again to explain Christ's mission on the cross.[23] Jesus, then, is the crowning guilt offering, who provides full compensation to God for our sin and frees us from the debts we owe him.

Some have sought to probe further and explain how both elements of the guilt offering – the sacrificial and the restitutional – are found in Christ. The act of restitution may occur through his consistent, active obedience, and the act of atonement through his voluntary surrendering of his life on the cross. As we participate 'in Christ', the benefits of both are made over to us (Phil. 2:8; Heb. 5:8–9). Kellogg sought an even more precise understanding of how Christ met the requirement of the guilt offering, and explained that not only did his perfect life make full restitution, but the 20% that was added 'came through the ineffable depth of his self-humiliation and obedience unto death, even death on a cross'.[24] But such a view is overly precise, and may even feed our fancy by its creativity instead of feeding our hearts in adoration.

d. The need for restitution

Surely it was the sacrifice of the guilt offering that Jesus had in mind when he told his disciples,

> if you are offering your gift at the altar and there remember that your brother or sister has something against you, leave your gift there in front of the altar. First go and be reconciled to them; then come and offer your gift.
> (Matt. 5:23–24)

Zacchaeus, who restored far more than the law required when he met Jesus, is presented as an illustration of how those living in the new covenant should behave (Luke 19:1–9). They should do more, not less, than the law laid down. The offering of worship is still no substitute for making practical amends for sin. Both are required.

---

[22] From 'Praise, My Soul, the King of Heaven' by Henry Francis Lyte (1793–1847).

[23] Wenham, ad loc., cites the following allusions: Isa. 53:1 in John 12:38 and Rom. 10:16; Isa. 53:4 in Matt. 8:17; Isa. 53:5–6 in 1 Pet. 2:24–25; Isa. 53:9 in 1 Pet. 2:22; and Isa. 53:12 in Luke 22:37. See also D. Tidball, *The Message of the Cross*, The Bible Speaks Today (Leicester: IVP, 2001), pp. 100–116, 137–141, 285–290.

[24] Kellogg, p. 172.

One wonders how often the presence of God seems absent from our worship services, not because the minister is ill-prepared, or the liturgy defective, or the songs ill-chosen, but because some of those in attendance are deluding themselves by thinking that by their much singing and praying they can conjure up the presence of God, when what is really needed is for them to go and pay their bills, apologize to their friends, repair bridges with their neighbours, meet their obligations to their families and make practical amends for any cheating in which they have been engaged. Just as significant is the cheating they have done on God, by their meagre offerings or the paucity of time they have set aside for him in daily devotion or in public worship. If reparation were made in these areas, might we not see God 'open the floodgates of heaven and pour out so much blessing that there will not be room enough to store it' (Mal. 3:10)?

The guilt offering speaks, once more, of a gracious God, who provides the means by which guilty sinners can be freed from their debt of sin. But it is no cheap grace. The grace that flows from God flows from an altar where the life of his Son was slain. And it flows into lives of those who, conscious of God's holy compassion, treat sin seriously, strive to live in integrity and make costly reparation when they fail.

Leviticus 6:8 – 7:38

6. Instructed by God: the priests' responsibilities

The role of the priests was critical in the life of Israel. They were the mediators of everything holy. They stood in the spiritual danger zone as go-betweens between God and his people, offering worship and interceding for forgiveness. Their task, defined in Leviticus 10:10–11, was to 'distinguish between the holy and the common, between the unclean and the clean', and to teach Israel 'all the decrees the LORD has given them through Moses'.

Up to this point, God, using Moses as his voice, has been addressing all the Israelites about their responsibilities as his covenant people (1:1–2; 4:1–2). Since these were responsibilities they had to fulfil in person and that could not be passed off to others to perform for them, it was right that the people should be taught directly about them rather than learning of them at second hand. But the priests were to play a special part in helping the people of Israel in their offering of sacrifices, so it was necessary that they also should be addressed and instructed in matters that would specifically concern them. So, at 6:8, we enter a new phase, with the Lord saying to Moses, *Give Aaron and his sons this command* (9). Much of the ground covered is familiar, but the perspective on it is distinctive and nothing is merely repeated. The ground is traversed again only if there is something new to be added.[1]

This command covers all five of the sacrifices to which the people of Israel have been introduced. Each offering here is introduced by the words

---

[1] Balentine, p. 60.

These are the regulations for . . . (6:9, 14, 25; 7:1, 11). These words not only serve as section dividers but also indicate the thrust of the material we shall find here. These *regulations* are about the ritual administration of the sacrifices and deal with matters that, while they would be of no concern to the laity, were of utmost concern to the priests. The fact that these verses were addressed to the priests also explains why the order in which the offerings are reviewed differs from the earlier order. Previously the voluntary offerings were introduced first, followed by the obligatory offerings of atonement. Here it is the *most holy* offerings (2:3, 10; 6:17, 25; 7:1, 6) – the offerings in which the priests had a more prominent part to play – that are dealt with first (6:8 – 7:10). The peace offering, which could be eaten by lay folk as well and was only a holy offering (as distinct from a most holy one) is considered last (7:11–21).[2]

The overwhelming impression these regulations leave is that of the duty of care that was laid on the shoulders of the priests. The worship they conducted was marked by 'scrupulous attention to detail and punctilious obedience to God's instructions',[3] without which an offering would not be accepted (e.g. 7:18). To our minds, some of the regulations appear to consist of niggling details that make us question what sort of God Israel served if he was so concerned about what priests wore or what pots they used. But the problem is ours rather than theirs, because each minute instruction, quite apart from having a particular significance, was sending out a signal that obedience to God's words and will was the most important service that Israel could render and so worship was to be conducted to a superlative degree of excellence and exactitude. The God of Israel was not to be worshipped in any slipshod manner, with rituals being hastily thrown together at the last minute according to the fancy of either the priest or the people. God's holiness made it essential for the Israelites to approach him with caution, reverence, humility and awe.

The responsibilities of those who lead worship under the new covenant are no less than those of the priests of old. No reduction in the standard of obedience to God's word, care with which worship is prepared, or the quality of excellence with which it is performed is acceptable just because we live in the age of grace rather than of law. It is Christian believers, not old-covenant Israelites, who are exhorted to 'be thankful, and so worship

---

[2] Milgrom, *Leviticus 1 – 16*, p. 382.

[3] Wenham, p. 127.

God acceptably with reverence and awe, for our "God is a consuming fire"' (Heb. 12:28–29). We require standards of professionalism and precision from our doctors, our engineers, our builders, our plumbers and our car mechanics. Shoddy workmanship on the part of any of them could well not only cause inconvenience, or require money to remedy what they have done defectively, but even cost lives. How much more should those of us who have the responsibility of leading worship – which involves people's eternal destiny – do so with diligent care!

A fatal misunderstanding often leads Christians to confuse worshipping God 'in spirit and in truth' with unprepared spontaneity and slipshod presentation. Many have begun to contrast spirit and form in a disastrous manner. Gordon Wenham, in a lengthy passage worth quoting in full, exposes our erroneous thinking:

> 'The letter killeth but the Spirit giveth life' is a text that out of context (2 Cor. 3:6) can be used to justify slapdash leading of services and other Christian activities. Spontaneity and lack of preparation are equated with spirituality. Lev. 6 – 7 denies this: care and attention to detail are indispensable to the conduct of divine worship. God is more important, more distinguished, worthy of more respect than any man; therefore, we should follow his injunctions to the letter, if we respect him.
>
> A glance at the performing arts dispels the illusion that a great and spirited performance can be achieved without practice and attention to detail. Indeed great actors and musicians spend hours studying and rehearsing the works they are to perform, so that they can recapture the spirit of the author and convey it in their performances. Audiences expect performers to aim at perfection in the concert hall. Worship is also a performance, a performance in honour of almighty God. As no orchestra can give of its best without a competent conductor and meticulous rehearsal, so no congregation is likely to worship our holy God in a worthy manner without careful direction by a well-instructed minister.[4]

How do the instructions given to the priests teach this?

---

[4] Wenham, p. 128.

1. Keep the fire burning (6:8–13)

The first duty of the priest concerned the burnt offering, which was offered daily both in the morning and again in the evening: it was the simple task of keeping alive the fire on the altar of burnt offering. The initial instruction to do so (9) is repeated for emphasis at the climax of this short passage: *The fire must be kept burning on the altar continuously; it must not go out* (13).

First and foremost, fire speaks of the presence of God among his people. The God who revealed himself to Moses in the fire of the burning bush (Exod. 3:2), and to Israel in fire on Mount Sinai, where 'the voice of the Lord flashes forth flames of fire',[5] and who led his people from a pillar of fire in the wilderness (Exod. 13:21), would often be compared by the prophets to a blazing fire (Isa. 10:17; 30:27; 31:9; 33:14; Dan. 7:9–10). Fire was a fitting symbol for God's active holiness. The fire on the altar in the tabernacle was to be ignited by God himself (9:24) as a sign of his acceptance of their offering and of his dwelling among them. The fire of God was no longer to be encountered in a distant desert, on a distant mountaintop or in a distant cloud, but on an altar at the heart of the community, and was to be kept burning perpetually to symbolize God's nearness to them. But the presence of their holy God, like fire, is at one and the same time comforting, warming, refining, purifying and terrifying in its potentially destructive power. So the priests were forbidden to 'play with fire' and commanded to tend it with care.

Fire speaks, second, of the worship of Israel. 'The perpetual fire on the altar', writes Baruch Levine, 'expressed the devotion of the Israelite people to God by indicating that they were attendant upon God at all times in the sanctuary.'[6] It was a symbol of their perpetual worship and, because it was on the altar of burnt offering, a reminder of their continual sinfulness, for which daily forgiveness needed to be sought.[7]

Whether it was the fire that comes from God, epitomizing his continual, holy presence among them, or fire that was offered up to God, enabling their worship to ascend continually to him, the priests had a task to perform and needed to be vigilant in executing it. None was to despise it

---

[5] Exod. 19:18. The quotation is from Ps. 29:7, NRSV.
[6] Levine, p. 36.
[7] Knight, p. 42.

as too menial an assignment for a priest of Israel to undertake. The humble role of removing the ashes and laying on fresh wood was not to be beneath them. They were the servants of God, called to do his bidding whatever it may be.

The priests were to do all this not as they chose but as he instructed. That meant that they were to perform the duty regularly, not periodically or when the mood took them. The careful daily ritual makes a virtue out of routines and exemplifies a spirituality that seeks to be constantly in touch with God. As Samuel Balentine comments, 'Regular – not occasional – acts of worship anchor life in God. Observance of the rites of faith that is disciplined – not haphazard or sporadic – keeps one in tune to truths that may otherwise slip or be overlooked.'[8]

The priests were also to change their clothes between one part of the task and the other (10–11). Priestly robes, right down to their priestly undergarments, were to be worn only within the precincts of the tabernacle – holy garments for a holy place. But when the priests left those precincts to dispose of the ashes *outside the camp* in a place that, although *clean*, was not holy and so was distant from God's presence, they were to change their clothes and wear ordinary garments. They were to guard against their sacred vestments becoming defiled. The changing of their clothes was a coded message about the need to prevent holy things from being devalued and made to be of no special importance. The things of God were extraordinary and ought to be treated as such.

2. Keep the aroma pleasing (6:14–23)

The next section concerns grain offerings. It deals first with the regular offerings presented by any Israelite (14–18) and then with the grain offerings presented by the priests at the time of their ordination (19–23). The text stresses that both offerings were made to the Lord and were his possession to be disposed of as he decreed. So God graciously allows the priests to eat a portion of the regular grain offering. The same is not true, however, in the case of the offerings they themselves brought, which God reserved wholly for himself. The priests were not permitted to benefit from their own offerings, since, logically, these offerings should cost the

---

[8] Balentine, p. 66.

priests something rather than provide them with a profit. And whereas any priest could prepare an ordinary person's grain offering, only the priest who was to succeed the high priest could prepare the high priest's own offering (22).

This offering is a *most holy* one (17), which means that only priests could eat it (18), because they alone had the status of holiness conferred on them by their ordination. Anyone else who ate it, perhaps inadvertently, would be committing sacrilege and would need to present a guilt offering, as prescribed in 5:14 – 6:7, by way of reparation. The importance of this is underlined by the last part of verse 18, which, according to the NIV margin, reads, in reference to the portion set aside for the priests, 'Whoever touches them must be holy.'[9]

Admittedly the translation of this verse is problematic. Does it mean that all who touch the sacred portion must be holy or else they will defile it, or that all who touch it will become holy and be sanctified by their contact with it? Milgrom, in a tour de force, has argued that it is correctly translated 'Whatever touches it will become holy.'[10] Anything, in other words, that comes into contact with a portion of the most holy offering will have holiness transmitted to it. This is not wholly good news as far as people are concerned. It could well lead to the person's death, as it did for Uzzah when he reached out to steady the ark on its way back to Jerusalem (1 Chr. 13:1–10; cf. Num. 4:15). 'Judgement falls', as Gordon Wenham remarks, 'when the unclean meets the holy.'[11] The balance of arguments, however, weighs in on the other side.[12] On the basis of Exodus 29:37 and 30:29, the context strongly suggests that holiness is a prerequisite for individuals who come into contact with the altar rather than a consequence of their touching it. And Haggai 2:11–13 is unequivocal in its teaching that sacredness is not contagious, whereas impurity is. Mere contact with the holy does not make a person clean, but contact with pollution defiles someone as quickly as anything. For these reasons this verse should be taken as a warning, underscoring the need of those who touch any part of the grain offering to be rightly qualified to do so.

The important message for the priests is that the grain offering must be performed with punctilious exactitude. Otherwise the aroma

---

9 NIV margin. See also v. 27.

10 Milgrom, *Leviticus 1 – 16*, pp. 443–456.

11 Wenham, p. 121.

12 E.g. Levine, p. 37, and Hartley, p. 97.

would not be *pleasing to the* LORD, but would be, rather, a bad odour that would cause him offence. Their task was to ensure that the aroma was pleasing at all times.

3. Keep holy things safe (6:24–30)

The same lesson is taught in the regulations about the sin offering. Everything about these instructions highlights the importance of treating holy things with care. Like the first two offerings in this section, the sin offering is *most holy* (25). So, after the animal had been presented at the entrance to the Tent, everything else relating to it occurred within the grounds of the tabernacle. It was slaughtered *in the place where the burnt offering is slaughtered* (25) and was also to be consumed within the confines of the Tent's forecourt.

The same point is made about the need for those who come into contact with the meat of the offering to be holy (27) as was made in respect of the grain offering – assuming the interpretation given above is accepted. But then a new point is added. What happens if the priest's vestments get soiled with the victim's blood, as was more than likely, given the violence of its killing? Could the priest take the spattered garment home for washing? The answer is a clear 'No'. Blood is the seat of a creature's life (17:11) and so it is a most sacred object – even more so since it had been offered up to God. So even the blood on the apron must remain within the environs of the tabernacle and the laundering must take place there. What is holy cannot be profaned by taking it outside the sanctuary and bringing it into contact with anything that could defile it.

The same logic lies behind the obscure instructions about pots and pans in verse 28. If an unglazed clay pot was used to cook the meat, because the pot was made of porous material, part of the meat might possibly have penetrated its sides. So it had to be destroyed. However, if the vessel was made of bronze, although it must be thoroughly cleaned before being used again, it need not be destroyed, for it was non-porous. Residual deposits of a sacred offering would contaminate anything they came into contact with rather than making it holy. So the priests had to avoid, at all costs, using the vessels that might still contain any fragments of a past sacred offering.

God draws the priests' attention to all these details for a very simple reason: ritual blood is sacred and used for the purpose of effecting atonement. 'It could not therefore be treated carelessly, as if it were ordinary.'[13]

4. Keep priests supplied (7:1–10, 28–36)

The regulations concerning the guilt offering (7:1–6) at first glance offer no new insights. But the focus quickly broadens from the guilt offering itself to all those offerings in which the priests were permitted to keep some of the meat as food for themselves. It is here that new elements in the regulations are brought to light. Mention is made particularly of the permission granted to the priest who officiated at the burnt offering to keep the victim's *hide for himself* (8). But the key issue seems to lie in the statement that the surplus from the offerings belongs *to the priest who makes atonement with them* (7–9). The grain offering is an exception and was to be distributed *equally to all the sons of Aaron* (10), perhaps because the grain offering was in less plentiful supply. The point is this: it was important that those officiating at the altars knew exactly how the surplus was to be handled and distributed. If this matter had been left to a vague generalization, all manner of disputes could have arisen, involving accusations of unfairness or favouritism. As it was, this matter still proved problematic and led eventually to the priests being divided into groups. It was said that Moses introduced eight or ten divisions, who came on active service by rotation. Within a division, each family served for just a day at a time, again on a rota.[14]

Behind this lay the important principle that those who served the Lord in the tabernacle should be supported by the Israelites who made use of their service as mediators with God. The priests were worthy of support. The same principle is repeated in the regulations for the peace offering, in 7:28–36, where the Lord draws towards a conclusion in his instructions to the priests.

The novel element in these instructions is that the particular portions with which the priests are supplied are identified and the way in which they are assigned is prescribed. The right breast was always to be given to *Aaron and his sons* (31, 34) – in other words, to the priesthood collectively. It was *their perpetual share from the Israelites* (34), relieving them of any

---

[13] Ross, p. 170.
[14] Noordtzij, p. 82; Hartley, p. 99. See 1 Chr. 24 and Luke 1:8–9.

anxiety that their support might be haphazard. They could not live on the basis of irregular gifts from the people of Israel, nor did God intend them to do so. By contrast, the right thigh of the sacrifice was presented to the priest who performed the rite, as his special share (33). The remainder of the animal, apart from that which had been burned on the altar, would be used for the fellowship meal and enjoyed by the people as well as any priests who were in attendance.

The way in which the breast was donated to the priests differed from the way in which the thigh was handled. Priests had no automatic entitlement to the right breast. As verse 34 emphasizes, it was the property of God, who graciously chose to return it to the priests. So, in recognition of God's ownership of it, before the priests took the breast away, they were to *wave the breast before the LORD as a wave offering* (30). For the breast to be brandished in this way would show it off, as it were, to God, while simultaneously reminding the priests that it was not theirs except by his gift. The right thigh, however, was subject to no such treatment. It was given to the officiating priest outside the sanctuary without ceremony as a matter of routine.

If these instructions teach those who lead others in worship of the need for extreme care in doing so, they equally teach that those who are led in worship have a duty to provide financial support for their ministers. In an enthusiastic discussion, I was told recently that those who wished to exercise an apostolic ministry should do so without expecting any financial support but rather that they should look only to the Lord for their maintenance. The point was well intended, but erroneous. True, Paul engaged in manual labour to support his ministry, but he made clear that this was his personal choice and so was not binding on others. In an extended passage in 1 Corinthians 9, which he based partly on the model of the support given to priests in the tabernacle and temple, he argued that 'the Lord has commanded that those who preach the gospel should receive their living from the gospel' (1 Cor. 9:14). And in his later correspondence he reinforced the point, quoting again from Deuteronomy 25:4, and commenting that 'the elders who direct the affairs of the church well are worthy of double honour, especially those whose work is preaching and teaching' (1 Tim. 5:17–18). The lesson seems incontrovertible. From the earliest writings of Moses to the closing letters of Paul, we read of God's concern that his servants should receive adequate support for their needs – a concern that has not always met with a ready response among his people.

5. Keep fellowship pure (7:11–27)

The peace or fellowship offering comes last in these instructions to the priests because, unlike the others, it was not a 'most holy' sacrifice. Parts of the sacrifice could be eaten by ordinary folk as well as by the priests, and outside the Tent rather than only within its boundaries. Despite this, however, these instructions share the concern already abundantly evident in the regulations about the other offerings: all should be done to preserve the purity of the offering. Three details hammer the message home. They involve the timing, the substance and the guests of the celebration meal.

First, the meat of the fellowship meal must be eaten on the day it was sacrificed if it was brought as a thanksgiving (15), or at the very latest on the next day if it was brought as a vow or freewill offering (16). To leave it to a third day would make it unclean, with the result that the offering *will not be accepted. It will not be reckoned to their credit, for it has become impure* (18). Second, if the meat became contaminated by touching *anything ceremonially unclean . . . it must be burned* and the worshippers were not permitted to eat it (19–20). Third, the people who ate it must be ceremonially clean (20–21). The participants were accountable themselves for ensuring both that the meat was fit to eat and that they were in a fit condition to eat it. It was a responsibility they could neither abdicate nor evade by seeking to pass it off to someone else.

Twice they were warned in the strongest terms about their liability. Those who ignored the regulations and chose to eat the meal even though they were unclean *must be cut off from their people* (20, 21, 27). The origin of the word *kārat* ('cut off') does not lie in the law courts but in the fields. A tree was 'cut off' when it was felled, and a bush when it was razed.[15] This penalty is thought to have covered a range of punishments, from being childless, through being denied a place in the afterlife, to having life suddenly terminated in death.[16] It did not, by any means, always imply immediate death, still less execution at the hands of fellow citizens. Where death did occur, it was usually as a result of an act of God.

The peace offering was, in a way, the happiest of the sacrifices of Israel since it led to the enjoyment of a celebratory feast. Even so, the priests knew that care must be exercised. The greater participation of the lay men

---

[15] Levine, p. 241, and Grabbe, *Oxford*, p. 99. For a full discussion see Milgrom, *Leviticus 1 – 16*, pp. 457–460.

[16] Examples of these are found in 20:21 and 24:10–23.

and women of Israel did not mean that standards could be eroded or attitudes towards holy things relaxed. If anything, the participation of others demanded even greater vigilance than normal. As with all the sacrifices, if the peace offering was to be acceptable, careful attention had to be given to matters of purity. It was inconceivable that the God of Israel, who was majestic in holiness, could be a party to anything that had a whiff of impurity about it, or that was in any way less than the best.

Christians, all of whom are priests of the new covenant (1 Pet. 2:9), have the same obligation to serve God with diligence as did the priests to whom these instructions were first given. While most of the regulations under consideration are addressed to those who led worship and occupied responsible positions of leadership among God's people, the regulations about the peace offering implicated everyone, not just the priests. They still call all of us to serve God with meticulous care, not simply in up-front leadership roles but also in daily living, pursuing holiness with a proper attention to the details of our lives. Taking their cue from these regulations, two New Testament writers encourage us to offer nothing less than what the children of Israel were required to give to God. James wrote: 'Religion that God our Father accepts as pure and faultless is this: to look after orphans and widows in their distress and to keep oneself from being polluted by the world' (Jas 1:27). Jude urged that we should 'show mercy, mixed with fear – hating even the clothing stained by corrupted flesh' (Jude 23).

Throughout this chapter I have applied the lessons of this section to the way we worship God. But there is a greater application that should be explored, and that is its application to the work of Christ – the supreme priest. This chapter reminds us that sinful people need a priest to serve as their mediator with God. Without a priest their approach to a holy God would prove fatally futile. This is a requirement that is as essential now as it was then. However, there is a difference: the priest to whom we look is not one of the many human beings duly ordained by church authorities to serve at an altar, but the 'one mediator between God and mankind, the man Christ Jesus, who gave himself as a ransom for all' (1 Tim. 2:5–6). From that premise, the other aspects of this chapter's teaching can be found pointing to Christ. In his life we see lived out to perfection the exacting obedience which effective worship requires. His blood was truly precious (1 Pet. 1:19). Just as the ministry of priests was sustained by food they received, so the ministry of Jesus was sustained by the Holy Spirit.[17] Just as they sought to preserve the purity of the fellowship meal, so Jesus is the one who was altogether pure (Heb. 7:26). Once more, the ultimate significance of Leviticus finds its fulfilment in Christ.

This section of Leviticus brings the consideration of the sacrificial offerings to an end.[18] The final verse says that God revealed his instructions to Moses *at Mount Sinai* (38), whereas the opening verse of Leviticus had said that they were given to Moses at 'the tent of meeting' (1:1). There need be no contradiction between the two statements, since the reference to Mount Sinai probably means the region of Sinai. Such details must never distract us from what is of supreme significance. The Lord has spoken. He has revealed his will. It is for us, his people, to respond in glad obedience to what *he commanded* should be done.

---

[17] E.g. Matt. 3:16; 4:1; 12:18, 28; Luke 4:1, 14, 18; 10:21.

[18] With the exception of the offerings of the Day of Atonement in Lev. 16.

B. The manual of priesthood: entering God's service (8:1 – 10:20)

Leviticus 8:1–36

7. Anointed for service

Preaching on the anniversary of his consecration as a bishop, Augustine of Hippo once referred to the enormity of the responsibility he carried:

> To rebuke those who stir up strife, to comfort those of little courage, to take the part of the weak, to refute opponents, to be on guard against traps, to teach the ignorant, to shake the indolent awake, to discourage those who want to buy and sell, to put the presumptuous in their place, to mollify the quarrelsome, to help the poor, to liberate the oppressed, to encourage the good and to suffer the evil and to love all men.
>
> To be preaching, disputing, reproving, edifying, to be on hand for everyman – that is the great burden and one which lies heavily on me.[1]

The duties of Augustine were as nothing compared with the responsibilities Aaron was to assume as the high priest of Israel. He and his family were to be the custodians of holiness, the teachers of the Israelites and the nation's intermediaries with God. It was important, therefore, that they should enter into office neither lightly nor without the full recognition of the people of God. Leviticus 8 reports the impressive ordination of Aaron to God's service.[2] The background to the ceremony is set out in Exodus 28 – 29,

---

[1] Quoted in F. van der Meer, *Augustine the Bishop* (London and New York: Sheed & Ward, 1961), p. 269; and D. Tidball, *Skilful Shepherds: Explorations in Pastoral Theology* (Leicester: Apollos, 1997), pp. 164–165.

[2] Contemporary scholarly opinion regards the account as 'a priestly fiction' rather than a description of an actual event. See Gerstenberger, pp. 99–107, and Grabbe, *Oxford*, p. 99. However, so much of the ceremony fits a very early period that there is no reason to question it as authentically Mosaic.

where the priestly garments are prepared and the order of events is fixed. What Exodus anticipated comes to fulfilment here in Leviticus.

Such was the importance of the ceremony that it lasted overall seven days. But attention is concentrated on the first day when, led by Moses, Aaron and his sons are conducted through a carefully crafted sequence of actions that transforms them from ordinary people, just like everyone else, to extraordinary servants of God who have a special status of holiness conferred upon them.

The minutiae of the developing ritual are full of meaning, as was the case for the sacrifices. Again, spiritual truth is conveyed through symbolic action. The details had significance first and foremost for those who participated in the event: for Aaron and Israel. But beyond this they point to the greater High Priest who was to come, and so reveal how Jesus fulfilled, and still fulfils, the priestly office with surpassing excellence. In many ways Jesus stands in continuity with the priesthood of Aaron, although there are some important respects in which he differs from it.[3] Like Aaron, Jesus was 'called by God' (Heb. 5:4); prepared for ministry;[4] set apart to serve in the sanctuary and to offer gifts and sacrifices, which in his case was the sacrifice of his own life (Heb. 8:2–3); and enters the Most Holy Place through the offering of blood (Heb. 9:12–14). Unlike Aaron, Christ was 'blameless', 'pure' and 'unblemished' in himself, not made so by the offering of sacrifices (Heb. 7:26, 28; 9:14). Furthermore, the high priesthood of Christ is permanent, and it is unnecessary for Christ to offer sacrifices either on his own behalf or repeatedly (Heb. 7:24, 27; 10:11–12).

At another level, Aaron's ordination is a particularly fitting model for those called into the service of God in special ways. But, since under the new covenant all Christians are priests of God (1 Pet. 2:9; Rev. 1:6), the template it provides is not restricted to those in 'ordained ministry' and has implications for all believers. Indeed, great care needs to be taken not to impose an Old Testament concept of priesthood on a New Testament understanding of ministry that in many respects is different and certainly does not assume the mediatorial role of the Aaronic priesthood, since that is reserved for Christ alone.[5] Even so, lessons about serving God are evident.

---

[3] The principal references are Heb. 5:1–5; 7:23 – 8:6; 9:11–14.

[4] Heb. 5:7–9. At this point Hebrews compares the priesthood of Jesus to that of Melchizedek rather than to that of Aaron.

[5] For a robust statement of this argument see Alec Motyer, 'The Meaning of Ministry', in Melvin Tinker (ed.), *Restoring the Vision* (Eastbourne: MARC, 1990), pp. 229–254.

1. Responding: as ordinary people they need to be called (8:1–5)

The call to serve God begins with his initiative, not ours. 'No one takes this honour on himself, but he receives it when called by God' (Heb. 5:4). Once more, then, the voice of God addresses Moses; his subject is no longer the offering of sacrifices, as it has been in chapters 1–7, but the installation of the priesthood. Each step of the way – eleven in all – we read that *the LORD commanded* (4, 5, 9, 13, 17, 21, 29, 31, 34, 35, 36), emphasizing that it is both God's will that is being revealed and his instructions that the people are following with scrupulous care. The introduction of the Aaronic priesthood was not a human invention but a divine creation. Several features marked the call, and still mark the call to Christian service today.

a. The call was necessary

Though some may set themselves up in leadership positions among God's people, unless God has called them their ministry will be self-serving rather than God-glorifying, and empire-building rather than kingdom-building. Furthermore, many who have entered the service of God without a clear call from him have found themselves overwhelmed by its responsibilities and unable to sustain the task in the face of numerous discouragements. It is for God to choose those whom he wishes to serve him, not us. Genuine ministry starts with our response to his voice addressing us.

b. The call was gracious

Aaron was a man with a history.[6] Much of that history was good, but there were some blotches on his record that might well have disqualified him from being a suitable candidate for the office of high priest. Most notably, Aaron had exercised fatally irresponsible leadership when he led the people in building a calf, similar to the idols they would have known in Egypt, and bowed down in homage before it (Exod. 32:1–35). This action was in direct contravention of the second commandment. It did not bode well that a future high priest was prepared to desert the Lord so soon and to compromise Israel's faith so readily. Immediately following the incident Aaron withdrew for a time, playing no part in setting up the tabernacle,

---

[6] See E. H. Merrill, 'Aaron', in *DOTP*, pp. 1–3.

a process recorded in Exodus 40.[7] Yet, following Aaron's discipline and repentance, God still called him to become high priest. Such is his grace. In his mercy he does not wait for people to be perfect before calling them into service. He specializes in using ordinary, flawed human beings to serve his purposes and to uphold his honour.

Jesus Christ alone is the one High Priest who had no record to hide and whose flawless life meant he had no need to offer sacrifices to atone for his own sins.

As 'one who is holy, blameless, pure, set apart from sinners, exalted above the heavens . . . he does not need to offer sacrifices day after day, first for his own sins', but sacrificed himself only for the sins of others (Heb. 7:26–27).

c. The call was indirect

The call of Aaron came through Moses. The priesthood was not yet functioning, and so Moses occupied the place of intermediary between God and his people.[8] On previous occasions, God had spoken directly to Aaron, especially in the days before Israel left Egypt (e.g. Exod. 4:27; 7:8; 9:8; 12:1, 43). But, given that Aaron himself was the subject at issue here, it was appropriate that God should speak this time through Moses.

The Bible gives ample evidence that God's call is never mass-produced, and that it comes to individuals in many different ways, often being shaped by the circumstances or personalities of those being called. Yet there is a kernel of wisdom in the way in which Aaron receives his call that should not be set aside lightly. To become a priest, let alone high priest, was to assume a prestigious office and a position of some status. It is far better that we occupy leadership positions because others have joined in issuing a call than that we put ourselves into such positions regardless of what others think or feel. There are, of course, celebrated exceptions to the rule, as those who know the story of Gladys Aylward[9] or Campbell Morgan[10] will attest. But this is rarely the way God works, and we should

---

[7] Kaiser, p. 1056.

[8] Hartley, p. 111.

[9] Gladys Aylward (1902–70) was a missionary in China who led a hundred children on an epic journey to safety after the Japanese invasion of 1940. Her application to serve as a missionary was rejected by several missionary societies.

[10] G. Campbell Morgan (1863–1945) was a famous Bible teacher and celebrated pastor of Westminster Chapel, London, who was turned down by both the Salvation Army and the Methodists when he applied to enter their ministries. He eventually became a Congregational minister.

claim exceptional status for ourselves only with due humility and caution. Usually he at least confirms his call through other brothers and sisters in the body of Christ, even if it does not come directly through them.

d. The call was public

The same point is repeated in a different way by the fact that the induction of Aaron took place in the presence of *the entire assembly* of Israel who had *gathered at the entrance to the tent of meeting* (3–4). Being high priest was a public leadership role and, consequently, it was fitting that Aaron should be invested publicly into office. This authenticated his position and provided him with the recognition he would need. In spite of this public acknowledgment of his calling, however, his position would not go unchallenged.[11] There are always some who wish to undermine those in leadership and claim to be equally, if not better, qualified for the task themselves. When such discouragements occur, the public authorization that confirmed one's call into service can prove to be an invaluable encouragement.

Christian service begins, not when we take initiatives or make moves that God has not commanded in response to some private vision or ambition, but when we respond to his initiative and obey his call. Aaron and his four sons showed their submission to God's call by being *brought . . . forward* (6) and undertaking the prescribed ceremonies. The choice of vocabulary for this apparently innocuous act of presentation is significant. The same word has been used until now for the presentation of a sacrificial animal.[12] Here, Aaron and his sons are 'presented' to the Lord, just like a sacrifice, so that they may offer their lives on the altar and be set apart exclusively to serve God (Rom. 12:1–2).

2. Washing: as sinful people they need cleansing (8:6)

The induction proper began when *Moses brought Aaron and his sons forward and washed them with water.* It was essential that those who were going to approach a God of purity were physically whole (21:16–23) and totally clean. So, on all important occasions, the priests bathed in the great washbasin that was situated in the inner courtyard (16:4, 24, 26, 28). This

---

[11] E.g. by Korah and his followers, Num. 16:1–50.

[12] Levine, p. 49, and Hartley, pp. 111, 115.

'outward physical action', as Gordon Wenham has said, represented 'the desire for inner spiritual cleansing'.[13] The one was a natural portrayal of the other. I can recall a man who, having come to Christ, experienced such a change in his heart that his first act was to go home and take a bath. He said to me that he had become clean on the inside and wanted to become clean on the outside as well!

In some respects this act anticipates the thorough cleansing from sin that Aaron and his sons would receive somewhat later, when the sin offering was presented on their behalf. But it immediately confronts those who aspire to leadership with the challenge not to embark on it while unacknowledged sin clings to them like dirt to a body. While, as we have seen, perfection is not a requirement (otherwise none but Christ would be called), seriousness in dealing with our sins and flaws is essential. How sad it is when Christian leaders stumble in their ministries, often at great cost to others, because they skipped over this step in their hurry to be 'ordained'! Denying the existence of a besetting sin that one day may prove fatal is a foolish way to begin ministry. Yet the cleansing required is concerned not only with the big sins, for even a speck of dirt soils. In the presence of a holy God no sin is trivial. Our approach must make us conscious of our unworthiness and desire to be rid of sin.

3. Clothing: as inadequate people they need equipping (8:7–9, 13)[14]

If the priests were sinful men who needed cleansing, they were also inadequate men who needed clothing. So, having bathed, Aaron, followed by his sons, donned the robes of office. The high priest was invested with eight garments, four of which were unique to him. His sons were dressed more simply in undergarments, tunics that were tied around with sashes, and headbands. Leviticus only lists the garments: we must look to Exodus 28 for a description of them in all their colourful detail. That passage leaves us in no doubt that the high priest would have looked resplendent in his robes and made a magnificent impression on the Israelites, contributing to the splendour and majesty of the worship of God.[15] Yet, for all the

---

[13] Wenham, p. 139.

[14] On this section see Alec Motyer, *The Message of Exodus* (London: IVP, 2021), pp. 262–267.

[15] Hartley, p. 112.

details given, no footwear is mentioned. The priests would have performed their duties barefoot, as was considered fitting for those who were standing on holy ground in the presence of the Lord.[16]

a. The clothing described

Wenham thinks it is now impossible to be certain what each item symbolized,[17] but this has not prevented many from having a try. Over Aaron's linen undergarment, which covered his nakedness (Exod. 28:42),[18] was placed a tunic. Both were made of fine linen and were gathered together by a sash 'to give them dignity and honour' (Exod. 28:40). However, it is the robe, ephod, breastpiece and turban that merit special mention.

The *robe*[19] was woven to make a single piece of blue cloth and trimmed with pomegranates and bells placed alternately around the hem. The pomegranate fruit was 'associated with fertility and abundance'.[20] The reason for the bells is less clear. There is some suggestion that they were used elsewhere to chase demons away,[21] but this seems inconsistent with Israel's approach to the demonic. More likely they were to warn of the high priest's approach (Zech. 14:20) and to summon Israel to pay special attention to the service the high priest was rendering on their behalf.

The *ephod* (Exod. 28:6–14) was a multicoloured apron, tied to the waist by a 'skilfully woven waistband' which was of one piece with the ephod itself. The fabric of gold, blue, purple and scarlet threads was identical to that of the tabernacle itself. Two onyx stones, each engraved with the names of six of the tribes of Israel, were mounted in the shoulder straps so that every time Aaron wore his ceremonial dress their names were borne 'as a memorial before the LORD' (Exod. 28:12). Attached to the mounted stones were pure gold chains. In this way the concerns of God's people would constantly be brought into his presence, and he would never be able to forget his people – as if he could.

The *breastpiece* (Exod. 28:15–30), again skilfully and beautifully woven, was 22 cm (9 ins) square, and on it were mounted four rows of precious

---

[16] Exod. 3:5; Josh. 5:15. Levine, p. 50, and Kaiser, p. 1060.

[17] Wenham, p. 137.

[18] Pagan worship often involved nakedness, and so this is more than an incidental reference and marks the priests and high priest of Israel out as different – 'holy to the LORD'.

[19] Exod. 28:31–35; 39:22–27.

[20] Num. 13:23; Balentine, p. 74.

[21] Milgrom, *Leviticus 1 – 16*, p. 504.

stones – three in each row – each having the name of one of Israel's tribes engraved on it. Evidently, with Aaron bearing the names on his heart in this manner, God was signalling that he had no desire to let his attention to the hopes and fears of Israel slip. Also, in pockets in the breastpiece were the curious *Urim and Thummim*. Although what they were and how they worked are unclear, they would appear to have been flat stones, perhaps of different colours, or with different-coloured sides, that 'worked in the manner of dice or lots'.[22]

Thummim carries the meaning of 'completion' or 'perfection'. The meaning of *Urim* is now lost, but could well mean 'curse'.[23] We know that they were used as a means to divine God's will because Exodus 28:30 says, 'Thus Aaron will always bear the means of making decisions for the Israelites over his heart before the LORD' (also Num. 27:21).

In the *turban* (Exod. 28:36–38) was *set the gold plate, the sacred emblem*. On the plate the words 'HOLY TO THE LORD' were engraved, reminding Israel that they were a special people, set apart for his exclusive service. This splendid regal diadem capped off the garments which exuded a royal quality, 'indicating that the high priest ministered at the altar for a people who were God's kingdom on earth'.[24]

The total effect of the garments impressed upon Israel the living presence of God among them, his loving concern for them and his commanding authority over them. They also reminded Israel that, for all his grace, they needed to approach God with care and live as his holy people in daily obedience to his will.

b. The clothing applied

The beauty and the glory of the garments reveal the grace of God in providing a priesthood to meet our needs, and point forward to the perfect priesthood of Christ, which was yet to come. The image of the high priest wearing his official garments calls to mind the vision of the ascended Lord, which the apostle John records in Revelation 1 (1:12–16). There, the 'Living One', who is 'the First and the Last', who died but now is alive for evermore, sits enthroned above the troubled world, where his subjects face distress and persecution. The picture of him robed in majesty, holding

---

[22] Levine, p. 50. This is partly on the basis that 1 Sam. 14:42 speaks of their being 'thrown down'.

[23] See Levine, p. 51, and Harrison, p. 96.

[24] Hartley, p. 115.

the symbols of authority and having the eyes, voice and feet of one who can execute judgment shows that God continues to be attentive to the needs of his people and to bear their concerns close to his heart. The outcome of the events on earth will be determined by him, and not by those who strut their bogus dignity through the corridors of human power. Dignity and power belong to him alone.

The image of clothing is frequently used in the Bible as a metaphor for the virtues God's people should display. The Bible's real concern is not with the design or make-up of material fabric, but with the qualities of character that clothe a person. The garments of our own worthiness should be set aside as amounting to no more than 'filthy rags' (Isa. 64:6). Instead, priests should be clothed with righteousness (Ps. 132:9); God's people should be clothed with salvation (Isa. 61:10; see also Isa. 52:1); Christian disciples should be clothed with 'compassion, kindness, humility, gentleness and patience' (Col. 3:12); and Christian warriors clothed with 'the armour of light' (Rom. 13:12): namely, with 'faith and love as a breastplate, and the hope of salvation as a helmet' (1 Thess. 5:8). Above all, those who wish to serve God must clothe themselves with the Lord Jesus and not 'think about how to gratify the desires of the flesh' (Rom. 13:14).

4. Anointing: as unqualified people they need empowering (8:10–12)

The heart of the ceremony lay in the act of anointing. A special oil was blended from four spices; it was particularly fragrant and used exclusively for the rite of consecration (Exod. 30:22–33). First, the tabernacle itself, together with its furniture and utensils, were sprinkled with oil to set them apart for God. Then Moses *poured some of the anointing oil on Aaron's head and anointed him to consecrate him* (12). Aaron alone is anointed because he alone is to serve as high priest.

Anointing was the customary way in which people were dedicated to God's service. When both Saul (1 Sam. 10:1–13) and David (1 Sam. 16:13) were anointed as kings, the Spirit of the Lord came upon them in power, and, in David's case, remained with him throughout his reign. In looking forward to the coming Messiah, Isaiah equally anticipated that the one who would bring good news to the poor would be anointed by 'the Spirit of the Sovereign Lord' (Isa. 61:1). None had a more perfect anointing on their lives than Jesus, the one whom Isaiah had foretold (Matt. 3:16–17;

Mark 1:9–11; Luke 3:21–22). At the age of thirty, the carpenter from Nazareth set out on his public ministry, and 'because he had become a man and was living in this world as a man, though he was still the eternal Son of God, he needed to receive the Spirit in his fulness, and God gave him the Spirit'.[25] If that was so for Jesus, how much greater the need of those who minister in his name! No-one dare serve the Lord without that enduement that comes from God himself.

5. Dedicating: as common people they need consecrating (8:14–30)

Following the anointing, Moses offered the sin and burnt offerings and the peace offering (or something like it). Aaron and his sons have still not entered into office: at this stage they are like any other worshippers who bring their offerings and identify with them by laying their hands on them. So Moses remains in the role of priest until the ceremonies reach their culmination in a further act of anointing (30).

a. The sin offering (8:14–17)

The high priest's sin offering follows the rubric set out for his use previously (4:1–12), but with one significant difference. Since the high priest is not yet in office, the blood of the offering is not sprinkled in front of the curtain of the sanctuary but daubed on *the horns of the altar to purify the altar* (15). As yet, the priests have not had the opportunity to pollute the Holy Place with their sin, so there is no need for them to cleanse the sanctuary, and they come, like any other in Israel, to offer a sacrifice for their own sin.[26]

It may seem curious that, having been bathed to symbolize their cleansing at the start of the ceremony, they are still required to offer a sin offering. But washing alone can never adequately bring about the expiation of sin and the removal of guilt. For that, a blood sacrifice is required. The washing of the body was a necessary preliminary and foretaste of the cleansing from sin that only the offering of a bull could effect.[27]

---

[25] D. M. Lloyd-Jones, *Joy Unspeakable* (Eastbourne: Kingsway, 1984), p. 48, cited in Tony Sargent, *The Sacred Anointing: The Preaching of Dr Martyn Lloyd-Jones* (London: Hodder & Stoughton, 1994), p. 61.

[26] Wenham, p. 141.

[27] Kaiser, p. 1061, writes, 'Apparently, the ablution can care only for the defilement of nature, by bringing renewal and regeneration through the Word of God and the Holy Spirit; but there remains the need for dealing with the removal of objective guilt and the need for forgiveness for the sin that caused guilt.'

b. The burnt offering (8:18–21)

Consistent with the usual order in which the sacrifices were offered, once forgiveness from sin had been obtained through the sin offering, Aaron and his sons were in a position to offer the burnt offering. It was offered exactly according to the rules previously set out (1:10–13), and signalled their willingness to offer up their lives to be used exclusively for the Lord's service. Through this act they were saying to God what many, in more recent times, have said through singing:

Take my life, and let it be
Consecrated, Lord, to thee:
Take my moments and my days,
Let them flow in ceaseless praise.

Take my will, and make it thine;
It shall be no longer mine:
Take my heart – it is thine own;
It shall be thy royal throne.

Take my love; my Lord, I pour
At thy feet its treasure store:
Take myself, and I will be
Ever, only, all for thee.[28]

c. The ordination offering (8:22–30)

The third offering has many similarities to the peace offering (3:1–17), but it is not called by that name here; the ram to be sacrificed is called *the ram for the ordination* (22). This, together with its distinctive features, suggests it was seen as a unique rite of ordination.[29] To be 'ordained' meant originally to have one's hands filled. Some see this as an allusion to the way in which Aaron's hands would in future be filled with the sacrifices people were offering to God.[30] R. K. Harrison, however, traces its use among the Mesopotamians, where, in the Mari texts, 'the allusion seems to have been to the sharing of booty among conquerors'.[31] This leads to a much more probable understanding of what it means to be 'ordained'. The

---

28 Frances Ridley Havergal (1836–79).

29 Demarest, p. 87.

30 E.g. Gorman, p. 58.

31 Harrison, p. 100. The Mari texts are dated 1750 bc.

hands of the priests are filled not with what they offer God, but with what God offers them: he himself bestows grace and blessing on those who would serve him, ill-suited and ill-equipped as they are in their own right.

The major difference between this rite and that of the peace offering is that the blood of the sacrificed animal is dashed against the altar only after first being placed *on the lobe of Aaron's right ear, on the thumb of his right hand and on the big toe of his right foot* (23).[32] The meaning of this part of the ritual is transparent. Priest and altar are inextricably bound together in the closest of associations.[33] Aaron was anointed on the right side because it was the favoured side, and the tip of the ear, the thumb and the toe were chosen as representative of the whole body.[34] The anointed ear speaks of the priest's need to be constantly attuned to listen to God's voice; the anointed thumb of the requirement to be continually willing to do God's work; and the anointed foot of the obligation perpetually to walk in God's ways. Only after Aaron has been anointed with blood does the rest of the sacrificial ritual unfold.

Already anointed with oil, and now with blood, Aaron, joined by his sons, undergoes a third anointing, consisting of both oil and blood (30). Both their persons and their clothes are sprinkled. With this final anointing the act of ordination comes to a climax. Again, the symbolism is clear. At last, Aaron and his sons are totally consecrated to the Lord.[35] The words that follow say it all: *So* Moses *consecrated Aaron and his garments and his sons and their garments* (30). They are now totally set apart for God's use and have said, in effect, as the words of the Methodist covenant service put it:

> I am no longer my own but Thine. Put me to what Thou wilt; put me to doing, put me to suffering; let me be employed for Thee or laid aside for Thee, exalted for Thee or brought low for Thee. Whether I have all things or nothing I freely and heartily yield all to Thy pleasure and disposal. And now, O glorious and blessed God, Father, Son and Holy Spirit, Thou art my Covenant Friend and I through Thine infinite grace am Thy Covenant servant. Amen. So be it.[36]

---

[32] Those who had overcome leprosy were similarly anointed by blood from the guilt offering once they took up their place in the worshipping community of Israel (Lev. 14:14).

[33] Levine, p. 53.

[34] Wenham, p. 143.

[35] Kaiser, p. 1062.

[36] From a Baptist version of the Methodist covenant service.

The sealing of the covenant developed naturally into the enjoyment of a covenant meal, as Aaron and his sons cooked the meat that remained and ate it *with the bread* that had been offered as *ordination offerings* (31).

Our great High Priest needed no sin offering (Heb. 7:27). Rather, Jesus became a sin offering for us, securing our forgiveness with his own blood. But he offered the other two offerings mentioned here in his own distinctive way. By offering himself unreservedly to God, Jesus fulfilled the meaning of the whole burnt offering. And none more than he enjoyed the intimacy with God of which the peace offering spoke.

All those who serve God must stand where Aaron once stood. Whatever our track record in Christian service, we remain sinners in constant need of forgiveness, for which we find ample provision in the atoning sacrifice of Christ. We need daily to renew our dedication to the Lord and make ourselves wholly available to him, as embodied by the burnt offering. Our heads must be anointed by his Spirit and our empty hands filled with his grace, for without him we have nothing to offer. He alone qualifies us for our calling. Our ears must be attuned to his voice, our hands ready to do his will and our feet quick to walk without deviation in his ways. Only so will a measure of consecration be reached that makes us useful to him, and only so shall we enjoy the blessed intimacy of being both in his presence and truly in his service. We are no more equipped to enter God's service than Aaron was.

Ministry remains a gift of God's mercy (2 Cor. 4:1), and he alone qualifies us to exercise that gift as ministers of the new covenant (2 Cor. 3:6).

6. Waiting: as unpractised people they need moulding (8:31–36)

After a full day, Aaron and his sons may well have been eager to commence their work as priests. But they are told they must wait a further seven days before embarking on their responsibilities. The wait is typical of the transition periods people undergo when passing from one significant status to another.[37] But the meaning of their delay is likely to be spiritually significant rather than merely reflecting the common pattern found in rites of passage.

---

[37] Hartley, p. 115. The time is often referred to as a 'liminal period'. An illustration would be the honeymoon period a couple take away from their family and friends immediately after their wedding. They leave as those who until that day were two individuals and re-enter their community as a couple.

The waiting period emphasizes the need not to rush headlong and insufficiently prepared into God's service. The week was to be occupied in offering sacrifices for themselves to keep themselves pure, in deepening fellowship with God and in making themselves ready. The delay testifies to the deep-rooted nature of sin and to the gradual character of the transformation that takes place through grace. 'A man may', as Gordon Wenham observes, 'defile himself in a moment but sanctification and the removal of uncleanness is [sic] generally a slower process.'[38] Fitness for service does not occur overnight. Knight has pointed out the remarkable parallel between the seven days that God took to create the world and the seven days he took to create and consecrate the priesthood.[39] It is almost as if the one was as difficult as the other, or, at least, as important.

Sadly, even this waiting period did not save Nadab and Abihu from fouling up their priesthood, with tragic consequences, not long after they took office (10:1–3). How much worse might the situation have proved if this period of reflection, worship and preparation had not been there at all!

Jesus' public ministry did not commence immediately after his baptism – the moment the Spirit descended on him. Mark tells us that the Spirit's first move in Jesus' life was to send him into the desert for forty days (not seven), there to strengthen himself, to pray, to endure temptation and to do battle with Satan (Mark 1:12–13). Only after that did he emerge to begin his priestly ministry of healing the broken and forgiving the fallen.

The experience of the disciples was similar. Their first calling was not to *do* anything for Jesus but just to be with him (Mark 3:14). Even after the resurrection, they were still instructed to wait in Jerusalem until the gift of the Spirit, whom God had promised, was poured out on them, rather than to become active in service immediately (Acts 1:4–5). It is only when disciples learn that God has first and foremost called them 'into fellowship with his Son, Jesus Christ' (1 Cor. 1:9) that they have any basis for service or anything to offer others, coming as it does from the overflow of their relationship with Jesus.

In our fast-paced society, and with well-meaning eagerness, some rush too hurriedly into God's service and allow themselves no time to have

---

[38] Wenham, p. 144.

[39] Knight, p. 51.

grown in holiness, no time to have been seasoned through the testing of life, and no time to have sought power from on high. Apart from the extra-ordinary grace of God, such impetuous presumption may well result in falling at the early hurdles of discouragement, temptation, testing or challenge, and only serve to show that they were inadequately prepared for the race. Even more significant may be the damage such impetuosity does to others who have looked to them as servants of God, only to find they have proved untrustworthy. Waiting is not an optional extra, but an essential component of the process of consecration.

Throughout Leviticus 8 special attention has been drawn to what the Lord commanded. The final note passes on the baton of obedience from Moses to Aaron. *So Aaron and his sons did everything the LORD commanded through Moses* (36). There could be no better way to commence one's ministry than by carefully obeying *all* that God has commanded. The priesthood was not a human invention, nor a sociological convenience, but a divinely instituted order of those who would stand in the gap between God and his people. Those who stand in that gap today are required to obey the Lord no less carefully than Moses and Aaron did centuries ago in the tabernacle in the wilderness.

Leviticus 9:1–24

8. The glory of the Lord appeared

The *eighth day* (9:1) is the first day of a new week. It signals a new beginning. The consecration of Aaron and his sons, which had occupied the whole of the previous week, is now complete and Aaron is ready to begin his ministry. But the inauguration of his priesthood heralds a change not only for him but also for the entire company of Israel. The *glory of the LORD* (6, 23) was to appear to them from within the tabernacle, which was God's permanent residence among them. God had made his home in the midst of his people and, in doing so, had restored to some degree the close fellowship he had once enjoyed with human beings in the Garden of Eden, though not, of course, the innocence they had once possessed.

1. The promise of God's appearing (9:1–6)

a. The promise to the leaders (9:1–4)

Moses took Aaron and his sons to one side and, in the presence of the leaders of Israel (1), instructed them to gather the materials needed for the numerous offerings Aaron was to present that day. He was to offer a sin and a burnt offering for himself (2), and the four major offerings – the sin, burnt, grain and peace offerings – on behalf of the community (3–4). Only one detail begs attention in these otherwise routine instructions. Aaron is instructed to offer *a bull calf* for his own sin offering (2), which is the only time this particular animal is stipulated. Later Jewish commentaries quite rightly explained that the choice of victim was due to the shameful incident of the golden calf in which Aaron had played such a crucial role (Exod. 32:1–35). With this offering 'the last stains of that grave sin' were being removed.[1]

All this, however, is a preliminary to the startling announcement Moses then made. *Today,* he said, *the Lord will appear to you.* The leaders of Israel had witnessed from a distance the Lord's appearance to Moses on Mount Sinai (Exod. 19:1–25) and had also once before encountered him enthroned in majesty (Exod. 24:9–10). But they had not previously been confronted by God so closely in person. Had they heard aright? Was the Lord really going to appear to them in the camp? They must have greeted such an announcement with a mixture of joyful anticipation and nervous apprehension.

b. The promise to the people (9:5–6)

When the priests had gathered the sacrificial materials together and brought them to the entrance of the tabernacle, *the entire assembly came near and stood before the Lord* (5). Moses then repeated his joyful announcement to them all: *This is what the Lord has commanded you to do, so that the glory of the Lord may appear to you* (6). The people had previously witnessed the glory of the Lord, but then it was in thunder and lightning, enveloped in thick cloud and smoke, and had the sound of a trumpet blast about it (Exod. 19:16–19). God had revealed himself on that occasion in awesome majesty, and the people had been warned to keep their distance lest he should break out against them in their unconsecrated state (Exod. 19:20–23). Not unnaturally, on that occasion the response of everyone in the camp was to tremble. But now his glory was going to appear, not from a distant mountaintop, but in their midst. Like their leaders, they must have been unsure whether to greet the news with delight or with fear.

What is this *glory of the Lord* that is referred to in Leviticus only in this chapter but is mentioned frequently elsewhere in Scripture?[2] *Kābôd* (the Hebrew word for *glory*) derives from the word for 'weight' or 'heavy', and hence came to mean something of worth and supreme value.[3] The proper response to such things is to treasure or honour them. The glory of the Lord refers to the 'weight of God'. He is worthy, and so not to be thought

---

[1] Hartley, p. 122.

[2] E.g. Exod. 24:9–10; 33:12–23; 40:34–35; 1 Kgs 8:10–11; Pss 24:10; 104:1–2; Isa. 2:10, 19, 21; 60:1–2.

[3] See C. John Collins, '*kbd*', in *NIDOTTE* 2, pp. 577–587.

of lightly, dismissed easily or dealt with casually. God's glory is almost 'a technical term for God's manifest presence' in Israel,[4] which shows itself in 'luminous unearthly brilliance' and in a display of intense majestic splendour.[5] Israel rightly approaches this God of glory with caution, listens to his words with care, and responds to them with submissive minds and diligent obedience.

The contemporary ills of the church have, in part, been attributed to our lack of appreciation of the glory of God. With good reason, David Wells has raised a prophetic protest against the understanding of God held by many Christians today. It is, he says, 'weightless'. The transcendence of God has been diminished to the point where we now believe in a god who serves us, satisfies all our needs and therapeutically fulfils our every whim, rather than a God we must obey and 'before whom we must surrender our rights to ourselves'.[6] God has been drained of glory, divested of majesty and denuded of authority. The fundamental problem of the evangelical church, Wells asserts, is not inadequate technique, poor organization or irrelevant music, but 'that God rests too inconsequentially upon his church'. And until we restore weight to God, nothing we do will 'staunch the flow of blood from [the church's] wounds'.[7]

Israel was in no such danger as she stood on that particular *eighth day* before the Lord. Yet she realized that the glory of God was to be not only viewed with caution but also greeted with delight. Israel did not respond to God's glory in prostrate worship alone but with joy as well (24). The only adequate response to the revelation of God's glory was this twin response of paradoxical emotions. Either joy or reverent fear on its own would have been deficient, because the glory of the Lord conveyed not only his awesome transcendence but also his gracious presence among them. He was not a distant God, still less an absent one, but a God who lived among his people. He protected, directed, comforted, guided and forgave, not by remote control, or from some far-flung planet, but from the very centre of the camp, in the Most Holy Place. He was neither removed from his people's concerns nor isolated in his holiness from their daily lives, but dwelt right among them. They could look to God at any time and know

---

[4] Ibid., p. 581.

[5] Mays, p. 43.

[6] David Wells, *God in the Wasteland* (Grand Rapids, MI: Eerdmans; Leicester: IVP, 1994), p. 114. See also pp. 87–93.

[7] Ibid., p. 30.

that he was with them. 'Without this truth,' as Allen Ross has said, 'the Book of Leviticus loses its meaning.'[8]

2. The preparation for God's coming (9:7–23)

As with the arrival of any important visitor, so it is with God: the way needs to be prepared for his coming. If his glory is to be revealed, his people must be in a state of readiness to receive it; so preparation was undertaken according to his plan (6).

a. Sacrifices are offered (9:7–21)

The preparation consisted mainly in the offering of sacrifices, with Aaron officiating at the altar for the first time. Before Aaron could act as a representative of the people, however, he first had to offer sacrifices on his own behalf (8–14). Once more, he must confess his own sinfulness and inadequacy before both God and the people.

One might think that, after a week of sacrifices presented on his behalf, further offerings would have been unnecessary. Some say that, in the face of this endless repetition, Aaron must have been struck by the inability of the sacrificial system to deal effectively with sin.[9] Perhaps; but such a view takes insufficient account of the fact that this was Aaron's first day in office – a day for which he had been preparing for some time. It was unlikely that he would tire of offering sacrifices so soon! It is also somewhat anachronistic and anticipates a Christian understanding of the deficiency of sacrificing animals as a means of making atonement. A truer reading of the situation is surely that daily atonement for sin, as indicated by the sin offering, and daily consecration to God, as symbolized by the burnt offering, were both needed then, and are still needed today, on the part of God's servants.

The procedures adopted on *the eighth day* differ in minor respects from those that were usually followed. The blood of the sin offerings, for example, is not dashed against the curtain or smeared on the horns of the altar of incense, as stipulated in 4:6–7, 17, but only daubed on the horns of the outer altar and poured out at its base (9, 15). This may be because the cultic apparatus had not yet fully come into operation and, therefore,

---

[8] Ross, p. 227.
[9] Kaiser, p. 1065, and Kellogg, p. 219.

sin had not yet had opportunity to defile the sanctuary and cling to the curtain separating the Holy Place from the Most Holy Place.[10] But the departure from the usual routines is much more likely to have been an acknowledgment that this day was to prove a special day, and anything but run-of-the-mill.[11]

Having offered his own sacrifices, Aaron then offers sin, burnt, grain and peace offerings for all the people. Only the guilt offering is missing from his repertoire, because that was reserved for occasions when specific sins were dealt with and these had no relevance on this special day of celebration. Otherwise, all the elements of Israel's worship were present and used to prepare for the coming of the Lord. The order of the sacrifices was carefully planned, not haphazard. It attests the only order that is truly acceptable in our approach to God. Sin is confessed first; consecration is renewed next; gifts are offered only after that;[12] and then, finally, fellowship is enjoyed as a result. The sacrifices, we should note, were never ends in themselves. The objective of Israel's worship was not that they should engage in religious theatre but that they should encounter God himself. But there could be no other way for sinful people to meet with a holy God except through the presentation of offerings of atonement and worship.

b. Blessing is pronounced (9:22)

With the sacrifices completed, *Aaron* stepped down from the altar,[13] *lifted his hands* – in a gesture characteristic of prayer – *towards the people and blessed them*. We are not told what words Aaron used on this occasion, but there is no reason to assume they differed from the blessing God provided for his use:

> The LORD bless you
>   and keep you;
> the LORD make his face shine on you
>   and be gracious to you;

---

[10] Wenham, p. 149.

[11] Hartley, p. 123.

[12] Note Paul's commendation of the generosity of the Macedonian churches, who gave support to the Jerusalem church. He comments that 'they gave themselves first of all to the Lord' (2 Cor. 8:5).

[13] Levine, p. 57. Aaron would have stepped down from the altar before offering the blessing in spite of the sequence of v. 22.

the LORD turn his face towards you
    and give you peace.
(Num. 6:24–26)

Unlike the benediction in many church services today, the pronouncement of this blessing was not a way of signalling that the service had
finished, but a meaningful, dynamic way of releasing the covenant promises of God upon his people. 'Blessing', as Raymond Brown has written,
'was multichrome; what was in mind was explicit, precise, almost tangible.'[14] It activated the blessings of the covenant found later in Leviticus
(and elsewhere) – the blessings of fruitful harvests, of peaceful days and
of growing strength (Lev. 26:3–13; Deut. 28:1–14). Worship is a two-way
transaction. In worship God delights to give as well as to receive. He gladly
pours out his rich benefits on those who draw near to him. So the human
participants receive as well as give. It was, in part, precisely to receive the
benefits of his blessing that the people of Israel offered worship to God in
the tabernacle.[15]

c. Prayer is offered (9:23)

Once the sacrifices were offered and the blessing pronounced, *Moses and
Aaron then went into the tent of meeting* to converse with God. A discreet
veil is drawn over the subject of their conversation. Perhaps Moses and
Aaron were pleading with the Lord to fulfil Moses' promise and reveal
himself in glory, since, in spite of Moses' expectation, there was no guar-
antee that he would do so.[16] More significant, though, is the fact that until
this point Moses alone had had access to God's intimate presence. Their
joint appearance before him marks the completion of the ordination
ceremonies and the handing over from Moses to Aaron of the full responsibility for intercession on behalf of Israel. From now on, Aaron too would
enjoy access to God.

It is hard to believe that the privileged right of immediate access to the
presence of God that all believers now enjoy through Christ (Rom. 5:1; Heb.
10:19–22) was once confined solely to Moses and Aaron. It is a mark of the
glory of the new covenant, in contrast to the old, that all who have faith

---

[14] Raymond Brown, *The Message of Numbers: Journey to the Promised Land*, The Bible Speaks Today
(London: IVP, 2021), p. 46.

[15] Hartley, p. 124.

[16] Milgrom, *Leviticus 1 – 16*, p. 588.

may approach God's throne of grace with confidence and there receive mercy and find grace to help in times of need (Heb. 4:16).

3. The realization of God's glory (9:23–24)

When Moses and Aaron came out from the Lord's presence, they blessed the people once more, *and the glory of the LORD appeared to all the people.* The promise made earlier in the day had now come to fruition. The God who had made himself known in majesty from Mount Sinai was now making himself known in splendour from the Tent.

a. The evidence of God's glory (9:24)

God, who had revealed his glory before with a variety of climatic signs, chose on this occasion to reveal himself through fire. *Fire came out from the presence of the LORD and consumed the burnt offering and the fat portions on the altar.* The meat and grain that had been slowly burning on the altar were now completely and supernaturally consumed. It was an unmistakable mark of God's acceptance of these offerings, and of his acceptance of the people who had brought them, that left no room for uncertainty or for timidity in their relationship. Similarly, remarkable fire from God would be seen at other times in Israel's history – when the birth of Samson was announced (Judg. 13:9–23), when David sacrificed an offering to appease God's anger (1 Chr. 21:26), when Solomon's temple was dedicated (2 Chr. 7:1–3) and when Elijah faced down the prophets of Baal on Carmel (1 Kgs 18:16–40). Each time, God sent fire from heaven to confirm his presence in a visible and majestic way and transform an ordinary, sometimes even desperate, situation by an infusion of his supernatural power.

That *fire came out from the presence of the LORD* makes this experience of Israel different from those reportedly found among their neighbours, as Milgrom notes.[17] Such events elsewhere signified the arrival of a tribal deity and his taking possession of his residence, but the God of Israel is already among them. The ark, his symbolic seat, is already installed. He does not come from the outside to enter his home but emerges from his home to bless them.

Fire is a fitting twofold sign of God's presence. To those who had reason to fear because their lives angered God, it spoke of his active holiness,

---

[17] Milgrom, *Leviticus 1 – 16*, p. 375.

warned of danger and threatened judgment. God's awesome presence could spell doom if taken lightly. His majestic holiness meant he was to be approached with reverent fear. But to those whose lives pleased him and who had reason to know his grace, fire spoke of warmth, acceptance, purity and blessing.[18] In both respects, fire epitomized the revelation of God's glory.

b. The response to God's glory (9:24)

When the people saw the fire they responded in the dual way anticipated earlier in our chapter – a way also mentioned in three out of the four accounts of when the fire of the Lord fell:[19] *they shouted for joy and fell face down.* Spontaneous, overflowing elation was tempered by sudden, submissive prostration in the presence of their awe-inspiring God. He truly lived among them. The object of worship had been achieved: they had met with God and encountered him in all his transcendent grace. God is still a consuming fire (Heb. 12:29), and authentic worshippers are still awestruck in his presence and respond to him in obeisance. Yet, simultaneously, they know what it is to join with thousands and thousands of angelic beings who gather in joyful assembly (Heb. 12:22), and with the myriads around the thrones of God and the Lamb, to sing:

> To him who sits on the throne and to the Lamb
>   be praise and honour and glory and power
> for ever and ever!
> (Rev. 5:13)

4. The unfolding of God's ways

This account of the events of *the eighth day* conveys enduring truth about the responsibilities of spiritual leadership, the nature of true worship, the work of the high priest and the limitations of the sacrifices of the old covenant. But it supremely points to the wonder of God's living among his people and paves the way for a fuller understanding of his glory.

It was not given to Israel in Aaron's day to see the fullest revelation of God's glory on earth; that experience was reserved for the people of Jesus'

---

[18] Levine, p. 57.
[19] 1 Chr. 21:26 alone does not record this response.

day and those who have lived since his time. When John came to explain the life of Jesus Christ, he employed the language and thought of Leviticus 9 as a framework. In Leviticus we learn that God resided among his people in the tabernacle and his glory was displayed from within it. In John's Gospel we learn that 'the Word became flesh and made his dwelling [tabernacle] among us. We have seen his glory, the glory of the one and only Son, who came from the Father, full of grace and truth' (John 1:14).

The true glory of God was manifested both in the life of Jesus and, paradoxically, even more in his death.[20] It was evident in the signs Jesus performed, in the truth he taught, in the compassion he showed and in the claims he made. But it was when Jesus was stripped of power, dignity, honour, and strength and hoisted on a cross that God's greatest glory was made known. In the weakness, humiliation, disgrace and abuse that Jesus endured there we see the true power and wisdom of God displayed – a power and wisdom that overcame sin and trounced the enemies who stood in opposition to him. The sacrifice of Christ on Calvary was certainly a strange way of sorting out the world's problems. We usually resort to 'shock and awe' to display our power, defeat our enemies and release those who are held captive. But God works in unconventional ways and his glory is revealed in extreme weakness and folly – weakness and folly, however, that prove far stronger than human strength and far wiser than human wisdom (1 Cor. 1:18–25).

We do not need to have stood with the entire assembly of Israel long ago on *the eighth day* in the wilderness to see the glory of God. We need only turn our eyes to Jesus and survey his wondrous cross to see a glory that outshines anything that Israel observed. And his glory will shine with increasing intensity until the hope we hold on to is fully realized (Col. 1:27) on the day of 'the appearing of the glory of our great God and Saviour, Jesus Christ, who gave himself for us to redeem us from all wickedness and to purify for himself a people that are his very own' (Titus 2:13–14). When that great day dawns, our voices will swell the choirs of heaven and cry, 'Glory!'

Until that day dawns, we make him the centre of our worship, joyfully trusting in the presence of a Saviour who will never desert us (Heb. 13:5) and respectfully bowing in obedient submission to his word.

---

[20] John 12:23 and 17:1 connect glory to the cross of Christ.

Leviticus 10:1–20

9. Fire from the Lord

After the ecstasy came the agony. The triumph of the eighth day, which inaugurated Aaron's ministry, was soon reduced to tragedy when Nadab and Abihu, newly ordained priests, *offered unauthorised fire before the LORD* (10:1). Fire that had come from the presence of the Lord to disclose his loving presence (9:24) now *came out from the presence of the LORD* (2) to deliver his stern judgment. It stands as a vivid reminder not to be carried away in moments of success, and never to allow enthusiasm to outdistance obedience.

Leviticus 10 is one of only two narratives in the whole book.[1] But it involves no deviation from the purpose of the book, which continues to teach God's law, using, on this occasion, the form of a case history rather than a more immediately recognizable and abstract legal approach. The story tells of the alarming incident when Aaron's sons offered illegitimate fire to the Lord (1) and its aftermath.

1. Provoking the Lord (10:1–7)

a. Who they were (10:1)

The central figures in the act of provocation were *Nadab and Abihu*, Aaron's eldest sons. They had received a privileged upbringing and witnessed God's revelation of himself to Israel from ringside seats. They had been among the select group who had approached Mount Sinai when

---

[1] The other is in 24:10–23. Noth, p. 13, believes the narrative character of Lev. 8 – 10 means it is the kernel of the book from which the rest grew.

Moses went up to speak with God and receive from him the tablets of stone that contained the commandments (Exod. 24:1). Freshly ordained, they had spent the previous week in the tabernacle communing with God and preparing for his service. They had seen with their own eyes the fire coming out from the Most Holy Place and consuming the sacrifices on the altar (9:24). All this made them next in experience, as well as in importance, to Aaron.

b. What they did (10:1)

In spite of their upbringing, their experience and their training, they *took their censers ... and they offered unauthorised fire before the LORD, contrary to his command.* Exactly what made it 'alien fire'[2] is uncertain. We can only speculate on the basis of possible clues scattered about elsewhere. The problem may have been that Nadab and Abihu were drunk when they officiated at the altar, as hinted at by the reference to alcohol in verse 8. It may be that they used the wrong utensils, *their* own personal *censers* (1) instead of the duly authorized, sacred censers. Perhaps they penetrated too far into the sanctuary, as Leviticus 16:1 might imply, and entered the Most Holy Place itself, which was out of bounds to them. The incense may not have been of the right kind, as prescribed in Exodus 30:9. Since, however, the stress is on the *fire* that they offered to the Lord, it is most likely that the fire they brought to the altar was not that which God had ignited but fire that came from an alternative, inappropriate source.[3]

However, all this is conjectural, leading to Samuel Balentine's comment that 'these and other questions about this story have evoked much speculation, some quite ingenious, but they mostly persist as dangling loose ends'.[4] With Andrew Bonar, we should probably conclude that 'the Lord had commanded neither the time, place, nor manner' of this offering.[5]

All agree on one thing: Nadab and Abihu were acting in flagrant disobedience to God. Their transgression was neither accidental nor inadvertent. In offering 'unholy fire' (NRSV), they were disregarding what God had commanded, claiming that their fire was as good as his, and perhaps seeking to step into their father's shoes – the shoes of the high priest. Their motivation may have been 'pride, ambition, jealousy or

---

[2] JPS translation. See Levine, p. 58.
[3] Milgrom, *Leviticus 1 – 16*, p. 597.
[4] Balentine, p. 83.
[5] Bonar, p. 195.

impatience', or perhaps even just an over-enthusiasm that led to care-lessness. But whatever it may have been, it was very far removed from living the life of holiness to which they had so recently been dedicated.[6]

c. How it ended (10:2–7)

It ended in tragedy as *fire came out from the presence of the Lord and consumed them, and they died before the Lord* (2). God abruptly put an end to the antics of Nadab and Abihu and intervened in judgment. They were 'cut off' in the most dramatic of ways. The severity of his punishment was not without cause (as we shall consider shortly), but for the moment we follow the line of the story.

Aaron was stunned into silence (3), and Moses was confronted with the problem of how to remove their dead bodies from the tabernacle. Priests could not defile themselves by touching a corpse, so *Mishael and Elzaphan, sons of Aaron's uncle Uzziel* (4), cousins of Nadab and Abihu, who were their nearest relatives among the Levites, were pressed into service and carried their corpses *outside the camp*.[7] The tunics worn by Nadab and Abihu had apparently survived incineration, suggesting that they died not because their whole bodies had been consumed by fire but because their faces had been blasted by the Lord's wrath.[8]

Neither Aaron nor his sons were permitted to show any signs of mourning (6). The refusal to allow the high priest to mourn the death of a relative, whatever the circumstances, was customary (21:10–12), but it was an exception to extend this prohibition to include such close relatives as sons (21:1–4), and testified to the seriousness of the offence Nadab and Abihu had committed. Other members of the family were able to mourn, showing that God was not insensitive to the distress his swift action would have caused (6). In addition to this restraint on their mourning, the priests were also commanded to stay within the precincts of the tabernacle, because they had been anointed with *the Lord's anointing oil* (7) and dare not risk defilement by contact with the outside world at this precarious moment in the relationship with God. By the standards of our culture the

---

[6] Harrison, p. 109.

[7] The mention of their names in no way supports the idea this account hints at 'the real story' behind this incident, which has been concealed and which concerns factions in the priesthood, as proposed by Noth, p. 84, and referred to by Gerstenberger, p. 120. Milgrom dismisses this fanciful idea as 'sheer speculation', *Leviticus 1 – 16*, p. 604.

[8] Levine, p. 60.

refusal to let Aaron express his grief seems unbearably harsh. But it witnesses not to an unfeeling God but rather to an appreciation of right priorities. Aaron had to put the service of God first, even before the concerns of family, and as the representative of Israel he needed to remain focused on his responsibilities. Put like this, these commands to Aaron are no different from the response Jesus gave to the man who wanted to bury his father before embarking on the path of discipleship. Jesus told him, 'Let the dead bury their own dead, but you go and proclaim the kingdom of God.'[9] There is an urgency about the work of God that gives it priority over all else and that insists that his servants should not divert their energies to attend to lesser matters.

d. Why it matters (10:3)

Why did God move so swiftly against Nadab and Abihu? Primarily because the honour of his name was involved. God had made himself known as jealous about his honour and was only acting in a way that was consistent with his holiness (Deut. 4:24). To have done anything else would have raised questions about whether God was really so pure, so alert or so powerful as Israel had been led to believe. Speaking to Moses, God reminds him that

> *Among those who approach me*
> *I will be proved holy;*
> *in the sight of all the people*
> *I will be honoured.*

God had upheld his honour against Pharaoh and would act again in precisely this manner against the rebels led by Korah (Num. 16:35). Why should priests be exempt from encountering God's holiness when they had done wrong? Should they be permitted to render obedience that was less exacting than that of others? The truth was quite the reverse. God is passionate about living among his people and will not permit anyone to prevent him from doing so by defiling his dwelling-place, not even priests.

God punishes Nadab and Abihu because, as priests, they worked in his immediate presence. The point is emphasized by the particular words that lie behind the translation *those who approach me*, in verse 3. This

---

[9] See Luke 9:59–62 (quotation from v. 60).

terminology usually referred to an official who had direct access to a sovereign and who had no need of an intermediary, or of one who enjoyed intimacy with a superior.[10] Scripture speaks with a united voice: the closer one is to God, the more careful one must be about his holiness and honour; the greater the privileges one has received, the more careful one must be to fulfil one's responsibilities. As Jesus warned, 'From everyone who has been given much, much will be demanded; and from the one who has been entrusted with much, much more will be asked' (Luke 12:48). Being close to God confers enormous benefits but, at the same time, places one in a position of danger, as the priests discovered. For all the grace he provides, he still requires prompt and exact obedience from his servants.

The priests were in a position of great influence in Israel. The attitudes they displayed towards God and towards the ceremonies of the tabernacle would soon be adopted by the people of Israel as a whole. Therefore, if God had tolerated slack service or slipshod obedience from Nadab and Abihu, especially so near to the start of their period in office, the whole of Israel might soon have been drawing near to him in a sloppy or disrespectful manner. It never ceases to amaze me what influence pastors exercise over their congregations. Their passion for God and his work rubs off. So, too, less fortunately, does their cynicism, half-heartedness or lack of holiness. It is hard to disagree with J. L. Mays' assertion that 'the attitude of the congregation depends on the character of its ministry'.[11] Though ministers are not to be seen as the direct heirs of Old Testament priests,[12] they still bear an awesome and personal responsibility for how mature their congregations are in Christ, even if the whole of this responsibility does not descend on their shoulders alone.

The fate of Nadab and Abihu has yet a further lesson to teach. While we cannot be sure what state of mind they were in when they offered *unauthorised fire before the Lord*, we do know that they were new to their responsibilities. Maybe their error was compounded by their inexperience. In presenting what they did to the Lord they may have meant well, and even felt that they were doing him a favour. What they did might have seemed right to them at the time. It might have been their zeal to offer as many sacrifices as possible that led them into error – but error it was

---

[10] Milgrom, *Leviticus 1 – 16*, pp. 600–601.

[11] Mays, p. 43.

[12] See p. 252.

nevertheless. Good intentions are no substitute for exact obedience, and well-meaning enthusiasm is no substitute for 'discipline and discretion in worship'.[13] It was a lesson Ananias and Sapphira learnt the hard way in the early days of the Christian church (Acts 5:1–11). They too made an offering to God which, while no doubt well meant, may have been motivated by an over-excited enthusiasm. In presenting their gift they sought to deceive the apostles and, like Nadab and Abihu, were executed by God as a result. 'Great fear', we read, 'seized the whole church and all who heard about these events' (Acts 5:11). The one God of the Old and New Testaments deserves to be approached in worship with respectful fear.

2. Hearing the Lord (10:8–11)

Immediately after the tragic deaths of Nadab and Abihu the Lord spoke to Aaron (8). It is the only time when we read that God addressed Aaron alone, since he usually did so in the company of Moses. God used the situation to remind Aaron of the core responsibilities he had accepted as high priest. There could never have been a more teachable moment than this.

a. What the Lord forbids (10:9)

The first item on God's agenda seems a peculiar choice of topic to us. *You and your sons are not to drink wine or other fermented drink whenever you go into the tent of meeting, or you will die.* The stark directness of the command has led some to think that it must have been alcohol that lay behind the folly of Nadab and Abihu.[14] It might well be so, but even if it is not, the prohibition on alcohol is not as strange as it may at first appear. Abstinence was a sign of total dedication to God, as we see in the vows undertaken by Nazirites (Num. 6:1–12), and total dedication was required from priests when they served in the sanctuary.

A second reason makes the ban on alcohol even more apposite for the priests. God reminds Aaron that at the heart of their role lies the task of making judgments and exercising discernment. The ability to do this would be seriously affected if the priests were in a state of intoxication. Judgments would be skewed and unreliable.[15] For priests to have their

---

[13] Hartley, p. 138. See also Kellogg, p. 239.

[14] But Noth, p. 86, among others, thinks this injunction is unrelated to the context.

[15] Levine, p. 61.

minds 'befuddled with wine' or to turn up at the tabernacle reeling from beer (Isa. 28:7) would show that the very people to whom Israel looked for wisdom were, in reality, people of great folly (Prov. 20:1; see also Prov. 31:4–7). Today, those who are in charge of any form of public transport rightly live under severe restrictions as far as alcohol is concerned so that the safety of their passengers is never endangered. How much greater should be the care of those who have responsibility for the eternal safety of God's people under their charge! Shunning substance abuse of any kind, they should be clear-minded, self-disciplined and, above all else, filled with the Spirit of God to teach rightly and guide the church with true discernment (Eph. 5:18; 1 Thess. 5:7–8; 1 Tim. 3:2–3, 8).

b. What the Lord requires (10:10–11)

Having removed an obstacle to effective ministry, the Lord then reminds Aaron of his core responsibilities: *so that you can distinguish between the holy and the common, between the unclean and the clean, and so you can teach the Israelites all the decrees the Lord has given them through Moses.*

Objects, people and places that had been consecrated to the Lord were holy. They included the instruments and utensils used in the tabernacle, the gifts and sacrifices offered on the altar, the lifeblood of sacrificial animals, and the priests who served in the tabernacle. But Leviticus throws up numerous examples where a judgment needed to be made as to whether something was holy or not, leading to the idea that 'the naming of distinctions is the essence of the priestly function'.[16] Our discussion of the guilt offering provided some relevant illustrations; the purity codes will provide plenty of others, as too will the final chapter of Leviticus. If something was not holy it could be used in an ordinary, everyday way. But if it was holy it was set apart for God alone; and Nadab and Abihu's experience taught the peril of abusing what belonged to him.

Things that were holy were not necessarily pure, although there was a good deal of overlap between the two qualities.[17] The central theme of the next section of Leviticus (chapters 11–15) will explore what was meant by being ceremonially clean or unclean. Something could be clean without being holy. But it would have been impossible for something impure ever to have been considered holy. Only clean food could be eaten by the

---

[16] Milgrom, *Leviticus 1 – 16*, p. 615. See Ezek. 44:23 and, in contrast, Ezek. 22:26.

[17] See the Introduction above, pp. 11–12.

Israelites, and only those adjudged clean could be permitted to draw near to God in worship. It was vital, therefore, that people knew where matters stood, and it was the task of the priest to guide them. For the children of Israel such concerns were matters of urgent daily spirituality.

The teaching role of the priests is more immediately intelligible to us. The Holiness Code, as it is sometimes called, of chapters 17–26 contains a wealth of ethical instruction setting out how God wants his covenant people to behave in their families and their finances, in their communities and towards their criminals, with their words and in their deeds. The Israelites would have needed to have all of these instructions patiently explained and carefully interpreted. It was the task of the priests to educate the ignorant as much as it was to correct the wayward. The remit of the priests never changed, as Malachi, centuries later, confirmed. 'The lips of a priest', he wrote, 'ought to preserve knowledge, because he is the messenger of the Lord Almighty and people seek instruction from his mouth' (Mal. 2:7).

Later still, in reflecting on ministry in the church, Paul continued to put a premium on the teaching responsibility of its elders[18] and on their need to pass on the gospel to 'reliable people who will also be qualified to teach others' (2 Tim. 2:2). The content of their teaching may have varied from that imparted by the priests of ancient Israel, but the task had not. Pastors were still required to expound the truth and to rebuke error. After surveying the evidence of the pastoral epistles, John Stott concludes: 'The Christian pastoral ministry is essentially a teaching ministry, which explains why candidates are required both to be orthodox in their own faith and to have an ability to teach.'[19]

3. Pleasing the Lord (10:12–20)

The conclusion of the chapter is still concerned with the aftermath of Nadab and Abihu's disobedience. Moses instructed Aaron, and Eleazar and Ithamar, his surviving sons, to eat up the portions of food that remained from the abortive sacrifices that Nadab and Abihu had offered. In giving this instruction, Moses was simply requiring the priests to follow

---

[18] E.g. 1 Tim. 3:2; 4:13; 6:2; 2 Tim. 4:2; Titus 1:9.

[19] John Stott, *The Message of 2 Timothy: Guard the Gospel*, The Bible Speaks Today (London: IVP, 2021), p. 85.

the sacrificial procedures through to completion and warning them to do so to the letter (12–15). It was important that they ate the offering, not only because by this time they must have been hungry, but also because half-finished offerings were never sufficient in God's sight.[20] Having spoken, it would seem that Moses left the tabernacle for a time,[21] only to discover, on his return, that Aaron and his family had burned the meat completely on the altar instead of eating the portion that belonged to them as they had been instructed (16–18). Moses was angry and immediately enquired as to why his instructions had been ignored.

Emotions that day would have been raw, and Moses at least had the sensitivity to raise the matter first with Eleazar and Ithamar, rather than going directly to Aaron, his inwardly grieving eighty-year-old brother. But it was Aaron who replied. *Today*, he explained, *they* [Nadab and Abihu] *sacrificed their sin offering and their burnt offering before the LORD, but such things as this* [presumably their deaths] *have happened to me. Would the LORD have been pleased if I had eaten the sin offering today?* (19).

Moses and Aaron had seen things from different angles and this had led them to conflicting conclusions as to how the law of God was to be interpreted. Moses had been anxious that the sin offering whose blood had been presented on the altar should be consumed, whereas Aaron had been worried that it had been contaminated by his sons' deaths and was therefore impure.[22] Clearly there was room for two godly people, both qualified in the law, and both handling it with perfect integrity, to see it differently. However precise its stipulations, there were always going to be areas where there was freedom to interpret it one way or another.

When Moses heard Aaron's explanation *he was satisfied* (20). Aaron wanted nothing more than to please the Lord, and consequently he had chosen to err on the side of caution and to make sure that there could be no possible further compromise to God's honour. It was a wise choice to make, not just on that particular day, but on any day. Aaron was not being casual about things that had been clearly revealed. He was being cautious about things that were less than clearly revealed. Though, as Walter Kaiser says, 'Aaron and his two youngest sons have not personally sinned, their

[20] Levine, p. 62.

[21] Milgrom, *Leviticus 1 – 16*, p. 622.

[22] Budd, pp. 156–157, summarizing Milgrom, *Leviticus 1 – 16*, pp. 635–640.

consciences are so awakened to the holiness of God, and to their tendency to sinfulness, that they hesitate to venture into areas where they have no explicit direction.'[23] To hold back, rather than to take liberties, with the things of God gave proof that the harsh lessons of the day had not been lost on Aaron and his remaining sons.

The debate between Moses and Aaron has a twofold import for today's church. On the one hand, there are those, like Moses, who are rigid in their interpretation of the Scripture and believe that their interpretation of it, and theirs alone, is legitimate. They need to face up to the fact that there are some matters on which those who have a desire to honour God and who handle Scripture with an integrity equal to their own may legitimately differ from them. The imposition, in some circles, of non-negotiable pet (and often petty!) interpretations is clearly not warranted by Scripture itself, which admits areas of debate, and can be damaging to the spiritual development of some believers, who need to mature by grappling with issues before the Lord rather than by having everything settled for them by others.[24] On the other hand, there are those, some in leadership positions, who play fast and loose with their handling of God's Word, and they need to be encouraged, both by the tragedy of Nadab and Abihu and by the example of Aaron, to approach the things that concern God with greater caution and respect. Make no mistake, 'God cannot be mocked' (Gal. 6:7). His honour will be served and his holiness made known to those who lead his people.

The fall from grace of Aaron's elder sons was rapid. The transformation of *fire* that *came out from the presence of the LORD* from being a sign of God's beneficial presence to being an instrument of God's awesome judgment was both sensational and tragic. The events that followed the inauguration of Aaron's priesthood stand as a permanent warning to all who would enter God's service. They should not, however, be taken as an indication that God is spiteful, merciless and vindictive. What we encounter most in Leviticus, as well as elsewhere, is a God of compassion and mercy, who is slow to anger and abounding in love and faithfulness (Exod. 34:6). He desires his people to draw near and longs for nothing more than to be like a Father who lives among his children, forgiving their wrongs and healing their hurts.

---

[23] Kaiser, p. 1072.

[24] Classically, Rom. 14 and 1 Cor. 7 – 8.

Paul once encouraged the Corinthians to wholehearted service for God in words that aptly capture the teaching of this sad episode for all believers: 'Dear friends, let us purify ourselves from everything that contaminates body and spirit, *perfecting holiness out of reverence for God'* (2 Cor. 7:1, emphasis added).

C. The manual of purity: encountering God's design (11:1 – 15:33)

Leviticus 11:1–47

10. Purity and the diet

Leviticus reads like a guidebook to a foreign land, and the sections that deal with questions about purity – 11:1 – 15:33 – introduce us to the strangest area within its boundaries. For five chapters Leviticus lays down detailed instructions about what foods may and may not be eaten; what to do when a woman gives birth; what to do when a person is afflicted by various skin diseases or when a house suffers from mildew; and what to do when men and women experience various discharges from their bodies. The obsessive style of these chapters has led one commentator to voice what many probably silently believe: these chapters 'are perhaps the least attractive in the whole Bible. To the modern reader there is much in them that is meaningless or repulsive.'[1]

But if all Scripture is inspired and useful (2 Tim. 3:16–17; cf. Rom. 15:4), we must not dismiss these chapters so easily. Nor need we do so. The purity laws have attracted considerable attention in recent years, with the result that much illumination has been shed on these ancient texts, revealing their message in new ways. Originally, they would have communicated to the ancient Israelites one main message, and would have done so with great lucidity: their God was holy and he required them to mirror his holiness in the way in which they lived. Holiness was never presented to them as an abstract ideal. It was always an 'attainable reality'[2] that dealt with the ever-present routines of daily life. Holiness

---

[1] N. Micklem, quoted by Douglas, *Purity*, p. 46.

[2] Harrison, p. 120.

encompassed the whole of life. It impacted what went on in the kitchen, the maternity room, the sickroom and the bedroom as much as what went on in the sanctuary. A God whose presence was felt in the kitchen was not a God you could marginalize, keep confined to a compartment of life marked 'spiritual', or serve only at special times designated for worship. He was a God who reigned over the totality of life and was to be served at all times and in all places.

1. Orientation: where do these issues fit?

Before looking at the details of the food laws, it might prove helpful to explore two general questions.

a. How do the issues relate to us?

Though, at first sight, the purity laws seem to usher us into an altogether foreign, unfamiliar world, a moment's reflection suggests that the territory is not as alien as it seems. Our own world operates along similar lines, as all cultures up to the present time have done. There are certain foods we will eat and others we regard as unfit to eat. One has only to contemplate the difference between English and French attitudes to horse meat or snails, without needing to venture further afield and think of the way some enjoy eating bugs in a jungle or dogs in the Far East, to grasp the point. Furthermore, our society is riddled with regulations over how food is to be stored and preserved – just think of sell-by dates, stipulations about freezer temperatures and the need to separate cooked from uncooked meat in a butcher's shop – which we account for in terms of hygienic necessity.

Moving away from food, we see a concern similar to that evident in Leviticus for the correct handling of what we consider to be unclean in the way we handle pollution in the atmosphere or body fluids in a hospital. We may draw the line in different places from where the ancient Israelites did, but we draw the line nonetheless. We may account for our attitudes from a scientific or hygienic perspective, but we hold as strongly to concepts of 'clean' and 'unclean' as they did.

Underneath it all, the matter is quite simple. It is about our view of what is safe and orderly in the world. Mary Douglas, whose many writings in this area have helped to shed light on its meaning, has said that the concept of 'uncleanness' is similar to, though not identical with, our concept of dirt.[3] We do not permit a pile of soil in the living room, not because soil in itself is 'evil' – it isn't, and it proves quite useful in the garden! – but because soil in the living room is out of place. Purity codes, as David deSilva has explained,

> are a way of talking about what is proper for a certain place and a certain time (however one's society fills in the content). Pollution is a label attached to whatever is out of place with regard to society's view of an orderly and safe world.[4]

So, though the details may differ, and our reasoning may be justified differently, it would seem that the idea of distinguishing between the clean and the unclean is not so strange after all.

b. How do the issues relate to the rest of Leviticus?

Leviticus 11 – 15 comes just at the right place as far as the wider context of Leviticus is concerned. The purity rules are placed immediately after the sacrificial system has been inaugurated, as if they were next in order of importance.[5] In the preceding chapter (10:10) we read that God had instructed Aaron that the responsibilities of the high priest included distinguishing between the unclean and the clean. These chapters are a self-conscious exploration of this task,[6] and it is very appropriate that five areas where this particular responsibility would come into play are covered in the next section of the book.

At the other end of this section readers find themselves introduced to the rituals of the great Day of Atonement. To some it seems as if they are moving from the ridiculous to the sublime. But the truth is that the Day of Atonement is intrinsically connected with what has gone before. On that day, the high priest undertook a special ceremony which was partly designed to cleanse the tabernacle 'from the uncleanness of the Israelites' (16:19) that had accumulated there in the previous twelve months. The impurities in question include those that are explored in chapters 11–15.

---

[3] Douglas, *Purity*, p. 35.

[4] David deSilva, *Honor, Patronage, Kinship and Purity: Unlocking New Testament Culture* (Downers Grove, IL: IVP, 2000), p. 242.

[5] Houston, p. 256.

[6] Lev. 11 closes by repeating this instruction in v. 47.

It is important to remember one further issue as we approach these chapters. The concepts of clean and unclean, though linked, are not synonymous with those of the sacred and the profane. Cleanliness has essentially to do with ritual purity, not moral purity, and is what makes a person fit to approach God in worship and live in his community without causing it damage. What is clean may be set apart for God and, by being sanctified, become holy. So the clean offerings presented to God are called *sacred* or *most sacred*. Similarly, ordinary men of the family of Aaron became priests when set apart for God through ordination, but it was essential that they were *clean* first. If, for any reason, by way of temporary ritual impurity or permanent physical deformity, they were unclean, then their service at the altar was not acceptable.

Uncleanness might be either permanent or temporary. On the one hand, temporary uncleanness could be overcome through an appropriate rite of cleansing – the subject of chapters 12, 14 and 15. On the other hand, some things were irredeemably unclean – like some of the animals listed in chapter 11 – and no amount of ritual cleansing could alter their status before God.

Given this, we must be careful not to equate being unclean with being a guilty sinner. It is true that sin may be implicated in uncleanness. But when a woman loses blood in the process of giving birth, or a person suffers from a skin disease or a bodily emission, it is not a symptom of having broken God's law: it is a consequence of living in the natural (fallen) world. Therefore, these chapters give no justification for identifying sexual matters with evil, and it is mistaken to think they equate childbirth, sickness or the menstrual cycle with sin. Indeed, while these regulations stress the need to approach God in a state of ritual purity, the greater stress is on the wonderful provision God makes to enable those to whom the pollutions of the world cling to be cleansed and restored to active participation in the community of those who worship him.

2. Exploration: what does the text say? (11:1–47)

Turning to the regulations concerning clean and unclean animals, we find that chapter 11 provides a systematic account of land animals (2–8), sea creatures (9–12), birds (13–19) and insects (20–23), before going on to answer a variety of questions that would inevitably arise, no matter how clear the lists provided were. Deuteronomy 14:1–21 gives a parallel account that concentrates more on questions of principle, whereas Leviticus provides a fuller list and applies those principles in specific ways.[7] Leviticus reviews the topic in a way that is both systematically comprehensive and symmetrically arranged.[8]

a. Land animals (11:2–8)

The primary marker that separates clean from unclean animals is whether the animal *has a divided hoof and . . . chews the cud* (3). If so, the animal is clean and may be eaten. If not, the animal is unclean and may not be eaten. Animals that fulfil one but not the other of these qualifications – the camel, hyrax, rabbit or hare, and pig are mentioned[9] – are *ceremonially unclean*. Clearly, caution was needed in determining whether an animal was in one category or the other. The camel, for example, has the appearance of being a clean animal because it *chews the cud* and has a split hoof but 'its sole is thick and cushiony so that the split does not appear'.[10] Therefore it is actually an unclean animal. Superficial interpretations were no more acceptable in approaching matters of ritual purity than casual performances were in the offering of sacrifices.

Being unclean means not only that these animals must not be eaten but also that their carcasses must not be touched, or else they would contaminate the one who had contact with them (8). This curious prohibition had the effect of preserving unclean animals and keeping them alive. In an overstatement, Mary Douglas explains that, while living, they could be 'harnessed, loaded, ridden, dogs can be beaten, cats can be kicked, mice can be trapped, without incurring impurity, but once they are dead they convey uncleanness'.[11] Once dead, they could not be skinned or dismembered. So no fur coats, leather waistcoats or wineskins could be made from their skin; no buttons or combs made from their bones and no musical strings created from their gut. To classify the dead animal as unclean meant that its carcass could not be exploited for economic gain, and, consequently, that living animals were not worth killing. The result was to ensure fertility

---

[7] Hartley, pp. 155–156.

[8] Houston, p. 231.

[9] Questions arise throughout the chapter about the exact identification of some of the animals mentioned, for which standard scholarly commentaries should be consulted.

[10] Hartley, p. 157.

[11] Douglas, *Literature*, p. 141. This should not be taken as justification for the mistreatment of animals, which some have wrongly understood God's command to humans to 'rule . . . over every living creature' (Gen. 1:28) to permit. The whole tenor of these prohibitions lies in the opposite direction; they are designed to *protect* species.

and 'the survival of the species'.[12] This prohibition resulted in the fulfilment of God's command to his creation to 'be fruitful and increase in number'.[13] Far from the label 'detestable' being a sign of God's curse on these animals, it was a sign of his blessing on them and protection over them.

Other peoples in the ancient world ate both camels and pigs without difficulty, as we know from archaeological evidence. So these regulations were not reflecting a general abhorrence of eating these animals; it is not that the animals were somehow inherently repulsive. These regulations were specific to Israel and called the people to live in a way that was distinctive from their neighbours. The pig played a role in the cult of the dead in Egypt and in Canaan, so the prohibition on eating pigs was a specific call to Israel to avoid imitating their neighbours in the way they lived. This particular way of working out the call to distinctive living is no longer relevant to Christian believers, but the call itself remains in force (2 Cor. 6:14 – 7:1) and the later chapters of Leviticus will give us an increasing understanding of how a 'separate' lifestyle may be lived in the contemporary world.

It is interesting to note that the animals that are clean are those that were the common domestic animals of the day – cattle, lambs and goats – as opposed to the wild animals. They were also the ones that were offered in sacrifice to God. The regulations have nothing to do with the superiority of a clean animal over others, since all creatures created by God are good. They reflect a sense of what worshippers saw as contributing to order and stability in their world, as opposed to those untamed animals that threatened to destroy it or cause it to revert to chaos. The clean animals were ones over which humans could exercise control.[14]

b. Sea creatures (11:9–12)

The basis for the distinction between fish is whether or not they *have fins and scales* (9). If they have them, they are clean; if they do not, they are unclean. Houston points out that few Israelites would have seen fish much and would not have sufficient knowledge to apply the criteria.[15] Even so, the criteria fall exactly in the right place to permit Israel to eat edible fish and avoid those that were inedible. Stronger language is used to outlaw

---

[12] Douglas, *Literature*, p. 142. For different reasons Milgrom argues that these laws are designed to restrict the diet and reduce the consumption of meat by rendering these animals unclean. *Leviticus 1 – 16*, p. 733.

[13] Gen. 1:28. Douglas, *Literature*, pp. 157–163.

[14] Houston, pp. 114–120, 176–177, 233; Budd, p. 159.

[15] Houston, p. 235.

the eating of unclean fish than was used to proscribe unclean meat. The Israelites are told that they are *to be regarded as unclean by you* (12), while their carcasses must be treated with utter contempt (11).

Mary Douglas proposed the idea that the basis for the criteria lay in distinguishing that which was natural in a category from that which was anomalous. Animals, fish, birds or other creatures that conformed to what was natural for their class were clean, whereas those that were somehow deviant were unclean. One would expect fish to have fins and scales, hence the ones that do are considered to be clean and may be eaten.[16] Originally, her basis for determining what was 'normal' was derived from the creation story in Genesis.[17] More recently, she has stressed the way in which these regulations emphasize God's care for creation. 'The law does not say', she writes, 'that there is anything inherently abominable about shrimps or eels or octopus, or even that they are universally to be abominated.'[18] Rather the law says they were detestable to the Israelites. And, pointing out that the word for 'scales' is the same as that used in 1 Samuel 17:5 to describe Goliath's coat of mail, she argues that the key issue is that unclean fish lack protection and were more vulnerable than clean fish. These regulations, then, were a further sign of God's desire to protect the vulnerable.[19]

c. Creatures of the air (11:13–19)

The section on birds is different. It does not state the criteria according to which the priests were to distinguish clean from unclean birds. Houston argues that no such criteria exist, or else they would have been mentioned.[20] In fact, no clean birds are listed. Rather, what is provided is a long list of some twenty names of *unclean* ones. These birds are primarily birds of prey which live in desert places and feed off the blood of other animals. As killers and blood-drinkers they break the law and so are outlawed.[21] In recent years, Mary Douglas has stressed that the key feature of both unclean land animals and unclean birds is that they are predators who live on blood and so violate the prohibition of eating blood, which is mentioned

---

[16] Douglas, *Purity*, pp. 41–57.

[17] She points out the threefold classification in the creation story where 'in the firmament two-legged fowls fly with wings. In the water scaly fish swim with fins. On the earth four-legged animals hop, jump and walk.' Douglas, *Purity*, p. 55.

[18] Ibid., p. 168.

[19] Ibid., p. 169.

[20] Houston, p. 235. See also Levine, p. 67.

[21] Wenham, p. 175. The prohibition on eating blood is found in Lev. 17.

in Leviticus 17.[22] Less certain, but possibly relevant, is the thought that they are the kinds of animals that were associated with demons.[23]

d. Flying insects (11:20–23)

The last group, flying insects, more specifically deals with 'swarming things'. They are a sign of God's abundance in his beautiful creation and, consequently, it is forbidden to attack them. They are protected by being declared *unclean*.

Unlike the other categories of creatures, 'swarming things' have no distinct method of movement and so are mostly unclean. Animals walk, fish swim and birds fly, but flying insects defy discrete categories of motion and sometimes fly in the air and sometimes walk on the ground. This same point is developed further in verses 41–42 and 45, where creatures that move about on the ground are referred to and labelled 'unclean'. Mary Douglas explains the problem with them in a colourful passage when she writes:

> Whether we call it teeming, trailing, creeping, crawling or swarming, it is an indeterminate form of movement. Since the main animal categories are defined by their typical movement, 'swarming', which is not a mode of propulsion proper to any particular element, cuts across the basic classification. Swarming things are neither fish, flesh nor fowl. Eels and worms inhabit water, though not as fish; reptiles go on dry ground, though not as quadrupeds; some insects fly, though not as birds. There is no order in them.[24]

Locusts and a few other insects, however, do have a distinctive means of movement and hop on the ground because they *have jointed legs* (21). So these insects are clean and may be eaten.[25]

e. Further questions (11:24–40)

Having set out the major position, the rest of the chapter provides further clarification, especially in relation to questions that would have been in the minds of the priests.

---

[22] Douglas, 'Forbidden Animals', pp. 15–18.

[23] Hartley, p. 159.

[24] Douglas, *Purity*, p. 56.

[25] Douglas, *Purity*, pp. 55–56. Milgrom, *Leviticus 1 – 16*, p. 666, rejects this view and says that locusts are an exception in view of the fondness with which people in ancient pastoral communities ate them. See Hartley, p. 161.

First, there are questions about people who come into contact with death (24–31). What happens when a person has touched the carcass of an unclean animal? The answer is: *Whoever picks up one of their carcasses must wash their clothes, and they will be unclean till evening* (25). The same penalty is laid down in a general way to begin with and then repeated for emphasis, first in respect of *animals that walk on all fours* (26–28) and, second, in respect of those that *move along the ground* (29–31). Whoever has contact with dead animals becomes defiled, but not in any major way, since the defilement is temporary, lasting only until the evening; the stain may be removed by washing and does not require the offering of a sacrifice.

Second, there are questions about objects that came into contact with the dead (32–38). The response shows a rapier-like logic. If a dead animal fell onto an item of clothing, the garment became unclean and required washing (32). However, if the corpse fell into a porous pot or an oven, those objects must be destroyed, together with any food that was in them at the time (33–35). Neither the oven nor the pot could be used again for cooking because it might be the means of spreading the uncleanness. Where the situation occurred, as it were, in the garden, rather than the kitchen, the effect of the unclean corpse is determined on the basis of whether running water was involved or not (36–37). If the water was running, as in a spring, then any defilement would automatically be washed away. But where, as in verse 38, any water had already been deposited on a seed and was static, the seed became unclean.

Third, there were questions about contact with the corpses of clean animals (39–40). The priests might wonder: Do the same rules as those to do with the corpses of unclean animals apply? Or is contact with the corpse of a clean animal to be handled differently? The reply is clear. The essential issue is not that the animal was one that the Israelites were permitted to eat, but that someone has come into contact with death. *Anyone who touches its carcass will be unclean till evening* (39) and, consequently, *must wash their clothes* (40).

f. Twin motivations (11:41–45)

While scholars debate the origin of these purity codes and compare them repeatedly with those found in other cultures, Leviticus attributes their origin to God and presents them as specific to Israel, his covenant people. Once more we find that the regulations, as others, are neither individually devised nor sociologically constructed, but divinely revealed. The regulations are based on the twin motivations of God's holiness and God's grace. *I am the* Lord *your God; consecrate yourselves and be holy, because I am holy* (44). Here is a breathtaking invitation – twice issued here (44, 45) – and one that is to be repeated three more times in the chapters that follow (19:2; 20:7, 26). Israel is to imitate God, their maker and covenant redeemer, in the routine of their daily living in the world. This calls for them to possess a distinctive lifestyle, which would mark them out as different from their neighbours. They were meant to be set apart from others, not indistinguishable from them. Having the Lord as their God laid particular obligations on them that affected even their diets.

Their motivation, however, was to lie as much in gratitude as in duty, and to be a response to God's gracious salvation as much as to his holy law. God says to them: *I am the* Lord, *who brought you up out of Egypt to be your God; therefore be holy* (45). His saving grace preceded his giving of the law. The giving of the law simply set out how this grateful people should live in response to the saving love they had received. They were set free to be holy. The law was not an unwelcome burden, cruelly imposed on them, but a continuing mark of his grace at work in their midst. Those who have experienced amazing grace today, and truly understand it, do not perceive the call to holiness as chaffing under the restrictions of law but as a glad response of gratitude for what Christ has done.

3. Explanation: why were the rules given?

While Leviticus sets out the dietary regulations in detail, it does not give any explanation as to why they take the form they do. There are those who say it is enough that God has spoken. He had no need to justify himself to Israel and has no need to explain himself to us. When he commands, Israel should obey without questioning, and so should we. The choice of clean and unclean may be purely arbitrary, such people argue – more in the manner of a test of obedience than making any sense for other reasons. While this may be true, it is uncharacteristic of the God of the covenant, who is often portrayed as explaining the wisdom of his laws to his people.

The silence of Scripture on the matter of explanation has not been matched by anything approaching silence among those who would speculate about the reasons behind these laws. Some of the theories that have been proposed have greater merit than others. Here we briefly review the main approaches.[26]

a. Hygienic

Among the traditional explanations is the idea that clean food was more hygienic to eat than unclean food, and that while the ancient Israelites may have had no knowledge of the matter – at least, no modern scientific knowledge – God's omniscience would have been all that was required to warn them away from food that would have been harmful to them. Maimonides, for example, the Jewish sage of the twelfth century, partially supported this view and explained that pork was forbidden because it was 'unwholesome' and contained 'more moisture than necessary . . . and too much superfluous matter'.[27] It is true that some foods on the forbidden list are prone to particularly harmful parasites, but no food is exempt from them, especially in hot climates, and it is evident that other nations knew how to overcome any potential problems by careful cooking. It would not have been beyond the wit of Israel to do so as well. So, while Laird Harris can write that 'the hygienic theory adequately explains the dietary laws, the laws covering disease, and the laws covering housing and sanitation', and adds that 'it is an old view worth defending',[28] the view does not commend widespread support today. Houston concludes that 'the idea has no explanatory power, and ought to be laid to rest'.[29]

b. Ascetic

Philo, an Alexandrian Jew and careful interpreter of Scripture who lived around the time of Christ, argued that the restrictions were imposed to teach Israel to live ascetically. Their purpose was to teach self-denial, to restrain self-indulgence and to prevent gluttony. Maimonides partly supported this perspective in arguing that the regulations were designed to encourage the practice of self-discipline. This view is still current in the writings of Jacob Milgrom, who argues that the rules are designed 'to discipline the appetite and to prevent human beings becoming dehumanised by the violence involved in the killing of meat'.[30] But, as Houston

---

[26] For an exhaustive discussion see Houston.

[27] Cited in Houston, p. 69.

[28] Harris, p. 528. Harris sees it as a fulfilment of God's promise in Exod. 15:26 not to inflict on them any of the diseases he brought upon the Egyptians, but to be 'the LORD, who heals you'.

[29] Houston, p. 70.

[30] Houston, p. 76. See Milgrom, *Leviticus 1 – 16*, pp. 718–736.

comments, it is difficult to see how this translates into the particular prohibitions included in Leviticus 11.

c. Allegorical

Mary Douglas says that 'Christian teaching has readily followed the allegorizing tradition'.[31] And there are plenty of inventive allegories that could be mentioned by way of example. Novatian, to give one, wrote in the third century: 'Fish with rough scales are considered clean, just as persons with austere, rough, unpolished, steadfast and grave traits are commended. Fish without scales are considered unclean, just as loose, fickle, insincere and effeminate traits are censured.'[32] Matthew Henry, to give another example, wrote in the eighteenth:

> Meditation, and other acts of devotion done by the hidden man of the heart, may be signified by chewing the cud, digesting our spiritual food; justice and charity towards men, and acts of good conversation, may be signified by the *dividing of the hoof*.[33]

While he may not have been wholly convinced about this particular analogy, Henry was less reticent with his own:

> We must not be filthy nor wallow in the mire as swine, nor be timorous and faint-hearted as hares, nor dwell in the earth as rabbits; let not man that is in honour make himself like these beasts that perish.[34]

Though the approach may initially have some advantages, in that it takes the animals as symbolic of spiritual wisdom (or lack of it), Douglas dismisses such comments as 'not so much interpretations as pious commentaries' that are neither consistent nor comprehensive. She is right in asserting that if this approach is adopted 'there is no end to the number of possible interpretations'.[35] There is no means of distinguishing the valid from the invalid, and the range of interpretations is limited only by the inventiveness of the commentators.

---

[31] Douglas, *Purity*, p. 47.

[32] *Jewish Foods* 3.13, quoted in Lienhard, p. 177.

[33] Matthew Henry, *Commentary on the Whole Bible* (London: Marshall, Morgan & Scott, 1953 edn), p. 485.

[34] Ibid., p. 486.

[35] Douglas, *Purity*, p. 48.

d. Cultic

The common thread that combines the various ideas that come under the cultic heading is that unclean foods were considered unclean because they were unacceptable in worship.[36] What made them objectionable was that they were associated either with pagan worship or with death. Though there is some evidence to support the former, it is difficult to apply it consistently to the lists in Leviticus 11. The latter works only if being associated with death is interpreted in the widest possible way and includes, for example, living underground as akin to death. The association of unclean animals with pagan worship cannot be completely ruled out and makes sense of this chapter as a call to Israel to live a distinct way of life.

e. Symbolic

Currently, the most popular approach is a symbolic one which owes its origin to the formative work of Mary Douglas. Building on the work of Emile Durkheim and of other anthropologists, she argues that the worship of Israel would have reflected the patterns that governed their social life. By symbolically representing their social structures and their values in their rituals, those structures and values would be reinforced, community life would be re-energized, and, as people came to worship, their commitment to what the community stood for would be renewed. Of particular relevance to the issue of clean and unclean food is her concept of normality and anomaly. The animals that conform to what is normal for their type are clean whereas those that are imperfect members of their class are unclean. She then connects this to the concept of holiness. 'To be holy is to be whole, to be one; holiness is unity, integrity, perfection of the individual and of kind. The dietary rules merely develop the metaphor of holiness on the same lines.'[37] This interpretation, she suggests, means that 'the dietary laws would have been like signs which at every turn inspired meditation on the oneness, purity and completeness of God'.[38]

The view has much to commend it and has been warmly accepted by Gordon Wenham, among others, who underlines its value in helping us to see how these regulations would teach the children of Israel the standards

---

[36] Noth, p. 92, and see Houston, pp. 72–74.

[37] Douglas, *Purity*, p. 54.

[38] Ibid., p. 57.

of righteousness that they required in approaching God.[39] But Douglas's views have not been uncritically accepted by all.[40] Some argue that the details do not support her theories and that it is more straightforward to see the basis for the difference between clean and unclean either as indicating the difference between those animals with which humans were comfortable or ill at ease, or as having to do with economics and issues of the food chain.[41] Edwin Firmage, while accepting that the rules are symbolic and reflect Israel's values, also criticizes her theory of anomaly and argues that the distinction mirrors the sacrificial system rather than the idea of holiness.[42]

Judging between these various interpretations is difficult, although some are patently more persuasive than others. Given that Leviticus teaches spiritual truth through symbolic action, those interpretations that stress this aspect of the purity rules are undoubtedly the most appropriate.

4. Interpretation: how do the truths apply?

The purity regulations subsequently became a matter of crucial import-ance for the Jews and were used to draw a clear boundary between themselves and other races. Christians quickly set them aside and only strictly orthodox Jews maintain their practice today. So what is their con-tinuing value?

a. What they teach about creation

First, the purity codes teach us about God's intention for creation. Thanks to the work of Mary Douglas, we now see that labelling an animal, fish, bird or insect as 'unclean', 'detestable' or 'abominable' was not, as is commonly supposed, a way of despising them or of suggesting that they were of less worth than those labelled 'clean'. On seeing his creation, God declared that all of it 'was very good' (Gen. 1:31). In the Psalms (e.g. 50:10–11), in Job (39:1–30) and in Proverbs (e.g. 30:24–28) God claims ownership over all creatures in his beautiful and diverse creation and

---

[39] Wenham, p. 171.

[40] See Houston, pp. 101–120, for a survey.

[41] Budd, pp. 159, 193.

[42] E. Firmage, 'The Biblical Dietary Laws and the Concept of Holiness', in J. A. Emerton (ed.), *Studies in the Pentateuch* (Leiden: Brill, 1990), pp. 177–208.

revels in their wonderfully playful and positive characteristics, specifically mentioning some of the very ones designated as 'unclean' in Leviticus
as he does so. So the purity codes cannot mean that God wants to rid his
world of some animals that he considers to be second-rate to others. There
is nothing wrong with them or inherently disgusting about them. Rather
the reverse is true. By declaring them 'unclean' and prohibiting the
touching or use of their carcasses, God is building a hedge of protection
around them and ensuring an environment in which it was possible for
them to thrive and multiply.

As stewards of creation our role is not to exploit the earth for selfish
gain but to preside over it in such a way as to enable the other species with
which we share the planet to thrive. God is as concerned about the well-
being of his creation as he is about the well-being of his sanctuary. He
reigns over all life and gives attention to the fortunes of all his teeming,
varied creatures.

b. What they teach about holiness

Second, the purity laws have much to teach us about holiness. Holiness is
no abstract, ethereal quality, removed from the business of everyday life.
Holiness has to do with the concrete realities of how we acquire our food
and what we eat, as much as with how long we spend in prayer. Biblical
spirituality, if not an earthbound spirituality, is an earth-focused
spirituality. It is this-worldly in its concerns as much as other-worldly.
'Holiness', as Walter Kaiser says, 'could not be practised merely in the
religious realm . . . God looked for wholeness, completion, and separateness in every aspect of one's life-style.'[43]

Food has always been a contentious issue. The Corinthians faced
the question of eating meat that had been sacrificed to idols (see 1 Cor.
8:1–13; 10:14–33). Some argued that it was a matter of freedom of conscience to be able to do so, and that, since idols had no real existence, it
did not matter that the meat had been offered in homage to them first.
Others, of a more sensitive conscience, argued that Christians should
avoid such meat completely because of its associations. Paul tells them
that they should balance their freedom to act in this area with sensitivity to the consciences of weaker believers, and that whatever they
did they should do it with thankfulness. 'So', he concluded, 'whether

---

[43] Kaiser, p. 1082.

you eat or drink or whatever you do, do it all for the glory of God' (1 Cor. 10:31).

In our world, food remains a contentious issue for a number of reasons. Not only is there a glaring and inexcusable gap between the 'haves' and the 'have nots', but modern methods of food production have thrown up a range of new ethical challenges, including that of genetic engineering, and the problem of obesity from which much of the Western world suffers. Some have been led to a new legalism, laying down rules about what should and should not be eaten. Whatever one's stance on these complex issues, it cannot be divorced from the Christian's commitment to holiness. Holiness calls upon us even to eat and drink 'for the glory of God'.

Holiness means that God's people will always live in a way that is distinct from those who do not follow their God. For Israel the differences were seen in the food laws, as well as in other ways. Other cultures had no inhibitions about eating the animals that were declared 'unclean' in Israel. In some cases, they even gave them a starring role in their worship performances. But God had drawn a line, and keeping to the right side of the boundary meant that Israel would show herself to be his unique people, called to serve him alone. The food laws of Leviticus are no longer binding on Christians and are not the means by which Christians display their loyalty to God in his world. But Christians are still required to live distinctively. In some areas, such as that of sexual ethics, the challenges remain constant. But other issues that distinguish Christians from the surrounding society may differ from generation to generation and from culture to culture. Not infrequently a particular context throws up a more transient issue that becomes symbolic of the dividing line. Compromise at these points would mean that Christian people living at that time would erode their distinctiveness altogether. For Daniel in Babylon it revolved around eating and drinking at the king's table (Dan. 1:8). For many Christians in Victorian Britain the boundary line concerned drink, debt or gambling. In Hitler's Germany it involved the Nazi salute. Today the place where the line is drawn may be different, but a line there will be. Christians will always be nonconformists in a world that marginalizes the living God.

The purity regulations teach us further that holiness is about being fit to approach our awesome God. People who infringed these regulations became unclean for the rest of the day and remained so until they had washed their clothes. That meant they were not able to join the community of Israel in worship and were unable to draw near to God. Those who wish to enter God's presence must be qualified to do so, not because of their own inherent goodness but because of the cleansing they have received from Christ.

c. What they teach about salvation

When Jesus came, he 'declared all foods clean' (Mark 7:19). By his time, the food laws (along with circumcision and the Sabbath laws) had become the key test of an authentic Jewish faith and lifestyle. Those who sought to uphold the law found Jesus' attitude to questions of purity lax.[44] In particular, they found him remiss in letting his disciples eat with 'unclean' hands. The ritual washing of hands had become a tradition, even though it was no more than a human extension to the dietary laws of Leviticus. It was on one such occasion that Jesus established the principle that 'nothing outside a person can defile them by going into them. Rather, it is what comes out of a person that defiles them' (Mark 7:15). Whatever went into a person, he explained, went temporarily into that person's stomach and passed through the body. By contrast, what came out of a person's heart was an expression of that person's real self. It was Mark who grasped the significance of this and drew the conclusion that this meant that what one ate no longer mattered. It was no longer important to categorize food as either 'clean' or 'unclean'. Other things, namely inner realities, were of greater significance.

The distinction between 'clean' and 'unclean' was inbred in all good Jews. So it took some time for the early Christians to break its stranglehold in their thinking and reconstruct their view of the way God worked. Peter confronted the issue near Joppa when he was on his way to share the good news of Jesus with Cornelius, a Roman centurion (Acts 10:1–48). In a vision, the Lord invited Peter to kill and eat 'unclean' food. When Peter protested that he could never do any such thing, the Lord replied, 'Do not call anything impure that God has made clean' (Acts 10:15). This was not the only occasion on which he had to unlearn human tradition and relearn the gospel (see Gal. 2:1–10). Yet learn it he did, and when, following Peter's vision, the leaders of the church met in Jerusalem to discuss what requirements should be laid on Gentile converts, they dropped the distinctive laws of diet, not out of pragmatism but out of theology. These laws

---

44 See Matt. 15:1–20; Mark 7:1–23. By drinking with a Samaritan woman, Jesus would have breached the rules of purity; John 4:7–10.

symbolized Gentile exclusion from God, an exclusion that the coming of Christ had brought to an end.[45]

The work of Jesus Christ had rendered the old distinctions void. The sharp separation that had existed between Jew and Gentile, symbolized by their distinctive food laws, no longer had any force. Where the laws divided, Christ unites. The blood of Jesus can make the least clean of people clean and those farthest away from God acceptable to him (Eph. 2:11–13).

The laws of Leviticus are like a photographic process. On the one hand, they set before us a positive image about creation and holiness. On the other, they function like a negative, setting before us a black and white image in which the tones are reversed and the image stands in need of further development. When it comes to salvation, Leviticus 11 is the photographic negative. When Jesus came the picture was printed in full, and we see that those who were 'excluded from citizenship in Israel and foreigners to the covenants of the promise, without hope and without God in the world' (Eph. 2:12), are now welcomed by him and, through faith, are equal citizens with the Israelites in the kingdom of God.

If, under the old covenant, 'the meaning of purity depends on the sense of God's awful majesty, manifest in creation',[46] under the new covenant the meaning of purity rests on faith in Christ's awesome grace, manifest in his blood shed on the cross.

---

[45] G. Wenham, 'The Theology of Unclean Food', *EQ* 53 (1981), p. 14.

[46] Douglas, *Literature*, p. 148.

Leviticus 12:1–8; 15:1–33

11. Purity and the body

From the strangest chapter in Leviticus, which deals with matters of diet, we turn to perhaps the most contentious chapters, those that deal with impurities that arise from our bodies. In seeking to understand these chapters it is important that we enter their world, rather than reading them condescendingly through the spectacles of contemporary liberal culture. Only so shall we unlock their meaning and avoid the erroneous idea that these regulations teach both that women are inferior to men and that sex is dirty and sinful. To be 'clean' meant to be in an appropriate state to draw near to God in worship. To be 'unclean' meant it would be improper to do so because of one's situation.[1] The categories are to be equated neither with modern ideas of cleanliness or dirtiness,[2] nor with being free from sin or full of sin. The regulations are designed to be good news, and spell out how people who found themselves in a state of uncleanness could rectify the situation and join with others again in worshipping God.

Chapters 12 and 15 deal with matters of purity in relation to the normal functions of the human body. In between there are two chapters that concern disease in humans and the contamination of property. For convenience we leave the chapters on disease and mildew for consideration later.[3]

---

[1] The NIV helpfully translates it, not as 'unclean', but as 'ceremonially unclean', which emphasizes the point that this has to do with ritual and not morality.

[2] Significantly, the purity regulations do not deal with urine or excrement, as they would have done if their concern was with physical dirt or filth.

[3] The reason for the particular arrangement of these chapters is hard to determine. Lev. 15 would seem to follow logically on from Lev. 12. See Kaiser, p. 1104.

1. Impurity caused by childbirth (12:1–8)

Only Moses is addressed in this section of the manual of purity, in contrast to the practice, since Aaron's ordination, of addressing both Moses and Aaron. This suggests that these regulations go back a long way and existed before being included here, as might be expected of regulations that deal with the most natural, the most powerful and the most awesome of human experiences, that of procreation.[4]

a. The waiting prescribed (12:1–5)

When an Israelite woman gave birth she became *ceremonially unclean* for a time and then had a further wait before being able to undergo rites of purification that would enable her to resume active participation in the worship of the tabernacle. During the time of waiting, the mother was allowed neither to *touch anything sacred* nor to *go to the sanctuary*. Uncleanness was contagious, and it was necessary that she should guard against contaminating sacred things or sacred places; if she did so, others would be prevented from benefiting from them. The length of her time of uncleanness and her waiting varied, depending on whether the child was a son or a daughter – and therein lies the offence in the eyes of some.

If the child was a boy, the mother was unclean *for seven days*; she would have the child circumcised *on the eighth day*; and then had to wait a further *thirty-three days to be purified from her bleeding* (2–4). Circumcision involved the removal of the foreskin of the penis and was the ceremony by which male infants were incorporated into the covenant of Israel (Gen. 17:9–14). It served both as a recognition that the newborn infant's life belonged to God and as a permanent, physical reminder of the promises and the obligations of the covenant.[5] Circumcision took place on *the eighth day*, the day that, since it was the first day of a new week, represented new beginnings and constantly stood as a sign of a new creation.[6] If the child was a girl, the prescribed period of uncleanness and of waiting was doubled, to fourteen days and sixty-six days respectively (5), but the girl was not subjected to circumcision.

---

[4] Hartley, p. 167, explains the absence of Aaron's name as due to the vital role he will play in offering the sacrifice of purification. He draws a parallel between this and 14:1.

[5] See P. R. Williamson, 'Circumcision', in *DOTP*, pp. 122–125.

[6] The phrase is found in 9:1; 14:10, 23; 15:14, 29; 22:27; 23:36, 39, and always signals a new start.

Little explanation is given as to why the new mother was placed in quarantine, but the regulations are clear that it is not the fact of having given birth that made the woman unclean (since that was a reason for joy) but the fact of *her bleeding* (4, 5), which is compared to her *monthly period* (2).

b. The purification available (12:6–8)

The condition of uncleanness that the new mother suffered is more severe than that experienced by those who infringed the regulations regarding unclean meat. Therefore, it was not to be removed either as quickly or as easily as that defilement, which merely required the washing of the offender's clothes at the end of the day on which the offence took place. Whenever someone's uncleanness lasted more than seven days, as it did in the case of childbirth, sacrifices were required to make the person clean again.[7] The new mother's period of uncleanness was not even brought to an end by the presentation of a single sacrifice; two sacrifices were required: a burnt offering and a sin offering. The former speaks of renewed dedication and the latter of fresh forgiveness for sin. Because they were obligatory offerings, provision was made for the more costly *year-old lamb* (6) to be replaced by *two doves or two young pigeons* (8) for those who were less well off.

The presentation of the sin offering was not required because giving birth is a sin. How could something be sin that God commanded his people to do (Gen. 1:28) and that was held in such high regard elsewhere as a sign of God's blessing (e.g. Gen. 15:1–5; 1 Sam. 1:1–28; Ps. 127:3)? This offering is not connected with any specific sin but shows an awareness that the new mother would have committed sin during the time she was absent from worship and that before she draws near to God again those sins need to be removed.

According to Luke 2:22–24, Mary undertook this ceremony of purification after the birth of Jesus and offered the cheaper sacrifice of 'a pair of doves or two young pigeons'.

c. The reasons proposed

These regulations pose two questions. Why was a period of purification necessary? And why was the waiting time before purification could be completed prolonged in the case of a girl?

---

[7] Wenham, p. 187.

Why was a period of purification necessary? These regulations, as mentioned, give an explicit answer to this question: it is because of a loss of blood (2, 4, 5). Any bodily discharge was considered defiling, as chapter 15 will underline; but to lose blood was of supreme consequence because of what blood represented. Blood is the symbol of life (17:11) and therefore the loss of blood is symptomatic of life being lost. It is associated with corruption and death. So, as Gordon Wenham explains, because of its symbolic import 'blood is at once the most effective ritual cleanser and the most polluting substance when it is in the wrong place'.[8] A flow of blood not only potentially put one's life in jeopardy but rendered one's body less than whole.[9] Before worship could be resumed, wholeness had to be restored and deficiencies overcome.

Giving birth was, in fact, hazardous for several reasons of both a spiritual and a physical kind. It was hazardous spiritually because it invoked the penalty God inflicted on women after the fall (Gen. 3:16) and challenged Satan's hold on the world (Gen. 3:15). It was also hazardous spiritually because, in the view of some, a woman's blood was thought to have magical, mysterious qualities and giving birth was thought to open the door for demonic and destructive, anti-life forces to enter. But while other nations believed this, there is no evidence that Israel did, and there is certainly no evidence that Israel was encouraged to oppose the demonic by using incantations and spells. There is, in truth, no hint of the demonic in these regulations.[10]

Giving birth, until very recent times, was also extremely hazardous physically and put the life of the mother, as well as the life of her child, in danger. Having delivered her baby, she would have been at a physically low ebb. 'By declaring a new mother impure, susceptible,' Baruch Levine explains, 'the community sought to protect and shelter her.'[11] These regulations, then, are a protective measure to enable her to recover fully before resuming an active life in the community. During her time out she could be expected to be treated with tender care.

Why was the waiting time prolonged for the birth of a girl? The usual modern assumption is that such regulations are extremely prejudicial and mirror the inferior status of women in Israelite society. It requires twice

---

8 Ibid., p. 188.
9 Hartley, p. 168, citing the argument of Mary Douglas in *Purity*, p. 51.
10 Noordtzij, p. 131.
11 Levine, p. 249.

the time, it is argued, for a woman to make herself clean if she gives birth to a girl than if she produces a boy, therefore girls must be twice as dirty as boys. But such a view is anachronistic and does not do justice to what the regulations state, or to what the rest of Leviticus teaches. It is not the birth of the child that makes a mother unclean, still less the gender of the child, but the loss of the mother's blood that is the cause of defilement. The resulting impurity is nothing to do with sinfulness or wickedness but with ceremonial uncleanness, as explained above. If it was about the value of the female child, one might also expect the legislation to cover children born with deformities or those who were sickly from the start, whose worth would have been considered less than that of others. But no such legislation exists. The truth is that Leviticus demonstrates a remarkable even-handedness in dealing with men and women. Women had more rights in Israel than in surrounding nations.[12] Admittedly, there is nothing like the total equality of the sexes that many would take for granted today,[13] but the fact that women could offer sacrifices alongside men and were subject, in chapter 15, to exactly the same penalties for uncleanness as men is astonishing, especially given the patriarchal climate of the age.[14]

What, then, can the differential mean? While there is no ultimately satisfactory explanation of the difference, a number of more or less credible explanations have been offered. A traditional view holds that it reflects Eve's role in the fall, as mentioned in 1 Timothy 2:13–15. An older view stated that the additional length of the quarantine was necessitated for medical reasons. The birth of a girl was commonly believed to be accompanied by greater difficulties than the birth of a boy.[15] Also, the vaginal discharge that accompanied the birth of a girl was said to last longer than in the case of a boy.[16] These views certainly imply that a greater recovery period was required by the mother if her child was a girl. But the basis for the differential probably lay elsewhere.

---

[12] Hartley, p. 168.

[13] For example, priests had to be male, and the stipulations of Lev. 27 show a marked differential between the economic value of men and women, although that had to do with their worth in the labour force, not their inherent status.

[14] Contra Noth, who argues that this proves 'the cultic inferiority of the female sex' (p. 97), and Wegner, p. 38. Milgrom refutes this by stating that greater defilement is not an indication of less social worth, as is evident from rabbinic law, where a human corpse, which is more valuable than a dead pig, nevertheless defiles more than a dead pig, which, in turn, defiles more than a dead frog. *Leviticus 1 – 16*, p. 751.

[15] Milgrom, *Leviticus 1 – 16*, p. 750; Noordtzij, p. 131.

[16] See Levine, p. 250; J. Magonet, 'But If It Is a Girl . . .', in Sawyer, p. 144; Pigott, p. 60.

Levine thinks that it 'may have reflected the apprehension and anticipation regarding the infant daughter's potential fertility, the expectation that she herself would become a mother some day'.[17] The birth of a daughter meant the creation of another woman who had the potential to give birth, and therefore her birth should be treated with greater significance. The daughter would herself, in due course, experience a menstrual cycle. Hence the birth of a girl meant that the equivalent of two women were involved, both of whom were generators of uncleanness; consequently, two periods of purification were required.[18]

Susan Pigott favours another view: that the period of uncleanness for a male child was shortened because of his circumcision – a sign of God's grace and incorporation into the community – in contrast to that of the female child, who did not undergo circumcision.[19]

Yet another, perhaps more persuasive, explanation of the difference is favoured by Walter Kaiser,[20] who relates it to passages in the later writings of the book of Jubilees and the Mishnah. They assert that Adam was created at the end of the first week and entered Eden on the forty-first day, while Eve was created at the end of the second week and entered Eden on the eighty-first day. The timing of the quarantine, therefore, may be an early expression of this belief about the birth of Adam and of Eve. But this view suffers from reading back later material into an earlier work and is by no means obvious.

Like other sections of the manual of purity, the regulations about purification after the birth of a child are a gracious provision of God to protect the vulnerable, not an excuse for the exercise of oppressive power that denigrated the worth of fellow creatures. They offered no excuse for men chauvinistically to flaunt their male superiority. Rather, the rules required men to exercise their calling as protectors and as wise and gentle stewards of all created life.

2. Impurity caused by bodily fluids (15:1–33)

The ceremonial impurities that are the subject of chapter 15 are those that occur because of an emission from a reproductive organ. In contrast to

---

[17] Levine, p. 250.

[18] Magonet, in Sawyer, p. 152.

[19] Pigott, pp. 60–61.

[20] Kaiser, p. 1085; Milgrom, *Leviticus 1 – 16*, p. 750.

the major event of childbirth referred to in chapter 12, they are either part and parcel of the routine of life or a symptom of a chronic condition. They involve both men and women. The regulations are designed with a remarkable symmetry, and the means of overcoming impurity shows a conspicuous equality between men and women. The path of the chapter may be charted as follows:

A¹ Introduction (1–2)
 B¹ Chronic male discharges (2–15)
  C¹ Short-term male discharges (16–18)
  C² Short-term female discharges (19–24)
 B² Chronic female discharges (25–30)
A² Conclusion (31–33)

a. What is the problem?

The first set of problems is set out in verse 3. When any man experiences a discharge, *whether it continues flowing from his body or is blocked, it will make him unclean.* The problems referred to are, by common consent, gonorrhoea on the one hand, and on the other a stoppage in the penis that makes passing urine painful.[21] The language used in this verse is rare and is more akin to medical terminology than is usual in the purity code. The discharge consists of a 'slimy juice' that cannot be restrained, while the stoppage means the penis has sealed itself up and the flow of urine is restricted.

Rather than providing a detailed diagnosis of the physical condition, however, this purity regulation is more concerned with a minute examination of its social and religious effects. Those who suffer from these conditions are unclean and liable to pass on their defilement to anything with which they come into contact. So, whether they lie on a bed or sit on a bench (4), or touch another person (7), or spit on someone (8), or ride on anything (9), or even use a clay pot (12), they will pass on their uncleanness. And the process of infection does not stop there, for it means that anyone who touches something that has become unclean also is infected by uncleanness. Those who contract this secondary defilement are unclean only until the evening, at which point they are to wash both themselves and their clothes to become clean again. Clay pots, as we have

---

[21] Harris, p. 586, unusually thinks that the illnesses in view are more general and include diarrhoea.

seen before, cannot be redeemed in this way, because they were made of porous material, and had to be broken (12) or else they would continue to circulate defilement.

The purity rules never provide a cure. They simply mark the recovery when healing has taken place. So a defiled man has to note when the sickness passes and then has to wait a further seven days before undergoing a ritual bathing and presenting two sacrifices in order to be readmitted to the worshipping community (13–15). As with childbirth, the sacrifices were those of the burnt offering and the sin offering, which expressed renewed commitment and renewed cleansing. The sacrificial animals required were not the expensive ones but the offerings of the poor.

The second cause of male uncleanness is *an emission of semen* caused either by a nocturnal emission or by sexual intercourse (16–18). This defilement is mild; it simply required the man to be ceremonially unclean until the evening, when he could remove the defilement by bathing. Anything that had been soiled by the semen was similarly in need of washing. The reason that an emission of semen defiled a man has nothing to do with sexual activity being dirty. Rather, it has to do with the fact that a loss of bodily fluids and sexual activity belonged to the realm of the common rather than the holy.[22]

The first item considered in respect of female uncleanness is menstruation (19–24). The female monthly *flow of blood* is treated in the same way as the male discharges mentioned at the beginning of the chapter. As with the men, anything or any person the woman comes into contact with becomes infected and needs washing at the end of the day (19–23). If a man has intercourse with her during her period, he incurs a more serious defilement and *will be unclean for seven days* (24).[23] The woman must wait until the period has passed, and then, after seven days, she must wash herself clean from her impurity. Gordon Wenham has pointed out that while menstruation is considered to be as contagious as gonorrhoea (2–15), no sacrifice is required to atone for the impurity. 'In this respect,' he writes, 'it resembles normal seminal emissions for men', which were considered in verses 16–17.[24] No guilt is attached to the woman for her monthly period, which is a natural physical condition.

---

[22] See discussion in Hartley, pp. 210–211.

[23] Lev. 18:19 categorically forbids a man to approach a woman during her period.

[24] Wenham, p. 220.

These regulations have sometimes been regarded as oppressing women by highlighting that the two things that are unique about a women's sexuality make her unclean. This is to misconstrue the purport of these regulations totally. The regulations are no more repressive of women than they are of men, if, indeed, they are repressive at all. In fact, as Chisholm-Smith has remarked in an article on menstruation, 'what is striking about Leviticus 15 is how consistently the laws regarding bodily emissions are applied to both sexes'.[25] Even so, could it really be that a woman would spend a week in every month out of circulation because of her menstrual period, as verses 19–23 imply? The apparent harshness of the regulations may be mitigated if Israelite women menstruated less frequently than today's Western women, as some scholars believe.[26] If not, the monthly time of rest is hardly a harsh restriction and may well have been welcomed as a blessing. Given the patriarchal context in which the laws were promulgated – a context in which women were often treated by men as mere property – these regulations placed limits on the power of men over women. They prohibited men from forcing themselves on their wives at inappropriate times. The rules, therefore, were again designed to offer protection and dignity to women and to prevent them from being demeaned and violated at vulnerable times.

Offerings were required in respect of the last category of leakage from the body that resulted in impurity. Verses 25–30 deal with the case of a woman who experienced a discharge of blood *for many days at a time other than her monthly period or has a discharge that continues beyond her period.* She remained unclean throughout the time of her bleeding, and a source of potential contamination for the duration of the illness (26–27). Any secondary contamination was dealt with through washing at the end of the day but, as in other cases, the woman herself had to wait until she was healed before taking action. Then she had to wait a further seven days and *on the eighth day* – the day of new beginnings – had to offer the cheaper version of the burnt and sin offerings *to the priest at the entrance to the tent of meeting* (28–30). In spite of Wegner's attempt to drive a wedge between the offerings brought by the men in verses 14–15 and those brought by the women here, which leads her to conclude that

[25] Lisa Chisholm-Smith, 'Menstruation', in Kroeger and Evans, p. 62.

[26] Ibid., p. 62, and Kaiser, p. 1105. The niv's use of 'monthly' in 12:2; 15:19, 24, 25, 26, 33; 18:19; 20:18 is an interpretative rendering of the original, which is less specific and refers to the time of a woman's impurity rather than specifying it as 'monthly'.

the procedures discriminate against women, the offering required and the procedures adopted put men and women on a level footing.[27]

b. What is the point?

If these regulations are emphatically not teaching that sexual matters are dirty, what are they teaching? Essentially, they are inculcating a respect for life. Some of the interpretations put forward to explain the differences between clean and unclean meat do not fit easily here. In the case of the animals, an essential difference was between what was normal and what was anomalous. Some of these impurities could be forced to fit that framework, but several of the experiences labelled unclean in chapter 15 are perfectly normal functions of the human body, so this explanation does not readily fit. Nor is it really convincing to say that the discharges breach the body's boundaries and so may, as it were, deposit the right things (blood and semen) in the wrong place.[28] Douglas adopts this approach and proposes that the physical body is a figurative representation of the larger social body. By declaring breaches of the physical body unclean, these laws are really seeking to discourage anyone from violating the integrity of the community's invisible social walls, as would occur, for example, if an Israelite married someone of another race.[29]

However, there is a more obvious and convincing explanation of these rules. What is clean is associated with life and what is unclean is associated with death.[30] The situations that are described as unclean in Leviticus 12 and 15 all involve the loss of the bodily fluids – blood and semen – that bring life. The key principle of Leviticus 17:11 – that 'the life of a creature is in the blood' – means that any loss of blood is a symptom of the ebbing away of life. To lose too much blood results in death. Equally, when a man's urethral tract is not functioning as it should, or when he spills his seed, for whatever reason, the possibility of new life is precluded and, in some cases, potential life may even be deliberately wasted. The protective hedges built around the mother who had just given birth, the male who experienced a penile emission, and a woman who

---

[27] Wegner, p. 42. Her reasoning is that v. 29, unlike v. 14, does not include the phrase 'and come before the LORD', and therefore she argues that the man may offer his sacrifice directly but a woman could only do so indirectly. But she hangs great weight on what may be no more than a stylistic difference.

[28] Bellinger, p. 93, and Budd, p. 214.

[29] See Wenham, pp. 222–223. Mary Douglas, *Natural Symbols* (Harmondsworth: Penguin, 1973), pp. 93–112, provides the background for this approach.

[30] G. Wenham, 'Why Does Sexual Intercourse Defile? (Lev 15:18)', *ZAW* 95 (1983), pp. 432–434.

experienced either her monthly period or chronic bleeding, mark out these people as deserving special attention and care. Matters of life and death are involved and should not be treated with indifference. God, the giver of life, wants his people to treat life itself with respect.

But why should that make them unfit to join in worship? There may be an element of the idea that people who approach God need to be whole when doing so – as the regulations about who is eligible to serve as a priest attest (21:16–23) – and that people who suffer these conditions are not whole.[31] But other nuances are just as important. Those who have been declared impure cannot approach God, who is pure, lest they defile the sanctuary and render it unfit for him as a dwelling-place (31). That is why a sin offering was required on their return.[32] Nor can those who have the imprint of death on them approach the Lord God, who is ever-living and the source of all life and creation. Until that imprint has faded and, in serious cases, the people concerned have been 'reborn' *on the eighth day* (14, 29), they are not permitted to approach him in worship.

3. Impurity and the new covenant

The imposing conclusion to these regulations turns them, in Levine's words, into 'a major statement of policy'.[33] *You must keep the Israelites separate from things that make them unclean, so they will not die in their uncleanness for defiling my dwelling-place, which is among them* (31). The Jewish rabbis took this injunction seriously and erected a huge framework of laws to prevent people from falling into the trap of uncleanness. By the time of Jesus Christ their traditions had become burdensome, and, far from encouraging the unclean to find a way back to God, served to keep them away from him. The bureaucrats of religious cleanliness were condemned by Jesus for tying up heavy loads and putting them on people's shoulders and for not being willing to lift a finger to bring relief (Matt. 23:4). The result was that they 'shut the door of the kingdom of heaven in people's faces', neither entering themselves nor permitting others to enter who were 'trying to' (Matt. 23:13).

---

[31] Douglas, *Purity*, p. 51. Levine, p. 92, argues that in Lev. 15 the conditions of illness and impurity are virtually interchangeable.

[32] Levine, p. 95.

[33] Ibid., p. 98.

Jesus, however, did more than condemn the system. He fulfilled it. His actions affirmed the need for people to be clean as they drew near to God. He did not lower the barrier or dumb down the requirements of holiness. Those who approach a holy God must be clean. But how? Jesus went beyond anything that the purity regulations of Leviticus could do. They could never effect a cure. They could only stipulate what people had to do to re-enter the worshipping community once they had experienced a cure and a certain amount of time had elapsed. But for some, whose chronic condition never improved, this would prove a policy of despair. What Jesus did was to bring about the cure. In the new age of grace, he enabled unclean people to draw near to God by making them clean; he enabled sick people who lacked wholeness to draw near to God by restoring them to perfect health. Then he sent them to the priest to verify their healing and to fulfil the ceremonial law (e.g. Matt. 8:4; Mark 1:44; Luke 5:14; 17:14). God has not changed. As Gordon Wenham has written, 'Leviticus declares that God is holy and the author of life and health: the Gospels show the same God saving the sick and sinful and giving life to the dead.'[34] Whereas under the old covenant the message to the unclean was, 'Keep out! You are unfit', under the new covenant and through the transforming work of Christ the message to the unclean is, 'Come near! Let me make you clean.'

The unnamed woman who one day had sufficient faith to reach out and touch Jesus' cloak found that 'her bleeding stopped and she felt in her body that she was freed from her suffering' after twelve long years.[35] She stands as a classic illustration of the redemptive power of Christ. No wonder she was reluctant to identify herself when Jesus asked the crowd who touched him, and no wonder she then trembled with fear as she fell at his feet. For years she had been excluded from the crowd going up to the temple. Her impurity meant she had no right to be in such a gathering. But the power of Christ stopped her flow of blood, cleansed her impurity and restored her to her place as a daughter of Israel who could draw near to God.

In healing her, Jesus both upheld the law and, at the same time, made it obsolete. What right had he to do so? How was it that he could accomplish what the law was powerless to do? The answer lies in his cross. At Calvary, Jesus, the pure one, was made impure; there, 'God made him who had no

---

[34] G. Wenham, 'Christ's Healing Ministry and His Attitude to the Law', in Harold H. Rowdon (ed.), *Christ the Lord: Essays in Christology Presented to Donald Guthrie* (Leicester: IVP, 1982), pp. 125–126.

[35] Mark 5:24–34. The quotation is from v. 29.

sin to be sin for us' (2 Cor. 5:21); there, his wounds brought about our healing (Isa. 53:5). His life-giving and life-restoring ministry is possible because he became the sacrifice that removed all our impurities and made us clean.

Leviticus 12 and 15 contain a number of important lessons: they teach us to respect life; to use God's gift of sex with restraint; to protect those who are physically and emotionally vulnerable; and to think holistically about our approach to God because the physical and the spiritual are all of a piece. But above all, these chapters teach us that we need Jesus, for only he can make us clean and only he can make us worthy to approach a holy God. Charles Wesley wanted a thousand tongues to celebrate the good news of Jesus' cleansing power because

> He breaks the power of cancelled sin,
>   He sets the prisoner free;
> His blood can make the foulest clean;
>   His blood availed for me.[36]

---

[36] From 'O for a Thousand Tongues', by Charles Wesley (1707–88).

Leviticus 13:1 – 14:57

12. Purity and disease

The priests' duty to distinguish 'between the clean and the unclean' involved them in making judgments about whether people who had symptoms of a skin disease and whether certain contaminated clothes or buildings were impure or not. In this respect they acted as early medical officers of health for the community and so needed a basis for making judgments – judgments that would have a profound effect on people's families and their fortunes. These chapters provide them with the required guidance, which stems not from scientific research, or from folk wisdom, but from God himself (13:1).

The work of the priests bore few of the hallmarks of modern medicine. While they were concerned about diagnosis, the priests showed no concern about providing a cure, nor were they able to do so. They simply certified someone (or something) unclean, and then, if and when the symptoms disappeared, certified this person (or thing) clean again. The description of the disease is general and imprecise, lacking the scientific rigour that would be expected today. Furthermore, the purpose of these chapters is less to preserve the good health of the Israelites than to determine who is fit to approach God. The sharp division between the physical and the spiritual that the modern world has mistakenly introduced would have been little understood in Israel. People were integrated unities in which all areas of life – body, mind and soul – had an effect on one's relationship with God. That God speaks to Moses and Aaron (13:1) about the nation's health shows once more that his knowledge, grasp and compassion are comprehensive, covering the whole of life.

Chapter 13 portrays the priests in their diagnosing role and is a chapter of almost unrelieved tension and gloom as people await the dreadful declaration of 'unclean'. This verdict, if pronounced, resulted in their having to leave the camp and sever all normal routines and relationships for a while. Chapter 14 stands in sharp contrast and presents the priests in their redeeming role. It mainly describes the great relief and complex ceremonies that followed the joyful announcement that a person was 'clean' again and therefore in a position to resume normal life within the camp.

1. Dealing with infectious skin diseases (13:1–46)

The onus for dealing with a skin disease lies with the person who is suffering from it or with his or her family. These regulations put a considerable amount of power in the hands of the priests by giving them the authority to exclude people from the camp. But they discourage the priests from conducting witch-hunts. The initial steps that might lead to a person being declared unclean do not lie with the priests, but rather with others, who are expected to assume responsibility in the matter. When individuals are suspected of having an infectious skin disease *they must be brought* [by their family and friends] *to Aaron the priest or to one of his sons who is a priest* (2). Unlike some other illnesses, a skin disease would have been highly visible and it would not prove easy to ignore it for long before taking the required action.

a. What was the priest to do?

The first task of the priest was *to examine the sore on the skin*, which involved paying attention to *whether the hair in the sore has turned white and the sore appears to be more than skin deep* (3). Several case studies follow to help the priest know what to do next.

In borderline cases infected people were isolated for seven days (4) and then re-examined. If the rash had not spread, a further seven days' 'sick leave' was granted, after which the person would be pronounced clean and was merely required to launder his or her clothes before resuming normal life (5–6). If the rash had developed, further appearances before the priest were required and the priest would *pronounce* the person *unclean* (7–8).

The second case (9–11) is where the chronic nature of the skin disease is obvious from the start because there is a *white swelling in the skin that has turned the hair white and . . . there is raw flesh in the swelling* (10). With these symptoms there is no need for a period of observation; the person is patently unclean and the procedures for treating an unclean person are put in place.

The third case (12–17) is when a skin ailment affects the whole body, from top to toe. It is not, however, the extent or the unsightliness of the disease that determines whether a person is unclean, but the nature of it. So, however extensive the rash, a person was considered unclean only if the flesh was ulcerated and raw, or if open wounds were exposed. Once the sores had turned white it was an indication that new skin was growing and the healing process was under way, so the person could be pronounced clean once more.

The fourth and longest section (18–46) considers a group of cases where the skin disease arises as a complication of other conditions,[1] such as inflamed scarring (18–23), burns (24–28), itchy skin under facial hair (29–37),[2] vitiligo (38–39) and baldness (40–46). Depending on the seriousness of the ailment, the suspects might be pronounced clean and required to wash their clothes or, alternatively, declared unclean and barred from the camp.

b. What is the illness referred to?

Since older versions of the New Testament speak of Jesus healing lepers, it has become customary to refer to the skin diseases mentioned here as leprosy. However, few would now consider *ṣāraʿat*, the Hebrew word in question, to refer to what we call leprosy today.[3] The symptoms are not consistent with modern leprosy, and leprosy is not now considered contagious. A few still take the view that Leviticus 13 is referring to leprosy, believing that it is possible to account for any difficulties involved, but in doing so they stand in opposition to the majority opinion.[4]

Dr Stanley Browne, who spent a lifetime treating leprosy, maintained that there was no positive proof that leprosy was referred to in the Old

---

[1] Levine, p. 79.

[2] The symptoms have led to a variety of diagnoses including psoriasis, eczema, dermatitis or favus. See Hartley, p. 192.

[3] Technically, Hansen's disease, named after Gerhard Hansen, who in 1873 discovered the bacterium that causes it.

[4] E.g. Kaiser, pp. 1094–1095, who argues that it is a generic term, that only the onset of the condition is described here, rather than fully developed forms of the illness, and that the symptoms are more serious than some other interpretations warrant.

Testament and certainly not here. To him, the symptoms described would not lead one to think of leprosy and, in any case, they lack scientific precision and are of a 'generic, non-scientific, inclusive and imprecise' nature. He thought ṣāra'at to be capable of such a wide range of meaning as to be 'virtually untranslatable'.[5] The significant thing about the skin complaints, Browne pointed out, is that at root the word ṣāra'at means 'to strike'. The person who suffered one of these diseases was a person 'stricken by God' and, equally, could be 'unstricken' or healed only by God.

After a detailed examination of the four primary symptoms (swelling, eruption, spot and itch) and the five secondary symptoms (changes to the colour of the skin or of the hair, infiltration of the skin, spread and ulceration), John Wilkinson reached a somewhat similar conclusion. The priests, he points out, were never required to identify the diseases 'and neither therefore are we'. The purpose of the descriptions is not to enable the priests to give a precise medical diagnosis but to draw attention to a number of features common to a variety of skin diseases that led to ritual uncleanness.[6]

c. What is the effect of being unclean?

What would it have meant for a person to be pronounced 'unclean'? The dreadful implications of uncleanness are spelt out in verses 45–46. Unclean individuals had to adopt a particular style of clothes, use a particular form of address and live in a particular place. They *must wear torn clothes, let their hair be unkempt, cover the lower part of their face and cry out, 'Unclean! Unclean!'* The torn clothes, untidy hair and covered lips were all signs of mourning, or signified a vexed attitude or even, on occasions, shame.[7] These diseases, like death, disturb order, threaten peace and remind people that life is precarious and that creation always stands on the brink of destruction and of reversion to chaos. These illnesses have disturbed normality, and things are not as they should be. Consequently, it was appropriate that those in the centre of the vortex should wear the symbols of grief or of disease. The cry of *Unclean!*

---

[5] Stanley Browne, 'Leprosy in the Bible', in Bernard Palmer (ed.), *Medicine and the Bible* (Exeter: Paternoster, 1986), pp. 101–125.

[6] John Wilkinson, 'Leprosy and Leviticus: The Problem of Description and Identification', *SJT* 30 (1977), pp. 153–169. On his scheme he believes that leprosy, if it was included in Lev. 13, would lack the necessary combination of symptoms to cause a person who had it to be declared unclean, and therefore would be among the clean diseases of the skin.

[7] Gen. 37:34; Num. 14:6; 2 Sam. 1:11; 2 Kgs 22:11; Ezra 9:5; Ezek. 24:17, 22; Mic. 3:7.

Unclean!, which they were to shout to announce their approach, was intended to distance people from them so that others did not catch the disease. Its purpose was to prevent the disorder from spreading rather than to bring shame on the individuals involved.

The worst element of the condition, however, was that those who were unclean had to live in isolation, *outside the camp* (46). As Gordon Wenham observes, this was not a wonderful opportunity to 'get away from it all' but a requirement that would have caused great distress.[8] It meant that sick persons would be cut off from their family, their friends and the normal activities of life, including their drawing near to God in worship. Living *outside the camp* meant living as far from the presence of God as possible and so being prevented from enjoying the blessings of the covenant. Those condemned to such an existence (as Miriam once was; Num. 12:1–16) and their loved ones would feel the dread of exclusion and would want to bring their exile to a conclusion as quickly as possible. But until the illness had passed and their skin was in process of being renewed, they were stuck, and contact with others was broken, or at least severely limited. The priests could offer neither hope nor cure. They were the custodians of ordered life and the guardians of creation, so their only option was to keep anything at bay that threatened the order of the created world.

In the light of all this, Samuel Kellogg's characterization of these skin complaints as 'a visible, perpetual and very awful parable of the nature and working of sin' is absolutely true. This is not to say that anyone who suffered from such a disease was any more of a sinner than anyone else. The uncleanness, it must be stressed, is a ritual one, not a moral one, and does not indicate that all who fell foul of one of these infections were guilty of sin. Nevertheless, it may be analogous to sin and its workings. Like the skin complaint, being almost imperceptible at the beginning, sin may appear insignificant at the start; but it is progressive, and gradually affects the whole of one's being and renders one's conscience insensitive (Eph. 4:18). To humans it is incurable and shuts one out from the presence of God and from fellowship with fellow believers. 'This is', Kellogg writes, 'indeed a dark picture of man's natural state, and very many are exceedingly loth to believe that sin can be such a very serious matter.'[9]

---

[8] Wenham, p. 200.

[9] Kellogg, pp. 335–343. Believing that Leviticus is referring to leprosy, Kellogg adds that the disease, like sin, is hereditary.

2. Dealing with contaminated fabrics (13:47–59)

Something very similar in appearance to the diseases that inflicted the human skin was also to be found in fabrics and leather; in other words, in clothing, bags or bottles. What was to be done when these were contaminated by mildew? The process for treating contaminated materials was analogous to the process for treating infected human beings. An initial examination of the colour of the blemish would reveal whether the contamination was serious or not. If it was *greenish or reddish* and appeared to be active, then the article was to be isolated for seven days (48–50). If at the end of that period the mildew was still found to be spreading, the article was pronounced unclean. There was no point in sending such materials outside the camp, so, instead of that, the article was to be destroyed by fire (51–52).

In the case of articles where the contamination did not appear to have advanced during the period of isolation, the cloth was to be washed and isolated for a further seven days (53–54). By then, washing should have cured the problem, but if it had not done so the affected article was to be burnt even if the stain was evident on only one side of the material (55). Even where the contamination seemed to have been contained and was fading, the priests were still required to exercise extreme caution. The affected area was to be torn out (56) and the rest of the material was to be washed again (58). 'Throughout the course of this procedure,' as Levine notes, 'every effort is made to save as much as possible of the materials by cutting away only the infected areas in the hope of containing the spread of the infection.'[10] Only when this was done would the article finally be considered clean. The slightest hint of the contagion returning would mean that the article was unclean and should be burned (57).

Here is a further parable of sin. If the skin diseases that afflicted humans were a parable of the effect of sin in human beings, mildew in clothing and leather goods served as a parable of the working of sin in the material creation in which men and women lived, as the curse of Genesis 3:17–19 predicted.[11] Such sin corrupts what is good and destroys what is wholesome, and cannot be treated with indifference, or else creation would swiftly degenerate into complete ruin. While the ultimate

---

[10] Levine, p. 83.

[11] Kellogg, p. 364.

containment of such sin does not lie in the hands of human beings, any more than the priests of old could bring about a cure for it, at least we, like them, can act quickly to contain the spread of corruption in our world, while leaving the ultimate solution – the recreation of the world – in the hands of the divine restorer (Rom. 8:18–21).

3. Dealing with healed people (14:1–32)

The Lord who wounds is also the Lord who heals (Deut. 32:39). No mention is made of how the sick person was made well. No medicine or other treatment is prescribed. But in the course of time and under the hand of God, the day would come when the skin disease would pass and those who had been excluded from the camp would be able to take up their place in the community once again and enter anew into the covenant blessings of Israel. How was their rehabilitation to be marked? Powerful, destructive forces had been at work and could not simply be ignored as if they had never existed. Restoration to normality, therefore, was 'not simply a matter of loving inclination', or of a mere decree, but of 'a carefully observed sacramental process'.[12] The ceremonies that led to their restoration were complex and 'among the most elaborate in the priestly laws'.[13] They consisted of three carefully worked steps and, like the ordination of Aaron, they lasted for eight days. Each step brought the cleansed individual nearer to God and to the Tent of Meeting.

a. Step 1: outside the camp – anticipation (14:1–7)

When a person believed himself or herself to be cured, the priest was summoned to go outside the camp, conduct an examination and then issue a verdict as to whether the excluded person really was in a fit state to return home. If the disease had cleared up, the priest undertook a puzzling little ceremony. He gathered *two live clean birds and some cedar wood, scarlet yarn and hyssop* on behalf of the healed individual (4). One bird was then killed and its blood caught in a pot, where it was diluted with fresh water. The other bird was then bathed in this bloody liquid and the wood, yarn and hyssop dipped in the mixture as well. The person who had been healed was then sprinkled *seven times* – to represent a complete

---

12 Brueggemann, *Theology*, p. 193.
13 Levine, p. 84.

number – before being pronounced *clean*. The priest then released the live bird in the open fields.

The meaning of several aspects of this ceremony is elusive, but there are enough hints about the elements involved to make some sense of it. The birds, as clean creatures, can bear the uncleanness of the excluded person, and birds are chosen rather than other animals because they fly up and away, removing the weight of impurity 'to far-off distances whence the impurity cannot return'.[14] The stick of *cedar wood* and the thread of *scarlet yarn* are chosen because they were both red, symbolizing the cleansing power of blood and to underline the use of the actual blood that one of the birds would shed.[15] *Hyssop*, though a tiny plant, was said to have roots that could penetrate the heart of rocks. So it came to symbolize a deep cleansing of the inward stains of sin, as mentioned in Psalm 51:7.[16] *Fresh water* was crucial if a thorough cleaning and removal of impurities was to take place. Stagnant or stale water would aggravate impurity rather than cure it.

The two birds inevitably point forward to the two goats that are central to the Day of Atonement (16:7–10, 15–22). As with the birds, one of these goats was killed and the other was set free. The blood of the goat that was killed was also sprinkled seven times, on this occasion on the horns of the altar, to effect cleansing. As a parallel ceremony, then, the dead bird represents the blood offered up to God for cleansing, and the bird that was released was similar to the scapegoat and represented the carrying away of sin.[17] Gordon Wenham, following the older commentator Keil, adds further that the bird that was killed served to remind the individuals who had been healed of what might have happened to them had God not cured them, while the living bird symbolizes the newly liberated life ahead of them.[18]

An initial cleansing then takes place *outside the camp* (3) that anticipates the deeper sacrifices of purification that would occur at the tabernacle after the healed person was back inside the camp. This cleansing functions, so to speak, as a down payment of the full atonement

---

[14] Milgrom, *Leviticus 1 – 16*, p. 834.

[15] Ibid., p. 835.

[16] Cassiodorus, *Exposition of the Psalms* 50.9, in Lienhard, p. 181.

[17] Hartley points out some differences between the released bird and the scapegoat, in that no confession is made over the bird, and the hands of neither the priest nor the presenter are laid on it.

[18] Wenham, pp. 208–209.

that will be experienced once the healed person has rejoined others in drawing near to God. Until that time the healed person would still be referred to as *the one to be cleansed*,[19] rather than the one who is cleansed. Such persons remained in a liminal state until the last sacrifice had been offered on their behalf and they were fit enough to take their place among the worshippers of the covenant God once more.

b. Step 2: on the fringe of the camp – confirmation (14:8–9)

Once the initial ceremonies were over, *the person to be cleansed* is permitted back into the camp but is still not ready to resume a normal place within it; only a partial resumption of relationships is permitted to start with. For seven days persons in this condition *must stay outside their tent*. After a week they were required to shave off any facial hair, bathe their bodies and launder their clothes. The act of shaving would ensure that no possible remaining sore or skin irritation could be hidden from anyone: it was an act of transparency. The bathing spoke of washing away the past with its scars and regrets, and of the cleansing of any lingering dirt brought in from outside the camp. The risk of contaminating one's family and spreading disease needed to be avoided at all costs.[20] The seven days – the time taken to create the world and inaugurate the priesthood of Aaron – indicated that what was happening was, in truth, a further act of creation. The healed person was being reborn.

c. Step 3: at the heart of the camp – purification (14:10–31)

Having been brought back into the right environment, the healed person is brought to the tabernacle on *the eighth day* (10), the day of new beginnings. The purpose is not only to bring sacrifices but to present the person to the Lord: *The priest who pronounces them clean shall present both the one to be cleansed and their offerings before the Lord at the entrance to the tent of meeting* (11). Four offerings are to be made – the sin, burnt, grain and guilt offerings. Permission was given to those who were unable to afford *two male lambs and one ewe lamb a year old* (10) to replace the lambs required by the burnt and sin offerings with *two doves or two young pigeons* (22). The offerings mostly follow the usual rituals, but with two

---

[19] The person at the centre of the drama is called *the one to be cleansed* throughout the chapter (4, 7, 8, 11, 14, 17, 18, 19, 25, 28, 29, 31).

[20] Hartley, p. 195.

significant differences: first in the order in which the sacrifices are offered and, second, in the act of anointing that takes place.

That those who are *to be cleansed* are commanded to offer the sin, burnt and grain offerings is easy to understand. During their period of absence, they would inevitably have committed unintentional sin, for which atonement was necessary. The burnt and grain offerings would have expressed their desire to dedicate themselves and their work to God once more.

But why was the guilt offering prescribed, and why is such importance attached to it? In a departure from normal practice, the guilt offering was the first sacrifice to be offered on the day of purification (23–24, 30–31), which gives it a place of prominence in the complex sequence of offerings that follows. Why? The guilt offering was required for specific sins that had to do with breaking faith with God or with one's neighbours. In what way had the healed person done this? Does the guilt element imply that the illness was caused by sin, and therefore had a moral basis, not merely a ritual one, after all? There might indeed be a fear that the illness had been caused by sin, and therefore the guilt offering was made 'just in case'.[21] The guilt offering was, as we saw, often presented as a cautionary measure.[22]

But, more likely, the guilt offering is required, not because the illness was *caused by* sin, but because the illness *resulted in* sin, especially the sin of not giving to God his due. Sick people who had been excluded from the camp would have been unable to render God the devotion of which he was worthy. So there were duties they had 'failed to do in regard to the holy things' (5:16), for which the guilt offering alone could make restitution. Its purpose was to compensate God for the loss of tithes, sacrifices and other offerings that had been missed during the sick person's period of uncleanness.[23]

Hartley offers the further interesting observation that a guilt offering was prescribed for a transgression against holy property. Perhaps, in this case, the 'holy property' in question was the healed person himself or herself. The divine image the person bore had been marred by disease. Therefore, a guilt offering would be required to make reparation and restoration. There seems no need to choose between these various

---

[21] J. Milgrom, *Cult and Conscience: The Asham and the Priestly Doctrine of Repentance* (Leiden: Brill, 1976), pp. 80–81.

[22] See p. 72 above.

[23] Wenham, p. 210.

explanations. The guilt offering served several purposes and was a wonderfully rich means of ensuring that from every conceivable angle all the guilt of the past had been washed away and that the person was cleansed.[24]

The second unusual aspect of the ceremony was that the *one to be cleansed* was anointed with blood from the guilt offering (14) and with oil from a *log of oil*[25] (15–18) that had been supplied for the occasion. Both the blood and the oil are placed on *the lobe of the right ear of the one to be cleansed, on the thumb of their right hand and on the big toe of their right foot* (14, 17, 25, 28). Additionally, the remaining oil, some of which had been sprinkled *before the LORD seven times* (16, 27), was to be poured on the head of the cleansed person (18, 29). By this means *atonement* – right standing before God – would be made for the cleansed person (18, 29).

This ritual of anointing inevitably reminds one of the anointing of Aaron as high priest of Israel (see 8:10–14, 22–30), by which he was consecrated to the Lord's service; a similar purpose must be signified here. Ears, hands and feet are dedicated anew to the Lord. Cleansed people are not only put back in a right standing with God, are not only purified from all sin and guilt, and do not only signal their confidence that God accepts them by their offering of voluntary sacrifices; they are also recommissioned as servants of the Lord to fulfil an active role of obedience among God's covenant people. The rites of purification, then, were not essentially about providing individuals with a sense that their sin was forgiven, or emotional reassurance, or even the experience of a personal audience with God, any more than our salvation in Christ is essentially about such subjective experiences. They were about restoring broken individuals to their place among those who were busy in the service of God. These rites took once-wounded, now-healed, soldiers, recommissioned them to active service, and sent them back to the front to engage once more in battle.

What a day of celebration this would have been. There is no mention of the fellowship offering here, but no doubt those who could afford further offerings would have gone on to celebrate their recovery by inviting their family and friends to a feast.

---

[24] Hartley, p. 198, points out that the repetition of *make atonement* in vv. 19–20 stresses that the person is 'thoroughly forgiven and fully cleansed'.

[25] See v. 10. A 'log of oil' is 'the smallest unit of capacity in the Bible' and is estimated to have been about a cup. Milgrom, *Leviticus 1 – 16*, pp. 846, 890–901.

4. Dealing with defiled buildings (14:33–53)

The last section of these complex chapters looks forward to the time when the children of Israel had entered Canaan and would be living in houses (34–35). What was to happen if fungus was discovered in the house? With necessary adjustments, the procedures to be followed are virtually identical to those given earlier in relation to soiled materials. The owner of the house was to empty it in order to prevent anything else within it becoming contaminated, and then summon the priest to examine it (35–37). The initial inspection was followed by a week of waiting before a second inspection took place (38–39). What happened next depended on what the priest then saw.

If the mould had *spread* (39–42), the stones from the contaminated area were removed and taken outside the town, and the house was repaired and totally replastered. As before, care was taken not to remove more of the contaminated material than necessary. Every effort was made to keep the problem small and to ensure that the family could continue to occupy their residence if at all possible. Having done this, it was hoped that the problem was cured and that that would be an end to the matter.

But if the mildew reappeared (43–45), more severe measures were invoked. The house was declared unclean and had to be demolished, and its materials taken outside the town *to an unclean place.*

If the house was entered (46–47) during the period of quarantine, the persons who had entered it contracted a minor dose of uncleanness themselves and were unclean for the rest of the day. Those with whom they were in close contact also had to wash their clothes to ensure they had not been infected by uncleanness.

What happened if the mildew disappeared (48–53)? If all the procedures had been followed and it was evident that the house was free from further problems, then the priest could declare it clean. But people were not to make light of the priest's happy verdict. They were to mark his words with due ceremony. Owning good property, like enjoying good health, was no light matter but something that called for the exercise of wise stewardship. So, as before (3–7), the ceremony of the birds had to be conducted, reminding people, on the one hand, of the fate they might have endured if the house had been condemned and, on the other, of the blessing God had graciously chosen to bestow on them in restoring their dwelling to them with a clean bill of health. But, since a house was an inanimate object, not a willing human being, and therefore had no choice in whether or not it contracted the fungus, further sacrifices would have been inappropriate and were not required.

5. Dealing with the continuing implications

What do these long and detailed regulations have to do with us? They speak to us about the nature of sin, the ministry of Jesus and the meaning of discipleship.

a. The nature of sin

To be unclean is not to be equated with being sinful. Although there were occasions when a person's sin may have resulted in sickness, as in the case of Miriam (Num. 12:1–15), there was no necessary connection between them. Inanimate materials cannot be compared to human beings, who are active moral agents and capable of wilful sin. Yet they too were encompassed by these regulations and could be declared by the priests to be unclean. Uncleanness, then, was a ritual status, not a moral evaluation. Even so, the various forms of defilement serve as a parable of sin. Kellogg, as mentioned, drew the parallels between sickness and sin. Both were seriously defiling even though sometimes initially thought to be unimportant; both were progressive; both were destructive; and both distanced people from God. He also pointed out that the mildew in fabric and leather represents the sin that affects every part of our material creation. The same could be said of the houses that were spoiled by fungus. The environment in which we live is tainted by sin. It is not only that men and women are sinful, but that creation itself is fallen and stands in need of redemption.

This approach should be taken one step further. The mildew that was embedded in the homes of people who had settled in the Promised Land is representative of the sin embedded in the institutions of our society. While the term 'structural sin' may be problematic,[26] not least in giving people an excuse to abdicate personal responsibility for sin, perhaps the term 'institutionalized sin' is more helpful. In contemporary parlance, some of the UK's national bodies are said to suffer from 'institutionalized

---

[26] See Greg Forster, *Sin, Structure and Responsibility*, Grove Booklet on Ethics 24 (Bramcote: Grove Books, 1978).

racism', or 'institutionalized sexism', or 'institutionalized ageism'. Institutions do have a life of their own and are more than the sum of the people who inhabit them. They throw up patterns of working and collective attitudes, and come to adopt inflexible rules and procedures. In other words, they create a culture, in which it is all too easy for sin to develop and multiply. Therefore, addressing the sin of the individual alone is never going to lead us to a complete answer to it, important though that is.[27]

John Hartley begins to move in this direction when he argues that the treatment of garments and houses suggests that we should take care of our possessions so that they do not threaten those who use them. 'In today's technological world,' he explains,

> this means that a person or a corporation is responsible to see that products produced by either not only perform their desired tasks, but also do not harm their users. To prevent a product or a process from harming a person and polluting the environment is an ethical responsibility. All of us have that responsibility in regard to taking care of what we own.[28]

But our responsibility is greater than 'a duty of care'. It is a responsibility to ensure that we do not harbour sin in the institutions with which we are connected, through producing cheap goods, by paying low and unjust wages, by using deception, or by treating any employee, client or customer unjustly in any way. This passage implicitly calls God's people to take issues of social justice and environmental care seriously.

Our understanding of sin is often too superficial. Sin is committed by individuals and is something for which we all bear responsibility. Sin also afflicts the individual and each of us is inherently tainted by it from the beginning. But sin also inhabits the institutions of our world and often affects us in ways that are more subtle and more difficult to identify than personal sin does. Finally, sin has damaged the environment in which we live. Planet Earth is both wonderful and cursed at the same time. For all these we need a cure.

---

[27] Christian Smith argues that evangelicals are well placed to convert individuals but will never have the impact they could on wider culture because of the individualistic fallacy that causes them to underestimate the significance of structures in society. *American Evangelicalism: Embattled and Thriving* (Chicago: University of Chicago Press, 1998), pp. 187–203. The commission to bring individuals to Christ has never been rescinded, but it is not the whole of our calling. See John Stott, *Christian Mission in the Modern World* (Eastbourne: Kingsway, 1986).

[28] Hartley, p. 200.

b. The ministry of Jesus

Some priests, it has been suggested, were especially trained for the ministry of purifying those who were to be cleansed.[29] But if so, their ministry was of a distinctly limited nature. They were powerless to cure anyone or to remedy any mildew that appeared in clothes or houses. All they could do was to take steps to contain the malady so as to prevent it spreading, and then affirm that the cure had taken place after God had restored a person's health or restored wholeness to an object. Valuable though these ministries might be, they are as nothing in comparison with our need to find one who has the power to bring healing into our lives. That priest, who is in a class of his own, is Jesus.

Throughout his ministry, Jesus did the unthinkable and accomplished the unimaginable. He touched the unclean and made them clean. On the road in Galilee he healed a leper who begged Jesus to make him clean, and 'immediately the leprosy left him' (Mark 1:40–45; cf. Matt. 8:1–4; Luke 5:12–16). On the outskirts of Samaria a whole colony of lepers was healed at his command (Luke 17:11–19). And these were just the tip of the iceberg, as can be seen from the message Jesus sent in response to a question from John the Baptist: 'The blind receive sight, the lame walk, those who have leprosy are cleansed, the deaf hear, the dead are raised, and the good news is proclaimed to the poor' (Luke 7:22).

By touching those whom the law declared unclean, Jesus vanquished their defilement, made them clean and brought them near to God again. The kingdom of God is full of leprosy sufferers who have been healed and others whose various defilements have been cleansed by Jesus.[30]

There is one other important respect, however, in which the purity laws foreshadow the work of Christ. The healed person was restored to fellowship with God through sacrifice. The mere passing of the disease was not sufficient to qualify the excluded person from resuming his or her place in the covenant community again. For that, sacrifices were required. Even in the case of contaminated clothes and buildings, where the usual sacrifices were inappropriate, there was still a rudimentary sacrificial ritual in which one bird lost its life and shed its blood as an act of atonement while another was set free. So it is with Jesus. The healing he brings, the cleansing he accomplishes and the lives he restores are all made possible

---

[29] As suggested by the terminology of v. 11. Levine, p. 87.

[30] Matt. 26:6; Mark 14:3; and, more inclusively, Luke 14:12–24.

by his greater sacrifice at Calvary. Miraculous and powerful deeds of healing are often associated with the giving of the Spirit at Pentecost. But what makes Pentecost possible is the self-giving of the Son at Passover.[31] What brings healing is Calvary love. On the cross Jesus gave himself to bear the impurity of those who were separated from God: the righteous one in the place of the unrighteous multitude, to bring them to God (1 Pet. 3:18).

For all the wonder of this work of Jesus, however, it is not limited to restoring the shattered lives of individuals alone. His death on Calvary was also the way in which God chose to vanquish the other dimensions of sin and to renew his marred and ruined creation. Eugene Peterson's marvellous paraphrase of Colossians 1:20 says it brilliantly: 'all the broken and dislocated pieces of the universe – people and things, animals and atoms – get properly fixed and fit together in vibrant harmonies, all because of his death, his blood that poured down from the cross'.[32]

c. The meaning of discipleship

While the primary emphasis of Leviticus 14 lies in the gracious provision God makes for those whose health temporarily excluded them from his presence to return to him, the chapter also throws up some interesting insights into what it means to be a member of God's covenant people or, in our terms, a disciple of Jesus Christ.

Disciples are those who have had their sin removed by Jesus and have been born again, like cleansed Israelites on the eighth day.

Disciples must constantly be in a state of cleanness when they approach God. Harbouring sin and neglecting repentance will distance us from God.

Disciples need to be aware that spiritual maturity involves the careful maintenance of our bodies as well as of our souls. God's concern is with the whole of our lives and with us as integrated persons, not just with the spiritual dimension of our lives.

Disciples must understand that the purpose of their rebirth is not only to provide them with personal comfort and reassurance, and still less with private spiritual privileges, but also to make them members of a community of priests who serve God and do his bidding.

---

[31] Christ was crucified at Passover.

[32] *The Message* (Colorado Springs: NavPress, 2002).

Disciples should daily dedicate their ears to hear God's word, their hands to do God's will and their feet to walk in God's ways.

Disciples must show a concern for the world God has made, protect its environment and exercise their stewardship of its resources, including our fellow human beings, with integrity and justice.

Christ did not abolish the Levitical regulations that have to do with purity. He fulfilled them. He fulfilled the regulations about diet by declaring all God's animal creatures clean. He fulfilled the regulations about our bodies by making us – the unclean – clean. He did so in order that we might offer our bodies 'as a living sacrifice, holy and pleasing to God' (Rom. 12:1).

D. The manual of atonement: ensuring God's forgiveness (16:1–34)

Leviticus 16:1–34

13. For all the sins of Israel[1]

The high point of Israel's year was the Day of Atonement. Like an annual spring clean that sweeps away the accumulated dirt of the previous twelve months, which the routine cleaning of a house had overlooked, so the Day of Atonement swept away all the accumulated sins of Israel that had escaped the attention of even the most conscientious worshipper in Israel.

Everything about the day underlines its supreme importance. It was celebrated on the tenth day of the seventh month (29), the most sacred of all months. The high priest wore a simple costume and underwent very careful preparation, heightening the sense of its solemnity. The rituals undertaken were unique and their effect unequalled. It was celebrated but once a year. The whole community was instructed to practise self-denial during the day. Information about this day is placed at the pivotal point of the book of Leviticus, further emphasizing its cardinal significance. Given all this, it is easy to understand why the rabbis came to refer to it simply as 'the Day'.[2]

The fullest account of the day occurs in Leviticus 16,[3] which sets out some reasonably detailed instructions. Although the Lord addresses Aaron through Moses, the people of Israel are the intended audience as much as the high priest. By the end of the chapter this becomes clear when the 'you' addressed in verses 29–34 is definitely the community as a whole.[4]

---

[1] For another exposition of Lev. 16 that partly overlaps with this chapter see the author's *The Message of the Cross*, The Bible Speaks Today (Leicester: IVP, 2001), pp. 68–84.

[2] Mays, p. 52, points out the rabbis devoted an entire book of the Mishnah to explaining this day.

[3] It is also mentioned in Exod. 30:10; Lev. 23:26–32; 25:9; Num. 29:7–11.

[4] Hartley, p. 225. Among other reasons for believing that this is addressed to the people, Hartley points out that some details, such as the identity of the altar in vv. 18–19, are a little too vague to provide the high priest with all the information he would need.

The structure of the chapter is complex, but may be understood as follows:

A¹   Prologue: a solemn warning from God (1–2)
    B¹   Drawing near: instructions from God (3–14)
        Preparation of the high priest (3–4)
        Preparation of the sacrifices (5–10)
        Preparation of the way into the Most Holy Place (11–14)
        C   Making atonement: purification from God (15–22)
            The goat that was sacrificed (15–19)
            The goat that was set free (20–22)
    B²   Taking leave: withdrawing from God (23–28)
        Changing back (23–24a)
        Renewing dedication (24b–25)
        Returning to camp (26)
        Disposing of waste (27–28)
A²   Epilogue: a lasting ordinance from God (29–34)

1. Prologue: a solemn warning from God (16:1–2)

Before the instructions proper begin, they are prefaced by a solemn warning from God that links this day to the sin of Nadab and Abihu, who were put to death by the Lord after offering unauthorized sacrifices (10:1–4).[5] This may imply that the cause of their offence was that they had strayed beyond their proper limits and tried to enter the Most Holy Place,[6] the innermost room in the Tent. But whether this helps us to understand their fatal mistake or not, the point is clear: not even Aaron, the high priest, has a right to enter God's awesome throne room *whenever he chooses*. Even he may dare to enter only when God invites him to do so on this one day in the year. The sin of presumption would lead to death.

To speak of God's throne room is inevitably to speak in foolish and paltry human terms. So great is the God of Israel that heaven is his throne and the earth merely his footstool.[7] Humans cannot provide shelter for him, nor can he be confined to any building they erect. And yet, although

---

[5] See above, pp. 117–119.

[6] *The Most Holy Place* is the NIV's term for what was traditionally called 'the Holy of Holies'. The NRSV terms it 'the sanctuary inside the curtain'.

[7] Isa. 66:1. See also 2 Sam. 7:1–29; Acts 7:48–50.

not restricted to this place, there was a sense in which God lived in the Most Holy Place among his people, at the very centre of their camp, and ruled over them from there.[8] This innermost room of the Tent was shielded from the Holy Place by a curtain. The room housed the rectangular box known as the ark of the covenant, which contained the tablets of stone Moses brought from Mount Sinai and was overshadowed by two golden cherubim (Exod. 25:10–22). The lid of the box served as a 'mercy-seat' (NRSV) or *atonement cover* (NIV). From this place God presided in majesty and grace over Israel. It was here that Aaron was to visit annually to make atonement for Israel.

2. Drawing near: instructions from God (16:3–14)

To enter the Most Holy Place was to expose oneself to the risk that God's dynamic holiness might break out and strike one dead. Aaron, therefore, had to approach God's majestic presence with extreme caution, as is underlined by the emphatic Hebrew, which has been lost in translation: the Lord does not tamely say, *This is how Aaron is to enter . . .* (3), but rather, 'Only in this way shall Aaron enter . . .'[9] Strict adherence to the prescribed preparations and procedures was required.

a. Preparation of the high priest (16:3–4)

Three things were required of Aaron by way of personal preparation. First, he was to make ready a bull and a ram to offer as his personal sin and burnt offerings (3). Second, he was to change his clothes. On this occasion he was to set aside the splendid robes of his office and appear before God in a *sacred linen tunic, with linen undergarments next to his body*, a *linen sash round him* and with *a linen turban* on his head (4). While some see this as a symbol of the purity that would be expected of anyone entering God's presence,[10] most see it as a mark of humility, a sign of one 'stripped of all pretence' and status.[11] The garment is the garment of a slave – 'a significant reminder that when the high priest enters the very presence of God he is nothing more

---

[8] When Solomon asked, 'But will God really dwell on earth?' (1 Kgs 8:27), he anticipated the answer 'Yes', which was wonderfully fulfilled in the coming of Jesus, John 1:14.

[9] Levine, p. 101.

[10] This view is consistent with passages such as Rev. 19:8. See Jenson, p. 200. Milgrom, *Leviticus 1 – 16*, pp. 1016–1017, sets out five explanations for this dress, including the possibility that it was the dress of an angel.

[11] Milgrom, *Leviticus 1 – 16*, p. 1016.

than a simple servant'.[12] Third, the high priest was to *bathe himself with water* before he dressed himself in the garments. The high priest, in fact, was to bathe himself frequently throughout the day. Complete physical cleanliness was necessary before he entered the heart of God's sanctuary, symbolizing the complete inner purity required of this servant of God.

In later years the preparation of the high priest was taken so seriously that it was commenced seven days before the Day of Atonement fell due.[13]

b. Preparation of the sacrifices (16:5–10)

Aaron had to prepare not only himself but the materials needed in the ceremonies. Altogether, five unblemished animals had to be gathered, ready for their part in the sacrifices. Two rams were needed (one for his own burnt offering and one for that offered for the people), a young bull for his own sin offering, and two goats (one to sacrifice as the people's sin offering and one to release in a solitary place in the desert).

Before the slaughtering of the animals began there was an additional task, which took place only on the Day of Atonement. Aaron *is to cast lots for the two goats – one lot for the* LORD *and the other for the scapegoat* (8). Nothing distinguished the goats from each other at first. Both were consecrated to the Lord to play a part in securing purification for Israel, but which one was to lay down its life and which one was to escape with its life is left entirely for the Lord to choose through the casting of lots.

The goat that was chosen to be the scapegoat is said to be 'for Azazel' (NRSV; cf. NIV mg.), which has caused a great deal of discussion. Several interpretations are given to this obscure term.[14] It might refer to an inaccessible place in the desert, as envisaged in verse 22. Or it might simply be a way of saying that this is the 'goat that goes away'. The Hebrew term is more than likely to be a compound of *'ēz* ('goat') and *'āzal* ('to go' or 'be led away').[15] Or it might refer to the demonic ruler of the wilderness, a desert demon, or perhaps the leader of fallen angels.[16] In favour of this is the symmetry that would then exist in the phrasing, between 'a goat for the Lord' and 'a goat for Azazel', and that this is how later Jewish interpreters understood it. But there are several reservations about this

---

[12] Demarest, p. 174.

[13] *Mishnah*, p. 265.

[14] For summaries see Levine, p. 102; D. P. Wright, *Disposal*, pp. 21–22.

[15] Favoured by Kaiser, p. 1112.

[16] Gerstenberger, p. 219; Grabbe, *Oxford*, p. 101; Noth, p. 125; D. P. Wright, *Disposal*, pp. 21–22.

interpretation, and we are certainly right to be hesitant about it in case it leads to a serious misunderstanding of what is being implied. The goat that is despatched to the desert is certainly not being sent as a sacrifice or ransom to a demon.[17] God does not owe anything to demonic beings and the Old Testament never gives the slightest hint that they should be appeased. God has the right to set his people free from sin by his own decree, not by the consent of opposing forces. The interpretation might be seen positively, however, if it is understood that what God is doing is returning evil to its source and removing it completely from Israel.[18] Of these, the second interpretation still has much to commend it, as it fits most neatly with 'the rite of riddance' that climaxes the Day of Atonement, as outlined in verses 20–22.

c. Preparation of the way into the Most Holy Place (16:11–14)

Still the careful preparations are not complete. On this day, and this day alone, the high priest is to enter the Most Holy Place and officiate in the immediate presence of God himself. God's holiness, emanating from his seat on the lid of the covenant ark, is a tangible force. As the high priest goes behind the curtain, which usually hid the ark from the priests who served in the Holy Place, he was entering dangerous territory. So he dare not enter without protection, and God provides a way in which he can safeguard himself. He was to *take a censer full of burning coals from the altar before the LORD and two handfuls of finely ground* [that is, high-quality] *fragrant incense* with him as he entered behind *the curtain* (12).[19] The fire and the incense served as a smokescreen forming a wall of protection, hiding God from Aaron. To look on God face to face would be to court death.[20] The smoke ensures that God's holiness is bearable by a sinful man, that God's being remains shrouded in mystery, and that his servant is preserved.

One further act is necessary before Aaron can present the offerings of purification on behalf of the people, and that is his need *to slaughter the bull for his own sin offering* (11). Before he can serve as a priestly representative, his own sin and that of his household must be expiated.

---

[17] Lev. 17:7 prohibits sacrifices to demons.

[18] Kellogg, p. 270, remarks that if Azazel is an evil spirit, sending the scapegoat to him has nothing to do with offering a sacrifice or ransom to him. Rather, Azazel is a form of Satan, who is the Accuser, and by this act God declares that the people's sins are forgiven, so his accusations no longer have any hold over them.

[19] Details of the incense are found in Exod. 30:34–38.

[20] Noordtzij, p. 165. Cf. Exod. 20:19; 33:20; Judg. 6:22–23; 13:22.

He follows the stipulated procedures for the high priest's sin offering, laid down in Leviticus 4:3–12, with the exception that, on this special day, the blood of the bull is sprinkled *on the front of the atonement cover* (14) instead of on the outside of the curtain as usual.

The awesome solemnity of Aaron's entering God's presence was well captured in Thomas Binney's[21] hymn 'Eternal Light! Eternal Light! How pure the soul must be . . .':

> O, how shall I, whose native sphere
> > Is dark, whose mind is dim,
> Before the Ineffable appear,
> And on my naked spirit bear
> > The uncreated beam?

To which question Binney replied:

> There is a way for man to rise
> > To that sublime abode;
> An offering and a sacrifice,
> A Holy Spirit's energies,
> > An advocate with God.

All these initial instructions leave one with a powerful impression of God as majestic in holiness. They thus begin to disclose the problem that the Day of Atonement was designed to address. The holy God has been offended in manifold ways by his people, and their offences have led to a growing mountain of defilement that must be removed. The uncleanness will not just disappear, it must be cleansed; the offences will not just go away, they must be taken away. And that is what the Day of Atonement is designed to accomplish.

3. Making atonement: purification from God (16:15–22)

Having engaged in careful preparation, Aaron is now ready to undertake the rituals that are at the heart of the day. The Tent of Meeting has

---

[21] Thomas Binney (1798–1874).

been vacated (17), and he stands, unassisted, as the solitary representative of the people, making atonement before God, *for himself, his household and the whole community of Israel* (17). The spotlight now falls on the two goats that had been selected. Only the casting of the lot had distinguished them, but that done, there was now to be a sharp difference in the parts they were to play and the destinies they faced – one would die at the heart of the Tent of Meeting and the other would be set free at the extremity of the camp.[22] In spite of these differences, they would be jointly engaged in one act of atonement, not two. Both their roles were necessary on this special day. Both would act as substitutes for the people of Israel. Both would bear the sins of Israel. Both would make for full atonement.

a. The goat that was sacrificed (16:15–19)

The first goat to which Aaron gives attention is sacrificed as *the sin offering for the people* (15), although this is a sin offering with a difference. On this occasion the blood of the bull is sprinkled not only in its customary location in the Holy Place (18) but uniquely in the Most Holy Place *on the atonement cover and in front of it* (15). The splendid gold that covered the ark and epitomized God's glory will henceforth be tarnished by blood because of the need for atonement from sin. Sprinkling behind the curtain is to take precedence over the sprinkling in the Holy Place. Only once this is done may Aaron then go out to the altar and continue to perform the usual ritual of the sin offering.

On the surface, the objective of this seems perfectly clear: as a sin offering its purpose is to make atonement for the people so that 'they will be forgiven' (4:20). But what is said about the sin offering on the Day of Atonement is somewhat different. We read that Aaron, in presenting this sin offering, *will make atonement for the Most Holy Place because of the uncleanness and rebellion of the Israelites, whatever their sins have been* (16). Similarly, verse 19 says that by sprinkling some of the bull's blood on the altar Aaron will *cleanse it and consecrate it from the uncleanness of the Israelites* – not 'them' but 'it'. And verse 20 speaks of Aaron *making atonement for the Most Holy Place*. Was the essential nature of this part of the ritual, then, not so much about forgiving the people's wrongs as about purifying the sanctuary from pollution?

---

[22] Jenson, p. 202.

This case has been strongly argued, not least by Milgrom.[23] The argument is that 'the God of Israel will not abide in a polluted sanctuary'.[24] Over time, the (often unintentional) failure of Israel to offer sufficient sacrifices to get rid of their impurities[25] meant that those impurities piled up in the Tent until God could no longer dwell there. The fog of pollution that accumulated became so dense that he was driven from his residence and estranged from his people. If this defilement was not removed, the people could expect the curses of Leviticus 26 to descend upon them for their failure to keep the covenant.[26]

According to its advocates, further support for this interpretation is found in the meaning of 'atonement' (*kipper*) and its relationship to 'atonement cover' (*kappōret*). The root of the word (*kpr*) may mean either 'to cover', as when one covers a road with pitch or covers a debt by payment, or 'to ransom', as in paying a price to achieve a favour, or 'to purge', 'to rub off' or to 'wipe away' and make something clean.[27] Traditionally, atonement has been thought to mean the second of these and to point to the way in which the debt of sin is met and expiated by means of a substitutionary sacrifice. But Milgrom and others are persuaded that, in the ritual texts of Leviticus, 'to rub off' or 'to wipe' is the intended meaning.[28] And what is wiped clean is not the sinner, but the sanctuary that had been polluted by ritual impurity.

Furthermore, it is said that this view is consistent with the way the priests viewed the world. The sanctuary was a microcosm of the world, and uncleanness there meant that the world itself was unclean and that its stability was under threat. Cleansing the sanctuary, then, restored to stability and normality not only the spiritual health of the people but also the world God had created.[29]

All this leads Milgrom to say that there are two different rites involved in the Day of Atonement: one that purifies the sanctuary from ceremonial uncleanness through a purification offering, and another that atones for people's moral guilt through the despatch of the scapegoat.

---

[23] Milgrom, *Leviticus 1 – 16*, p. 1033, backed by his fuller note on pp. 258–261.

[24] Ibid., p. 258.

[25] It is argued that the impurities referred to here are the ritual impurities set out in chapters 11–15, rather than are moral wrongdoings, which are the concern of the next part of the ritual.

[26] Douglas, *Literature*, p. 192.

[27] R. E. Averbeck, '*kpr*', in *NIDOTTE* 3, pp. 689–710.

[28] Milgrom, *Leviticus 1 – 16*, p. 1081. See full discussion on pp. 1079–1084.

[29] Balentine, pp. 128–129, gives a clear exposition of this view. See also Bellinger, p. 103.

However, in an extensive linguistic study of *kipper*, N. Kiuchi[30] argues that it is inadequate to interpret it as meaning 'to wipe the sanctuary clean' and insists that all the evidence leads one to interpret it as providing expiation for the sanctuary. While recognizing that there were two forms of the sin offering – one that atoned for people and one that atoned for the sanctuary – they were both atonement offerings that dealt with moral guilt, not just ritual impurity. And the blood of both of them removed guilt, and did not simply act as a spiritual detergent, cleaning up what had been unfortunately made dirty. In the special rite of the Day of Atonement the sanctuary is indeed cleansed, but it is cleansed because Aaron temporarily bears the guilt of the Israelites and then subsequently transfers it to the live goat by laying both his hands on its head and sending it away into the wilderness.[31]

This seems to do greater justice to the whole tenor of the sacrificial system, where guilt, not mere ritual impurity, is a major concern, and where atonement is acquired by blood substitution, not by mere washing. The sanctuary is indeed purified on this one day of the year. But it is purified not only from the ritual pollution but also from the moral pollution of Israel's *rebellion* (16, 21), *wickedness* (21) and *all their sins* and wrongdoings (21). The rich and varied vocabulary of sin cannot be avoided in this chapter. Woven through the central rituals of the day is a consciousness of sin in all its varied forms. To pull the thread of sin, and consequently moral guilt, from the garment knitted together by these ceremonies is to cause the whole garment to unravel, not just a part of it to be defaced. The goat that was killed both purifies the sanctuary and atones for people, no less than the goat that was released.

b. The goat that was set free (16:20–22)

Once the sin offering has cleansed the Tent of Meeting, from its innermost shrine to its outermost courts, Aaron is to *bring forward the live goat* and lay both his hands on its head as a symbolic act of transference, and *confess over it all the wickedness and rebellion of the Israelites* (21). This goat is then handed over to the *care of someone appointed for the task* (21), who escorts it away from the Tent, out through the camp and to the regions beyond, where he releases it in the desert. What had been effected

---

[30] Kiuchi, *Purification*, pp. 87–109.

[31] Ibid., pp. 148, 156. Exod. 28:38 speaks of Aaron bearing the people's guilt.

in private, between God and Aaron alone, was now made public for all to see.[32] As Gordon Wenham comments, 'the symbolism of this ceremony is transparent'.[33] *The goat will carry on itself all their sins to a remote place* (22), thus physically removing them from the people and depositing them as far away as possible from the camp, where they can trouble the people no longer. It is what the psalmist celebrated when he wrote that 'as far as the east is from the west, so far has he removed our transgressions from us' (Ps. 103:12).

The ritual is evocative. Sin is being removed from the camp and banished to a barren, essentially uninhabited place. It is being taken to where it truly belongs, because sin has the effect of turning fertile pastures into desert wastes. The desert was thought to be the place where demons and evil powers had their home; perhaps one of them was even called Azazel.[34] Sin belonged, not among the covenant people of God, but among the wild and malevolent spirits of the wasteland. In sending sin there, God is saying, 'Here are the sins you have engineered. You can have them back. They have power over us no longer.'[35]

The rabbinic writings tell us that whereas at first the goat was left simply to wander around, in later history the escort, when he had reached his destination, would tie the goat to a rock and then push it from behind over a precipice, where it was torn to pieces before it was halfway down. This was to ensure the scapegoat's complete destruction and that it would never return to the camp.[36] There was, for sure, no way back. Sin had been irretrievably banished and irrevocably forgiven.

The geographical movements involved in these rituals were wider than those involved in any other act of sacrifice. And these, too, serve to underline the comprehensive scope of the forgiveness available on the Day of Atonement. The sacrificial drama was usually played out in the courtyard of the Tent of Meeting and in the Holy Place. The drama of this special day reaches into the innermost core of the Tent, the Most Holy Place, and is not completed until the scapegoat is let loose in the region beyond the camp. Philip Jenson has pictured the layout of Israel's camp as if it were

---

[32] Alec Motyer, *Look to the Rock* (Leicester: IVP, 1996), p. 54.

[33] Wenham, p. 233.

[34] Azazel is mentioned in v. 8 (cf. NRSV). See discussion there.

[35] Demarest, p. 50.

[36] In later Jewish tradition the arrival of the scapegoat in the desert was communicated all the way back to Jerusalem by the joyful waving of towels. *Mishnah*, p. 276.

five concentric circles reaching from Zone 1 at the centre, the Most Holy Place, through to Zone 5, beyond the circumference, the desert region outside the camp. Only the ceremonies of the Day of Atonement covered the complete geography of holiness in Israel, from the most sacred spot of all to the least clean place in the world. Atonement reaches right to the heart of God and propels sin to the furthest part of the earth. Cleansing comes from an act of God in his dwelling-place and leads to the removal of the problem as far away as it is possible to conceive.

The two central acts of the Day of Atonement seem to be two not different rites but inextricably bound together. It is not that the cleansing of the sanctuary comes first and then the cleansing of the people. Cleansing the sanctuary involves cleansing the people, and vice versa. It is not that the former has to do with ritual impurity, and the latter with moral impurity. The terminology of uncleanness and sin is blended as if the rituals are one. It is not that the former has to do with atonement by blood, and the latter with atonement by some lesser means. The scapegoat would be inadequate but for the dead goat. The acts are mutually complementary, like two sides of the same coin. If there is a difference, it is best described as Kaiser does: 'The one goat makes possible the expiation of the sins laid on it, and thus it is a *means* of expiating and propitiating Israel's sins, while the other goat exhibits the *effects* of that expiation.'[37] Sin has been both forgiven and forgotten.

The joint rite of 'blood brought near and a ram being driven away'[38] meant that once a year the people had the assurance that *all* their sin had been forgiven, whether a ritual transgression or a moral rebellion, whether consciously done or unconsciously committed, whether previously confessed or unintentionally missed. On this day cleansing was available for all the sins of Israel (30, 34). On this day, 'all bases are covered'.[39]

4. Taking leave: withdrawing from God (16:23–28)

Having despatched the scapegoat, Aaron has further work to do to draw this remarkable day to a conclusion and to return the business of the Tent of Meeting to normal for another year.

---

[37] Kaiser, p. 1111.
[38] Jenson, p. 202.
[39] A. D. Hayes, 'Atonement in the Book of Leviticus', *Int* 52.1 (1998), p. 13.

a. Changing back (16:23–24a)

The clothes that had been appropriate for this day – the clothes of penitent humility – were exchanged for the normal, ornate robes that Aaron wore as the high priest of Israel. But before he resumed the wearing of those magnificent garments, he was required to immerse himself completely in water. All in all, the rabbis calculated that the high priest was required to bathe himself five times and wash his hands and feet a further ten times on this day, although this seems an excessive calculation.[40] Aaron's ablutions before he went into the Most Holy Place were to ensure that his body was clean, but those he undertakes as he withdraws from the immediate presence of God may serve a different function. Aaron would have borne the aura of holiness about him as he came out from the Most Holy Place. Unless that aura had been toned down to some degree, those who now joined him in the more regular offering of sacrifices in which he was about to engage might have been endangered by him.[41]

b. Renewing dedication (16:24b–25)

The return to normal clothing signalled the resumption of the routine responsibilities of the high priest. So his next act was to *sacrifice the burnt offering for himself and the burnt offering for the people.* The rams that had been selected early in the morning were now put to good use as Aaron, on his own behalf and then as a representative of the community, killed them and burned them wholly on the altar. Having been set free from sin, Aaron and the people were in a position to express renewed dedication to God and offer themselves once more to him for obedient service. Without going this extra mile, Israel might have taken for granted God's grace, which had been freshly bestowed in the rituals of that day. They may have made the dangerous assumption, expressed in the reputed last words of the satirist Heinrich Heine, that 'Of course God will forgive me; that's his business.' Such audacity would be fertile soil in which to grow a spirit of ingratitude and in which to reproduce further sin. The presentation of the burnt offerings would remind Israel that receiving forgiveness had to be accompanied by both a change of heart and an amendment of life.

---

[40] *Mishnah*, p. 268. See Milgrom, *Leviticus 1 – 16*, p. 1047, for details.

[41] Hartley, p. 242.

c. Returning to camp (16:26)

While this was going on, the one who had escorted the scapegoat into exile was making his way back to camp. But, since he had ventured into unclean territory, he was not able to return until he too had bathed himself and washed his clothes.

d. Disposing of waste (16:27–28)

The final act of the day is the disposal of the carcasses of the sin offerings. They are taken to the ash heap outside the camp and burned. Although the remains are taken *outside the camp*, they are taken to a clean place because they derive from holy offerings and must therefore be treated with an appropriate degree of respect (4:12, 21). This contrasts with the live goat that, bearing the sins of Israel, has become unclean and is despatched to an unclean place.

As the servant who disposes of the remains re-enters the camp, the familiar requirement that he *wash his clothes and bathe himself with water* is repeated for the last time. He must not risk bringing any defilement back into the community of Israel.

With this final act the momentous Day of Atonement draws to a close. But the chapter itself does not. It is rounded off with a final word addressed to all Israel.

5. Epilogue: a lasting ordinance from God (16:29–34)

The chapter concludes with an epilogue of solemn affirmation to balance the prologue of solemn warning with which it began. Only now are the people of Israel addressed; until this point they have been mere spectators (though with a very restricted vision of what was happening). The Day of Atonement was not a temporary expedient but was to be *a lasting ordinance* (29, 31, 34), perpetually observed by Israel. When Aaron had passed from the scene, his successor was to preside over the day (32) and ensure that the annual removal of all sin still took place.

These final words prescribe the time – *the tenth day of the seventh month* (29); the manner – *you must deny yourselves and not do any work . . . It is a day of sabbath of rest* (29, 31); and the participants – *whether native-born or a foreigner residing among you* (29) of the annual ceremony. The date is chosen because the *seventh month* is the most sacred month of the year,[42] and *the tenth day* is selected, it has been suggested, because ten is a composite of the sacred numbers three and seven.[43] The solemnity of the festival is underlined by the call for self-denial. It is to be marked by abstaining from all routine activity, including, but not limited to, work and feasting.[44] As with the burnt offering, this was intended to ensure that the presenting of this special sin offering would be accompanied by a genuine sense of repentance on the part of all those who would benefit from it. The day was to incorporate all who lived in the community of Israel, not just those who were Israelites by birth. Every individual, Israelite and foreigner alike, had contributed to the piling up of sin and, by the grace of God, on this day every individual, Israelite and foreigner alike, was to be a recipient of his mercy and know his or her sins forgiven.

The closing sentence of the chapter (34) issues what Hartley terms the 'compliance report' of the first Day of Atonement. What God commanded, Moses communicated and Aaron completed. Israel had been restored to a state of holiness by the grace of God through the offering of sacrifices and by their own obedience. Peter speaks of God's new royal priesthood and holy nation in remarkably similar terms. They are, he says, 'chosen according to the foreknowledge of God the Father, through the sanctifying work of the Spirit, *to be obedient to Jesus Christ and sprinkled with his blood*' (1 Pet. 1:2, emphasis added).

6. A lasting ordinance?

The rituals of this great day effected atonement for Israel, but not because the sacrifices themselves were adequate, for they were not. Their rituals were only shadows of the reality that was to come. Yet they were effective for Israel because by undertaking them they demonstrated obedient faith in God's word and, unknown to them, anticipated the work of Christ. In Calvin's words, 'If anyone asks whether the sins of the fathers were remitted under the Law, we must hold … that they were remitted, but remitted by the mercy of Christ.'[45] They pointed to one who would serve

---

[42] See further Lev. 23.

[43] Hartley, p. 242.

[44] *Mishnah*, p. 277, states that self-denial was to include abstinence from sex, bathing, anointing and even the wearing of sandals. Acts 27:9 refers to the Day of Atonement as 'the Fast' (NRSV).

[45] J. Calvin, *Calvin's Commentaries*, ed. D. W. Torrance and T. F. Torrance (Edinburgh: St Andrew Press, 1963), vol. 12, p. 122.

as a perfect High Priest, who would offer a perfect sin offering by his death, who would by his life render a perfect burnt offering, and who would become the perfect scapegoat who takes away the sin of the world. The lasting ordinance that Israel was commanded to observe annually would no longer be needed once the Day of Atonement had metamorphosed into the day of Calvary.

It is curious that the New Testament does not identify the work of Christ with that of the scapegoat in any overt or explicit way.[46] That was left to the *Epistle of Barnabas*, around the year AD 130, after which the parallel became more popular in the early church. But, in spite of the absence of any specific reference to the scapegoat, the New Testament alludes to the Day of Atonement as a whole on numerous occasions, especially in the letter to Hebrews.[47] The allusions all go to prove the infinite superiority of the sacrifice of Jesus Christ as he brings the Day of Atonement to its ultimate fulfilment.

The superiority of his work is seen both in points of comparison and in points of contrast.

a. The superiority demonstrated by way of comparison

By comparison, the blood of Jesus Christ was poured out as a 'sacrifice of atonement' (Rom. 3:25), just like the sin offering, and put those who were alienated from God back in a right standing with him. Like the scapegoat, Jesus had the burden of our sin transferred to him. In Paul's words, 'God made him who had no sin to be sin for us' (2 Cor. 5:21). In Peter's words, 'He himself bore our sins in his body on the cross' (1 Pet. 2:24). And in bearing the burden of our sins, Christ bore them away. 'Christ was sacrificed once to take away the sins of many' (Heb. 9:28). Jesus is the ultimate 'rite of riddance' and removes people's sins far from them.

Another allusion to the scapegoat is found in Hebrews 13:12. Just as the scapegoat was sent outside the camp, so Jesus died outside the city.

A final comparison lies in the ministry of the high priest as a mediator. As our great High Priest, Jesus continues to be our 'advocate with the Father' (1 John 2:1). Even here, however, the differences in their ministries begin to emerge, since Aaron conducted his intercession for Israel in a

---

[46] John 1:29 and 1 Pet. 2:24 may allude to the scapegoat but may equally have the Passover lamb or the suffering lamb of Isa. 53 in view.

[47] Heb. 9:7–14 makes an explicit connection.

humanly built sanctuary, whereas Christ speaks to the Father on our behalf in heaven itself (Heb. 9:24).

b. The superiority demonstrated by way of contrast

For all the points of connection between the work of Christ and the Day of Atonement, it is the points of contrast that the New Testament develops most, helping us to see the greater splendour of Christ's atoning sacrifice for us.

The high priests of old were sinners who had to offer sacrifices for their own sins before they could offer any on behalf of others. Jesus, however, is unblemished in his perfection and has no such need. The High Priest who can truly meet our need both identifies with us in our humanity and yet remains one who is 'holy, blameless, pure' and to be distinguished from sinners (Heb. 7:26–28).

The high priests of old offered the blood of bulls and goats. But however good that was, such blood was inevitably in the end an inadequate substitute for wilful human beings. But Jesus offered his own blood, the blood of a sentient human being. His blood provided an adequate substitute indeed, and one that would not only provide outward cleansing but cleanse the conscience as well (Heb. 9:9, 12–14).

The high priests of old were compelled to offer the sacrifices of the Day of Atonement annually. The regular repetition of the day could only serve to underline its ultimate inadequacy. The repeated ritual, as Thomas Long points out,

> is like a sledgehammer, pounding away year after year with its constant battering away at the theme of sin. In other words, it doesn't work to heal; it works only to drub it into us that we are sinful, sinful, sinful – guilty and unacceptable to God.[48]

The rituals of that day could never make perfect those who participated in them (Heb. 10:1). But Jesus releases us from that depressing treadmill, needing only to offer the sacrifice of himself once for it to prove sufficient for all time as well as for all people (Heb. 7:27; 9:12, 26, 28).

The wonderful result of Christ's atoning death is that now 'we have confidence to enter the Most Holy Place by the blood of Jesus' (Heb. 10:19).

---

[48] Thomas Long, *Hebrews*, Interpretation (Louisville, KY: John Knox, 1997), p. 101.

Every believer has direct and unimpeded access into the presence of his or her holy God and loving Father because Christ died. In claiming this, the letter to the Hebrews is only stating propositionally what the Gospels had demonstrated visually. When Christ was crucified, the curtain in the temple that separated the Holy Place from the Most Holy Place was ripped in two,[49] providing all who trust in him with unhindered access to the presence of God. No longer would this privilege be reserved for the high priest and his annual encounter in a smoke-filled room. From Good Friday on – the Christians' great Day of Atonement – all God's children have daily and immediate access to him.

However great the celebration of the Day of Atonement, the day of Calvary exceeds it by far. The annual event by which Israel secured cleansing has been replaced by a unique historic event that secured forgiveness for all who seek it. As the great preacher C. H. Spurgeon once proclaimed:

> The blood of Christ, *it is all-sufficient*. There is no case which the blood of Christ cannot meet; there is no sin which it cannot wash away. There is no multiplicity of sin which it cannot cleanse, no aggravation of guilt which it cannot remove.[50]

Jesus is both priest and sacrifice, both the goat who dies to atone and the scapegoat who lives to bear sin away, both the sin offering and the burnt offering. He lived and died in total submission and dedication to God. He removed the defilement of our sin and paid the price for our iniquity. He ripped open the curtain and gave us constant, privileged access into the presence of God. In him our alienation from God because of our sin, and God's distancing himself from us because of his holiness, are overcome. All sin is forgiven and we are reconciled to a holy God. Every aspect of the work of this wonderful, yet complex, Day of Atonement finds its fulfilment in Christ. He is indeed the all-sufficient sacrifice for sin.

---

[49] Matt. 27:51; Mark 15:38; Luke 23:45.

[50] C. H. Spurgeon, *Sermons on the Blood and Cross of Christ*, ed. C. T. Cook (London: Marshall, Morgan & Scott, 1961), pp. 112–113.

E. The manual of holiness: enacting God's word (17:1 – 26:46)

Leviticus 17:1–16

14. God's word about lifeblood

Chapter 17 is a bridge. It connects the first part of Leviticus, which is mainly concerned with ritual matters, to the second part, mainly concerned with ethical matters. The former has to do with holiness within the sanctuary, and the latter with holiness outside the sanctuary. This chapter shares the earlier agenda and continues to show an interest in matters to do with sacrifice and with blood. But it begins to open the door to the sorts of issues that will increasingly occupy the attention of the chapters that follow, as, for example, when it focuses on what the Israelites do 'in the open fields' (5).

Chapters 17–26 are often referred to as 'the Holiness Code'.[1] Their central theme is found in 19:2: 'Be holy because I, the LORD your God, am holy.'[2] The absence of any specific language about holiness in chapter 17 has led some to deduce that it does not belong in the Holiness Code but should be seen as the conclusion of the section on matters of sacrifice and purity. But the absence of explicit vocabulary is unimportant where the implicit meaning is clearly about living a holy life.

We should be wary of a preoccupation with slicing the document into sections in the misguided belief that if we can do so properly we shall somehow unlock its message more clearly. Scholars have too often used this analytical approach as an excuse for consigning difficult sayings to a position of secondary importance, if not to the waste bin completely. Even if the book of Leviticus was originally composed of independent sections,

---

[1] For details see the Introduction above, pp. 5, 8.

[2] The command also comes in 11:44, 45; 20:7, 26.

it comes to us in canonical Scripture as an integrated document, the whole of which demands our attention. In any case, chapter 17 brilliantly spans the concerns of the earlier and the later chapters of Leviticus and serves as a wonderful means of moving the agenda gently along to the next items of business.

Moses remains God's mouthpiece, but his words are now addressed to the whole community without distinction: from his brother Aaron, the high priest, to the lowliest member of Israel (2). The commands even take in the non-Israelites who have chosen to live among them (8, 10, 13, 15). Holiness was a matter that embraced them all and was not just of interest to the religious professionals who worked in the tabernacle. Every member of the Israelite community was called upon to live by a distinct code of ethics that would set them apart *from* their neighbours and *to* their God. The demands of holiness are egalitarian.

1. The actions it prohibits (17:1–16)

Like many subsequent parts of the Holiness Code, this chapter seems heavy on negatives. But the 'thou shalt nots' of Leviticus have a gloriously positive purpose and are designed, not to suppress life, but to release it in all its fullness. They set before Israel a vision of an ideal way of living, which they are encouraged to adopt.

The chapter breaks down into five paragraphs, all of which have something to say about the use of blood. The first four begin with the words *any Israelite* (3, 8, 10, 13) while the fifth paragraph begins with a more inclusive formula and is simply addressed to *anyone* (15). In fact, the second, third and fourth laws are just as inclusive as the fifth and mention resident aliens alongside Israelites in their opening words (8, 10, 13). Non-Israelites are included so that the distinctive lifestyle of Israel would not be compromised. To make exceptions to this lifestyle, for whatever reason, would result in Israel's holy way of life being undermined and would before long end in the total erosion of their particular calling as God's covenant people. While safeguards were put in place to ensure that resident aliens were not exploited, those who chose to live within the boundaries of Israel were, for the most part, expected to abide by the Israelite way of life.

These laws prohibit five different specific actions in relation to blood: two of these pertain to sacrificial offerings and three of them pertain to the blood of dead animals. We shall examine them using these two main concerns as our framework.

a. Random sacrifices forbidden (17:1–9)

The first action that is forbidden is the slaughtering of any *ox, lamb* or *goat* – domestic livestock that were the principal animals offered in the sacrifices – anywhere except *in front of the tabernacle of the* Lord (4). The command is repeated twice in different forms, first in verses 1–7 and then again in verses 8–9. It is backed up by the most serious penalties invoked against those who contravened it: *that person shall be considered guilty of bloodshed; they have shed blood and must be cut off from their people* (4).[3]

To us, this rule is as vague as it is demanding. Was it prohibiting the slaughter of any domestic animal unless it was offered in sacrifice to God? Or was it merely forbidding the slaughter of an animal for use as a sacrifice except at the tabernacle, so ruling out the offering of sacrifices to other gods?

If the former, it would mean that families could not slaughter their animals to eat whenever they chose, and it would limit the slaughtering of all meat to the occasion of a fellowship offering. Some[4] take it in this first sense, and argue that it has to do with controlling the killing of animals that were considered to be more valuable as a source of milk and for their reproductive abilities than as food.

But most see it, justifiably, as prohibiting the killing of animals for use in idol worship, and as banning the offering of sacrifices wherever a worshipper fancied. The context, and the use of the word *šāḥaṭ* ('to slit the throat'), suggest that it is ritual slaughter, not ordinary butchering, that is in view. This would leave people free to kill domestic animals for their own tables whenever they wished, as Deuteronomy 12:15 gives them permission to do in locations other than at the Tent. And, as Hartley points out, if this law banned the butchering of all edible domesticated animals except as a sacrifice, these rules would have been grossly inadequate, since they do not cover questions of what to do, for example, in the case of animals with a defect, which would not have been acceptable in sacrificial worship.[5]

---

[3] The penalty was as serious as that for murder. On the meaning of *cut off* see p. 245.

[4] Grabbe, *Oxford*, p. 102; Milgrom, *Leviticus 17 – 22*, pp. 1452–1454.

[5] Hartley, pp. 270–271.

This law teaches, then, that people who offer pagan sacrifices *shall be considered guilty of bloodshed* (4). This verdict seems to assume a well-established principle rather than being of any obvious relevance to the issue being discussed. To understand it we need to trace the background to the law. God abhors the shedding of blood and says that anyone who sheds it will be culpable and liable to severe punishment (4). God's hatred of bloodshed was made known in his covenant with Noah in Genesis 9:3–6.[6] There, he gave Noah and his family permission to kill 'everything that lives and moves about' so that they could eat, but insisted that the blood be drained from the slaughtered animals before they consumed them. God said he would require 'an accounting' for the eating of any meat that still contained blood, and put drinking it on a par with shedding the blood of a human being. Blood assumes this position of importance because it is symbolic of life, as will be stated in Leviticus 17:11. The argument in Leviticus 17 is something of a shorthand argument but amounts to saying that the illegitimate slaughtering of sacrificial animals is like shedding the blood of a human being and so deserves the same penalty. 'As is often the case,' Levine explains, 'biblical statements draw on other, preceding verses, lending a different nuance to traditional language.'[7]

In addition to the need to respect blood, another reason for this prohibition is made explicit when the law is restated in verses 5–7. It bans Israel from offering sacrifices randomly. Sacrifices are not to be offered *in the open fields* or *to goat idols* or demons.[8] 'Do-it-yourself spirituality' was to have no place in Israel. Once people began to set up their own forms of sacrifice, and perform them when, where and how they liked, elements of pagan worship from surrounding cultures would soon be imported to 'improve' the liturgy of Israel. No doubt it would be argued that the 'improvements' were harmless or even necessary for the emotional satisfaction of the worshippers (while in reality probably satisfying their baser instincts). But God does not mince his words. Since the incident of the golden calf (Exod. 32:1–35), the folly of worshipping idols should have been seared into Israel's consciousness. To commit idolatry was not to be compared to committing an unfortunate, but forgivable, breach of social

---

[6] Arguably it can be traced even further back, to Gen. 4:8–16.

[7] Levine, p. 113.

[8] See discussion of Azazel on pp. 179–180. Kaiser, p. 1118, suggests that the worship of these 'hairy ones' evolved into a belief in mystical creatures that were half human and half goat, the worship of which flourished in Lower Egypt. See Josh. 24:14.

etiquette. Rather, it was to be compared to sexual promiscuity; it was to *prostitute* oneself spiritually (7), to turn one's back on a faithful and powerful God and sell oneself to gods that would fail.[9]

The first time the prohibition is introduced it is tied to the fellowship offering (5), but on the second occasion (8–9) it is connected to the other sacrifices as well. No blood sacrifice was to be offered other than at *the entrance to the tent of meeting*, where it would be offered in the proper manner *to the LORD* and not in an improper manner to another deity. The regulations about sacrifices had reinforced the importance of approaching God with care over and over again. But nothing that concerns the worship of a holy God is left to chance. What was implicit in the earlier regulations – that only the prescribed forms of sacrifice should be offered and only in the prescribed place – is now made explicit. Nothing is left in doubt. The Israelites have no possible excuse for any disobedience in which they might engage.

b. Eating blood forbidden (17:10–16)

The next group of prohibitions focuses on the practice of eating blood – a practice that was common among other peoples in the ancient world.[10] No-one who lived within the borders of Israel was permitted to eat or drink the blood of a dead animal, again on pain of the most serious of penalties. The general prohibition is set out in verses 10–12 and is then amplified by two additional and more specific paragraphs.

The first specific application is to animals that had been killed in a hunt (13–14). The blood of these animals was as precious as the blood of those whose throats were slit in sacrifice or that were butchered for the family's dinner table. So, no blood was to be eaten.

The second specific application, in verses 15–16, has a slightly different remit from the previous ones, and announces an absolute ban on the eating of animals found dead either from natural causes or because they had been killed by a wild animal. The infringing of this rule, however, was

---

[9] Some argue that these regulations are designed to ensure that worship is centralized. But the basic contrast is not between a central sanctuary and dispersed sanctuaries but between sanctuary worship and pagan worship; Demarest, p. 202, and Wenham, p. 243. Wenham also points out that these regulations assume that the community is small and gathered around the Tent and that meat-eating is a luxury. Scholars who assume they come from a much later period have to solve all sorts of problems to make them fit a time when the population of Israel was dispersed throughout the land and able to enjoy a more luxurious diet.

[10] Hartley, p. 273.

only a minor offence and meant that the guilty persons would be unclean until the evening, when they would have to undergo the washing of their bodies and their clothes to attain a state of cleanness again.

The reason given for the taboo on eating blood is because of what blood symbolizes. The statement is repeated that *the life of a creature is in the blood* (11; cf. 14). The connection between life and blood seems obvious. Loss of blood leads to loss of life – blood shed is life terminated – so it is natural to assume that blood carries the essence of life in it. God has determined that it is by the means of shed blood that atonement should be made. It is not, therefore, for human beings to seek to make use of blood for other purposes or to appropriate it for themselves. It belongs to the Lord alone.[11]

2. The principles it proclaims

From these apparently arcane regulations, four important, timeless principles stand out.

a. The uniqueness of God

The Holiness Code endorses the Ten Commandments in a variety of ways. These regulations begin at the beginning and remind Israel that they were to have no other gods besides God (Exod. 20:3). He alone had delivered them from Egypt and made them his people, and he alone was to be the God to whom they were bound by a covenant commitment.

Consequently, they were to offer sacrifices only at his sanctuary, and not to set up altars elsewhere and offer devotion or sacrifices to any other so-called gods. The existence of idols as living beings was commonly assumed. (Even that, however, was called into question by Israel's belief and experience. For them there was but one God, from whom everything came and for whose glory all were to live.[12]) Yet, even if they actually existed, idols certainly had no power and were totally devoid of grace. Therefore, it was both a gross insult to the Lord and an act of gross absurdity on the part of the worshipper to offer sacrifices to them. It would be like forsaking the good and faithful blessings of marriage for the titillating but unsatisfying experience of a one-night stand. What good

---

[11] Alec Motyer, *Look to the Rock* (Leicester: IVP, 1996), pp. 52–53.

[12] 1 Cor. 8:6. See more widely Paul's argument in vv. 4–13.

would it do them? It could only lead them into fresh forms of bondage and sorrow, as the references to Molek in the succeeding chapters illustrate (18:21; 20:2–5). God deserved their undivided and undeviating loyalty. He was not merely to come first in their affection but was to be the sole recipient of it.

b. The sanctity of life

The root of the prohibition against shedding blood, as we have seen, is to be found in the covenant with Noah, where the treatment of the blood of animals and the blood of humans are closely connected. The intention of the restriction on eating blood in that covenant was partly so that life, and especially human life, could flourish once again on earth after the near-total destruction of the flood.

Those who regard the regulations of Leviticus 17 as forbidding the Israelites to kill any animal except in the context of a fellowship meal see them as underlining this message about the sanctity of life and as illustrating God's desire that animal life should prosper. But one does not have to adopt this narrow interpretation to see the whole tenor of these regulations as reinforcing the truth that life is sacred in God's eyes. While God may have given permission for humans to kill animals in order to eat, his permission is severely qualified so as to restrain people's blood lust and to prevent their appetite for blood from growing.

At the council of Jerusalem, in a judgment that reflects the connection Leviticus 17 makes between idolatry and the shedding of blood, the early Christians maintained the same attitude of reverence for life. In the very letter that the leaders of the early church wrote to publicize a relaxation of many of the ceremonial laws of purity, Gentile Christians were instructed still to avoid eating blood.[13]

The regulations of Leviticus 17 relate to the killing of animals, but, given the origin of the taboo, this cannot be divorced from the killing of humans. With the exception of occasions when God commands people to kill others for judicial reasons or legitimate reasons of warfare, God alone has the right to shed human blood and take life. All life bears the hallmark of sacredness.

Life is sacred because all humans bear God's image and, as John Wyatt, Emeritus Professor of Neonatal Paediatrics at University College London,

---

[13] Acts 15:29. Kaiser, p. 1121, thinks the restriction is still binding on Christians.

has written, 'any being made in God's image deserves a range of responses: wonder, respect, empathy, and above all *protection*: protection from abuse, from harm and from manipulation'.[14] The bearing of God's image means more than that all humans have dignity. It also means that all humans belong to God and are his possession. So someone who extinguishes a life is accountable to God on two counts: such a person has both desecrated God's image and fatally damaged God's property. We hold life as a sacred trust from him.

The sanctity of life is called into question today in a frightening number of ways: from the ethical discussions provoked by advances in biotechnology, through the widespread demand for freedom of choice, to the acts of global terrorists. Assaults on the sanctity of life come in a number of guises, some of which have the appearance of being respectable medical philosophy. Ronald Dworkin, for example, argues for the primacy of the right of individuals to decide for themselves what they do with their lives, or with the lives of embryos planted within their wombs.[15] Humans are the only ones that matter; God, the creator, is irrelevant. And Peter Singer, to quote a second example, argues that we should drop the pretence that all lives are of equal value, since this traditional religious view is unable to cope with the dilemmas of modern medicine, and recognize that some lives are more valuable than others. Medicine should treat only those who give evidence of a worthwhile life, defined in terms of relationships and a reasonable capability for physical, social and mental interaction.[16] On this argument, not only are abortion and euthanasia quite acceptable, but a number of mentally ill or severely incapacitated people might find their lives prematurely terminated.

Faced with these challenges, which are based on reductionist and Darwinian views of human beings, it is important that we not only reassert God's bottom line – that all human life is sacred – but that we put forward a fuller, meaningful Christian response. John Wyatt confidently asserts the Christian view of the sanctity of life because it is true and because it fits with reality, because it works and is beneficial for individuals and the community, and because it feels right and accords with human intuition.

---

[14] John Wyatt, *Matters of Life and Death* (Leicester: IVP, 1998), p. 192.

[15] The view is expounded in Ronald Dworkin, *Life's Dominion* (London: Harper & Row, 1995), p. 239. For a discussion of the varying positions see Wyatt, op. cit., pp. 36–47.

[16] Peter Singer, *Rethinking Life and Death* (Oxford: Oxford University Press, 1995), summarized in Wyatt, op. cit., pp. 43–45.

Building on this basis he then develops his response to those who argue like Peter Singer, stressing that the Christian perspective 'enshrines a holistic perspective of human identity', provides stability and ensures values throughout the whole of life, promotes social cohesion and mutual respect, provides a basis for a consistent legal framework, fits with widespread human intuition, furnishes motivation for sacrificial caring, and provides a safeguard against abuse and manipulation.[17] In putting forward these views, Wyatt is no armchair philosopher but one who struggled every day in his medical practice with life-and-death decisions and the agonizing tragedy of scarce resources. Yet he believes it to be possible, credible and, indeed, essential to affirm that, since God is the giver of life, all life is sacred.

c. The meaning of blood

Leviticus 17:11 enshrines one of the most important principles in the whole book. It says not only that *the life of a creature is in the blood* but also that God gives it to his people to make *atonement for one's life*. As a result of this gift, forgiveness for sin is possible. The principle enshrined in this verse is that of substitutionary atonement; that is to say, atonement is made by a victim that takes the place of a sinner and sheds its blood in the sinner's stead. 'The wages of sin is death' (Rom. 6:23). So those who sin are bound for death and, since we all sin, that includes us all; death is our inescapable destiny. The only hope is if a ransom were to be offered on our behalf – a life laid down in the place of the life that is spared.

This traditional interpretation has been challenged in recent times by those who wish for a softer view of God and find it unacceptable that he should exact such a price for sin. Milgrom believes that 'the substitutionary theory of sacrifice, based on this verse and championed by so many in the scholarly world, must once and for all be rejected'.[18] Instead he proposes that this verse means that if blood is drained and sprinkled *against the altar of the LORD at the entrance to the tent of meeting* (6), the victim's life will be returned to its creator and atonement will be made. Others see the offering as bringing God a gift of worship in which the life of the animal is set free, rather than its having anything to do with expiation from sin

---

[17] Wyatt, op. cit., pp. 228–230.

[18] Milgrom, *Leviticus 17 – 22*, p. 1477. See full discussion, pp. 1472–1478.

or deliverance from death 'by exchanging one life for another'.[19] Paul Fiddes, for example, writes: 'The idea seems to be that the tainted and unclean life of the offending community is renewed by the pouring out of the fresh life present in the blood of the animal.'[20]

But such arguments seem tendentious – especially for the sacrificial victim. However one seeks to argue it, the pouring out of the sacrificial victim's blood meant that the sacrifice died. With Alan Stibbs, one must conclude that shedding blood does not stand 'for the release of life from the burden of the flesh, but for the bringing to an end of life in the flesh. It is evidence of physical death, not spiritual survival.'[21] And why physical death? Because a holy God exacts the just penalty of death from those who sin unless a substitute is made available, as Nadab and Abihu, among many others, discovered all too tragically.

The new covenant no less than the old is a covenant of blood (1 Cor. 11:25), and it still holds that without the laying down of a life and the shedding of blood there is no forgiveness of sins (Heb. 9:22). But the new covenant does not require the endless offering of blood sacrifices, because the offering of one blood sacrifice, the sacrifice of Christ, the perfect human, is sufficient to cover all our sin. The value of his blood, the blood of a 'lamb without blemish or defect', far exceeds that of all the litres of blood shed on Israel's altars (1 Pet. 1:19). His blood is the redemption price that sets us free from the consequences of sin and the cleansing agent that purifies us from every defilement (1 John 1:7).

In a curious reversal, however, though the people of Israel were forbidden to drink blood, the people of Christ are commanded to do so. For the exchange to be complete, not only has Jesus to take the sinner's place and lay down his life as a ransom, but sinners have to absorb his life so that they may begin to live for God. This is why Jesus said, 'Very truly I tell you, unless you eat the flesh of the Son of Man *and drink his blood*, you have no life in you' (John 6:53, emphasis added). To drink his blood is to assimilate the benefits of his death and infuse every part of our being with his life. The sacrament of communion serves as a regular, enacted reminder of this. Nothing is achieved, however, by mere outward

---

[19] Kaiser, p. 1120.

[20] Paul Fiddes, *Past Event and Present Salvation: The Christian Idea of Atonement* (London: Darton, Longman & Todd, 1989), p. 69.

[21] Alan Stibbs, *The Meaning of the Word 'Blood' in Scripture* (London: Theological Students Fellowship, 1954), p. 11.

observance. It is only as we grasp the meaning of it and participate[22] in Christ by our eating and drinking that the ceremony translates into reality in our lives and produces holy living.

d. The grace of forgiveness

In the battle over the meaning of the statement that *the life of a creature is in the blood* (11), we too often fail to notice the emphasis in the words that follow: *I have given it to you to make atonement for yourselves.* Here is the wonder of God's grace. The blood that is required to release us from our sin is not blood that God exacts from us but blood that he provides for us. From the beginning to the end of Scripture, the message remains the same. God does not require from us what we cannot give, but graciously overcomes our poverty and spares our lives by providing an alternative sacrifice in our place. He did it for Abraham on Mount Moriah, when a ram was provided in place of Isaac, just as Abraham had confidently expected him to do (Gen. 22:1–19, esp. 8, 13–14). As a result, Abraham renamed the place 'The LORD Will Provide' (Gen. 22:14). And he provided for us, at the same location, centuries later, when he supplied his own Son as the ultimate sacrifice of atonement.[23]

The provision of God is nicely balanced with the responsibility of humans. 'Life', God says to his children, 'has been given *to you* so that you can make atonement *for yourselves* on the altar' (11). The atonement did not happen automatically, with no involvement on the part of sinners. They had to bring the gift, identify with it, slaughter it, and offer it to God as a sign of a penitent attitude and of obedient faith. It could not be done by proxy or sacrificed at arm's length. Only with their personal involvement would the benefits of the atoning blood flow into their lives, forgiving their sins. God has provided in abundance, but all to no avail unless we appropriate the gift of his Son by faith.

The five prohibitions in this chapter seem forbidding. They appear to cry out, 'Thou shalt not.' But in reality each of them is an expression of the goodness of God, saving us from the folly of worshipping worthless idols, causing us to value life, even the lives of dead animals, and pointing us to his gracious provision of atoning blood. His prohibitions do not lead us

---

[22] 'Participation' is a key word in Paul's understanding of communion. See 1 Cor. 10:16.

[23] See the comment by C. S. Lewis about those who objected to the doctrine of hell, in *The Problem of Pain* (London: Fontana, 1957), p. 116.

to the restricted lives of prisoners but set our feet free in a spacious place (Pss 18:19; 31:8). They do not impair life, but enhance it (Ps. 119:32, 37). They do not kill joy, but release it (Ps. 119:35). For his laws are laws of liberty and life (Ps. 119:45; Jas 2:12).

Leviticus 18:1–30

15. God's word about family health

Within two chapters of reaching the heights of the Day of Atonement, Leviticus finds itself dealing with matters that are more usually associated with the gutter press; matters like incest, adultery, homosexuality and bestiality. With even a cursory glance at chapter 18, which covers these issues, the command 'Do not' leaps out.[1] Beyond this, words such as 'dishonour', 'wickedness', 'defile', 'perversion' and 'detestable' seem to abound. No wonder contemporary liberal society considers this chapter a relic from the past, which is best forgotten and which is injurious to the values of personal liberty and choice that we prize so highly today. The chapter has provoked the special ire of those who champion the cause of gay rights.

To read these laws in this negative way, however, is misguided. To do so wholly misconstrues the intention of God's words and gives a distorted surface reading that ignores the direction finders within it that give us our bearings when we come to interpret it. God is not a puritanical killjoy, out to prevent his people from enjoying themselves, but rather the reverse. As the one who created humans to be sexual beings, he knows the power of the sexual drive and its ability to bring happiness or to breed misery. He wants to save his people from experiencing distress and to establish those foundations on which healthy families can be built and from which healthy communities can spring. Turn the 'do nots' into 'dos' and it will soon become apparent what an ugly, destructive and damaging society would be created if God's word were to be ignored.

---

[1] 'Do not' occurs nineteen times in the NIV translation of this chapter.

1. Israel's vocation (18:1–5)

Before listing the various sexual practices that will be harmful to family life, God first explains through Moses the basis for his addressing Israel in the way he does. A threefold call is wrapped up in the opening paragraph, the threads of which are picked up later in the chapter.

a. The call to be loyal (18:2, 4)

The call begins as God reminds his people who he is, using the words, *I am the* LORD *your God.*[2] The phrase, or its shorter version, *I am the* LORD,[3] reads to us as if God is asserting his authority right at the start and, given that the phrase is repeated a further five times in the chapter (4, 5, 6, 21, 30), doing so in a heavy-handed manner. It sounds as if he is saying, 'I'm the boss; do what I say, or else . . .' But that is not the intent of these words. In addressing his people like this, God is using his personal name and speaking with them out of a committed and intimate relationship. He is using the name that is associated primarily with his promise to deliver Israel from Egypt.[4] It communicates not so much his authority and right to command, as his 'incomprehensible grace'. He is the God who is faithful to his promises.[5] The title is closely tied to his action in saving his people in the exodus. Beyond that, as Wenham notes, the name is mostly used when Israel is invited to imitate her God, a God who in his very essence is holy.[6]

Here, then, God is using a name that would remind them of the great things he had done for them and the close binding relationship they had entered into in the covenant. It was not a name to crush them by the assertion of overwhelming authority but a name to uplift them by the recollection of overwhelming grace. The same name is used in Exodus 20:2, at the head of the Ten Commandments. His words are not laws to be grudgingly obeyed because God has imposed them on his reluctant people,

---

[2] Milgrom refers to this title of God as the Holiness Code's 'signature seal'. Milgrom, *Leviticus 17 – 22*, p. 1517.

[3] The phrase *I am the* LORD is an English translation of 'I am Yahweh'. Yahweh is the personal name of God and therefore was considered too sacred to pronounce. Consequently, it was usually replaced by the word *'ǎdōnāy*, meaning 'Lord', which accounts for the translation in our English texts. The addition of *your God* emphasizes that Yahweh is divinely sovereign over Israel. The phrase occurs most often in the Holiness Code of Leviticus, Isaiah 40 – 55 and Ezekiel. See further Hartley, pp. 291–293.

[4] See, e.g., its early use in Exod. 6:6–8.

[5] Hartley, p. 292.

[6] Wenham, p. 251.

but principles to live by as a response to God's saving action in their lives, in the knowledge that obeying them will lead to a fuller and more wholesome way of life.

First, then, in the giving of these regulations about sexual practices, there is a call to Israel to be loyal to the gracious God who set them free, by being like him.

b. The call to be different (18:3)

Loyalty to God inevitably results in being distinct from one's neighbours. So Israel is told: *You must not do as they do in Egypt, where you used to live*, and then, *you must not do as they do in the land of Canaan, where I am bringing you* (3). The need to reject the seductiveness of past lifestyles in Egypt, and to resist the temptation they will face in the future to assimilate to the lifestyles of the occupants of the Promised Land, is underlined with the blunt command, *Do not follow their practices* (3).

How, then, did they live in Egypt and Canaan and what were the practices that Israel was to avoid at all costs? In both nations sex was deified. Knight sums up the situation as far as Egypt is concerned: 'Egypt was a pagan nation. In Moses' day the people worshipped some eighty different gods. Some of these were manifestations of human violence, nationalistic chauvinism, or lust for power; others again were the apotheosis of mere sexual lust.'[7] Egypt was recognized for its licentiousness, and it was well known that incest was practised by the Egyptian royal family, where brothers regularly married their sisters.[8] Canaan was famed for its encouragement of homosexuality and bestiality,[9] and the practices condemned in this chapter[10] were enshrined in the fertility rites in which temple prostitutes (both male and female) incited their deities to grant fertility to the land by performing sexual acts in their presence.

The vocation of Israel was to live a different sort of life, one in which all people were treated with respect rather than used merely as objects to gratify uncontrolled sexual lust. The people of Israel were called to channel their sexual drives within the boundaries of faithful marriage as God had decreed, in the sure and certain knowledge that it would be more

---

[7] Knight, p. 103.

[8] Milgrom, *Leviticus 17 – 22*, p. 1518; Wenham, p. 251.

[9] Milgrom, *Leviticus 17 – 22*, p. 1520.

[10] Levine, p. 118, thinks there is little evidence for the widespread practice of incest in either Egypt or Canaan, but confirms that the other practices that are condemned were common.

beneficial for them to do so than to live promiscuously. To live in line with God's commands would reflect God's life-creating purity rather than the destructive and untamed powers of chaos.

Their vocation was also to trust in God – a God who was willing and able to look after his people without their having to resort to frantic fertility ceremonies with a view to twisting his arm to provide them with good harvests.

Israel had been set free to be holy.

c. The call to life (18:5)

The call of Israel was a call to abundant life.[11] Obedience to God's commands would result, not in poverty, death or destruction, but in a fullness of life denied to those who lived by their own laws instead of by God's word.[12] God promised to look on those who obeyed the terms of his covenant with favour (26:9) and to bestow on them the blessings of peace and prosperity. Rich and fruitful lives would be theirs. By contrast, the story of Adam and Eve's expulsion from the Garden of Eden served as a standing reminder of the death-inducing and destruction-bearing results of failing to live as God commanded (Gen. 3:1–24).

Some might wish to object to God's right to say how his people should live, but it should really come as no surprise that the God who made us knows better than we ourselves know how we should function in his world. It should not surprise us that obeying the maker's instructions is likely to bring the best out of us and lead us to live life to the full.

2. Sexual regulations (18:6–23)

'As a result of the all-pervasive presence of sin,' writes Stanley Grenz,

> our sexuality, which was intended to be a vehicle for expressing the nature of God, can easily be twisted. Sexual passion, designed as the foundation for the bonding that leads to community, can be misdirected and expressed in unhealthy and damaging ways.[13]

---

[11] This verse is quoted in Ezek. 20:11, 21, where Ezekiel reiterates the same message: obedience leads to life; disobedience leads to destruction.

[12] Levine, p. 119, cites the rabbinic interpretation of this verse, 'That one may *live* by them, not that one should *die* because of them.'

[13] Stanley Grenz, *Sexual Ethics: A Biblical Perspective* (Louisville, KY: Westminster John Knox, 1997; Carlisle: Paternoster, 1998), p. 53.

Aware of this, God sets some limits on our sexual expression in order to prevent others, especially those who are close to us in the family, from being hurt and damaged by our lack of control. Having a sexual drive is like being in charge of a car; we need to know how to handle it if we are to avoid causing mayhem. As a powerful river needs banks to keep it on its course and prevent it from ruinously flooding what is around it, so our sexual drive needs strong boundaries if it is not to cause untold misery in the lives of those around us.

a. Forbidden sexual practices in the family (18:6–19)

Verse 6 serves as an introduction to the first set of sexual actions that are proscribed. The command that *no-one is to approach any close relative to have sexual relations* essentially forbids incest. Literally, the words say that no-one is 'to come near anyone of his own flesh to uncover naked-ness'.[14] Except between a man and his wife, sexual intercourse within the close family is vetoed.

What follows is a list of the particular relationships that are out of bounds so that people have a clearer definition of who might count as a *close relative*.[15] The list functions like the table of affinity in the marriage laws of the UK. The people mentioned in the list as being within the forbidden zone are a man's mother (7) or stepmother (8); sister or half-sister (9, 11); granddaughter (10); aunt, on either side or by marriage (12–14); daughter-in-law (15); sister-in-law (16); and stepdaughter or step-granddaughter (17). Curiously, a man's own daughter is not mentioned in the list, but the prohibition on sex with one's daughter should go without saying and is in any case ruled out by other laws; so its absence here cannot be taken to mean that an incestuous relationship between a man and his daughter is condoned.[16] The prohibition on sexual relations with children is particularly relevant to our contemporary concern about child abuse.

The reason given for banning these sexual relationships is that they involve people who, as we would say, are our own flesh and blood.[17]

---

[14] Levine, p. 119.

[15] The rules are written from a cultural perspective where the male head of household was dominant, and therefore do not include all forms of incest that are relevant today, such as that between a brother and a sister. The principle behind these laws is undoubtedly intended to prohibit all incestuous relationships.

[16] Gen. 19:30–38 records Lot's daughters as sleeping with him, as a result of which Moab and Ben-Ammi were born. That the liaisons resulted in giving birth to the fathers of the Moabites and the Ammonites, who proved a perpetual thorn in Israel's side, is intended as a warning.

[17] Cf. Wenham, p. 255.

Marriage creates close blood relationships vertically, both up and down the generations; upwards towards parents and downwards towards children. It also creates a close set of intimate relationships horizontally, as a man marries into his wife's family. To abuse the closeness of any of these relationships in order to satisfy one's sexual needs is dishonouring all round. It dishonours the Lord through disobedience. It dishonours the perpetrator of the act by bringing shame on him for his unfaithfulness. It dishonours the woman who has been violated. It also dishonours the one whose wife, daughter or sister she is. Wives and children were not seen in the culture of the time as discrete individuals, but as extensions of the man to whom they belonged, so to violate a woman was inevitably to violate her husband as well. (The notion is not altogether absent even in our culture of advanced individualism; to hurt my son is still to hurt me.)

This is brought out better by the NRSV's more earthy translation than by the more prudish NIV translation. The dishonour involved was more than a mere lack of respect. To commit any of these forbidden acts was to 'uncover [a woman's] nakedness',[18] and since these women were already bound in a 'one-flesh' relationship of some sort with someone else, to uncover her nakedness was tantamount to uncovering his nakedness. It was to violate the sanctity of a 'one-flesh' relationship that had already been formed.

When a man commits incest with his granddaughter, he is said to be uncovering his own nakedness and lacking respect for his own sexual integrity (10). Why is he not said to be uncovering his son's nakedness? The reason is that in the patriarchal context of the day the grandfather would remain the head of the household until he died, and would continue to rule over his son even after his son had married and become a father himself. So the shame devolved on the grandfather's own head.[19]

Gordon Wenham sums up the basic rules like this: 'a man may not marry any woman who is a close blood relation, or any woman who has become a close relative through a previous marriage to one of the man's close blood relations'.[20]

One exception to these regulations needs to be noted, and that concerns what is called Levirate marriage, mentioned in Deuteronomy 25:5–10.

---

[18] 'To uncover nakedness' is a reference not to nudity but to having sexual intercourse.

[19] Hartley, p. 295.

[20] Wenham, p. 255.

Leviticus 18:16 forbids sexual relations with *your brother's wife*. But if the brother died and had not produced a son, it became the responsibility of his surviving brother to have sexual intercourse with the widow in order that the name of the dead brother might be carried on. The prohibition in Leviticus assumes that the brother is still alive.

Two clauses are appended to this section on prohibited sexual behaviour within the family. The first forbids a man from marrying his *wife's sister as a rival wife* (18). This action should in any case have been proscribed by the previous regulations, but even so, the practice was not unknown. The story of Jacob amply illustrates the folly of marrying sisters and is a commentary on the reference to rivalry in this verse (Gen. 29:14 – 30:24). Equally, the briefer story of Hannah, whose distress at her childlessness was made harder to bear because of the fertility of Elkanah's other wife, illustrates the harmfulness of having rival wives (1 Sam. 1:1–20).

The second appendix prohibits a man from having *sexual relations* with his wife *during the uncleanness of her monthly period* (19). This rule has already been covered in our discussion of the purity regulations of 15:19–23.

In a close-knit society like Israel, it was essential for the continuing physical health of the nation, as well as the continuing emotional health of the family, that the law forbade incest.[21] Inbreeding would have soon led to physical debility as well as creating a multitude of arguments and jealousies in the dynamics of the nuclear family. The story of Amnon and Tamar in 2 Samuel 13 provides all too tragic an account of the perils of incest.

b. Forbidden sexual practices outside the family (18:20–23)

When the camera, as it were, draws back from focusing narrowly on the family and uses a wider-angle lens, four other sexual practices are caught in its eye and are forbidden. They are adultery (20); the sacrificing of children (21); homosexuality (22); and bestiality (23).

i. Adultery

The condemnation of adultery was plain in the Ten Commandments (Exod. 20:14; Deut. 5:18). Adultery is defined in terms of having sexual

---

[21] Harrison, p. 189, provides evidence of the detrimental effects on the health of children born as a result of incestuous relationships. M. A. Swann, 'Incest', in *NDCEPT*, p. 480, lists the negative psychological impact of incest on the victim as including traumatized sexuality, stigmatization, a sense of betrayal, and powerlessness.

relations with another man's wife, and the person who commits it is said to lack judgment and to be set on a course of self-destruction (Prov. 6:32).

The condemnation of adultery is maintained in the New Testament[22] but intensified in two ways. First, Jesus moves beyond the outward act to draw attention to the inward attitude of lust that leads to it (Matt. 5:27–30). Lust is unbridled sexual desire that denies the humanity of its quarry and treats its object as a thing. Second, the rest of the New Testament intensifies the prohibition by broadening its scope to include sexual intercourse not only with a married woman but with any woman outside of marriage.[23]

The vocation of God's people, now as then, is fulfilled not simply by avoiding actions that are wrong, but by living wholesome lives that are full of goodness. Hence Paul wrote to the Thessalonians that 'God did not call us to be impure, but to live a holy life' (1 Thess. 4:7). Hebrews similarly encourages believers not only to keep 'the marriage bed . . . pure, for God will judge the adulterer and all the sexually immoral', but to hold marriage itself in high honour (Heb. 13:4).

ii. Child sacrifice

The next item on the list of prohibited sexual behaviour outside the family says, *Do not give any of your children to be sacrificed to Molek, for you must not profane the name of your God. I am the LORD* (21). In our present context it is ironic that this prohibition should follow so hard on the heels of the prohibition of adultery. Popular opinion today would regard the regulation on adultery as unnecessarily restrictive. 'We should be able to do what we like with our own bodies,' it is said. 'Morality is my private concern. Who gives anyone the right, let alone God, to dictate how I should live?' But the very same society that manifests an addiction to almost unbridled sexual licence also manifests a new Puritanism about the treatment of children. In contemporary (early 2000s) Western society the paedophile occupies the place reserved in seventeenth-century New England for witches. Strong, even obsessive, measures have been put in place to ensure the physical, sexual and emotional protection of children.[24] So this command

---

[22] Matt. 19:9, 18; Mark 7:21; 10:11–12, 19; Luke 16:18; 18:20; Rom. 2:22; 13:9; Rev. 2:22.

[23] Eph. 5:3; Col. 3:5; 1 Thess. 4:3–8; Heb. 13:4.

[24] Elsewhere the situation is different. On the day I wrote this, a story appeared in *The Times* (of London) reporting the tragedy of a father's strangling his son on the advice of a Hindu holy man in order to combat the curse he believed was on his marriage. *The Times*, 3 March 2004.

would be as warmly applauded by contemporary society as its predecessor would be fiercely derided.

The particular form of fatal child abuse that is prohibited by Leviticus is the offering of one's children to Molek. Molek, who is mentioned on several occasions in the Old Testament,[25] was a detestable god of the Ammonites. His cult, located at the foot of what was to become the Temple Mount in the Valley of Ben Hinnom, was popular among the people, and even Solomon was enticed to take part in it in his old age. Molek's name, Budd suggests, means 'the king of shame'.[26] The rituals associated with his name were certainly shameful and involved the sacrificing of children, probably by requiring them to pass through fire to their deaths.[27] Budd picks up the similarity of terminology between this and the previous verse and points out that 'to give one's seed' to a woman in an adulterous relationship was as serious an offence as 'to give one's seed to Molech'.[28]

While not strictly a sexual action, it was sensuous behaviour that hovered on the borders of sexual behaviour. The reasons it is included in this list are because its practice would undermine the well-being of the family and would be detrimental to family survival; and because it was practised by the Canaanites, and Israel's vocation was not to do what they did in Canaan (3). For Israel to engage with the cult of Molek was to *profane the name of your God* (21), because it dragged God's holy name in the muck as far as the surrounding nations were concerned and made him the object of their ridicule.

The practice is not mentioned in the New Testament[29] because by that time the cult of Molek was no longer an issue. But the New Testament does address the way God's people should treat their children. Jesus gave time to children in a way that would have been unheard of among the rabbis, and treated them with an unprecedented respect.[30] Paul twice spoke to fathers about their need not to push their children and 'wind them up', but rather to give them positive encouragement and training in the Lord (Eph. 6:4; Col. 3:21).

---

[25] Lev. 20:2–5; 1 Kgs 11:5, 7, 33; 2 Kgs 23:10, 13; Isa. 57:9; Jer. 32:35; 49:1, 3; Zeph. 1:5. See also Ezek. 23:39.

[26] Budd, p. 259.

[27] For details see Milgrom, *Leviticus 17 – 22*, pp. 1551–1555.

[28] Budd, p. 259.

[29] With the exception of a passing reference in Acts 7:43.

[30] Matt. 19:13–15; Mark 10:13–16; Luke 18:15–17. The statement that 'the kingdom of God belongs to such as these' has nothing to do with sentimental views about the innocence or trustfulness of children. It means that the kingdom of God is open to nobodies and nonentities, which is how children were viewed in Jesus' day.

iii. Homosexuality

The third forbidden sexual practice is that of homosexuality (22).[31] The plain meaning of this verse is that homosexual actions are considered totally unacceptable among God's people. Several factors support this straightforward interpretation. Genesis 1:27–28 and 2:24–25 teach that God's original design was that a man should overcome his isolation through an intimate and binding relationship with a woman and that children would be born through their becoming one flesh. Thus, the fulfilment of personal needs and the blessing of biological fruitfulness can only really be achieved through a committed heterosexual relationship. Homosexual practice clearly flies in the face of the consistent advocacy of heterosexual marriage in Scripture. In the immediate context of Leviticus 18, the purpose of which was to create an environment in which healthy families could flourish, it is easy to see how homosexuality would subvert that aim but hard to see how it would contribute to it. Homosexual partners are, by biological definition, unable to procreate. The rest of the Bible speaks with one voice in reiterating the condemnation of homosexual practice (or, at least, has been thought to do so until very recently), in the few but varied places where it is mentioned, which span a wide range of cultures and times, in both the Old and New Testaments. The chief references in addition to this passage are Genesis 19:1–29; Leviticus 20:13; Judges 19:1–30; Romans 1:18–32; 1 Corinthians 6:9–11; 1 Timothy 1:9–10. Later Judaism consistently maintained an attitude of abhorrence to homosexual acts.[32] Homosexual activity, then, seems taboo for God's people of any era, including our own, or under either covenant.

But this verse, together with Leviticus 20:13,[33] has recently become the storm centre of the debate about human rights and equal opportunities. A vast number of people today find it offensive that matters that they

---

[31] I am aware of the acutely sensitive nature of this issue and the pastoral complexities this topic creates, especially in the current climate. Space does not permit as full an exploration of these issues as one might wish. Our task is to expound the message of Leviticus, in which the prohibition on homosexuality is one issue among many. For further consideration, refer to Stanley Grenz, *Welcoming but Not Affirming* (Louisville, KY: Westminster John Knox, 1998), and Thomas E. Schmidt, *Straight and Narrow? Compassion and Clarity in the Homosexual Debate* (Downers Grove, IL, and Leicester: IVP, 1995).

[32] Robin Scroggs, *The New Testament and Homosexuality* (Philadelphia: Fortress, 1983), pp. 66–98. He concludes (p. 97) that later Judaism considers homosexual activity to be a vice and that their view of it was uncompromisingly negative.

[33] This verse enjoins the death penalty for this offence. A discussion of the implications of this will be left until chapter 17 below.

consider to belong to people's fundamental identities should be pilloried in this way, especially when such an attitude results in those who adopt this pattern of sexual expression finding themselves subject to discrimination. Most simply regard the Bible as an irrelevant relic of a bygone age that no longer has any authority in the modern world.

Others, who want to support the legitimacy of same-sex relationships and yet do not want to let go of the Bible altogether, sometimes adopt the strategy of taking this text, and other relevant texts, and reinterpreting them.[34] So, with regard to the Leviticus prohibitions, some emphasize the context in which the prohibition is found. Israel is to set itself against the practices of Canaan, where male temple prostitutes played a significant role.[35] So the real sin, it is said, is not that of homosexuality but that of idolatry. Since homosexuality today no longer plays a role in idolatry (though this is highly questionable, since sex would seem to be a modern idolatry), the prohibition on this form of behaviour need no longer concern us. Others are keen to argue that the prohibition on homosexuality belongs to the ceremonial law rather than to the moral law, and that since the ceremonial law has been abolished, this particular law need no longer exercise authority over us. Milgrom stresses that what these rules have in common is a concern for 'procreation within a stable family', and concludes, by a giant leap of logic, that if this is correct, 'a consolatory and compensatory remedy is at hand for Jewish gays (non-Jews . . . are not subject to these laws): if gay partners adopt children, they do not violate the *intent* of the prohibition'.[36]

All these recent interpretations, however, seem like special pleading and fly in the face of the obvious meaning of these texts. If the purpose of the Levitical regulations is to bolster family life and create a stable environment in which children can be born and nurtured, it naturally

---

[34] The main revisionist interpretations are: (1) Gen. 19:1–29 is taken to be about a breach of the laws of hospitality rather than the laws of sexuality; (2) Rom. 1:18–32 is interpreted as referring, not to what is unnatural from creation or in general, but to what is unnatural for the individual involved; and (3) 1 Cor. 6:9–11 and 1 Tim. 1:9–10 are said to condemn not homosexuality in general but only particular forms that involve passive partners or (especially) male prostitutes. Among the huge literature in this area a popular version of this position can be found in Michael Vasey, *Strangers and Friends: A New Exploration of Homosexuality and the Bible* (London: Hodder & Stoughton, 1995), pp. 124–138. For rebuttals of these interpretations, see not only the books by Grenz and Schmidt mentioned above, but particularly William J. Webb's excellent *Slaves, Women and Homosexuals: Exploring the Hermeneutics of Cultural Analysis* (Downers Grove, IL: IVP, 2001), which gives superb guidance on how to distinguish between issues in Scripture that are locked into one particular culture and those that are transcultural. Webb concludes that, unlike slavery and the secondary role of women, the prohibition on homosexual practice is for all time.

[35] For details see Levine, p. 123.

[36] Milgrom, *Leviticus 17 – 22*, p. 1568.

follows that homosexuality, along with the other practices that are condemned in this chapter, has no place among God's people, because it would prevent them from reaching this goal. The fact that among the Egyptians and the Canaanites homosexual practice had a place within the cult is an additional reason, but not the only one, for the Israelites to abstain from this activity. That their avoidance of homosexuality is partly because they are called to be different is true; but their abstaining from it is primarily because the Lord is their God, and he has made known his desire (and design) that sexual needs should be fulfilled within the bonds of the heterosexual relationship of marriage.

It is sometimes pointed out that lesbianism is not mentioned in these regulations. The observation is correct, but the explanation for its absence is simple. The silence about lesbianism does not mean that it is permitted, but rather that 'the framer of the laws may not have envisaged that such even existed'.[37]

iv. Bestiality

The final forbidden sexual act is that of bestiality, a restriction that is applied to both men and women (23). Given that Israel was an agrarian society, in which people lived cheek by jowl with animals, it would have been all too easy to be tempted in this direction. Ancient literature testifies that such practices were acceptable in other cultures.[38] But to engage in such actions reduces human beings to the level of mere animals themselves, and rides roughshod over the boundaries God has created between his human and his animal creatures.[39]

3. Closing exhortation (18:24–30)

A lengthy exhortation brings the chapter to a close. It does more than sum up what has been said already and broadens our understanding of the laws in important respects.

a. Why?

To the reasons already given at the start of the chapter for behaving in accordance with the will of God, a further reason is now added. The

---

[37] Grabbe, *Oxford*, p. 103.

[38] Hartley, p. 297.

[39] On the question of boundaries see chapter 10 above.

lifestyle of unbridled sexual licence that characterized the Canaanites had become so repulsive that even the land in which they lived was sickened by it. Unless Israelite men exhibited greater respect for women and for children by restraining their sexual passions, they would also defile the land as the Canaanites had done and, God promises them, *it will vomit you out as it vomited out the nations that were before you* (28). Creation itself contains moral vitality, and consequently will reach its limits of tolerance and react to repel such depraved behaviour.

The first fulfilment of these words came as God drove out the tribes that lived in Canaan so that it could be occupied, as promised, by the Israelites. But sadly, there was to be another dreadful fulfilment of these words, a longer-term one, when Israel, having failed to heed the warnings, were themselves driven from the land into exile. God always keeps his promises.

b. Who?

To this point the regulations have clearly been addressed to the Israelites, especially to the male heads of their houses. But in this concluding exhortation two other groups are brought within their ambit.

First, the *nations* are implicated in these rules (28). The tribes of Canaan were not party to the covenant treaty God had entered into with Israel. Even so, God still held them accountable for their sexual and religious behaviour. The absence of any specific covenant that spelt out in detail how God wanted his chosen people to live did not mean they were not answerable to him. There was a creation covenant that set out in general terms how God wanted all his created people to live. They had ignored it completely and therefore would be punished for their sin.

The prophets constantly made the same assumption. Israel may have experienced special grace, and may consequently be subject to more exacting standards, but all nations were (and are) accountable to God for how and what they worshipped, how they treated others, how they used the resources of creation and how they occupied God's world. The prophecies of Isaiah (Isa. 13:1 – 21:17) and of Amos (Amos 1:1 – 2:3), among others, illustrate this.

When Paul wrote to the Romans he took up the same theme at the beginning of his letter (Rom. 1:18 – 2:29). The nations of the world, he explained, were without excuse. They may have lacked the privileges of the Jews and the benefits of the law and the covenant, of which circumcision was a sign, but they knew God well enough to be held accountable for their shameful, sinful behaviour. God had made himself known to them sufficiently: 'Since the creation of the world God's invisible qualities – his eternal power and divine nature – have been clearly seen, being understood from what has been made, so that people are without excuse' (Rom. 1:20). True, they did not have the law, and therefore it would have been unjust for God to judge them by its standards. But God would judge them on the basis both of what they knew and of what their consciences taught them, and he would do so according to the standards of his perfect justice.[40] So, while the sexual disciplines of this chapter may place God's people of the old and new covenants under special obligations, they have inescapable implications for others as well.

Second, *the foreigners residing among you* (26) are brought within the purview of these rules. Foreigners who had chosen to make their homes among the Israelites were under obligation to live according to the moral framework of their hosts (see e.g. 16:29; 17:8, 10, 13). They could not import their morals and argue for living by their own rules on the basis that they were not born as Israelites. That was beside the point. Nothing they did could be permitted to undermine the faith and morality of Israel; therefore, they were required to conform in matters of sexual practice as well as in a range of other matters.

The contemporary world faces the challenge of multiculturalism as never before. Various nations adopt different solutions to the challenges it throws up. Some, such as France, rigorously try to exclude from the public arena anything that would mark people out as distinctive, especially if that marker carries with it an element, real or imagined, of superiority. This leads them, for example, to ban the display of religious symbols in public places. But it is difficult in practice to exclude all such markers, especially where people are required by their religion to display their faith in distinctive dress or by adherence to a strict calendar. In the USA and the UK, the solution is to permit all cultural groups to live alongside one another without discrimination and to allow them to practise their own customs and religion freely and even to speak their own language. But this raises serious questions as to how such diverse subcultures can be integrated into a unity and how a nation can function coherently without fragmenting. In practice, many in the majority, host

---

[40] See particularly Rom. 2:12–16.

culture feel threatened by such a policy. Israel's approach, and it is not alone in adopting it, is to say that those who lived among them should live like them, at least in regard to ethical issues.

c. What if?

What if members of the community did what was forbidden? If the offenders were individuals they were to *be cut off from their people* (29), a penalty explained elsewhere. If, however, the sins were committed on a widespread scale in the nation, then exile would follow.

In spite of this strong warning, God's desire was not to threaten but to woo. His longing was that his people should live in such a way as to enjoy the benefits he desired to shower on them, but if they chose to ignore his warning and disobey the stipulations of his covenant they should know the consequences that would follow.

Unlike the purity regulations outlined in previous chapters, the sexual ethics laid down in this chapter remain in force for the people of God. Nowhere in the New Testament are they abrogated. In so far as they are referred to at all, they are confirmed, and, as in the case of adultery, even intensified. The vocation of God's people is still to avoid sexual immorality (including incest, adultery, fornication, homosexuality and bestiality) and to learn to control their bodies. We are not called to live according to media ethics or popular opinion, but according to the will of the one who loved us and delivered us from the kingdom of darkness. Rejecting this framework of Christian behaviour is to reject, not human wisdom, but God's divine word, the whole purpose of which is to give us life. To live according to God's will helps us avoid doing wrong to others and stops us taking advantage of those who are vulnerable. In summary, 'God did not call us to be impure, but to live a holy life' (1 Thess. 4:7).

What happens if we fail? Paul's stern words to the Thessalonians smack of the warnings given to the Israelites: 'The Lord will punish all those who commit such sins' (1 Thess. 4:6). But there is a difference between the person who struggles courageously against temptation, only to fail, or the person who occasionally fails and is contrite, and one who wilfully disregards God's law. As in ancient Israel, there is always a way back for the sinner who is penitent, through the atoning sacrifice of Christ. But for the one who flagrantly lives in opposition to God's word, there is no hope.

These laws may be addressed specifically to the covenant people of God, but they supply wisdom to any people of any time and any culture.

They are the building blocks out of which strong families can be formed, and where there are strong families there can be healthy societies. The absence of strong families in contemporary society is causing untold personal misery, impairing our children emotionally and costing our society countless millions in the provision of legal, social, psychological and medical support for those who have been damaged by people who have chosen to go their own way rather than God's. Nothing would serve our world better than a return to this ancient wisdom revealed from on high to Moses in the wilderness.

These laws, which seem to be full of 'do nots', are in reality good news because they lead to respect for women, honour between marriage partners, value being placed on relationships, protection for children, regard for boundaries and even care for the land. They result in people reaching their potential as human beings instead of lowering themselves to be mere animals. They are the path we must tread if we are to experience life in all its fullness.

Leviticus 19:1–37

16. God's word about society's welfare

One of the most popular stories of Jesus is the story of the good Samaritan (Luke 10:25–37). But few realize that the crucial statement it illustrates, 'Love your neighbour as yourself', has its origin in Leviticus 19:18.

By any measure, Leviticus 19 is one of the world's greatest ethical charters. Those who question the value of the rest of Leviticus see value here. It covers every one of the Ten Commandments explicitly, except the first, which is assumed throughout and not far beneath the surface of the opening verses.[1] But these commandments are not used to shape the structure of the chapter, which ranges far and wide, mixing major issues with minor ones, ritual issues with ethical ones, and theological issues with behavioural ones. Its almost random character means that any neat analytical framework eludes us. Perhaps it is a deliberate jungle because life is like that – one thing after another. If there is a framework, the chapter can be seen to deal with foundational issues in verses 3–10; friendship issues in verses 11–18; and far-reaching issues in verses 19–37.[2] One reason for supporting this analysis is that the terminology about God changes between these sections, as will be mentioned when each of them is introduced below.

1. The heart of the matter: a call to holy living (19:2)

The previous chapter dealt with ethical issues to do with the family, the fundamental building block of society. This chapter broadens the scope

---

[1] The Ten Commandments are referred to as follows: second, v. 4; third, v. 12; fourth, vv. 3, 30; fifth, v. 3; sixth, v. 16; seventh, vv. 20–22, 29; eighth, vv. 11, 13; ninth, vv. 11, 16; and tenth (less clearly), vv. 17–18. For a full discussion see Milgrom, *Leviticus 17 – 22*, pp. 1600–1602.

[2] Milgrom, ibid., pp. 1586–1587, and Wenham, p. 263.

and is concerned about how people should live to create a healthy society, one in which it would be a pleasure to live and in which its citizens are at ease with one another. The factors that go to make for social harmony are numerous. But the perspective from which this chapter comes is that all individuals have responsibility for the society to which they belong, and by their actions and attitudes they either contribute to its health or destroy it. These instructions from God are addressed to *the entire assembly of Israel* (2). They are not the responsibility of the government, the leadership or the priesthood, but of every member of the community.

Sociologists are increasingly speaking of the need for 'social capital' if a society is to function smoothly.[3] Any society needs more than financial capital and physical infrastructure in order to be prosperous; it also needs quality social relationships and secure networks that share a common set of values. A society that has made a good investment in social capital will not be one in which people are distrustful and suspicious of one another, or one that has to devote endless resources to dealing with crime. It will be comfortable to live in, and its members will enjoy sharing common resources. It will function much more efficiently than those in which the society's social capital is low. The fear of many today is that the social capital of all cultures of advanced individualism is disappearing fast.[4] From one viewpoint Leviticus 19 is about how every member of a community can invest in its social capital.

Yet we must be careful not to advance down this particular road too fast. For though the laws of Leviticus 19 will lead to the creation of a wholesome community and the banking of wonderful reserves of social capital, this is not the chapter's *raison d'être*. The rules are designed first and foremost not as a matter of social convenience but as a matter of divine holiness. They arise from God's invitation to *be holy because I, the LORD your God, am holy*.

'Holiness', explains John Hartley, 'is the quintessential quality of Yahweh. In the entire universe, he alone is intrinsically holy . . . that God is holy means that he is exalted, awesome in power, glorious in appearance, pure in character.'[5] Yet in spite of his separateness, astonishingly, his holiness reaches out and his people on earth are called upon to mirror his

---

[3] See e.g. Robert Putnam, *Bowling Alone* (New York: Simon & Schuster, 2001), pp. 18–24.

[4] For a British exposition see Jonathan Sacks, *The Politics of Hope* (London: Jonathan Cape, 1997), especially pp. 198–209.

[5] Hartley, p. 312.

character. The life of holiness is in essence a life of the imitation of God. This is, as Christopher Wright has remarked, 'quite breathtaking'. Israel's quality of life 'must reflect the very heart of God's character'.[6] It was the same demand that Jesus made of his disciples when he said to them, 'Be perfect, therefore, as your heavenly Father is perfect' (Matt. 5:48). Peter later reiterated the command and encouraged the early Christians to 'be holy in all you do' (1 Pet. 1:15). The call to holiness has never been revoked and still remains the primary call of God's people today.[7]

Holiness was never some abstract, ethereal quality which was remote from the real world. It was always a quality that could be translated into practical daily living and measured by what could be seen on earth.[8] Holiness was also brought within the reach of every member of the community. Holy living involved goals that were manageable, by God's grace, rather than goals that were so far out of reach that people were condemned to perpetual failure. Moreover, holiness was not a private experience that could be cultivated in the interior dimensions of life by isolated individuals. Holiness was eminently social. It was a community affair, traced in the quality of one's relationships and the ethical goodness of one's life in community. The daily practice of reaping in the fields, of selling in the marketplace, of speaking in a court, of gossiping on the street, even of cutting one's hair, was to do with holiness.

Applying the laws today

What are we meant to do with these laws today? Does holiness require that we avoid all that they forbid and comply with all the actions they commend? In some cases, this would be extremely difficult. I do not possess a field, so I cannot leave its edges untouched (9). Nor do I own a vineyard, and so I cannot leave the fallen grapes on the ground for others to pick up (10). Even if I did, it would not benefit the poor and the alien whom these regulations were originally designed to help. And do I always have to 'stand up in the presence of the aged' (32), who in some cases are more sprightly than I am? Is tattooing one's body still forbidden? The commands given seem to oscillate between mighty ethical giants and trivial ethical midgets. Do they all still matter? Are they all still to be observed literally?

---

[6] C. J. H. Wright, *Ethics*, p. 39.

[7] 1 Cor. 1:2; Eph. 5:3, 26; Col. 1:22; 1 Thess. 4:7; Jas 1:27; 1 Pet. 1:15–16.

[8] Levine, p. 256.

Recent study helps us understand how these laws functioned in Israel and encourages us to avoid the fundamentalist error of seeking to impose them 'neat' on everyone, whether or not they have any allegiance to God. The Introduction above contained a discussion of the various approaches. Here I make use of what, to me, is the most satisfactory approach, as outlined by Richard Bauckham.

Old Testament law, he reminds us, is not to be confused with modern detailed legislation. Their law worked with general principles that were sometimes made explicit and at other times were silently assumed and left buried within specific commands that applied them. Where the principles are implicit, it is our responsibility to dig behind the specifics and unearth and reapply them. In contrast to contemporary law, they were never designed to be exhaustive and to cover every eventuality. Where the law does supply specific rules, as it frequently did, 'they are still only *illustrations* designed to educate people in the spirit of the Law, so that they will learn by analogy how to behave in cases the Law does not mention'.[9] Like other chapters of law, Leviticus 19 should not be regarded as a statute book for use in the courts. 'Rather its purpose is to educate the people of God in the will of God for the whole of their life as his people, to create and develop the conscience of the community.'[10] Its purpose was to cultivate healthy values rather than prosecute sick criminals.

Given this, we can see how foolish it is to think that we can read these laws straight off the page and translate them into modern legislation in a pluralistic, secular and democratic society. Though law has an important part to play in shaping morality, people cannot easily be made good by law. Contemporary Christian believers, then, will achieve their longing for a moral society not by imposing laws on unwilling citizens but first by taking these laws seriously themselves as a means of promoting holiness in every area of their own lives. And then, given that the laws do make for good sense and build up healthy social capital, they will seek to engage in debate with legislators and unbelievers in the wider society about its collective values and, using these laws as a basis, raise questions as to what sort of society we want to live in.

---

[9] Bauckham, p. 25.
[10] Ibid., p. 26.

2. Foundation principles (19:3–10)

In the first group of laws each concludes with the phrase *I am the LORD your God* (3, 4, 10), which is picked up from the overall introduction that comes in verse 2. Chosen by God in eternity and liberated by God in history, the Israelites are now his people and owe exclusive loyalty to him. Since he is the kind of Lord he is, they should live in imitation of him. Three areas of their lives, which are fundamental to all else, are raised in this opening section.

a. There are things to honour (19:3)

Two of the Ten Commandments are mentioned in this single verse. Society will be healthy where respect is shown for parents, not only because they are key to the most elementary unit in the social structure, but also because they play the primary role in introducing their offspring to God.[11] The wording of the command is interesting. *Respect* is a strong word, meaning 'fear' or 'revere', and calls for an attitude of devotion. The fact that the mother is mentioned before the father puts them on a level and recognizes the important part both parents play in the family.[12]

The second thing to honour was the Sabbath, a command repeated in verse 30. The Sabbath provided freedom from the tyranny of work and space for people to cultivate their relationship with God. A society that is addicted to commercial activity and never ceases from the endless task of creating wealth is an unhealthy one. Its riches in material terms will only be matched by its poverty in spiritual terms. Its citizens will be cogs in the industrial machine or bytes in the information network, but they will not be people who are fully alive.

b. There is something to repudiate (19:4)

Idolatry is to have no place in Israel. People become like the gods they worship. Why should Israel want to exchange the worship of their living, all-powerful, morally incorrupt and graciously compassionate God for the worship of some second-rate, impotent and impure deity of their own making? Yet such is the corruption of the human heart that often people

---

[11] Kaiser, p. 1132.

[12] Wegner, p. 43, somewhat grudgingly (and erroneously) comments that 'only in the capacity of parenthood does Leviticus grant women equality'.

choose this absurd course in the misguided belief that it will somehow bring them greater satisfaction. Furthermore, no attempt was to be made to capture their infinite and invisible God in some humanly created image. People were made in his image, not he in theirs. To attempt to represent him was inevitably to misrepresent him and to open a door that would lead to their own destruction.

c. There are things to remember (19:5–10)

At first, the next paragraphs do not seem to fit. A relatively lengthy comment is made about the fellowship offering, with a reminder of the restrictions, which had been set out previously, about when and by whom it may be eaten.[13] This is followed by the novel idea that fields and vineyards are not to be harvested to the nth degree, but that their owners are to leave wide edges and windfalls unreaped so that *the poor and the foreigner* (10) may help themselves. What do these regulations have in common, and why do they come so high up the list of ethical commandments?

The common thread between them is food, which is a fundamental factor of life.[14] The former concerns food enjoyed in the presence of God, the latter food that was required by those on the margins of society. Treating God's food as if it was insignificant and ordinary attracted serious penalties (8). But treating God's hungry people as if they were insignificant and of no value was just as heinous. The vertical dimension of spirituality that was expressed in sacrifice, and the horizontal dimension of spirituality that was expressed in social care, while not identical, were indivisible.

The provision of food for the poor by this means achieved more than establishing in Israel an elementary welfare system. To leave some food unharvested was a sign of thanksgiving for God's abundance, a mark of trust in his provision, a way of restraining greed and a reminder of Israel's own story, as they too had once experienced times of great hardship. Hartley points out the wisdom as well as the practicality of these instructions. To leave grain on the edges of the field and grapes lying on the ground would free the landlord from extra expense, since he did not have to collect them or pay for them to be collected, but would leave the poor with the

---

[13] Details are found in 3:1–17 and 7:11–21. In this book it was called the peace offering.

[14] Hinted at by Milgrom, *Leviticus 17 – 22*, p. 1596, who nevertheless thinks that vv. 9–10 have more to do with the verses that follow than with the verses that precede them (p. 1623).

dignity of working to supply their own needs rather than depending on handouts.[15] The story of Ruth, of course, provides a wonderful illustration of this principle at work (Ruth 2:1–23). Holiness, then, involved generosity. It also involved horticulture. Holiness was measured not only by what went on in the sanctuary but by what went on in the fields as well.

3. Friendship issues (19:11–18)

The next group of instructions is composed of four subsections, each of which ends with the words *I am the Lord* (12, 14, 16, 18). Gordon Wenham has noted in them the frequency of the words 'fellow citizen', 'people', 'neighbour', and even 'brother', and concluded that they have to do with friendship and relationships between those who live close to one another. This makes sense especially in view of the words that come at the climax of the section, *love your neighbour as yourself* (18).[16] What are the characteristics that would make for good neighbourliness? Four hallmarks of quality relationships are mentioned: integrity, non-exploitation, justice and love.

a. Integrity (19:11–12)

Resuming the reference to the Ten Commandments, the eighth and ninth commandments are quoted to forbid any dishonest action or speech. Both these are reinforced by the summary statement, *Do not deceive one another* (11). Further reinforcement comes in verse 12, which refers to the third commandment. Profaning God's name – the name would represent the whole of his being – by using it falsely in an oath is not a new issue, separate from what has just been said, but a continuation of the same theme. In any dispute, God's name may well have been invoked as a means of covering up an act of deception. The citizens of Israel needed to be people of plain dealing and plain talking, marked, through and through, by integrity.

The Harvard political scientist Robert Putnam points out the obvious benefits of such integrity. Social capital 'greases the wheels that allow communities to advance smoothly. Where people are trusting and trust-worthy', societies are less costly to run than those which have to keep

---

[15] Hartley, p. 314.

[16] Wenham, p. 276. Grabbe, *Oxford*, p. 103, finds Wenham's arguments persuasive.

checking on whether people have done what they said they would.[17] How much more economically efficient and socially at ease we would be if the multitude of surveillance systems and the army of inspectors, checkers and 'policemen' who have been appointed in recent days could be made redundant because people were honest and their inspections were no longer necessary! These people could do something productive themselves rather than examining a decreasing band of active producers. This ancient law has a wonderfully modern relevance, and this ancient wisdom proves timeless once more.

b. No exploitation (19:13–14)

Neither neighbours nor employees nor the disabled are to be exploited. In the simple economic system of Israel a labourer could expect to be paid at the end of the day. If the employer failed to pay, whatever the reason, it could cause the labourer real hardship. Though not actually illegal, such behaviour would fail to show the standard of respect and consideration that was expected among the children of God and therefore should be avoided at all costs. It might well be to the disadvantage of the employer to meet this exacting standard, especially as the wages of a hired worker were twice those of a slave,[18] but better that the employer should be disadvantaged than those whose labour he had hired.

Another group of people who could easily be exploited were those who were deaf or blind. The deaf would not hear if they were cursed, and the blind would not see who was responsible for putting a stumbling block in their way. 'So,' some might say, 'where is the harm in having an "innocent" laugh at their expense? They won't know any better.' But such discourteous actions fail in the duty of care that neighbours have for one another and demonstrate that the offender does not understand who these people really are. They may have a disability, but they are still people made in the image of God and deserve to be treated with respect. If the offender does not fear them, then he or she should at least fear God.

c. Justice (19:15–16)

The courts of ancient Israel were much more like our civil than our criminal courts. Courts would be local and enmeshed in the community,

---

[17] Putnam, *Bowling Alone*, p. 288.

[18] Budd, p. 275, citing Deut. 15:18.

not separate from it. Two parties would plead a case before a judge (without the paraphernalia of professional lawyers with which we are familiar), whose duty it was to decide who was in the right. So Christopher Wright explains, 'Against this background, the careful instructions on applying the law with rigorous fairness and the warnings against bribery and favouritism are all the more pertinent.'[19] Discussing a parallel passage in Exodus 23:1–8, Wright concludes that witnesses were expected to testify with integrity, antagonists to behave with courtesy, and judges to preside with impartiality and incorruptibility.[20] The scales of justice required by these regulations should be evenly balanced. Wealth and status should not influence the court's judgments. The poor should not be favoured just because they were poor, or the rich treated more harshly just because of their wealth. All were to be treated as equals.

The penultimate sentence in verse 16, *Do not do anything that endangers your neighbour's life*, does not appear to fit easily in the context. To endanger life is literally to 'stand in the blood' of a neighbour. But we should probably read it as a complement to the first half of verse 16 and take it to mean that uttering lies in court could easily result in an innocent person being convicted and even condemned to death as a result.[21] False testimony, then, could too easily endanger life.

d. Love (19:17–18)

From outward actions and words, the spotlight turns inwards to attitudes. These verses concern *the heart*, which includes one's mind and will as much as one's emotions.[22] Holiness is more than just abstaining from doing wrong. It is even more than doing right, since there are people who, in Mark Twain's reported words, are 'good in the worst sense of the word'. Unless doing right is accompanied by right attitudes and dispositions it can be Pharisaical rather than godly. These verses forbid hatred and the harbouring of negative attitudes that are likely to lead to acts of revenge, and commend instead a better way of dealing with disputes.

Negative and positive are neatly balanced in both verses. In place of hatred, relationships should be of such a quality that to *rebuke your neighbour frankly* would be both accepted and free from abuse (Prov. 15:31;

---

[19] C. J. H. Wright, *Ethics*, p. 303.

[20] Ibid., p. 304.

[21] Milgrom, *Leviticus 17 – 22*, p. 1645, who notes the connection with Exod. 23:7.

[22] Budd, p. 175.

17:10; 27:5–6). Openly dealing with issues of tension is nearly always preferable to letting them fester beneath the surface, only for them later to erupt in anger and cause needless devastation. If there is justice to be meted out, it should be left to God and pursued in the way he has stipulated, through the courts. The dispute should not be an excuse for the wreaking of personal vengeance. On this, Scripture speaks with one unequivocal voice (Matt. 5:38–42; Rom. 12:19–20). In place of resentment there should be love: *love your neighbour as yourself.*

The exhortation to love one's neighbour as one loves oneself needs explanation, especially in days when feelings are the touchstone of everything, and when, instead of taking this as a command genuinely to love their neighbours, people often use it as an excuse for self-love. Neither here, nor when Jesus repeated and endorsed this command,[23] was narcissistic self-love advocated. The phrase *as yourself* is a recognition not only of the situation as it is but of the wisdom of having self-respect. People naturally care for themselves and in general terms do not hate their own bodies (Eph. 5:29). This command is saying that, granted this, others should be treated with the same respect and shown the same consideration as we instinctively apply to ourselves (and as we certainly want others to apply to us). Self-love is sin (2 Tim. 3:2). Gary Demarest shows pastoral wisdom as well as theological soundness when he writes on this issue:

> Many contemporary expositions emphasize loving oneself as the first step towards loving your neighbour. However, this may result in self-love that never gets to loving others . . . a low self-image need not be a block to loving others and certainly is never an excuse for a failure to do so. As a matter of fact I am convinced that one of the best ways to deal with a negative self-image is to act intentionally in love towards someone else, no matter how one feels about oneself.[24]

This positive summons to love one's neighbour releases us from understanding holiness as legalistic and negative and sets us free to fulfil its generous and constructive spirit. Samuel Balentine comments, 'If the

---

[23] Matt. 22:39; Mark 12:31; Luke 10:27.

[24] Demarest, p. 222. See also John Stott's astute comments in *The Cross of Christ* (Leicester: IVP, 1986), pp. 274–276.

summons to holiness in 19:2 constitutes the keynote message of Leviticus, the command to love and not hate each other in 19:17–18 brings us to the epicentre of the book.'[25] He is right. How different our communities would be if we lived by this simple yet demanding rule. Indeed, the shockwaves would radiate from us and begin to transform the wider communities we belong to for good.

4. Wider issues (19:19–37)

The third section is headed by the command *Keep my decrees* (19).[26] When the word *decree* is used it suggests a boundary that has been fixed by God in perpetuity and should not be crossed. It stands in contrast to human judgments, which, however wise, never have the same quality of infallibility or permanence about them.

This section contains a collection of diverse commands that give the appearance of 'multiple layers and colours'.[27] They all have the common theme of respect. Any society that wishes to enjoy healthy community life will be one in which due regard is given not only to people but also to boundaries. A society in which such respect is absent will soon degenerate into anarchy. Here respect for social relations, environmental issues and ritual observance are all rolled into one, witnessing again to the truth that biblical holiness affects the whole of life. While, for purposes of clarity, we may analyse the text in a particular way and separate out some verses that especially emphasize respect for God, the need to honour God is interwoven into every area to which our attention is drawn.

a. Respect for boundaries (19:19)

Three illustrations are given of cases where boundaries need to be respected: those between *different kinds of animals*, between *two kinds of seed*, and between *two kinds of material*. In each, unnatural combinations are to be avoided. Different animal species have an autonomy of their own,[28] as have different families of seeds and different materials,

---

[25] Balentine, p. 166.

[26] Milgrom, *Leviticus 17 – 22*, pp. 1656–1657, thinks that the heading refers only to v. 19 itself, contra others.

[27] Gerstenberger, p. 273.

[28] The primary reference is probably to the mating of animals, though Harris (p. 606) thinks it has more to do with mixing animals in a load-bearing partnership than with breeding mules.

and they should not be arbitrarily mixed together. The only reason given for respecting these boundaries is that God has decreed that we should; any further reasoning is now lost to us.[29] This probably has nothing to do with not wishing to disturb the demons, as Gerstenberger proposes,[30] but everything to do with God's creation order as already reflected in the purity rules of Leviticus 11. As explained there, we still demonstrate an acute sense of boundaries and of things needing to be kept in their rightful place in our modern world.[31] Caution should certainly be exercised in applying this command today, because it has been used to justify unacceptable and unbiblical racist behaviour. Even so, such a decree should make us wary about rushing headlong into areas of genetic manipulation, where we mix genes from different species without knowing what consequences might result, or where we cross boundaries in, for example, techniques of human fertilization, purely on the basis that science has made it possible to do so without regard to wider ethical questions.

b. Respect for people (19:20–22, 29, 32–36)

A number of situations are presented that share the common theme of respecting people. The first (20–22) concerns a slave. Slavery was not the cruel institution it became in later centuries and we must rid our minds of images of Africans enslaved on the plantations of the Caribbean or the southern states of America. Slaves were more like live-in apprentices than shackled prisoners, and they enjoyed certain rights.

This particular case, about a man who sleeps with his female slave *who is promised to another man but who has not been ransomed or given her freedom*, is the most problematic of the cases that follow. The owner's action is clearly wrong and *due punishment* is required (20). It lacks respect for the woman who is about to marry, even though she is not yet free to do so, as well as for the man to whom she will shortly be betrothed. So why does the offender seem to be treated leniently in comparison with other acts of adultery, for which the death penalty was prescribed (see 20:10)? The fact is that the situation is not straightforward. Although the woman's destiny might be fixed, she is, at the time of the offence, still owned by the

---

[29] Craigie says they may 'combat certain practices in other countries, which may have had magical associations', or that each law may have had a different intent behind it. P. C. Craigie, *The Book of Deuteronomy*, NICOT (London: Hodder & Stoughton, 1976), p. 290.

[30] Gerstenberger, p. 273.

[31] E.g. mud belongs in the garden, not in the living room.

man who has slept with her. From the viewpoint of her present status, an aberration but not perhaps a legal offence has taken place, but in view of her forthcoming betrothal a disrespectful action has certainly taken place. Because the case is marginal, the punishment required is serious but not severe. It would have been wiser for the offender to show respect both to the woman and to her future partner and avoid such foolish behaviour.

The blunt command of verse 29 should need no further explanation. How could a man treat his daughter in such a degrading way as to make her a prostitute? But some people's financial situation becomes so desperate that they see this as the only option. The second half of the verse may suggest that the type of prostitution in mind is cultic prostitution, whereby the daughter is forced to participate in the ceremonies of a Canaanite fertility cult.[32] But the verse need not be narrowed to this interpretation for the warning that one sin breeds another to apply.

The elderly (32) are the third particular case where respect is enjoined, shown by the act of rising in their presence. The elderly were to be respected for the wisdom they had acquired through their long experience.[33] Traditional societies today still show much greater respect for the older generation than many so-called advanced societies do, where the elderly are often written off as a drain on resources. But the contrast is not a matter of traditional versus progressive societies so much as a matter of biblical holiness versus unprincipled arrogance. Where the elderly are not a treasured resource of wisdom, society is soon likely to decay (Isa. 3:5).

The next group who call for respect are the *foreigners* who live among the children of Israel (33–34). The frequency with which this command appears stresses the importance God attaches to it.[34] Israel is in no way to exploit those from other nations who have taken up residence among them just because they are not native-born. It is not only exploitative behaviour that is ruled out; racist and superior attitudes are condemned as well. Long before the contemporary race-relations industry came into being, God commanded his people to abstain from prejudicial behaviour

---

[32] Milgrom, *Leviticus 17 – 22*, p. 1695.

[33] Prov. 16:31; 20:29. As with so many of the laws and precepts of Scripture, this discussion is expressed in general terms. Sadly, this does not mean that every senior citizen is going to be wise!

[34] Noordtzij, p. 207, says the Old Testament reminds 'Israel of its obligations towards aliens, widows and orphans no fewer than thirty-six times'.

and to treat immigrants with love. For the second time in the chapter the directive is given to *love them as yourself* (34). The first time this was said it was in relation to one's neighbours. This time it is in relation to strangers. The reminder *for you were foreigners in Egypt* gives further encouragement to treat incomers with respect. Israel was never to forget the treatment it had received in Egypt. The memory of it, however, was not to provoke them to 'get their own back' when the time was ripe, but to inhibit them from ever treating others in the same way. The dread of slavery was to inspire them to handle all those on the margins of their society with consideration and to hold them in honour.

Three groups of vulnerable people have now been highlighted in this chapter: the disabled (14), the elderly (32) and immigrants (33–34). Each of these could all too easily be abused or brushed aside as unimportant, but Israel must never do so. Interestingly, when these commands are issued, the Lord is always explicitly mentioned. Verses 14 and 32 (the commands about the disabled and the elderly) conclude with *I am the LORD*, and verse 34 (the command about immigrants) concludes with *I am the LORD your God*. Every person who belonged to these groups bore the image of God and so none dare despise or mistreat them in any way. To ill-treat them was to ill-treat God; to dishonour them was to dishonour God.

The final area where respect for others is demanded is in the marketplace (35–36). In one's business dealings there was (and is) to be no short-changing and no selling of short measures. Nor are the devious entrepreneurs who wish to make a fast buck to protest their innocence by claiming that they are keeping the letter of the law while offending against its spirit. All one's business transactions were to be infused with total integrity.[35] In concluding this command with *I am the LORD your God, who brought you out of Egypt*, God is hinting that any person who was less than honest was on the same level as the oppressors they had known in Egypt. Surely, they had been set free to escape such exploitation! They had been set free to be holy.

c. Respect for nature (19:23–25)

A different area of concern is raised in verses 23–25. Here care for the natural world is encouraged. The Hebrew of these verses is difficult and calls for the fruit of a tree to be regarded as 'uncircumcised' for the first

---

[35] This is consistent with v. 11.

three years after its planting, to be offered to the Lord in the fourth year and to be eaten by the people themselves only in the fifth year. Omitting to pluck the fruit of a tree for three years would stunt its growth and would have the opposite effect of increasing the harvest, which, as verse 25 tells us, is the purpose of this rule. So what can this mean?[36]

Milgrom believes that sense can be made of the circumcision analogy if the verse is taken to mean that during the first three years the tree should not be pruned but that its buds should be picked out before the fruit emerges.[37] This, he says, is consistent with contemporary horticultural practice and enables the trees to grow healthily in their early years.

The command is certainly clear about the need to put God first, even when it came to harvesting one's crop of fruit. In doing so, the people of Israel would experience the blessings of obedience in measurable ways, because God promises them that *In this way your harvest will be increased.* The command also has the effect of reinforcing 'the community's consciousness that Yahweh is the owner of the land'.[38]

d. Respect for God (19:26–28, 30–31, 37)

All the commands have to do with respect for God, but several have this as their main focus. The prohibition on eating meat with *blood still in it* (26) has been explored earlier.[39] But its positioning next to the prohibition on divination may indicate that a particular ritual in pagan worship, which was designed to contact the spirits more easily and increase the power of telling the future, is in view here.[40]

Divination, a means by which the future is supposedly predicted, and sorcery, a means by which the future is supposedly altered, is flatly and consistently condemned (see 2 Kgs 17:17; 21:6; Isa. 2:6; 8:19). God had provided various means of making his will known,[41] but Israel was to trust God, even when his ways were not clear, rather than resorting to the use of divination and mediums (26b). He, not blind fate or lesser powers, was in charge of Israel's future, and it was safe in his hands. With

---

[36] What it cannot mean is that the fruit for the first three years belongs 'to the tree deities and field spirits', as suggested by Gerstenberger, p. 275, since this is totally at odds with Israel's monotheistic beliefs and totally inconsistent with the attitudes in Leviticus to demons and spirits.

[37] Milgrom, *Leviticus 17 – 22*, p. 1679.

[38] Hartley, p. 319.

[39] Verse 26a is passed over here because of the discussion of the topic on pp. 197–198.

[40] Hartley, p. 320.

[41] E.g. the Urim and Thummim, mentioned at 8:8.

irresistible logic, Isaiah asked the people of his day, 'Should not a people enquire of their God? Why consult the dead on behalf of the living?' (Isa. 8:19). With the living God as their God, Israel had no need for such flawed and useless means of discerning and fixing their futures.

Why should God make a particular hairstyle (27) or the absence of tattoos (28) a sign of holiness? The phrase *for the dead* (28) holds the secret. The trimming of sidelocks of hair, shaving one's head and gashing one's body were all associated with the cult of the dead, the worship of ancestors and Baal worship.[42] Furthermore, hair was a sign of a person's vitality. On two counts, then, that of engaging in pagan worship and of subtracting from the life God had given, God would be dishonoured by these actions. Here is a call to be separate for God, as the parallel passage in Deuteronomy makes clear:

> Do not cut yourselves or shave the front of your heads for the dead, for you are a people holy to the LORD your God. Out of all the peoples on the face of the earth, the LORD has chosen you to be his treasured possession. (Deut. 14:1–2)

The threat of ancestor worship also lay behind the prohibition in verse 31 against resorting to *mediums* and *spiritists*. Turning to a 'knower' to consult the dead was forbidden on the grounds that it was idolatry and would make the seeker unclean. Again, they were made to ask why the living who had faith in a living God thought that conferring with the dead would resolve any questions on which they sought guidance. Saul's desire to consult Samuel through the medium at Endor is a permanent lesson in the folly of such disobedience (1 Sam. 28:1–25).

The call to observe the Sabbath is repeated (30) from verse 3, with the call to show reverence for God's sanctuary added to it.

The words of verse 37, which is introduced with *Keep all my decrees*, bring full circle the section which began at verse 19 with a reference to *decrees*. But they also bring the whole chapter, which began with the statement *The LORD said to Moses* and has repeatedly stressed the nature of the Lord who commands these things, to a fitting conclusion with the refrain *I am the LORD*.

---

42 Milgrom, *Leviticus 17 – 22*, pp. 1689–1695.

5. Conclusion

Some of these illustrations of the call to holiness no longer have the force that once they did. These laws do not bind Christians to hire only day labourers, or prevent them from wearing wool and polyester suits, or stop them visiting the hairdresser. The significance of these particular issues has changed since the time when the laws were first pronounced in the wilderness. In any case, the rules, as explained, sometimes explicitly provide us with general principles and sometimes only give us typical applications of principles that are implicitly assumed. But in spite of the need for careful application, the call to holy living in the variety of our social lives is unaltered, as the New Testament teaches by its frequent references back to this chapter.

Within one short paragraph Jesus twice referred to this law, first telling his disciples that they should love not only their neighbours but their enemies as well, and then going on to say that they needed to imitate the perfection of their heavenly Father (Matt. 5:43–48). Peter teaches similar truth, actually quoting the words of Leviticus 19:2 (cf. 1 Pet. 1:16) and making it central to his call to his readers not to live in conformity to their previous way of life but to live in obedience to Jesus Christ.

But perhaps the letter of James provides the most outstanding example of the New Testament's use of this chapter. In 2:8, James speaks of 'the royal law found in Scripture'. We know this to be his 'title' for Leviticus 19 because he immediately quotes from it twice – citing both verses 18 and 15. But his interest in Leviticus 19 is much wider than this. Luke Johnson has worked out that there are 'certainly four, and possibly six further verbal or thematic allusions to Lev. 19:12–18' in James's letter.[43] The call to integrity, impartiality, mutual correction, forgiveness, trust in God's provision and, above all, to love is the royal law that is still binding on Christian believers. New Testament holiness is riddled with the spirit of Leviticus 19.

These words are addressed to the people of God and primarily have relevance to the way they relate to one another within the Christian community and within the wider society. They teach us that holiness has to do with social relationships as well as with spiritual devotion. The way we

---

[43] Luke T. Johnson, 'The Use of Leviticus 19 in the Letter of James', *JBL* 101 (1982), p. 399. In his analysis v. 12 = Jas 5:12; v. 13 = Jas 5:4; v. 15 = Jas 2:1, 9; v. 16 = Jas 4:11; v. 17 = Jas 5:20; v. 18 = Jas 5:9; v. 18 = Jas 2:8. Verse 14 seems to be missing, but arguably is covered by James's demand for impartiality.

treat God cannot be divorced from the way we treat one another. But though they are addressed to God's covenant people, these words contain wisdom that would be beneficial for any society, at any time. If we lived according to their wisdom, we would rapidly increase the social capital that has become so depleted in Western nations. Living with respect, relating in honesty, letting go of revenge, caring for the marginalized, guarding the environment, trusting in one another as well as in God, creating space for him – these and the other qualities advocated in this chapter would make for the creation of much more wholesome societies than the ones to which many of us currently belong.

Leviticus 20:1–27

17. God's word about the penal code

Should Christians advocate the death penalty, and if so, for what crimes should they demand it? Though long abolished in the UK and hardly even a matter of discussion, the debate about capital punishment elsewhere in the world is fierce. Christians are often to be found speaking with a divided voice on different sides of the debate. Those who advocate its use as a penalty for murder may be heard quoting the Old Testament law in support,[1] whereas those who oppose it may argue that such laws have been abolished by Christ. On one extreme wing of the debate, there are a few who want to go much further than those who merely favour its use in cases of premeditated murder. These people say that the Old Testament law advocates the death penalty for a whole series of 'crimes' and that it should also be applied in cases of adultery, incest, sodomy, Sabbath-breaking and incorrigibility in children.[2] They find vital support for their arguments in Leviticus 20, a section of the Holiness Code that demands the death penalty for a wide range of offences.

1. The chapter in context

a. The immediate context – Leviticus

At first glance, Leviticus 20 seems like a repeat of Leviticus 18. The list of sins covered is virtually identical and the same apparently condemnatory attitude is evident in both chapters. But whereas in chapter 18 the law was

---

[1] Especially Gen. 9:5–6 and perhaps Num. 35:31.

[2] This represents the view of Reconstructionists, a movement that began in the 1960s in the USA. One key statement of their views is found in Greg. L. Bahnsen's *Theonomy in Christian Ethics* (Nutley, NJ: Craig Press, 1979).

cast in apodictic form (an imperative form that simply states without further qualification that certain actions are wrong), in chapter 20 the law is cast in casuistic form – an 'if . . . then . . .' form that spells out the consequences of wrongdoing. Chapter 20, therefore, introduces the new element of punishment to the discussion and functions as something of a penal code for Israel.

b. The intermediate context – Pentateuchal law

This chapter is one of a number of passages that give us an insight into Israel's penal code. In itself it does not give us the complete picture, and makes, for example, no reference to crimes such as murder. Its interest is focused on offences that will undermine the stability of the family and the purity of worship. The penalties prescribed for these offences are severe because they are foundational to the social and religious life of Israel.[3]

A wider consideration of the law in the Pentateuch puts this chapter in context. After researching the nature of the laws of the Pentateuch in comparison with other penal codes of the time, Gordon Wenham has argued that the outstanding feature of the Old Testament law is its humanitarianism.[4] Three factors lend support to his verdict. First, crimes against people are treated with greater seriousness than crimes against property. In Israel the death penalty was mandatory for murder, whereas in other cultures it could be commuted to mere monetary compensation. In contrast to Israel, Babylonian law prescribed the death penalty for crimes against property – crimes of breaking and entering, theft and looting. Second, in Israel it was not permissible for a substitute to bear the punishment for a crime, as it was elsewhere (Deut. 24:16). Third, the primary objective of the law was to reconcile parties in dispute, and to do so by requiring restitution rather than by imposing fines or imprisonment. Even where an offender was sentenced to corporal punishment, it was restricted so as to preserve the dignity of the guilty one (Deut. 25:2–3). Physical mutilation was virtually unknown as a judicial punishment.[5]

The offences for which the death penalty was prescribed in Israel totalled seventeen.[6] They included murder, kidnapping, culpable negligence,

---

[3] C. J. H. Wright, 'Leviticus', p. 149.

[4] Wenham, pp. 281–288. For another overview see C. J. H. Wright, *Ethics*, pp. 281–326.

[5] It is commanded once in Deut. 25:11–12, where, as Wenham, p. 284, comments, the offence is extreme and 'the penalty is mild compared with some of those in the Assyrian laws'.

[6] Milgrom, *Leviticus 17 – 22*, p. 1733.

persistent disobedience, adultery, homosexuality, some forms of incest, false prophecy, breaking the Sabbath, blasphemy, idolatry, magic, and divination. It should be remembered that this means that the number of capital offences in Israel was far lower than in medieval England.

The fact that the death penalty was prescribed does not mean that the sentence was always carried out, and there is some suggestion that it was not enforced as much as we think. The basis for this supposition is that Numbers 35:31 specifically rules out commuting the death penalty in the case of murder, leaving open the possibility that it was (even routinely) commuted for other offences. But Wenham, who argues along these lines, thinks it unlikely that capital punishment would be commuted where the manner of execution was stipulated. The truth is that we know too little to be sure how these laws were put into practice.

Contemporary views of justice favour restorative rather than retributive justice, and some think that contemporary views of punishment major on the rehabilitation of offenders rather than on their receiving their just deserts. Early Israelite society would not have been as squeamish about retributive justice as we are, but their penal code was not solely driven by the desire for retribution. Wenham discerns, in fact, five principles in the Old Testament approach.[7] Punishment serves the purposes of awarding the offender his or her legal desert; of purging evil from their midst; of deterring others from offending; of making atonement and fostering reconciliation with society; and of providing recompense for the injured.

c. The wider context – theological discussion

In a brilliant discussion of capital punishment, Oliver O'Donovan rightly points out that it is impossible to discuss the issue without discussing the nature of the state and the limits of its authority over its citizens.[8] On the one hand, the Bible confers on governments a key role in administering justice on God's behalf. Romans 13:4 says that they are God's servants and bear the sword on God's behalf to mete out his wrath on wrongdoers. On the other hand, the Bible also recognizes that governments can become corrupt and, in taking powers to themselves that belong to God alone, can even become idolatrous. John's view of oppressive world

---

[7] All captured in Deut. 19:19–21. See Wenham, pp. 282–284.

[8] Oliver O'Donovan, *Measure for Measure: Justice in Punishment and the Sentence of Death*, Grove Booklet on Ethics 19 (Bramcote: Grove Books, 1977), p. 6.

governments in Revelation 13, including the Roman Empire of his day, represents that stream. In this case, the state is certainly not in a position to execute justice on behalf of God, since it stands in opposition to God. Just where any particular government falls on the continuum between Romans 13 and Revelation 13 will always be a matter of debate and discernment.

For Israel, however, the position was clear. Israel was a theocracy, directly under God's government and collectively subject to living according to his law. Israel was not a pluralist community where a variety of religious, political and ethical views jostled with one another to gain the people's adherence. There was one law to be obeyed, arising from one central source of authority, namely God himself. In the tight-knit community of Israel it could be expected that his laws would be obeyed, and it made sense that any deviation from them should be punished in the severest of ways.

Reconstructionists believe that we should reject secularism as the basis of society and also repudiate the sacred–secular dichotomy. Our moral standards, they say, should be taken directly from God's written Word and applied to the societies of the twenty-first century. They argue that not a single element of the law and its penal code, including Leviticus 20, has ever been withdrawn,[9] and therefore that we should consider actions that the Bible labels as crimes still to be illegal and apply the penalties that the Bible prescribes.

However, it is extremely doubtful that we should seek to be building society on these lines today. First, we do not live in a theocracy but in secular democracies. Second, as Bahnsen, one of the key exponents of this position, himself confesses, we are never told in Scripture to impose these rules on others. Bahnsen argues that we should seek the regeneration of individuals and take the path of re-education and social reform to achieve our objectives.[10] Third, in arguing for the restoration of Old Testament law, Reconstructionists do not sufficiently distinguish between the different types of law found in the Pentateuch. The enduring moral law is too easily taken to include transient civil law. Most important of all, there is more debate than they acknowledge about whether these laws have been

---

[9] They quote Matt. 5:17–18 in support.

[10] Greg Bahnsen, 'Christ and the Role of Civil Government: The Theonomic Perspective – Part II', *Transformation* 5.3 (1988), p. 28.

superseded by Christ. They overstress the continuities between the Old and New Testaments at the expense of the discontinuities. It is not just the ceremonial law that has been fulfilled and so abolished in Christ. There is also a clear discontinuity between the Testaments regarding the Sabbath, to take one example.[11] And as far as the death penalty is concerned, Christ might be said to be ambiguous about it, at best. Matthew 15:4 stands in tension with John 7:53 – 8:11. Christ came to save rather than condemn (John 3:17). On the death penalty it would seem that there is no clear guidance and, in the words of Oliver O'Donovan, 'from a Christian point of view, the death penalty is neither categorically demanded nor categorically forbidden'.[12]

2. The offences it catalogues

With this background we turn to the text of Leviticus 20. The evils it lists overlap substantially with chapter 18, but they are organized differently. In chapter 18 they were listed from the closest to the most distant family relations. Here they are listed chiefly according to the severity of punishment they merit. The wrongdoings listed are:

Sacrificing children to Molek (20:1–5; cf. 18:21)
Necromancy (20:6, 27; cf. 19:31)
Cursing parents (20:9; cf. 19:3)
Adultery (20:10; cf. 18:20)
Incest (20:11–12, 17–21; cf. 18:6–18)
Active homosexuality (20:13; cf. 18:22)
Marriage to a woman and her mother (20:14; cf. 18:17)
Bestiality (20:15–16; cf. 18:23)
Sex with menstruants (20:18; cf. 18:19)
Marriage to sister-in-law (20:21; cf. 18:16)

3. The punishments it prescribes

Four kinds of sentences are passed on those found guilty, according to the offence committed. The most severe punishment is to be put to death by

---

[11] See further pp. 263–264.

[12] O'Donovan, op. cit., p. 3.

one's fellow humans and to be cut off by God. Next in order of severity is the death penalty alone, then excision and finally childlessness.

a. The double sentence (20:2–6)

The crime of Molek worship is a double crime involving both idolatry and murder, and therefore it merits the double sentence of *death* (2) and of God setting his face against offenders and cutting them off (3). Necromancy incurred a similar double penalty, although verse 6 mentions only *mediums and spiritists* being *cut . . . off from their people*. This appears, however, to be an abbreviated pronouncement of the sentence, because verse 27 adds that practitioners of these forbidden arts are to be stoned, and the Mishnah stipulated the death penalty for these crimes.[13]

b. The death penalty (20:9–16)

Adultery, incest, homosexuality, polygamy involving a woman and her mother, and bestiality all incur the death penalty. Only in the case of a man who marries *both a woman and her mother* (14) is the mode of execution stipulated. In this case *they must be burned in the fire, so that no wickedness will be among you*. This probably means, as Hartley suggests, that their bodies were to be burned after they had been put to death rather than that they were executed by being burned alive. The case of Achan seems to confirm this.[14] Otherwise the manner of execution is not stipulated, but might be assumed to be by stoning. Usually condemned persons were taken to a high point and thrown off, and stones would have been rained down upon them only if the fall had not killed them. It was considered the most humane form of execution possible.[15] This method of execution also served to underline that it was a community punishment because it was carried out not by an individual but by a group, who expressed their collective disapproval of the reprobate behaviour. It should also be noted that in such cases not only the one who initiated the offence but all the parties involved in it were judged guilty of evil (presumably because they had consented to the action) and so were

---

[13] Levine, p. 137.

[14] Hartley, p. 339. See Josh. 7:1–26.

[15] "'Love your neighbour as yourself" (19:18) is applied even to condemned criminals, whom you love by giving them the most humane death possible . . . and the body should not be destroyed or mutilated' (Milgrom, *Leviticus 17 – 22*, pp. 1732–1733). Contemporary penal systems have a lot to learn about treating criminals humanely. Whether life imprisonment or lengthy incarceration in the prison system is humane is open to question.

sentenced to death. So, for example, adulterer and adulteress (10), incest villain and incest victim (11–12), homosexual perpetrator and partner (13), and human and beast (15–16) were all to be killed.

c. Being cut off (20:17–18)

The third group merited the punishment of being *cut off from their people*. These offences consisted of marrying a half-sister, having sexual intercourse with a woman during her monthly period, and having sexual intercourse with a paternal or maternal aunt. The most likely meaning of being *cut off* is that they would die prematurely, perhaps even immediately, or that their line would be cut off or their children would die before them.[16] By one means or another the flow of life through the family would be brought to an end. It was an action of God rather than a punishment meted out by the community and, consequently, these acts were not subject to trial in a human court. But, although the culprits were spared that shame, they did not altogether escape humiliation. The phrase in verse 17 that they were to be cut off *publicly ... from their people* means that though they had sinned in secret, and perhaps hoped as a result to get away with it, they would be punished in public (cf. 2 Sam. 12:12).

d. Childlessness (20:19–21)

The final offences, sex with an uncle's wife and marriage to a sister-in-law while one's brother was still living, are punished by childlessness. To be childless was literally to be 'stripped' and therefore carried overtones of shame.[17] Children were viewed as a sign of God's blessing, and therefore barrenness – being stripped of children to enjoy one's legacy (Gen. 15:2) – was seen as being stripped of God's blessing and raised the spectre that those who were childless had sinned against God.

4. The principles it enshrines

If it is not our duty to impose these laws on others and exact the penalties prescribed for the various offences, what are we to make of these regulations? They teach us several important truths, which have already been

---

[16] Levine, p. 241; Milgrom, *Leviticus 17 – 22*, p. 1754.

[17] Budd, p. 296.

taught in different ways earlier in the book. An analysis of the chapter's structure[18] serves to highlight the real import of its message, which lies not in exacting the death penalty but in encouraging holiness.

    A[1] Worship of the gods of the underworld (1–6)
        B[1] Exhortation to holiness (7–8)
            C   Penalties for sin (9–21)
        B[2] Exhortation to holiness (22–26)
    A[2] Worship of the gods of the underworld (27)

a. God is important (20:22–26)

Bill Shankly, the great post-war football manager, once famously said, 'Some people think football is a matter of life and death. I don't like that attitude. I can assure them it is much more serious than that.'[19] This chapter is a way of declaring, in a form that would have been easily understood among the Semitic people at the time, 'that obedience to God is a life and death matter'.[20] They would not have concluded, as we might, that it painted a picture of God as cruel and barbaric. They would rather have understood it to indicate that the gracious God of salvation has a right to be supreme in our lives and that by giving him pre-eminence and obeying his commands we shall live.[21] Only through obedience would Israel enjoy the prosperity of the land they were to inherit. The path of disobedience was the path of treason and could only lead to death and disaster. Refusal to obey him would mean that the land to which they were going would spit them out, as it had done to the occupants who were there before them (22–23; cf. 26:1–46).

Penal codes reflect the various values we assign to things. The heaviest penalties are reserved for offences against what we value highly, the lighter penalties for what we hold lightly. Israel attached the greatest value to knowing God, who required his people to abstain from worshipping other deities and to do all within their power to ensure the integrity of their families. Consequently, when people transgressed in these areas, severe penalties were exacted.

---

[18] The following is patterned on Milgrom, *Leviticus 17 – 22*, p. 1728.

[19] *Sunday Times*, 4 October 1981.

[20] Knight, p. 126.

[21] See the instructive incident in 1 Sam. 6 as an example, especially v. 20.

b. Sin is serious

The obverse of saying that God is important is to say that sin is serious. Sin is not a neutral activity in which we can ever indulge nonchalantly. It always entails a price. The penalties prescribed for the offences here are a dramatic way of expressing this inescapable truth. Even without them, the price of sin would have been all too obvious on a human level: children would have died in the arms of Molek, families would have been ruined, jealousies would have been stoked, and society would have crumbled. In prescribing these penalties, God was putting down a marker about the seriousness of sin with a view to deterring his people from committing it. These judicial sentences only bring into sharp focus what people would know in their own fuzzy experience all along: sin has a price tag.

The penalties, though, are more than a statement about the impersonal consequences of sin. They are an expression of the personal wrath of a holy God against actions that are an offence to him. 'Supreme in the intention of this law', Kellogg claims, 'is the satisfaction of outraged justice.'[22] This is seen particularly when God says, *I myself will set my face against him and his family* (5). God's personal wrath is evident when he himself steps in to execute the sentence of cutting *them off from their people* (5, 6). Why is it so difficult for people to grasp that the God who intended people to enjoy a relationship with him, and made his world to be good and full of life, would take offence at those who by their actions alienate themselves from him and destroy his creation? What sort of a God would it be who was indifferent to the presence of evil in his world?

Christopher Wright wisely points out that, though the penalties may have changed, the New Testament still regards the offences as 'serious moral evils' and Christians should still view them with repugnance.[23] And though the expression of God's wrath may be delayed or take a different form, Paul still warns the early Christians that on account of sins such as immorality, impurity and idolatry, 'the wrath of God is coming' (Col. 3:6). Sin remains serious.

c. Humans are responsible

In the current climate, sin is always said to be someone else's fault – we blame our parents, our schools, the government, or just society in general.

---

22 Kellogg, p. 422.

23 C. J. H. Wright, 'Leviticus', p. 149. See Matt. 15:4; Rom. 1:18–32; 1 Cor. 5:1–5.

Many seek to abdicate any personal responsibility for their wrongful actions. (It must be admitted that this is not just a contemporary attitude, since passing the buck goes back to the Garden of Eden – Gen. 3:12–13.) The Israelites were not allowed to adopt the status of a victim quite so easily. These regulations underlined that they had both a collective and a personal responsibility for sin that they could not avoid. The buck could not be passed.

The collective responsibility is mentioned in verses 4–5: *If the members of the community close their eyes when that man sacrifices one of his children to Molek and if they fail to put him to death, I myself will set my face against him.* God created people to be responsible moral agents, and the limits of this responsibility are not confined to their own lives or immediate families; they also have a responsibility for the community to which they belong. Shutting their eyes to evil, and pretending evil was nothing to do with them, were not permissible. Such cowardly indifference would only exacerbate the situation and lead God himself to intervene in judgment. It was better if people took the action that lay within their own power rather than exhausting God's patience.

Collective responsibility is balanced by individual responsibility. Neither is sufficient on its own and neither can take the place of the other. Five times when the sentence of death is pronounced the words *their blood will be on their own heads* (9, 11, 12, 13, 16) are added. It means that by their actions the guilty persons have forfeited their right to life.[24] The guilty have caused their own deaths and are involved in self-murder. Consequently, those who engaged in judicial executions were not guilty of shedding blood and were not liable themselves to the penalty for murder. Improvements in contemporary society will never be experienced until there is a renewed acceptance of both individual and corporate responsibility for wrong.

d. Holiness is imperative

The pronouncements regarding the death penalty are framed by two calls to holiness (7–8, 22–26), which are made up of several strands woven together.

Holiness is about consecration (7). Holiness does not just happen. It is not a warm fuzzy feeling of saintliness. It develops from intentional

---

[24] Hartley, p. 339.

decisions and affirmative actions. As it was for the Israelites, so it is for us. To be holy means to commit ourselves to following God and abstaining from actions that offend him. Obedience – *Keep my decrees* (8, 22) – is the key.

Holiness is about separation (23, 26). Much of the behaviour outlawed here played a significant part in the lives and the worship of Israel's neighbours. These practices were forbidden both because they were wrong in themselves and because of their associations with pagan culture. Hence Israel was told, *You must not live according to the customs of the nations I am going to drive out before you* (23). Being holy still entails living a lifestyle that runs counter to the customs of the people around us where they live in ignorance or opposition to the revealed will of God (2 Cor. 6:14 – 7:1). Our calling is not to be fashionable, acceptable or conventional but to be the best we can be for God. The reason for our separation, however, is not negative but positive. It is because we belong to God and enjoy a special relationship with him: *I have set you apart from the nations to be my own* (26).

Holiness is about sanctification (8). God says, *I am the LORD, who makes you holy.* The process of being made holy is one that God himself brings about in our lives. Every time the Israelites obeyed God's word they activated the presence of God in their midst and strengthened the bonds of union between them.[25] In becoming closer to him they became more like him, and less like their pagan neighbours, from whose deities they were required to distance themselves. God still brings about the transformation of our lives into his likeness by his Spirit (2 Cor. 3:18; see also Acts 5:32). But he does it in the lives of those who are obedient.

Holiness is about purification (25). Many struggle with the inclusion of a verse about clean and unclean animals at this juncture, as it seems like an interruption to the flow of the chapter and a deviation from the topic being addressed. But it serves as another reminder that holiness has a comprehensive reach into our lives. It is neither just about piety nor just about morality. God claims total allegiance in every department of our lives and calls us to live with purity.

Holiness is about imitation (26). Reduced to its essence, to be holy is to reflect the purity and character of God in one's life, as we saw in considering 19:2.

---

25 Hartley, p. 338.

While this part of the penal code of Israel may give us little guidance about judicial penalties in contemporary, secular and pluralistic societies, it has contemporary relevance for society. It shows how 'false religion leads to base living, but pure religion leads to holy living'.[26] It gives us insight into the administration of divine justice. And it sets before us the moral code by which God's people are still required to live in holiness. How glad we must be that for all failures there is a way of atonement and a God waiting to forgive!

---

[26] Ross, p. 378.

Leviticus 21:1 – 22:33

18. God's word about spiritual leadership

Israel's call was to be a holy people. If they were to fulfil this calling it was essential that they were led by spiritual leaders who were committed to the pursuit of holiness. So it is far from incidental that Leviticus 21 and 22 address the priests and set out the qualifications and standards they were expected to meet.

It is sometimes said that a church cannot grow spiritually beyond its leaders. That is to claim too much. The sovereign Lord is capable of blessing a people way beyond anything their leaders merit. God is also capable of bypassing leaders and raising up those who do not occupy any position of authority to encourage (or provoke) his people to higher things. But it is true nevertheless that leaders set a tone and exercise an enormous influence on the spiritual vitality of their people. Leaders occupy a strategic role, and it is wise, therefore, that careful consideration should be given to the qualifications they should be expected to have before they are admitted to leadership and to the standards they should be expected to reach once they are in that role.

These chapters cover issues in the priests' personal lives and their physical make-up before introducing a code of professional conduct. High standards of holiness were expected of the general population, but even higher standards were required of priests, and even higher standards still were demanded of the high priest. 'The principle observed here', notes Walter Kaiser, 'is the abiding one that special privilege and honor place those on whom they are conferred under special obligations to a higher level of holiness of life.'[1] In the words of Jesus, quoted previously: 'From

---

[1] Kaiser, p. 1147.

everyone who has been given much, much will be demanded; and from the one who has been entrusted with much, much more will be asked' (Luke 12:48). James writes in a similar vein to leaders in the New Testament church: 'you know that we who teach will be judged more strictly' (Jas 3:1).

The weight of responsibility to achieve the required standards does not fall on the shoulders of the priests alone. The people share some responsibility for ensuring that the priests live according to God's word, and are encouraged to adopt the right attitude towards them, regarding them and considering them holy (8). Perhaps some congregations are too quick to lay the blame for failure at the feet of their pastors when they should be looking to themselves to see if they have cared enough, prayed enough, encouraged enough, even corrected enough, and kept their leaders focused enough on their calling.

More significant still is the phrase *I the* Lord *am holy – I who make you holy*, which occurs in varying forms in 21:8, 15, 23; 22:9, 16, 32.[2] The Lord himself makes them holy as his transforming power works in their lives, affirming the good, convicting them of wrong, and cleansing out the bad. Holiness is not achieved by their own unaided effort. Even so, God's role in sanctifying them works in partnership with their own commitment.[3] The first reference to the phrase occurs in 20:8[4] and the last in 22:31–32. These 'bookend' references show that the process of holiness is advanced as the people keep the decrees God has given. There can be no holiness apart from obedience: God does not confer holiness on people irrespective of their own desire to walk in his ways.

1. Personal qualifications (21:1–15)

In this passage the *sons of Aaron* are first addressed as a group (1–9), before Aaron, *the high priest*, is addressed in his own right and as a representative of the subsequent holders of that office (10–15). The issues at stake largely concern mourning rites and marriage practices. Death and marriage are obviously two of the most crucial transition stages in the life of any family. But while we may understand what is said about marriage, the

---

[2] The phrase is taken by some as lending structure to the passage, which it does to a considerable extent.

[3] Hartley, p. lxi; Milgrom, *Leviticus 17 – 22*, pp. 1741–1742.

[4] Lev. 20:8 refers to God making all the people holy, not just the priests.

comments about mourning seem obscure. Both concern the need for priests, of whatever rank, to make God their absolute priority and to put him before loyalty to family or personal feelings. In their own way they illustrate the leadership principle enunciated by J. Oswald Sanders: 'Only the disciplined person will rise to his highest powers. The leader is able to lead others because he has conquered himself.'[5]

a. The personal life of the priests (21:1–9)

i. Mourning (21:1–6)

To touch a corpse rendered any Israelite unclean for seven days and required the defiled person to wash himself or herself on the third and the seventh day to remove the uncleanness (Num. 19:11–22). For a lay member of Israel such defilement was not too serious, but for a priest to be rendered incapable of representing his people before God for such a period was a different matter. However, the ban on a priest mourning his relatives was not absolute, and a concession was made in the case of his closest blood relatives – *his mother, father, son, daughter* and *brother*. (His brother's widow would be equated with his brother, assuming the priest had responsibility for her.) The NIV translates verse 4 as ruling out any concession in the case of relatives by marriage. The context favours this as the correct translation of a somewhat obscure original.[6] This would mean that priests were not even permitted to engage in the mourning ceremonies for their own wives.[7] The purpose was not to denigrate human relationships – they were important – but to exalt the priest's relationship with God, which was even more important.[8]

These apparently harsh restrictions on the expression of personal grief find some justification in verses 5–6. To shave one's head or beard, as we saw when considering 19:27, was to adopt pagan mourning customs and to be associated with the worship of the dead. That is why these practices would *profane the name of their God*. In view of the popularity of cults connected with the dead, it was essential that priests should visibly distance themselves from such practices and demonstrate unswerving loyalty to the Lord alone.

---

[5] J. Oswald Sanders, *Spiritual Leadership* (London: Lakeland, 1967), p. 44.

[6] Hartley, p. 348, contra Wenham, p. 290, who interprets it as an anticipation of v. 7.

[7] The scribes later relaxed the ruling and permitted a priest to attend his wife's funeral; Levine, pp. 142–143.

[8] Kellogg, pp. 434–435.

ii. Marriage (21:7–9)

Priests also had to be careful whom they married, so that their family life could be above reproach and so that nothing could taint their service for God. Prostitutes of any kind, but especially cult prostitutes, would make unsuitable partners because of the licentious nature of their sexual and religious habits. And divorcees[9] were also deemed unsuitable because their histories would undermine the integrity of the family, an integrity that priests should be striving to uphold.

A wayward daughter might be as capable of undermining the high standards required of a priest's family as much as an ill-chosen wife. Should a daughter resort to prostitution, it would reflect badly on her father, who should show no mercy towards her. No special privileges were available because she was the daughter of a priest; rather the reverse. The full punishment of death, probably first by stoning and then by the burning of her corpse,[10] should be meted out so that the disgrace she had brought on the family could be removed.

Though the specific applications had changed, Paul continues to assert the importance of church leaders having a family that can be held in respect by all (1 Tim. 3:2–5, 12; Titus 1:6). A family that is the seedbed for children who neither believe nor behave as Christians inevitably calls into question the credibility of the very leadership a pastor or elder is seeking to exercise.

b. The personal life of the high priest (21:10–15)

The same two issues are raised in respect of the high priest. The greater status of the high priest's office is emphasized by the allusions to his anointing and his robes of office.

i. Mourning (21:10–12)

The high priest is not permitted to show any of the customary signs of mourning, even if for most people they are entirely innocuous. He is certainly not to indulge in any custom associated with pagan cults. He *must not let his hair become unkempt or tear his clothes* (10). Furthermore, he is not even permitted to avail himself of the concessions available to

---

[9] Levine, pp. 143–144, thinks that divorce was likely to have been caused by marital unfaithfulness, and related to adultery, rather than being caused by something else. Thus, the integrity of marriage would be undermined.

[10] Hartley, p. 349.

the ordinary priests. He is not to show grief or participate in the funeral rites even of his closest blood relatives. During the period of mourning, the high priest cannot leave his post but must stay on duty throughout.[11] Loyalty to God and service to others eclipse any obligations towards oneself and override personal needs and preferences. The verse is silent as to whether these restrictions apply to the death of the high priest's wife, and so we cannot know what would have happened in this case.

ii. Marriage (21:13–15)

The high priest's bride *must be a virgin* (13). The list of those he is forbidden to marry covers prostitutes and divorcees, as before, but also in his case includes widows (14). The reason given is *so that he will not defile his offspring among his people* (15). As Wegner points out, these restrictions are designed to ensure that the purity of the line is safeguarded and that there is no uncertainty about the paternity of the priests, and even more of the high priests.[12] The removal of any possible suspicion was essential, since the high priesthood was an inherited office.

All these regulations signal that the spiritual leaders of Israel were to put God before all else and serve him with absolute dedication and in total purity of life. Service was never to be half-hearted and holiness was never to be compromised. In Paul's words, leaders must be 'above reproach' (1 Tim. 3:2).

2. Physical fitness (21:16–24)

The unblemished lifestyle of the priests of Israel had to be matched by their unblemished bodies. *No man*[13] *who has any* [physical] *defect may come near* and minister at the altar (18). This general interdict is followed by the naming of twelve physical disabilities that disqualified a priest from offering sacrifices. The list is probably intended to be not exhaustive but illustrative.[14] Its order is organized on a continuum from the most to the

---

[11] Kaiser, p. 1148, says that no living quarters were provided in the Tent and therefore this is purely a reference to being there while on duty. In contrast, Hartley, p. 349, writes that 'the high priest is not permitted to leave his dwelling place in the sanctuary'.

[12] Wegner, p. 42.

[13] Only men were permitted to be priests in Israel, essentially to distinguish their priesthood from those of their pagan neighbours, who had priestesses. For a full and balanced discussion see Mary Hayter, *The New Eve in Christ: The Use and Abuse of the Bible in the Debate about Women in the Church* (London: SPCK, 1987), pp. 60–79.

[14] The twelve listed here are probably general categories. The rabbis expanded the list to 142; Milgrom, *Leviticus 17 – 22*, p. 1825.

least severe disability. Milgrom suggests that these twelve conditions are selected to complement the twelve blemishes that disqualify animals from being suitable for sacrifice, which are listed in 22:22–24.[15]

The list raises as many questions as it answers. Why were these physical disfigurements considered sufficient to disqualify a person from serving at the altar? Is the list not extremely discriminatory, and would it not lead inevitably to a group of second-class priests who were valued less than those who enjoyed physical health? What happened to these priests? And why are only physical defects mentioned; why no mention of moral or psychological deficiencies?

Some of these questions are answered by the text itself. No unfit priest was eligible to offer sacrifices because, like the sacrificial victim itself, only perfection could be brought so close to the presence of a perfect God, lest his vital holiness break out against that which was not whole. Anything that was not excellent would be unworthy of him. The interests of those priests who were excused from offering sacrifices were guarded by the very law that forbade them to stand at the altar or go near to the curtain in front of the Most Holy Place. Verse 22 guarantees that they should not miss out on the portions of food that were the chief means of their support. Indeed, the point is laboured when it is said that they *may eat the most holy food of their God, as well as the holy food.* Their remuneration was safe. There would have been numerous other jobs that they could do as part of the priestly team in the outer court of the tabernacle without their having to offer sacrifices. Clearly, no judgment about the value or dignity of the person is intended.[16]

Milgrom's idea that only physical blemishes are mentioned because they are counterpoised with the physical defects of animals that were unfit to sacrifice may have some merit, but is surely not the whole story. Other parts of the law, including the verses that immediately follow, detail the moral and ceremonial grounds on which a priest might be disqualified. So they need not be repeated here. Israel would not have thought in terms of mental disabilities as we do, and so, even if they had been listed, such 'blemishes' may not have made sense in the culture of their day. It is likely, though, that the physical dimension is chosen to represent the whole person. As so often in a context where spiritual truth is symbolized by

---

[15] Milgrom, *Leviticus 17 – 22*, pp. 1821, 1836–1841.

[16] Demarest, p. 237.

dramatic, physical action, the outward is taken to signify the inward. Here, the body is taken to signify the totality of the person. As Gregory of Nazianzus put it, 'It was required by the law that perfect sacrifices must be offered by perfect men – a symbol, I take it, of integrity of soul.'[17] To this, we must surely add that it is also a preview of the perfection of Jesus Christ as our great High Priest.

3. Professional conduct (22:1–33)

From personal qualifications the Lord's concern now turns to the actual performance of the job. Chapter 22 mentions a number of circumstances in which the priest's handling of a sacrifice would make it unacceptable. The fact that a priest reached the personal and physical standards required to officiate at the altar did not mean he was free to do what he liked. There were other considerations to be borne in mind. Failure to perform one's duty before God with care showed lack of respect for God (2) and amounted to treating his words with *contempt* (9). It could even result in death. These instructions teach us that 'the Christian leader never equates mediocrity with the things of God but is always committed to the pursuit of excellence'.[18]

a. Service that was not admissible (22:1–9)

An otherwise fit priest might be temporarily disqualified from service because he had become *ceremonially unclean* (3). There were no special privileges in this area just because the person in question was a priest. If there was a suspicion of a skin disease, the usual procedures had to be put into effect (4; 13:1–46; 14:1–32). And if he came into contact with anything that was unclean (4–5), the usual limitations and requirements came into force,[19] with the added restriction that sacred food could not be eaten until the evening, when any minor defilement would have been washed away (6–7). Priests (8) also had to observe the regulations regarding dead animals, like anyone else (17:15–16).

Like present-day Christian leaders, priests might be tempted to plead that they were a special case, that others depended on them and that regulations did not apply to them in quite the same way. It is one of the

---

[17] Gregory of Nazianzus (fourth century), 'Oration 2: In Defence of His Flight to Pontus', in Lienhard, p. 192.
[18] Ted Engstrom, *The Making of a Christian Leader* (Grand Rapids, MI: Zondervan, 1976), p. 199. On pp. 103–104, 199–200, he discusses excellence versus mediocrity in Christian work.
[19] The relevant regulations are woven into other regulations in Lev. 11 – 14.

occupational hazards of the clergy to think that God's word applies to everyone else but them. But these regulations are unequivocal. The priests need to obey the rules like everyone else; indeed, even more than everyone else, since they are dealing with sacred things so close to the presence of their holy God. Failure to do so would result in their becoming guilty and might lead to their paying the ultimate price for their presumption (9).

These reminders are a way of saying that priests have to keep themselves holy, an imperative that still rests on the shoulders of those who would lead God's people today (2 Pet. 3:11).

b. Negligence that was not permissible (22:10–16)

The next set of regulations relates to a second occupational hazard found among Christian leaders. They become so familiar with the things of God that they begin to treat them casually. The particular issue raised here concerned the eating of offerings. Two illustrations are given of where the boundaries between what was and what was not permissible might easily be blurred.

The first illustration relates to who was permitted to eat *the sacred offering* (10–13). The food set aside from the offerings for the priest and his family were to be eaten only by his family and not by any *unauthorised person* (13). But who constitutes the family? Are guests, hired workers and married daughters included? The answer is a strict 'no'. The responsibility for feeding them belongs to someone else. Guests and hired workers are only temporarily in contact with a priest and he bears no permanent responsibility for them. A married daughter, similarly, became the responsibility of her husband on marriage. If the daughter returned home permanently, for whatever reason, then she became a family member again and was then permitted to eat the sacred meat. Slaves were in a different situation (11). They belonged to and were the responsibility of the priest. Consequently, they had a right to eat the sacred meat. It would be easy to say that these boundaries did not matter and to argue that one piece of meat was much like another. But the meat set aside for the priests from the sacred offerings remained the Lord's, and he, not the priest, had the right to determine who would sit down to enjoy it.

The second illustration is a similar type of situation. In this case it relates to when a priest might eat a sacred offering *by mistake* (14–15).[20]

---

[20] It is not entirely clear who the offenders are, but they are usually taken to be the priests; Hartley, p. 356.

It was this sort of situation that the sin offering covered (4:2–12), and when mistakes were made, priests, like everyone else, were required to confess their wrongdoing, offer sacrifice and make restitution. Overfamiliarity with the things of God was no excuse.

c. Sacrifices that were not acceptable (22:17–33)

The final area where priests needed to exercise great care was over the quality of the sacrifices that were offered. They played a crucial role in saying whether a sacrifice reached the required standard,[21] and so, although the gist of what is spelt out here has been said before, further detailed guidance is provided. The key principle is that for a sacrifice to be accepted by God it must be perfect. Worshippers were not doing God a favour by giving him these gifts. He was doing them a favour by accepting them and making atonement because of them. It was essential, therefore, that the quality of gifts presented was determined not by the worshipper but by God himself.

The new features contained here include a list of blemishes that would make a sacrifice unacceptable (22, 24); the concession that a freewill offering need not be perfect unless offered as a vow (23);[22] that damaged offerings purchased from foreigners were no more acceptable than if they had been bought from an Israelite (25);[23] that any sacrificial animal had to be at least a week old (26); and that a mother and its young should not be sacrificed on the same day (27).[24] To attempt to cut corners and give an imperfect gift would indicate that the worshipper had little understanding of the absolute perfection of the God with whom they were dealing.

Chapter 22 amounts to something of a 'guide to good practice' for priests. It warns that standards must never be eroded in God's service nor advantage taken of the privilege of being close to God. Those who lead must be careful to obey. They must 'set an example for the believers in speech, in conduct, in love, in faith and in purity' (1 Tim. 4:12). Though worthy of support, they must not serve because of greed, either for money or for

---

[21] This is a further example of the role as formulated in 10:10.

[22] Levine, pp. 151–152, points out the wholly exceptional nature of this concession and stresses that it does not apply to votive offerings or where people had a duty to thank God. It was the voluntary nature of the offering that made a blemished animal acceptable.

[23] It is not envisaged that the offering is presented by a foreigner, but that it would be sold to an Israelite, who would then present it. Milgrom, *Leviticus 17 – 22*, pp. 1881–1882.

[24] Exod. 23:19; 34:26; Deut. 14:21. Wenham, p. 296, says that this law is not due to sentimentality, but arises from a concern for conservation and a desire to avoid the wanton destruction of creation. But it may also reflect caution about pagan customs designed to increase fertility; Hartley, p. 362.

status. They must be 'eager to serve', not to rule (1 Pet. 5:2–4). 'They are not to be executives, lusting for power, but models of God's redeeming grace.'[25]

4. Perfect fulfilment

Behind the specific issues raised in this chapter are principles that are relevant to all Christian leaders. Effective leaders will put God above all else, including personal convenience, the dictates of feelings and the desire to be fashionable. Committed leaders will strive for holiness. Godly leaders should not be 'unduly preoccupied with the affairs of this life, which have the kiss of death on them'.[26] Wise leaders will care for their bodies as temples of the Holy Spirit (1 Cor. 6:19; see also 1 Tim. 4:8). Skilful leaders will shun mediocrity and perform all their duties with excellence. Dedicated leaders will watch the special temptations and occupational hazards of dealing regularly in holy things. Presumption, negligence and compromise are to be avoided at all costs. Then good leaders will enjoy the tremendous privilege of connecting people with their God and helping people to bring sacrifices that are acceptable to him.

Although the focus may be on leaders, however, these chapters do not apply exclusively to them, and the assumption must not be made that Christian ministers are identical to Old Testament priests, offering atoning sacrifices. Under the new covenant, all Christians are priests (1 Pet. 2:9), so no disciples of Christ can say that these matters do not concern them. The same passion for holiness and desire to serve God acceptably is incumbent on us all.

Under the new covenant, too, there is only one great High Priest, who alone can and does offer a sacrifice for sin. So the perfect fulfilment of these ideals is found, not in any human leader, who may occasionally fail, or in any animal sacrifice, which is an inadequate substitute for human beings, but in Christ, our great High Priest in heaven (Heb. 4:14; 7:26) and our perfect sacrifice on Calvary (Heb. 9:14; 1 Pet. 1:19). He lived a life of total consecration, performed his duties with excellence, and gave himself without reservation so that one day he might present to himself 'a radiant church, without stain or wrinkle or any other blemish, but holy and blameless' (Eph. 5:27).

---

[25] Hartley, p. 357.
[26] Hartley, p. 351. See Matt. 6:25–34; Luke 12:33–34.

Leviticus 23:1–44

19. God's word about times of celebration

Any society needs its special days; days that mark the passing of times and seasons and that recall some of the historic events that have shaped them as a people. Without these regular rhythms, life would be extremely tedious. Israel had more than its fair share of such days that regularly punctuated the routine monotony of the calendar. Unlike most societies, however, they had not sat down and worked out what would be convenient for them. These days were *the appointed festivals of the Lord* (2), determined by him and announced through Moses.[1] Because the Lord claimed these days as his own, they were permeated with his character. They spoke of his generosity, his provision, his justice, his salvation and his promise.

Before the chapter launches into the details of the annual round of festivals, it introduces the weekly Sabbath (3–4). Starting here is not merely a way of separating a weekly observance from annual festivals but also stresses the significance of the Sabbath. Seven, the number of completion and perfection, is the most significant number in the whole chapter. There are seven festivals and seven days of rest, and several of the celebrations occur in the seventh month. The Sabbath principle underlies all the other celebrations.

Though Moses issued these instructions in the wilderness, the feasts were given to Israel as an abiding gift (*a lasting ordinance*) and were to be observed long after they had settled in their permanent home in Canaan (14, 21, 31, 41). Undoubtedly the festivals were reinterpreted as time went

---

[1] 'The Lord said to Moses' occurs five times, in vv. 1, 9, 23, 26, 33.

on and Israel became less a migrant, pastoral people and more a settled, urban nation.[2] But in essence they remained unchanged – permanent reminders of God's goodness.

The days of celebration cluster in the spring (4–22) and the autumn (23–43). The chapter acknowledges this main division by concluding the two sections with the words *I am the* LORD *your God* (22, 43). This title, we should remember, had overtones of God as gracious in salvation, not merely as powerful in command.[3] Although the shape of each feast was different, they were observed by the holding of a *sacred assembly* (2, 3, 4, 7, 21, 24, 27, 35, 36, 37), when the people would come together to engage in collective worship and, for part of the time at least, abstain from work.

1. The Sabbath: God rests (23:3)

The Sabbath was one of the great innovations of Israel.[4] Others shaped their calendars according to the lunar cycle and divided them into months. Israel, at God's command, divided time into regular weeks that had nothing to do with the course of the moon. The Sabbath was essentially a day of rest: *You are not to do any work; wherever you live, it is a sabbath to the* LORD. The very word *Sabbath* is derived from the verb 'to cease', 'to rest'. Though the text hints at some collective act of worship, nothing specific is commanded and the accent always falls more on what people should not do than on what they should.

Taking its cue from the Genesis account of creation, where God rested on the seventh day after he had finished making the world (Gen. 2:2–3), the Sabbath had assumed additional significance because of Israel's relentless 24/7 experience in Egypt. A fuller understanding of the Sabbath is provided in Exodus 20:8–11 (cf. Exod. 31:15; 35:2–3) and Deuteronomy 5:12–15, which explain that the command to stop working applied not only to the members of an Israelite family but to all those dependent on them or associated with them, be they servants, resident guests or even animals. Having experienced non-stop forced labour in Egypt themselves, they were not to subject others to such tyranny. The Creator provided the day

---

[2] Bailey, p. 89, for example, points to how the Feast of Weeks (15–22) became a commemoration in the synagogue era of God's gift of the Torah on Sinai.

[3] On this phrase see p. 137.

[4] Levine, p. 261.

to allow one to 'catch one's breath'.[5] God had set them free from un-remitting drudgery; the weekly Sabbath would serve to remind them regularly that they had experienced his saving justice in their own lives and to prompt them regularly to treat others with similar mercy and justice.

In the light of this, it is tragic that what God intended as an instrument of freedom was subsequently refashioned into a tool of oppression. God gives his people no more than a general principle, which required them to work out its detailed application for themselves.[6] At a later date, well-intentioned religious bureaucrats sought to help the less able members of the community by spelling out exactly what could and could not be done on the Sabbath. In practice, what they were doing was to forge fresh chains with which to bind people once more. It was these petty interpretations, rather than the liberating Sabbath principle itself, to which Jesus objected when he proclaimed himself 'the Lord of the Sabbath'.[7]

Walter Brueggemann finds it astonishing that this day should assume such importance in the ethical system of Israel and become a crucial factor in determining whether God's presence would be among them or withdrawn from them. And yet, he comments, one can see why it became so significant. The Sabbath 'means desisting from the frantic pursuit of securing the world on our own terms'.[8] It curbs our drivenness; it interrupts our acquisitiveness; it realigns our values; it draws us back to basics, to depend on God again; and it gives us space to renew our relationship with him.

Observing the Sabbath is the only one of the Ten Commandments not to be commended in the New Testament. The New Testament's silence is probably to be explained on two fronts. First, there was the need for the early Christians to distance themselves from the distorted understanding of the Sabbath held by the Jews of their day. Such references to the Sabbath as there are suggest that observing the day is no longer legally binding but considered optional (Rom. 14:5; Gal. 4:8–10; Col. 2:16). Second, the import-ance of the seventh day has been somewhat overtaken by the importance of the eighth day – the day that Leviticus has constantly used as a symbol

---

[5] Cf. Kaiser, p. 1157.

[6] Hartley, p. 375.

[7] Matt. 12:1–14; Mark 2:23–28; Luke 6:1–11; 13:10–17; John 5:1–30; 9:1–41.

[8] Brueggemann, *Finally*, p. 95.

of new beginnings,[9] and the day on which Jesus rose from the dead. In honour of Christ's resurrection, the early Christians met for worship, not on the last day of the week, but on the first day of the week.[10]

There is no room for legalism in the life of liberty that Christ has won for us (Gal. 5:1). But there is wisdom still in observing and working out the Sabbath principle in our lives.[11] Creating regular space for God, ceasing from the work that so easily becomes a tyrant, refocusing our spiritual values, and recalling our need not to oppress others, as well as joyfully celebrating the irrepressible life of our risen Lord, all remain crucial elements in the formation of the spiritual life.

2. The Passover: God delivers (23:4–5)

The Lord's Passover meal was to be observed annually on the *fourteenth day of the first month*. Its timing was significant.[12] As the first sacrifice to be observed in the year it spoke of the new beginning Israel had enjoyed, thanks to a sovereign act of God. It celebrated that fateful night, long ago in Egypt, when the angel of death passed over the bloodstained homes of the Israelites and meted out God's judgment on the tyrants who had oppressed them. The details are found in Exodus 12:1–51, which not only records the original event but lays down instructions as to how it was to be observed in the future.[13]

The central act of the meal was the sacrificing and eating of the Passover lamb. As with the sacrifices of Leviticus, the meaning is to be found in the details, and the particulars of which lamb was chosen and the use of its blood are all highly suggestive of the sacrifices that Leviticus later enshrined. The meal heralded the freedom of Israel from Egypt and their commissioning as priests.[14] Their exodus has served as a paradigm

---

[9] Lev. 9:1; 12:3; 14:10, 23; 15:14, 29; 23:36, 39.

[10] John 20:1; 1 Cor. 16:2. For a full discussion see D. A. Carson (ed.), *From Sabbath to Lord's Day* (Grand Rapids, MI: Zondervan, 1982).

[11] Isa. 58 provides a vigorous exhortation to keep the Sabbath, which illustrates the way in which doing so both liberates individuals and serves the purposes of social justice.

[12] The first month, later known as Nisan, occurs not in January, as in our calendar, but in the spring, in March–April.

[13] For a full exposition see Derek Tidball, *The Message of the Cross*, The Bible Speaks Today (Leicester: IVP, 2001), pp. 51–67.

[14] Desmond Alexander has drawn out some striking parallels between this meal and the account of the ordination of Aaron and his sons as priests in Lev. 8. T. D. Alexander, 'The Passover Sacrifice', in R. T. Beckwith and M. J. Selman (eds.), *Sacrifice and the Bible* (Carlisle: Paternoster, 1995), p. 8.

for many liberation movements down through history. But, unlike so many that depend merely on human effort and political agency, this liberation movement was an act of God. The Passover meal would constantly bring Israel back to that fact. They had gained their freedom, not because of Moses' acute political organization or Aaron's diplomatic skills, or because there was a popular uprising, and even less as a result of mounting a powerful army in opposition to Egypt's military forces, but because God intervened in judgment and salvation. It was for ever to be *the Lord's Passover.*

The communion meal that Christians enjoy evolved from this Passover feast. The setting in which Jesus commanded his disciples to eat bread in remembrance that his body had been given for them, and to drink wine in remembrance that his blood had been poured out for them, was that of a Passover meal (Matt. 26:17; Mark 14:12; Luke 22:1–23). He claims for himself the role of the Passover lamb, and as we eat bread and drink wine, we celebrate the salvation he has won for us through his sacrifice on the cross.

3. The Feast of Unleavened Bread: God nourishes (23:6–8)

The Passover merged into the Feast of Unleavened Bread, which began the next day and lasted for seven days. It marked the start of the barley harvest and was one of the three occasions during the year when Israelite men were mandated to appear at the sanctuary (Exod. 23:17). This feast began and ended with days of *sacred assembly*, which were days that were free from work. In between, the people were required to eat the thin wafers of bread that had been baked without yeast, having first removed all yeast from their houses (Exod. 12:15). This recalled the unleavened bread that Israel ate in Egypt on the night of the Passover (Exod. 12:8). Originally, the reason for eating unleavened bread was that Israel left Egypt to commence their pilgrimage in haste and there was no opportunity for them to let their bread rise. (The Hebrew title of the festival emphasizes its connection with pilgrimage.[15]) Unleavened bread would serve people on the move better than leavened bread.

Later on, yeast became a symbol for corruption and its removal from their houses was taken as a sign of removing all corruption from their

---

[15] Levine, p. 156. The full title is 'the Pilgrimage Feast of Unleavened Bread of the Lord'.

lives. It is interesting that in 1 Corinthians 5:7, which is the only explicit statement of Christ as the Passover in the New Testament,[16] Paul does not focus on the lamb, which is not explicitly mentioned in the original Greek, but on the secondary element in the Passover meal, which required the cleansing of yeast from the house. 'How can anyone celebrate the Festival',[17] he goes on to ask in effect, unless 'the yeast of malice and wickedness has been removed?' Free from any taint of sin, the regular diet of the Christian should be 'the unleavened bread of sincerity and truth'.

Christians have no equivalent to this festival, but it serves as a reminder of at least four important 'oughts' of the Christian life. First, Christians ought to be in haste to obey God's will. Second, Christians ought to be a pilgrim people, always making spiritual progress and never settling into a state of smug spiritual complacency. Third, Christians ought regularly to examine their lives and throw out the corrupting influences of sin. Finally, Christians ought to feast themselves on the nutritious food of truth instead of on the seductive junk food of compromise that is often mistaken for it.

4. The offering of firstfruits: God claims (23:9–14)

The next festival anticipates the time when the Israelites will have taken possession of the Promised Land and will enjoy reaping the early barley harvest. It was an event, rather than a festival. Of necessity, no date is set for it because it could not be fixed too far in advance. It depended on when the first grain was ripe.

When the barley was ripe, *a sheaf of the first grain you harvest* was to be given to a priest who would *wave the sheaf before the LORD*, in a gesture that represented the giving of a present to God (10–11). God had the prior claim over all things; the first, the freshest and the best belonged to him. Only after the first pickings of the harvest had been offered to him were the people allowed to enjoy the rest of the harvest themselves (14). The 'wave offering' was to be accompanied by a burnt and a grain offering. The day would have been one of great celebration.

---

16 There are many implied references, e.g. John 1:29, 36; 1 Pet. 1:18–19; Rev. 5:6, 8, 12, 13; 12:11.

17 What Paul means by 'Festival' in 1 Cor. 5:8 is unclear in the context. It may be an allusion to the Lord's Table, but, partly because the present continuous tense is used, it may be a reference to the daily sacrifice of our lives. See A. C. Thiselton, *The First Epistle to the Corinthians*, NIGTC (Grand Rapids, MI: Eerdmans; Carlisle: Paternoster, 2000), p. 406.

This liturgical action differentiates Israel sharply from her neighbours. In the fertility rituals of the surrounding nations people sought to manipulate their deities into providing abundant harvests. But Israel's God could be trusted to provide for them without the need to resort to such arm-twisting. In offering him the first sheaves to be reaped they were acknowledging that he was the source of all good things and that the rich earth belonged to him and was under his control (Jas 1:17).

The New Testament makes a great deal of use of the image of 'firstfruits'. It stands for a first instalment and for the conviction that more of the same will follow. Christ's resurrection made him 'the firstfruits of those who have fallen asleep' (1 Cor. 15:20). The full harvest of the resurrection is yet to come. Christian believers enjoy 'the firstfruits of the Spirit' and will one day enjoy much more of his recreative ministry in their lives (Rom. 8:23). Christians themselves are spoken of as the firstfruits of the new creation, forerunners of the age to be consummated when Christ returns.[18]

5. The Feast of Weeks: God provides (23:15–22)

If the presentation of the firstfruits signalled the beginning of the barley harvest, the Feast of Weeks signalled its end. Its name[19] is derived from the practice of counting seven weeks from the offering of firstfruits as a way of determining when this festival should be held. On the fiftieth day the people enjoyed another *sacred assembly* and had a day off work (21). On this occasion the ritual consisted of presenting God with two loaves baked from the fresh grain but this time baked *with yeast* (17), making them representative of Israel's normal and richer fare.[20] Given that they contained yeast, the loaves were not to be placed on the altar but were 'elevated' before the Lord in an act of dedication. Their presentation was accompanied by seven burnt offerings, a grain offering, a sin offering and a fellowship offering. Here, indeed, was a mega-celebration of God's provision.

An interesting footnote is appended to these regulations. In the midst of their celebration of abundance the children of Israel are reminded of

---

[18] Jas 1:18. Both Jas 1:17 and 18 have their roots in this offering; the former acknowledges that God is the provider of all good things, and the latter makes use of the imagery of the firstfruits.

[19] The name is absent in Leviticus but mentioned in Deut. 16:10. It is called 'the Festival of Harvest' in Exod. 23:16.

[20] Noordtzij, p. 236.

their obligations to the poor (22).[21] Harvests and holiness belonged together (Neh. 8:10). They could not truly express dedication and thankfulness to God while being indifferent to the needs of their neighbours.

The fifty days mentioned in verse 16 led to this feast being known as the Feast of Pentecost. Much later the feast became associated with the giving of the law, another of God's rich provisions for his people. But for Christians it is inextricably associated with yet a third gift – the gift of the Holy Spirit to the church. Fifty days after Jesus rose from the dead, as his waiting disciples were 'all together in one place', 'all of them were filled with the Holy Spirit' (Acts 2:1–4). What they saw and what they heard led them to have confidence that God had sent the 'gift' he had promised (Acts 1:4), and with new boldness they went outside among the crowds and preached Jesus as 'both Lord and Messiah' (Acts 2:36). The spiritual harvest they reaped that day was overwhelming and amounted to the addition of three thousand people to the church.

6. The Feast of Trumpets: God remembers (23:23–25)

At this point the interest shifts to the festivals that fall in the autumn. The first *sacred assembly* in the latter part of the year took place on *the first day of the seventh month*.[22] The seventh month of the year held great significance for the Israelites. It would have been the lightest month in the agricultural year and therefore gave the opportunity for some 'time out'. But its real significance lay in the fact that seven was the number for perfection, and several celebratory events fall during this month. The Feast of Trumpets heads the list.

Little is said of this feast. We know that it was one of the seven days on which people were expected not to work, and that a special burnt offering was presented (Num. 29:1–6). The distinctive feature of the day, however, lay in the blowing of loud blasts on a trumpet (which, for them, was not a brass instrument but a ram's horn – cf. Ps. 81:3). The trumpet blasts had something to do with stirring up a memory, indicated by the use of the word *commemorated*. Literally it is 'a memorial day with resounding'.[23] But whose memory is being jogged, and what is the memory being stirred?

---

[21] The verses repeat the instructions of Lev. 19:9–10.

[22] The month was later known as Tishri (September–October).

[23] Noordtzij, p. 237.

In other cultures the blowing of trumpets at New Year was associated with warding off evil spirits and attracting the attention of their gods so as to win their favour for the days ahead. But these attitudes do not fit with the beliefs and practices of Israel. With God on their side, they need not placate evil spirits, and their futures lie safely in his sovereign and loving hands. Here the point seems to be, as suggested by John Hartley, a mutual reviving of memory between God and his people.[24] Trumpets had been sounded when the law was received at Sinai (Exod. 19:16) and were blown on other significant occasions (Num. 10:10). The trumpet blasts remind Israel that they are party to a covenant. Are they obedient to its stipulations and faithful in following God? Equally, the trumpet blasts remind God of the covenant he has made with Israel, not in the sense that he needs it to be recalled to his mind because he has forgotten it (cf. Isa. 49:15), but as a way of renewing his commitment to them to keep his promises.

In later Judaism this day became New Year's Day. There is no Christian equivalent to this day, although the practice of observing a watch-night service as the New Year dawns, or an annual church anniversary, both of which entail the renewing of commitment, may be modelled on this festival.

7. The Day of Atonement: God forgives (23:26–32)

The annual Day of Atonement, during which total expiation for the sins of Israel was obtained, has been extensively covered earlier (16:1–34). This day, with its unique rituals, must have been the high point of the year. Whatever sins had been committed during the previous year were now swept up and removed in a ceremony that reached its climax when the two specially chosen goats were dealt their different fates. One died as a sin offering for the people, and its blood was sprinkled in the Most Holy Place and the Tent of Meeting. The other lived. After the high priest's hands had been laid on it and the wickedness of Israel confessed over it, it was sent away into the desert and, carrying the sins of the people with it, it was never to return. In this way, 'whatever their sins have been' (16:16), atonement was made.

---

[24] Hartley, p. 387. This is contrary to Noordtzij, who, citing Josh. 6:4; Matt. 24:31; 1 Cor. 15:52; 1 Thess. 4:16; and Rev. 8 – 11, believes it to be a warning of God's judgment.

The regulations here repeat that the day was to be celebrated on the *tenth day of this seventh month* (27; cf. 16:29),[25] and add that failure to observe it would attract the severest of penalties as the Lord himself stepped in in judgment (29). Levine points out that scheduling this event a few days before the major pilgrimage feast of the year 'ensured that the sanctuary and, hence, the people would be restored to a state of fitness' in time for those celebrations.[26]

8. The Feast of Tabernacles: God reminds (23:33–43)

The final celebration of the year was a seven-day festival that concluded the agricultural cycle. It was, in Hartley's apt words, 'the most gala feast of the year'.[27] The regulations clearly have in view the time when the Israelites had settled in the Promised Land and lived in scattered communities.[28] This feast was another of the three occasions a year when Israelite men were required to make pilgrimage to Jerusalem.

It began *on the fifteenth day of the seventh month* (34), during which a continuous round of sacrifices was offered, climaxing with the offering of a special sacrifice *on the eighth day* (36). On both the first and the last day, work was forbidden. The offerings prescribed were in addition to any routine offerings, such as those normally presented on the Sabbath, and to any personal votive or freewill offerings that might be presented during the duration of the feast (37–38).

Two distinctive features of this feast are set out in verses 39–43, in a paragraph that supplements the basic regulations. First, citrus fruit and olives were to be harvested and, together with branches from the palm, myrtle and willow trees, were taken in joyful procession to the altar (40; cf. Ps. 118:27). Second, the pilgrims were told to construct temporary shelters, like those that would have been erected in the fields during harvest time (42). *All native-born Israelites* were required to live in these makeshift structures because all had benefited from the events they commemorated.

---

[25] The reference to *the evening of the ninth day* in v. 32 alludes to the fact that the Israelite day went from sunset to sunset.

[26] Levine, p. 162.

[27] Hartley, p. 388.

[28] Many scholars see vv. 39–43 as a post-exilic addition to the original instructions. See Milgrom, *Leviticus 23 – 27*, pp. 2036–2038. Milgrom contains fascinating details of the later development of the feast.

The rationale for their temporary accommodation is given in verse 43: *so that your descendants will know that I made the Israelites live in temporary shelters when I brought them out of Egypt.* After Israel had settled in their own land and enjoyed the comfort of permanent housing, it would be all too easy to forget that it was the Lord who led them out of Egypt and provided food and shelter for them during their wilderness journey. They were likely to think of themselves as self-sufficient and to assume that the food and security they enjoyed were the result of their own labour rather than of the Lord's generosity.[29] But such arrogance would, at least annually, be deflated by the observance of this ceremony, which reminded them of their past. Many understand the chief purpose of this feast as being to remind pilgrims of the hardship they had experienced in the wilderness and to encourage a spirit of thankfulness for what they subsequently enjoyed. But the practice can be given a more positive spin. The purpose may have been to draw attention not so much to their hardship in the past as to the Lord's provision in the present. He had kept them and provided for them in the harsh wilderness; would he not now provide for them in the land of promise? Hartley argues for this interpretation, pointing out that the booths were built out of the glorious trees of the Promised Land, not the barren shrubs of the wilderness.[30]

One of the main objectives of the day, as we learn from its later practice, was to pray that God would provide rain for the crops. 'The waving of the branches in all directions is a summons to the four winds to bring rain.'[31] So, too, was the water libation that became attached to the feast. By the time of Jesus Christ an essential element of the celebration was the bringing of water from the Pool of Siloam through the Water Gate to the temple, where it was poured out as a supplication to God. The rabbis argued that the ritual went back to Moses and derived from the time when he struck the rock with his staff in the wilderness at Meribah in order to provide the people with water (Num. 20:1–13; see also 1 Sam. 7:6). As God had done it before, so, they prayed, he would do it again.

But another hope had become bound up with the quest for water. It came to symbolize the day of the Messiah, when life-giving water would flow from the very heart of the temple, as prophesied by Ezekiel (47:1–12)

---

[29] Deut. 8 warns of the spiritual danger of forgetting what the Lord has done in the past.

[30] Hartley, pp. 389–390.

[31] Milgrom, *Leviticus 23 – 27*, p. 2043.

and Zechariah (14:8). The Jews believed that when the Messiah came, their enemies would be defeated and the day of supreme peace and prosperity would arrive. Centuries later, Jesus went as a pilgrim to this feast, and 'on the last and greatest day of the festival' – a day when it is thought they did not observe the ritual of carrying the water in procession as they had on the previous days – he cried, 'Let anyone who is thirsty come to me and drink. Whoever believes in me, as Scripture has said, rivers of living water will flow from within them.' In this stunning and controversial call, recorded in John 7:37–44, he was declaring that with his coming the day of the Messiah had indeed arrived.

There is no equivalent festival for Christians since the hopes and aspirations of the feast have been fulfilled in Jesus. But we are, nevertheless, wise to keep in mind some of the lessons it embodies. Recalling the past is important. God's people forget it at their peril. In lean days, the memory of God's gracious provision in past times can provide the stamina needed to keep trusting. In prosperous days, the memory that God was the source of the provision can encourage humility and keep us from foolish feelings of self-sufficiency. Memory matters. The feast also reminds us that we are called to be a pilgrim people. It is all too easy, as Israel found after entering the Promised Land, to settle and become spiritually complacent. We are to enjoy the material things that God provides, if we accept them with thanksgiving (1 Tim. 4:4). But the very blessings designed for our comfort can easily become traps. So we are to hold loose to the things of earth and cultivate trust in God rather than wrongly placing our hope and trust in material possessions (1 Tim. 6:6–10, 17–19). On this earth, God's people will never be anything other than a pilgrim people, always on the move, always growing, always making spiritual progress, until their final destination of eternal rest is reached (Heb. 4:11).

Walter Kaiser has summed up the significance of the feasts, somewhat sweetly, like this: 'A sabbath or a festival was like a kiss between lovers. It gathered into a special moment what was always true.'[32] It is always true that God desires his people to know the restfulness of trusting in him, but once a week the frantic round of busy lives is brought to a standstill to recall his resting on the seventh day and his desire that no-one should be exploited in the labour market. It is always true that God saves, that he nourishes his people, claims their commitment, provides for their needs,

---

[32] Kaiser, p. 1160.

recalls his covenant with them, forgives their sin and reminds them of their identity. But it is helpful to have particular days spread through the calendar which mark these truths in a special way and stave off the presumption that takes them as read. Some Christians still find the observance of a special calendar helpful to their spiritual lives, though none are obliged to observe one. Since the coming of Christ, it is important that we do not judge one another on the basis of external religious observance. In this area we must do what our consciences dictate before God. Above all, we must not hold on to these shadow days too tightly, since they merely point forward to a future reality. Rather, we must hold firmly to the reality of Christ himself: our redeemer, protector and provider, and the Lord who claims the freshest and best of our lives (Rom. 14:5; Col. 2:16–17).

Keeping the feasts was no hardship. It gave people space and led them to reconnect with God as well as with one another. It led them to reflect on the goodness of their God, to refocus their lives and to renew their trust in him for the future. Rather than being a chore, these feasts testified to the joy Israel experienced in knowing God.[33] Their combined message is captured in Joseph Hart's short hymn:

> How good is the God we adore,
>   Our faithful, unchangeable Friend!
> His love is as great as his power,
>   And knows neither measure nor end!
>
> 'Tis Jesus, the first and the last,
>   Whose Spirit shall guide us safe home;
> We'll praise him for all that is past,
>   And trust him for all that's to come.[34]

[33] Kellogg, p. 473.

[34] Joseph Hart (1712–68).

Leviticus 24:1–23

20. God's word about safeguarding the sacred

Sacred times, places, objects and actions are considered by many today as helpful aids to their spirituality, even by some evangelicals who have historically proved very suspicious of them. Evangelical suspicion can be traced back to the Reformation and to the way Martin Luther and others reacted against pilgrimages, the veneration of relics, and the acts performed by the priests that were often treated as superstitious magic. Behind these sacred things there lurked the ever-present danger of idolatry and a belief in salvation by works. Nowhere does the New Testament even commend, let alone command, the observing of certain days, places, objects or actions as 'sacred'.[1] In fact, its teaching runs in the opposite direction. We saw in the previous chapter that its attitude to special days is one of indifference (Col. 2:16–17). To this we might add that no special persons are given the status of priests and marked out as deserving of veneration (cf. Acts 14:8–20). Nor is any place recommended as worthy of pilgrimage, not even Jerusalem.[2]

In the Old Testament, however, the matter was different. Places, times, actions and items were designated as sacred and served as object lessons in spirituality and as 'types' (prefigurings) of the reality that would one day be realized in Christ. The tabernacle was a sacred space, with the Most Holy Place being the most sacred of all. Sacrifices were sacred actions. The

---

[1] For a recent discussion see Peter Adam, *Hearing God's Words: Exploring Biblical Spirituality* (Leicester: Apollos; Downers Grove, IL: IVP, 2004), pp. 148–162.

[2] Acts 6:8 – 7:59 teaches that Jesus, not Jerusalem, is to be the centre of our faith and the place where we encounter God.

Sabbath and the festivals were sacred times. There were also sacred objects, which had to be handled with care and could not be treated as if they were ordinary.

Many find little coherence in chapter 24, and little obvious reason for its inclusion at this point.[3] It is, however, about the need to maintain and protect three sacred items – the lamp and the bread on the table in the Holy Place, and the sacred name of God. Each of these deserved special care. The importance of this is taught in the first two cases by the issuing of words of command (1–9), and in the third by recording a sad incident in the life of Israel (10–23).

1. Safeguarding sacred objects (24:1–9)

a. The importance of unremarkable service

The brief instructions about maintaining the lights and caring for the bread include the word *continually* four times (2, 3, 4, 8).[4] This gives us both the clue to why they are included at this point and the key principle they seek to inculcate. Chapter 23 had outlined the major events of the year. By contrast, these verses deal with the routine events of every day and every week. The lamps are to be tended daily and the bread on the table replaced weekly. It was by any measure unspectacular, mundane and routine service for God, but, for all that, it was no less important than presiding over the big celebrations or offering a multitude of sacrifices.

The danger of much of today's Christianity, with its concentration on major gatherings and celebrity speakers, is that it sets wrong aspirations before emerging Christian leaders. Some see the glamour and glitz and want to have a prominent place in the celebration event or on the big platform before they are ready. They do not see, and they fail to grasp, the significance of serving God faithfully in the unremarkable, small and routine work that characterizes most service for God.

In the school of Jesus, disciples were trained to grasp the need to serve God in the ordinary, small things that others dismissed as unworthy of their time. His attitude to children, his stress on watching over 'these little ones' (Matt. 10:42; 18:6, 10, 14), by which he meant weak disciples, and the

---

[3] Mary Douglas has attempted to explain the order of Leviticus as a cycle in which the defiling of the sacred name in this chapter corresponds to the defiling of the sacred place in Lev. 10. These chapters contain the only narrative sections in the book. Douglas, 'Forbidden Animals', p. 11. See Introduction above, p. 8.

[4] NIV translates the last of these as *regularly*.

significance he saw in a simple 'cup of cold water' (Matt. 10:42; 25:35) give us one insight into what he considers important. So, too, do his comments following the parable of the shrewd manager. While the parable itself may be difficult for us, because on the surface Jesus seems to be commending dishonesty, the lessons he draws from it are crystal clear.[5] In God's service, servants have to prove themselves faithful in the little things before being entrusted with the bigger things, faithful with material responsibilities before being entrusted with spiritual ones, and faithful in handling other people's property before being entrusted with their own (Luke 16:10–12).

The priests of old would have understood that in 'the trivial round, the common task' there was 'a road to bring us daily nearer God'.[6] The tending of the lamp and the replenishing of the bread were simple routine tasks, the one a daily chore and the other a weekly offering, that enabled God's light to shine in a dark world and God's food to be available for a hungry people.

The truth is that many of us get worn down by the endless round of tedious tasks and do not find ourselves being brought nearer to God through them. When this happens, we need to look to Jesus. A prayer by Ruth Etchells puts it brilliantly. Having complained about discouragement and 'the weariness of grinding routine', she continues:

And then I turn my eyes to you, Lord Christ:

You gave up the infinite space of eternity,
The shining serenity of heaven;
Surrendered your power, honour and rightful glory
To the crushing finitude of our human life.

O my Lord Christ, for what? for whom?
Yes, Lord, I hear you. For us. For me.

You gave up the lovely companionships of eternity,
The totally trusting, totally trustworthy loves of heaven;

---

[5] Luke 16:1–15. The parable does not commend dishonesty; interpreted in the business context of the day, the steward shows determination and acute shrewdness in reducing the liabilities of those in debt to his master. For a brilliant exposition see Kenneth E. Bailey, *Poet and Peasant* (Grand Rapids, MI: Eerdmans, 1976), pp. 86–118.

[6] From 'New Every Morning Is the Love', by John Keble (1792–1866).

Were subject to pettiness, scorn, misunderstanding,
And the limited love your friends could give you
And the humiliations and death your enemies planned for you.

Yes, Lord, I hear you. For us. For me.

O my Lord, forgive me. For you took to yourself the tedium and
frustration of this ordinary human life of mine, and so lived it that
it gave glimpses of the glory and the richness of the life within it of
heaven, for which we were created and for which I long. You showed
how the life of heaven was present to be lived here and now; and you
opened up for us the way to do it.

   O Lord, help me to grasp hold of that truth today, so that the
ordinary things I do and my every encounter, reflect, however dimly,
the lambency[7] of heaven. To which heaven bring me in fullness,
my dear Lord Christ, one day.

Amen.[8]

b. Tending the lamps (24:1–4)[9]

The people are instructed to bring *clear oil of pressed olives* (2) to the
priests so that they may *tend the lamps before the LORD* and ensure that
they burn continually, day and night. The priests had the duty of ensuring
that the oil never ran dry and that the wicks were kept trimmed. The lamp
was the six-branched lampstand that was made of pure, beaten gold and
stood on the south side of the Holy Place.[10] It reminded them that God
was the creator of light, and that even when the sun went down at night
he forfeited none of his powers but continued to rule over his world.[11] The
burning of the light at night testified to God's continual presence among
them, without which chaos and darkness would soon encroach. Against
this background, light stood for God's 'order, goodness and stability'.[12]
The lamp was a sacred object, full of meaning, and needed to be

---

[7] 'Lambency' means 'light' or 'brilliance'.

[8] Ruth Etchells, *Just as I Am: Personal Prayers for Every Day* (London: SPCK, 1994), pp. 58–59. Used with permission.

[9] The command is repeated in Exod. 27:20–21.

[10] The details are given in Exod. 37:17–24; 40:24–25.

[11] Gerstenberger, p. 356.

[12] Bellinger, p. 143.

maintained with love and care if people were truly to understand, in however rudimentary a way, that 'God is light; in him there is no darkness at all' (1 John 1:5). We need to guard our relationship with the Lord Jesus with the same regularity, affection and degree of care that the priests of old demonstrated in caring for the lamp.

c. Replenishing the bread (2:5–9)

Opposite the lamp in the Holy Place, on its north side, was another sacred symbol, namely the table on which was placed the 'bread of the Presence'. Also made of gold, it stood about 750 cm high, almost a metre long, and 50 cm wide, and was made to be portable (Exod. 37:10–16). The sacredness of this table was not to be neglected by letting the loaves stay on it week after week. So, each week, on the Sabbath, twelve fresh loaves were placed on it in two rows, and then incense was placed beside them.[13] The twelve loaves represented God's sufficient provision for the twelve tribes of Israel. The bread is literally 'the bread of the face', that is, bread that keeps the children of Israel before the face of God. The incense is *a memorial portion . . . to be a food offering presented to the* LORD (7) that wafts the needs of his people into God's presence. All these symbols, together with days such as the Feast of Trumpets, ensure that God is never for a moment unmindful of the covenant he has entered with his people, or of their concerns.[14]

d. The symbols through New Testament eyes

Jesus claimed for himself the titles of both 'the light of the world' (John 8:12) and 'the bread of life' (John 6:35). As light, he cuts through the searing darkness of our sin and deceit, and leads us to walk in the life-giving light of God. As bread, he nourishes our famished spirits and satisfies the deepest hunger of our lives, a hunger that other food can never touch.

Yet, though the symbols reach their ultimate fulfilment in Jesus, they also have implications for the work of his disciples in the world. We are commissioned by Christ to reflect his light among the nations and, ourselves, to be 'the light of the world' (Matt. 5:14). The life-giving light of

---

[13] Hartley, p. 401, points out that, since Aaron and his sons ate the loaves (v. 9), it was less likely that the incense was sprinkled on them than that it was placed alongside them. Given that the loaves were eaten a week after they were first baked, the bread must have been unleavened.

[14] Hartley, p. 402, adds, 'It is possible that the priests' partaking of this bread symbolized that all members of the twelve tribes are in table fellowship with Yahweh.'

Jesus is not something we are to hide, as if ashamed of it, but to display in all its splendour through our lives. And while we are never told that we are 'bread for the world', the command Jesus gave to his disciples, as he was on the verge of feeding the five thousand, is one that reverberates down the centuries to us as well: 'You give them something to eat' (Matt. 14:16). For the light to shine brightly and the bread to be fresh food, disciples of Jesus need to maintain regular – daily and weekly – contact with the Lord. There is much benefit in observing routine spiritual disciplines rather than 'tending the lamps' or 'replacing the bread' irregularly, when we feel the need to do so.

2. Safeguarding the sacred name (24:10–23)

The latter half of the chapter concerns the safeguarding of *the Name* (11), arguably the most sacred entity of all. The name stood for the whole person, so to curse the name of God was to curse the sacred person of God himself.

a. A tragic incident (24:10–16, 23)

The incident reported here is one of only two narrative interludes in the book of Leviticus.[15] It occurred when a half-Israelite, whose father was Egyptian but whose mother was an Israelite, *used the Name blasphemously with a curse* (11). The details of the curse are not repeated for us, but it was obviously considered a serious infringement of the third commandment by those who heard it. George Knight suggests that the offender must have been more than merely using God's name as a swear word, and 'was actually trying to destroy the faith of the people of Israel by saying that Yahweh, the Lord, was not like his name. He would therefore be insinuating that the ideal of the covenant was a lot of nonsense.'[16] Blasphemy was high treason against God.

The man was held in temporary *custody*[17] [a rare reference in the Old Testament to incarceration] *until the will of the Lord should be made clear to them* (12). Again, the details are missing. How were they to determine

---

[15] The other is 10:1–19.

[16] Knight, p. 148.

[17] Wenham, p. 286, quotes (approvingly?) Driver and Miles as saying that imprisonment, 'which is expensive to the community, generally corrupting the prisoner, and often bringing unmerited hardship on his dependants, is the invention of a later age'.

the will of the Lord? It reads as if the will of the Lord came directly to Moses rather than by Aaron using the Urim and Thummim. Whatever the means of communication, the verdict was that the man should be subjected to the death penalty. The offence was a capital crime, since it dishonoured God and undermined the whole basis of Israel's identity and calling. An offence of this nature, though primarily an offence against God, was also 'an offence against the state that depended on him'.[18] So he was taken out and stoned to death by *the entire assembly* of Israel (14), probably acting through their tribal leaders and representatives. It made no difference that the man was not a pure Israelite. Full Israelite, half-Israelite or foreigner, the brazen insolence shown to the sacred name of God and all that it stood for could in no way be tolerated. The sacred name must be safeguarded.

b. A general principle (24:17–22)

This particular case leads to a consideration of wider law, but it does so in a way that forges a close connection between the particular and the general. The arrangement of the verses, with the command to execute a murderer following immediately on the execution of a blasphemer, suggests that blasphemy is seen as equivalent to murder: the one a grievous assault against God, and the other a grievous assault against a fellow human being made in the image of God.[19] Both, therefore, merit the death penalty.

The general principle of law is known as the *lex talionis: life for life . . . fracture for fracture, eye for eye, tooth for tooth* (18–20). Justice was to be based on the principle of exact reciprocity. This law fulfilled a number of purposes. It emphasized, as other laws in Leviticus had previously done, the sacredness of life. No-one could take a life without surrendering his or her own, although due allowance was made for the difference between premeditated murder and manslaughter.[20] If a violent offender robbed his or her victim of a limb or organ, the offender forfeited the right to that limb or organ in his or her own body. The law was also designed to set a limit on the punishments meted out, to check the unleashing of vengeance and to forestall the igniting of spirals of retaliation. If an eye was lost,

---

[18] C. J. H. Wright, 'Leviticus', p. 152.

[19] Balentine, p. 187.

[20] Deut. 19:1–7 established three cities as refuges for those who have killed unintentionally.

no-one had the right to take a life in return, or to blow up a house and render a family homeless. The punishment had to be equal to the crime, not more, not less. The punishment also had to be administered on behalf of the community and the offended parties by the courts and magistrates (Exod. 21:22; 22:8–9). This was not a charter for taking the law into one's own hands.[21] The Deuteronomic version of this law begins with the words 'Show no pity', which, in addition to ruling out undue sentimentality in the administration of justice, also underlined the need for courts to be utterly impartial in their execution of the law.[22]

The *lex talionis* applies to human beings. Injuring animals falls in a different category (21). Any injury to an animal would be serious because it would almost certainly mean a loss of revenue for its owner, who, therefore, must be compensated for it. But the value of an animal's life was not to be equated with the value of a human life. Therefore, though restitution was required, the same penalties were not exacted.

Both in valuing human life above that of property and in setting limits on the punishments that might be sought, the Old Testament laws exemplify a humanitarianism that is unmatched in the other laws of the day.

Whether these laws should determine the way modern courts approach their policies on sentencing is a moot point, discussed earlier in reference to capital punishment in chapter 17.[23] One cannot help but feel that the emphasis on restitution, at least, would lead to a great improvement in the current system of sentencing. To sidetrack this, however, into a discussion of penal policy may mean that we miss the main thrust of the chapter. That which is sacred needs to be safeguarded. We must be watchful so as not to let the sacred be denigrated or despised in any way. We must watch over the small and routine things, as well as the momentous and exceptional things, to ensure that God's honour is upheld.

As Christians, we may no longer have sacred places, days, objects or actions that require protection. They belong to a past day. If some use them as aids to spiritual growth, that is fine, though they dare not judge the spirituality of others by how much they use them, and they should be

---

[21] Jesus' comments on this law seem designed to rescue it from those who sought to administer it personally, and to restore its execution to its proper place in the courts. See Matt. 5:38–42.

[22] Deut. 19:21. Deut. 19:15–21 sets some wider principles and a wider philosophy of justice than Lev. 24. See Wenham, p. 282.

[23] For a discussion of the blasphemy laws in contemporary society see A. J. Rivers, 'Blasphemy Law in the Secular State', *Cambridge Papers* 1.4 (1982).

alert to the danger of stopping with the sign and not looking beyond to the reality.

The person of God, however, remains sacred. The name of God the Father and all that it represents, together with the sacred person of Jesus, the new centre of our faith, must be venerated still. What does it mean for us to do so? And how can we encourage others to do so, who belong to a society that regards very little as sacred? We cannot impose our will on others. But we may encourage them to treat with respect the name and the person we hold dear by our example and our own devotion. For us to honour that name will certainly mean that we avoid using it as a swear word. It will mean that people should know that it is entirely unnecessary for us to use it in swearing an oath because we always speak with integrity. As James said, 'Above all, my brothers and sisters, do not swear – not by heaven or by earth or by anything else.[24] All you need to say is a simple "Yes" or "No". Otherwise you will be condemned' (Jas 5:12). More than this, it will mean that we do nothing to malign the name of God or denigrate the person of Jesus, and nothing that mutinies against their sovereign authority in our lives. We shall hold the triune God, by life and lip, in high honour.

---

[24] The later Jews avoided using the name for God in oaths and resorted to circumlocutions: heaven was God's dwelling-place and earth his footstool.

Leviticus 25:1–55

21. God's word about radical economics

The *Observer*, a newspaper known for its progressive views, is not normally the place you would look for a commendation of Leviticus. But on 3 October 1999, its headline ran, 'The Jubilee line that works: Debt-relief campaign Jubilee 2000 can now claim its great victory, thanks to Leviticus.' In welcoming the success of the Jubilee 2000 campaign, which subjected governments to unprecedented international pressure to reduce the debt of the world's poorest countries, Will Hutton paid tribute to Leviticus and wrote,

> At the end of an increasingly secular century, it has been the biblical proof and moral imagination of religion that have torched the principles of the hitherto unassailable citadels of international finance – and opened the way to a radicalism about capitalism whose ramifications are not yet fully understood.

The inspiration for the campaign came from the year of Jubilee, set forth in Leviticus 25, the main purpose of which was to provide a way out for those who fell into debt.

The structure of the chapter is complex and the issues wider than the Jubilee alone. But the heart of it all lies in verse 23: *The land must not be sold permanently, because the land is mine and you reside in my land as foreigners and strangers.* When the Israelites took possession of the Promised Land, they could enjoy its benefits but were to be aware that 'they had no ultimate title to the land – it was owned by God'.[1] Consequently, their

---

[1] C. J. H. Wright, *Ethics*, p. 201.

status in Canaan was just like that of the resident foreigners who lived in their midst. They belonged, and they had a certain measure of protection, but at the end of the day they did not possess it. Ownership of land was, and is, an essential component in economic activity as well as in providing a family with its identity and the basis of its security. If a book such as Leviticus, which aims to set out what it means to be holy, had omitted to address this issue, it would have been deficient in a crucial area. The demands of holiness embrace our economic decisions as much as our church activities.

1. The sabbath year (25:1–7)

The chapter begins with a discussion of the sabbath year rather than the Jubilee year. Every seventh year *the land is to have a year of sabbath rest* (4) that is as sacred as the weekly Sabbath the Israelites themselves enjoyed, because it is named *a sabbath to the LORD* (3).[2] The normal activities of sowing, pruning, tending and reaping were to be set aside for a year and people were to live on whatever the uncultivated fields yielded during that time. There were to be no loopholes: strict observance of this sabbath was required by all who lived in Israel. Israelite householders could not get round it by arranging for others to till the land on their behalf.

The sabbath year effectively meant that it would be two years before a proper harvest could be reaped again. The harvest of the sixth year would have to sustain them not only then but during the seventh and eighth years as well.[3] That was an awful lot to ask of it. How would they cope? Would the food supply be sufficient, or run out? Did it not make more sense to exploit the earth's resources rather than wasting them for a year? Why risk relying on God when human effort could solve the problem?

The sabbath year served a number of purposes, as becomes clear later in the chapter. It prevented Israel from raping the land and turning it into an arid dustbowl. It allowed the land to replenish itself naturally.[4] It also

---

[2] The sabbath year is also mentioned in Exod. 23:10–11 and Deut. 15:1–16; in the latter it is associated with the cancelling of loans owed by fellow Israelites.

[3] The matter was more difficult at the Jubilee because that required two successive fallow years. See v. 20.

[4] Levine, pp. 170, 272, points to the horticultural advantages underlying this regulation. It would prevent the build-up of alkalines, sodium and calcium in the soil, especially where it had been irrigated. Modern methods of farming have introduced different techniques for replenishing the soil.

provided the people with a year of rest and space to accomplish other things. But it served deeper purposes as well. The land belonged to God, and it was his right to determine its use as he chose (23). He rested on the seventh day of creation and longs for his earth to enjoy the same privilege. Since the people belonged to God no less than the land, he promised that he would care for them. The question was whether they would show that they trusted him by obeying this apparently nonsensical command. The promise was harder to believe when it was a Jubilee – the sabbath year of sabbath years. But in reference to that year, God promised,

> I will send you such a blessing in the sixth year that the land will yield enough for three years. While you plant during the eighth year, you will eat from the old crop and will continue to eat from it until the harvest of the ninth year comes in.
> (21–22)

Would they take him at his word?

Two issues arise from this law for Christians today. First, as God's people we should care for the environment. Our own lifestyles should reflect our belief that this is God's earth, that Jesus Christ is Lord over it (Col. 1:15–17) and that therefore we should do all within our power to use its resources wisely, not for short-term, selfish gain but in such a way that they can be renewed healthily for the benefit of those who follow us. We should also be among the most ardent supporters of those who advocate care for the environment.

Second, the law challenges us, as it did Israel, to question where our real trust lies. Does our security genuinely rest in the ability of the living God to provide for us in the future, or does it lie in the pension schemes, the insurance policies and the bricks and mortar we accumulate? Richard Foster observed that 'because we lack a divine Centre our need for security has led us to an insane attachment to things'.[5] Describing what he considers a psychotic lust for possessions in Western society, he points out how we have revised our language to reduce our guilt about our consumerist lifestyles. 'Covetousness we call ambition. Hoarding we call prudence. Greed we call industry.'[6] How would we fare, I wonder, if the

---

[5] Richard Foster, *Celebration of Discipline* (London: Hodder & Stoughton, 1980), p. 70.

[6] Ibid., p. 71.

Lord said to us that we were to take a sabbatical year, not once in a lifetime, but as a regular spiritual discipline to free us from our dependence on things?

2. The Jubilee year (25:8–55)

a. The initial announcement (25:8–13)

After seven sabbath years a special year was to be observed. The Jubilee fell every fifty years and extended the fallow of the forty-ninth year for a further period.[7] It started with the blowing of the trumpet on the Day of Atonement *to proclaim liberty throughout the land to all its inhabitants* (10). The year began on the day of fresh beginnings, when the whole nation had just received forgiveness for their sin. The entire year was to be characterized by the twin ideas of liberty and return. Freedom from labour and freedom from debt were to go hand in hand with restoring broken family ties and repossessing lost family property. The hope of returning to one's roots at the Jubilee would sustain many who had fallen on hard times.

b. The initial implications (25:14–22)

Two implications are immediately explored. The first is the implication of the year for property rights and values. Verses 14–17 explain that the price to be paid for any property between Jubilees depends on how distant the next Jubilee is. The further away it is, the higher the price to be paid. The nearer it is, the lower the price to be paid. This is because in the Jubilee all property that has changed hands since the last one is returned to its original owners. Purchasing property was like purchasing a lease, rather than a freehold, and therefore its value was calculated on a descending scale according to how near the redemption date was. With this system in place there was no room for property speculation.

The system was not a matter of political convenience but the inevitable outworking of a number of key spiritual principles. All property was ultimately owned by God (23) and no-one could ever treat it as a personal possession. In reality, people only ever occupied it by God's gracious permission for a period, be that period long or short. Then there was the

---

[7] There has been some discussion of whether the Jubilee occurred in the fiftieth year, coincided with the forty-ninth year, or was a special shortened year that lasted only forty-nine days, rather like our 29 February every leap year. See Wenham, p. 319.

principle of community solidarity. The command *Do not take advantage of each other* occurs twice in this short paragraph (14, 17). Neighbours who had fallen on hard times and had to sell their land in order to survive were not to be exploited by others. Debt could easily undermine the social foundations of Israel and their respect for one another as equals.[8] These regulations were designed to ensure that this did not happen. A third spiritual principle lay in the respect felt for the family and the clan. Family land was passed from generation to generation and was held almost as a 'divine right'.[9] At the Jubilee, property was returned to those who had disposed of it, so that the family and clan structure of Israel could be sustained intact. All this leads to the other great principle lying behind these regulations. They are designed to prevent the rich getting richer at the expense of the poor, who thus get poorer. Jubilee sets a limit on greed.

The second implication addressed is the question, already referred to, of how people were to sustain themselves without engaging in agricultural activity during the Jubilee. The normal cycle of sabbath years meant that there would be no humanly produced harvest every seventh year, and the harvest of the previous year would have to stretch to two. When a Jubilee year was added to the end of the seventh sabbath year, the previous harvest would have to cover three years. Verses 18–22 recognize the fears this would provoke. But God promises to send them sufficient for their needs (22). The bumper crops of that year would last them through until they could reap the harvest again in the ninth year. Here was, as mentioned above, a test of how far Israel would trust her covenant God.

c. The theological foundation (25:23–24)

The theological foundation on which all these provisions were built was explained earlier in the chapter. God owned all the land but let his people lease it under certain conditions. It was never to be used as a pawn in the game of economic one-upmanship. This legislation endorses the legitimacy of the private ownership of property, especially when it is invested in the family. Although there is a recognition that some land is in common ownership (see e.g. v. 34), this is the exception rather than the norm. As Robert North points out, while socialism says that none

---

[8] Hartley, p. 424.

[9] C. J. H. Wright uses the term in *God's People*, p. 119. His work shows how inextricably property rights and family structure were bound together.

shall own property, the message of Leviticus is that none shall lose property.[10] So, when bankruptcy threatened, ways of redemption had to be found.

d. Steps to Jubilee (25:25–55)[11]

The Jubilee was a method of last resort for releasing those who had fallen into financial trouble. Debt was seen as a major evil, both debilitating and dehumanizing for those who suffered it. Everything had to be done to overcome it as soon as possible. So none need wait for the fiftieth year if they could extricate themselves in the meantime. But Jubilee meant that at least once in a lifetime freedom could be acquired, even if all other means of achieving it had failed. The remaining verses of chapter 25 set out the steps that might be taken before the Jubilee year dawned. But woven into these instructions is a consideration of three special cases, namely that of a *house in a walled city* (29–31), that of the Levites (32–34) and that of non-native slaves (44–46). We shall explore the main path first and return to the bypaths afterwards.

The main path is marked by the phrase *If one of your fellow Israelites becomes poor* (25, 35, 39, 47). The path begins gently, outlining the steps that can be taken in the case of a minor debt that can easily be redeemed, and then climbs with increasing difficulty until it reaches its high point with the words *Even if someone is not redeemed in any of these ways, they and their children are to be released in the Year of Jubilee* (54).

i. Step 1 (25:25–28)

If for any reason Israelites fell into debt, their first recourse was to *sell some of their property* (25). If the property was sold on the 'open market' then ideally it would be bought by *their nearest relative*[12] as soon as possible, on the basis that land should be kept within the family if at all feasible. If that proved impossible, and the debtors' own fortunes improved so that they were in a position to redeem it themselves, they were entitled to do so at any stage. There was, however, to be no haggling over the price. The value of the property was to be fixed by the number of years that still remained before the Jubilee. If all else failed, it would return to them then.

---

[10] North, p. 175.

[11] The following section follows C. J. H. Wright, *God's People*, pp. 119–125, and *Ethics*, pp. 203–206.

[12] The nearest relative is the *gō'ēl*, the kinsman-redeemer, as illustrated by the story of Ruth.

ii. Step 2 (25:35–38)

If the situation got worse and the selling of property did not resolve it, then it was the obligation of the nearest relatives to support debtors by hiring them as labourers and by loaning money to pay off the debt, interest-free. On no account should a relative exploit a kinsman's misfortune for profit.

iii. Step 3 (25:39–46)

In extreme situations poor people might even *sell themselves* to their relatives (39). But if they did so, the relatives who hired them had to understand that there were several conditions attached. They were to treat their fellow family members not as slaves but as hired labourers, the implication of which was not so much that they should be paid as that they should be treated with respect.[13] They could not be sold on to other owners. They were not to be treated ruthlessly – literally, 'with backbreaking labour'.[14] And the arrangement lasted only until the Jubilee, when the whole of the poor Israelite's family was to be restored to freedom. The redeemer could not claim ownership of any children born while a poor father was in his service. These instructions emphasize again the strong ties of kinship and remind the one who came to the rescue not to exploit his brother's vulnerability. The rescuer was to *fear . . . God* (43). Remembering that God sees all would encourage people to resist the temptations of power and make them realize that they would never get away with abusing their role.[15]

The main thrust of these verses is underlined by the contrasting treatment of *slaves* from *the nations around you* (44). They could be purchased and treated like other property and could be passed on as an inheritance to their children. But an Israelite was never to enslave an Israelite. To do so would make nonsense of the covenant that made them all equally *servants* of God (42).

iv. Step 4 (25:47–53)

In the event that a poor Israelite sold himself, not to a family member, but to a rich *foreigner or to a member of the foreigner's clan* (47), the poor person never forfeited his right of redemption (48). Two routes to freedom

---

[13] Hartley, p. 441.

[14] Levine, p. 179. Such labour would, of course, remind them of the slavery in Egypt from which they had been delivered.

[15] Levine, p. 173.

might be followed. First, a close relative, not necessarily a brother, would be encouraged to buy the rich man out (49), or second, if the slave's own circumstances changed, he could redeem himself (49). Again, the tariff that set the redemption price was calculated according to the period remaining before the next Jubilee and was not a matter for negotiation.

v. Step 5 (25:54–55)

If all else failed, the *Year of Jubilee* would herald liberation. In fact, the Jubilee provision was wider even than this. It not only restored property that was in the hands of aliens or temporary residents, but restored all property to its original owners, even if it was still in the clan and had been redeemed by close relatives. The Jubilee was the 'override'[16] factor that, when it came, leapfrogged over all other solutions to poverty.

e. The exceptions (25:29–34, 44–46)

The Jubilee regulations applied to traditional family land in rural areas, not to houses in *a walled city* (29–31). In this case a house could be purchased back up to a year after it had been sold, but not thereafter, and was *not to be returned in the Jubilee.*

The case of the Levites (32–34) is more problematic than it seems, but need not detain us here.[17] This is the first mention of *the Levites* in Leviticus.[18] The Levites had no sacrificial duties, but seem to have served as assistants in the tabernacle, although their status is not altogether clear.[19] They had distinguished themselves at the time of the golden-calf incident and were blessed by God as a result (Exod. 32:26–29). Originally the Levites held no property (Deut. 10:9; 18:1), but lived in forty-eight towns that were allocated, together with the pasture land surrounding them, for their use (Num. 35:1–8; Josh. 21:1–45). Wenham correctly takes the meaning of these verses in a straightforward manner.[20] In contrast to town houses owned by others, any town house the Levites owned could

---

[16] C. J. H. Wright, *God's People*, p. 123.

[17] For a discussion of the problem see Budd, pp. 352–353, and Milgrom, *Leviticus 23 – 27*, pp. 2202–2203.

[18] In Hebrew the book is known by its opening words, 'And he called'. The name 'Leviticus' became attached to it because the Septuagint entitled it 'Relating to the Levites'. Harrison, p. 13, remarks that the title is not altogether inappropriate, since even though the book contains instructions for (the Aaronic) priests, and the Levites are mentioned only here, 'the Hebrew priesthood was essentially levitical in character (cf. Heb. 7:11)'.

[19] Deut. 17:9, 18; 18:1 suggest that they were considered priests.

[20] Wenham, p. 321.

be redeemed at any time up to the Jubilee, and not simply during the first year. And when the Jubilee came, again in contrast to other town houses, any property they had mortgaged was to be returned to them. If this did not happen, the Levites would end up homeless. The land surrounding the towns, however, must never be sold, as it was *their permanent possession* (34).

The third exception (44–46), already mentioned above, relates to the ownership of slaves rather than to the ownership of land. It was acceptable to own slaves provided that they belonged to other nations or came from those who had taken up temporary residence among the Israelite community. Doing so turned these people into property, as if they were land, and therefore meant that they could be inherited by children like any other property.

3. More than theory?

The idea of Jubilee 'is probably the most radical social and economic idea in all the Bible'.[21] Its effect was to rule out speculation and prevent economic exploitation. It enshrined in law the cessation of land abuse, the cancellation of debts, the restitution of land to its original owners, the repair of the family and the termination of slavery. Its proclamation of liberty and its policies of justice have, like the exodus, fired the imaginations and inspired the hopes of many subsequent movements of liberation. But was it ever put into practice in Israel?

Robert North in his seminal study of the Jubilee concludes that 'there is an absolute silence in the later books of the Bible regarding the theory and practice of the jubilee'.[22] At most there is a hint of it in Isaiah 37:30,[23] but there is no clear statement that it was practised in Israel. Absence of evidence, however, is never evidence of absence. There are many things, in both Testaments, which are never said explicitly to have been performed which we know full well were undertaken. Some aspects of the Jubilee are reflected in Nehemiah 5 and Jeremiah 32:6–15 and 34:8–10, as well as in the moving story of the kinsman-redeemer in Ruth. But these are not the full version, and the release of slaves perhaps owes more to Exodus 21:1–8

---

[21] Hartley, p. 265.

[22] North, p. 36.

[23] C. J. H. Wright, *God's People*, p. 126 n. 9, thinks this may refer to a double year of fallow enforced by foreign invasion rather than voluntarily undertaken in obedience to God's command.

and Deuteronomy 15:12–18 than to the Jubilee legislation of Leviticus. The prophets condemned the acquisition of land by the rich and the royal.[24] But perhaps they would not have needed to do so if the Jubilee concept had been taken seriously in Israel.

So, was it only an ideal and never a reality? Walter Brueggemann objects to the question because it is too often asked with self-serving intent, implying that it was unworkable and utterly unpractical, and thereby gives people an excuse to abdicate responsibility for their destructive economic policies. He responds to the question by saying, 'What I judge to be important about this text is that Israel, through this provision, asserted it [the Jubilee], hoped it.' It gave Israel 'its fundamental identity' as a nation committed to freedom, and set before them a vision which, even if it is still to be implemented, established a goal to which they should aspire.[25]

4. The continuing application

Whether Israel ever put the legislation into practice or not, the principles enshrined in the Jubilee have continuing significance for many aspects of our Christian lives. John Bright claims it to be 'normative ethics' that speaks with eternal relevance to the Christian.[26]

a. Jubilee calls us to promote social justice

The Jubilee makes it unmistakably clear that God champions the cause of the poor and the destitute. He not only sympathizes with their plight but provides Israel with a practical way of rescuing them from it. He requires his people to show compassion to all, however poor, and never to take advantage of those who are financially vulnerable. He is opposed to a brother's reducing another brother to slavery. He forbids the ruthless management of slaves and employees. He refuses to countenance indifference to the needs of a family member. He sets his face against the concentration of property in the hands of a few. He sets a limit on the rich getting richer and the poor getting poorer. He oversees all business transactions, and watches to see if they show evidence that he is feared, or whether property tycoons think of themselves as unaccountable to

---

[24] E.g. 1 Kgs 21:1–29; Isa. 5:8; Amos 5:11; 8:5; Mic. 2:2.

[25] Brueggemann, *Finally*, p. 102.

[26] John Bright, *The Authority of the Old Testament* (Grand Rapids, MI: Baker, 1975), p. 153.

anyone beyond themselves. He counters the belief that debts can never be forgiven. He contests the selfish exploitation of both land and people.

b. Jubilee calls us to practise authentic worship

Leviticus 25 is a political document and serves as a manifesto of social and economic policies. But it is also an intensely spiritual document. God's fingerprints are all over it. He speaks (1), he cares (17, 36, 43), he provides (21), he owns (23), he rules (55) and he gives hope (54–55). Three times the Israelites are warned to fear him (17, 36, 43) by submitting to his will with respect and reverence. God was to be worshipped in the financial sector as well as in the sanctuary. Unless mercy was shown in one's business life, all the sacrifices offered in the tabernacle or the temple would prove futile (Hos. 6:6). God is to be honoured in every area of life.

This cry was taken up by Isaiah, who denounced the empty worship of the people of his day because, while they were pretending to seek God in the temple, they were oppressing the poor in the marketplace:

> Is not this the kind of fasting I have chosen:
> to loose the chains of injustice
>   and untie the cords of the yoke,
> to set the oppressed free
>   and break every yoke?
> (Isa. 58:6)

'All worship', as Robert North contends, 'is animated by charity which in one act reaches God and neighbour; all worship gains in effectiveness by the widest possible distribution of economic wealth.'[27]

c. Jubilee calls us to pursue merciful living

Some have viewed the Jubilee as a complete paradigm for personal spirituality.[28] The heart of this perspective on personal spirituality lies in the call to exercise mercy in our dealings with one another. To do so will prove profoundly countercultural, for our society is based on people

---

[27] North, p. 231.

[28] See Maria Harris, *Proclaim Jubilee: A Spirituality for the Twenty-First Century* (Louisville, KY: Westminster John Knox, 1996). She identifies five 'traditions' from the core of Jubilee teaching: fallow land, forgiveness, freedom, justice and jubilation. See also Ross Kinsler and Gloria Kinsler, *The Biblical Jubilee and the Struggle for Life* (Maryknoll, NY: Orbis Books, 1999).

receiving what they deserve and gaining what they have worked for, and on people getting their own back. Astonishingly, there is no discussion in Leviticus 25 about the causes of poverty. Perhaps some who fell into debt deserved to do so because of laziness, folly or incompetence. Perhaps for others the misfortune was no fault of their own. But no distinction is made between them, no inquiry into the cause is conducted. Whether the poor were deserving or undeserving, the Jubilee was for them, and their family and fellow citizens were called upon to exercise mercy, to release, to forgive.

In an equally astonishing way Jesus spoke of God as being 'kind to the ungrateful and wicked', on the basis of which he instructed his disciples to 'be merciful, just as your Father is merciful' (Luke 6:35–36). James took up the same call to be merciful and echoed both the Jubilee and Jesus when he wrote, 'Speak and act as those who are going to be judged by the law that gives freedom, because judgement without mercy will be shown to anyone who has not been merciful. Mercy triumphs over judgement' (Jas 2:12–13).

d. Jubilee calls us to possess unwavering hope

The prospect of Jubilee kept hope alive when debtors may have been tempted to despair. Jubilee became a metaphor for future hope, for the dawning of a day of the Lord's favour, when the blind would see, the deaf hear, the lame walk and the dumb speak (Isa. 35:5–6). It serves us still as an image of a future salvation when the restoration of all creation will take place (Rom. 8:18–21; 1 Cor. 15:24–28; Col. 1:20). Its forward thrust encourages us to look ahead rather than to look around at the experiences that cause us discouragement and doubt, and to persevere in hope (Rom. 5:3–5). The day of liberation was originally proclaimed by the blowing of a ram's horn, just as our day of liberation will be announced by the sounding of another trumpet: 'the Lord himself will come down from heaven, with a loud command, with the voice of the archangel and with the trumpet call of God' (1 Thess. 4:16; see also Matt. 24:31; 1 Cor. 15:52).

e. Jesus is Jubilee[29]

Several of these threads come together in Jesus. His 'Nazareth Manifesto' (Luke 4:16–21), in which he claimed that he had come to fulfil the prophecy

---

[29] For the background discussion see C. J. H. Wright, *Ethics*, pp. 205–206, and especially John Howard Yoder, *The Politics of Jesus* (Grand Rapids, MI: Eerdmans, 1972), pp. 34–40, 64–77.

of Isaiah 61:1–2, puts him firmly in the centre of the trajectory that began in the Jubilee legislation of Leviticus 25.[30] Isaiah 61 reverberates with the images of Jubilee. The anointed one would 'proclaim the year of the LORD's favour', which meant that good news would be brought to the poor, the broken-hearted would be comforted, and those held in prison would be set free. Jesus says that with his arrival that day had come.

Throughout his ministry he gave evidence to justify his claim. People were set free from a multitude of diseases, disabilities, demons, defilements, debts and sins. Mercy and forgiveness flowed freely and justice was at work for the benefit of the poor. He did not inaugurate a national restructuring of economic life. He inaugurated a greater Jubilee in which people of all nations were (and are) set free from the stronger forces that enslaved them and the deeper debts that they owed.

The Jubilee is a model of God's relationship with his world. In it the sovereign God takes an initiative to deal with the realities of an unjust and sin-riddled society. He shows special compassion to the weak and vulnerable members of the community. He calls his people to obey his word and have faith in his providence. He also calls them to reproduce his mercy and justice in their dealings with one another. He gives us the opportunity for new beginnings in the present, while drawing out from us a hope in the future.

Jubilee speaks about:

1. our relation to the environment: the need for rest and renewal;
2. our mission in the world: the need for liberty and justice;
3. our worship in the church: the need for authenticity and charity;
4. our relations in the family: the need for compassion and support;
5. our growth in the Spirit: the need for mercy and forgiveness;
6. our faith in the Saviour: the need to trust Jesus; and
7. our hope in the future: the need to look forward to his coming again.

---

[30] Joel Green rightly argues that the Jubilee is the backdrop for Jesus' ministry rather than controlling it, and that there is no need to think of Jesus immediately implementing it. See his *The Gospel of Luke*, NICNT (Grand Rapids, MI: Eerdmans, 1997), p. 212 n. 33.

Leviticus 26:1–46

22. God's word about future prosperity

Natan Sharansky, an Israeli politician, was imprisoned for several years by the Soviet regime. After his release he commented that each day of his imprisonment started with the choice of saying either 'yes' or 'no' to the KGB.

> From morning to night you think about the essence of life – the difference between light and dark, good and evil. You are enriched by the answers that you find. Compared with that the choices when you are free in the Western World are a little shallow and boring. What shoes shall I buy? Where shall I go on vacation?[1]

As the Holiness Code draws to a close it confronts the children of Israel – and us – with a stark choice. The choice God's people have to make has to do with the essence of life, with light and dark, with good and evil, with future prosperity or future ruin. As the rest of the Bible says, obeying God will bring reward; disobeying God will bring nothing but trouble and disaster.

Leviticus 26 differs from the chapters that have gone before.[2] The characteristic legal and ritual formulations are left behind and their place is taken by the language of 'blessing' and 'cursing'. The language and the

---

[1] *Sunday Times*, 17 July 1988.

[2] Milgrom, *Leviticus 23 – 27*, p. 2274, argues that Lev. 26 is a continuous unit with Lev. 25, because Lev. 26 includes no introductory formula, both speak of deliverance from Egypt, both have an interest in the sabbatical year, and they share the single theme that disobedience to God's commands will lead inexorably to exile. These are astute observations, but even so, the formulation of Lev. 26 seems to make it a section separate from what has gone before.

structure of the chapter, which parallel those of Deuteronomy 27 – 28, conform to the way in which treaties in the Ancient Near East would have been concluded.[3] Once the stipulations of the covenant had been set out by the sovereign party, the agreement would be concluded with a statement of the benefits of keeping the covenant and the perils of ignoring it. In adopting this approach, God is saying to the Israelites that the world is not capricious, nor are their futures unpredictable. The world runs, and their futures will unfold, on lines that can be anticipated, because he, the sovereign Lord of all and the saving God of Israel, is faithful to his word.

In a discussion of the theology of blessing and cursing, Mary Evans[4] has laid a number of important foundations that need to be borne in mind if we are to understand this chapter aright. She explains that the blessings and curses are to be read in reference to the covenant people collectively, rather than applied to individuals; that they are not intended to imply an iron law of consequences; and that the material expression given to blessings and curses is expressive of something deeper, namely the people's relationship with God. She writes:

> To be part of God's covenant people, to belong to God, is to be blessed.
> To be out of relationship with God is to be cursed. The curses are equally
> presented in materialistic terms (as were the blessings), but it does not
> appear that they were ever intended to be applied in a mechanistic way,
> with a one-to-one relationship to individual lawbreaking. They are there
> to show the Israelites that God must be taken seriously, that turning
> away from God's will for them will have devastating consequences, that
> being 'outside Yahweh' is a terrible state, to be avoided at all costs. But
> just as the blessing in fact rests on God's promise and is not portrayed
> as a reward for keeping the law, so the curse is not, strictly speaking,
> a punishment for not keeping the law, but a description of the
> consequences of being outside of God's blessing.[5]

This is the first chapter since chapter 11 not to begin with the words 'The LORD said . . .' Instead, the opening verses link the chapter with what

---

[3] The treaty structure is even more evident in Deut. 28, which is the counterpart of Lev. 26.

[4] Mary Evans, '"A Plague on Both Your Houses": Cursing and Blessing Reviewed', *Vox Evangelica* 24 (1994), pp. 77–89.

[5] Ibid., pp. 81–82.

has gone before, highlight a couple of issues as representative of others, and then lead into promises and warnings about the future. Through it all God is speaking and using not 'mere words' but 'performative language', that is, language that does something, that activates and accomplishes what is said. So, when blessings are pronounced, blessing follows. But equally, when curses are pronounced, the curse will inevitably follow. The chapter falls easily into three sections. Verses 3–13 speak of the blessings that will accompany obedience. Verses 14–39 describe the curses that will accompany disobedience. Verses 40–45 concern the restoration that will accompany confession of sin. The section concludes with a reminder that his claim on them lies in the fact that he delivered them from Egypt. A final verse brings the Holiness Code, containing *the regulations that the* LORD *established at Mount Sinai between himself and the Israelites through Moses* (46), to a conclusion.

1. 'If you follow . . .': the blessings of obedience (26:3–13)

There are a number of ways of grouping the blessings after the introductory headline of verse 3. Wenham says there are three groups (4–5, 6–10, 11–13),[6] Hartley finds four (4–5, 6–8, 9–10, 11–13),[7] and Milgrom, among others, identifies five (4–5, 6, 7–8, 9–10, 11–12).[8] Though a little fragmentary, the advantage of this scheme is that it complements the five groups of curses that are evident in the next section. For this reason, we shall follow the fivefold scheme.

a. The blessing of plenty (26:4–5)

The most basic human need is the need for food. In the hot climates of the Middle East the provision of food could not always be counted on because water – the basic element needed to produce food – could not be guaranteed. Two seasons of rain were required. Heavy rain was needed in the autumn to water the freshly planted soil, and lighter rain needed in the early spring to bring the crops to full harvest. God promises that if they obey his covenant, he *will send . . . rain in its season, and the ground*

---

6 Wenham, p. 329.

7 Hartley, p. 457.

8 Milgrom, *Leviticus 23 – 27*, pp. 2286–2288.

will yield its crops and the trees their fruit. Verse 5 gives a picture of the abundance that would result. The harvests would be so bountiful that the reaping of one crop would be followed by the planting of another without interruption.

b. The blessing of peace (26:6)

The next promise is that of *peace in the land.* Our use of the word 'peace' usually conjures up a very shallow understanding in comparison with the deep harmony that the biblical word conveys. Here the focus is on security in the land. The peace that is promised will lead people to feel so protected by God that they can sleep without worrying about any threats arising within their boundaries. They will enjoy safety from any harm, whether harm from strife in the community or danger from the wild beasts that still roamed the land. Furthermore, God promises that *the sword will not pass through your country,* which implies that Israel's borders would be secure and that raiding parties would not be able to destroy their abundant harvests.

c. The blessing of victory (26:7–8)

From internal threats, God now turns to external threats and promises that, in return for their obedience, they will know victory against their enemies. This was a necessary promise for the fragile, fledgling state of Israel as they entered the Promised Land. Surrounded by hostile nations, and the object of hatred by displaced peoples, they would regularly come under attack and be drawn into war. But God promises that they will triumph over their enemies. The dramatic nature both of the odds against them and of the astonishing nature of their victories is captured in the image of a mere handful of soldiers chasing off a hundred, and a hundred despatching ten thousand. Under David's and Solomon's reigns, in particular, Israel would enjoy the fulfilment of this promise beyond all that they could have imagined (2 Sam. 5:1 – 1 Kgs 10:29).

d. The blessing of prosperity (26:9–10)

A further sign of prosperity is now mentioned as the reward of obedience. God promises, *I will . . . make you fruitful and increase your numbers.* High fertility rates combined with low infant mortality would lead to large families and a strong nation as a sign of God's favour and of his continuing commitment to his plan of creation. This echoes the promise God made to Abraham when he said he would greatly increase his numbers and make him the father of many nations, which was also a promise made in the context of cementing a covenant agreement (Gen. 17:1–8).

The growth in population, however, could cause Israel some apprehension. With so many mouths to feed, would the food supply be sufficient? To quieten this fear God repeats his promise of verse 5 and even amplifies what he pledged there. The harvests would be so abundant that *you will still be eating last year's harvest when you will have to move it out to make room for the new.* It could even be, as Milgrom suggests, that the intention of verse 10 is to stand as something of a contrast to verse 5. In verse 5, 'the abundance is natural; here, however, in prospect of the teeming population, the abundance is supernatural'.[9]

e. The blessing of presence (26:11–13)

The ultimate blessing was found in the presence of God among them. Though the tabernacle would be his residence, he would not confine himself to it, as if under some self-imposed divine house arrest, but would walk freely among them. He had secured their freedom so that he could enjoy their company and take pride in their relationship. Moreover, he would want to show them off as a great example to other nations of what a people who enjoyed his favour could be like. Given that this was his plan, they need not lack self-respect just because they had once been slaves in Egypt. They were to reject the victim mentality that imprisons so many people in their past. A failure to break free from the cringing mentality instilled in Egypt would reveal that they lacked gratitude for what God had done and had no faith in his continuing love for them and his power to protect them. God had healed the stoop caused by their bearing heavy loads in Egypt.[10] So now they were to walk among the nations of the world *with heads held high.*

All the other blessings were as nothing compared with the blessing of walking in companionship with God. In Augustine's words,

God will be the source of every satisfaction, more than any heart can rightly crave, more than life and health, food and wealth, glory and honour, peace and every good work – so that God, as St Paul said,

---

[9] Milgrom, *Leviticus 23 – 27*, pp. 2298–2299.

[10] Hartley, p. 265.

'may be all in all'. He will be the consummation of all our desiring – the object of our unending visions, of our unlessening love, of our unwearying praise.[11]

2. 'If you will not listen . . .': the curses of disobedience (26:14–39)

'It is very easy', Gordon Wenham writes, 'to take the blessing of rain, peace, and even God's presence for granted. It is salutary to be reminded in detail of what life is like when his providential gifts are removed.'[12] That is what the curses, which are twice as long as the blessings,[13] do. Like the plagues of Egypt,[14] they are listed in order of increasing severity, and warn Israel to get off the path of disobedience immediately, well before it takes them to its inevitable destination in exile and destruction. The five-stage curse begins with the measured phrase *if you will not listen* (14). But this is followed by phrases of increasing urgency: *If after all this you will not listen . . .* (18), *If you remain hostile . . .* (21), *If in spite of these things . . .* (23), until the axe falls and the final curse is pronounced in verse 27.

While some might see this as God wielding 'the big stick' with a view to frightening his people into obedience, it is actually nothing of the sort. It is, in reality, a measure of the way in which God treats his people as grown-up, responsible moral agents. He compliments them by refusing to hide anything from them and, unlike many a cheap salesman who tries to secure a deal by hiding the penalty clauses in a contract, he lays everything out on the table from the start.

The first step towards disaster, it should be noted, was to refuse to listen to the voice of God. Moses had continually spoken the words of God. The children of Israel were distinguished from other nations in that they had received the oracles of God and had covenanted to live by them. To be the people of God meant that they were people of the word of God. These revelations of God's will were more than sufficient as they sought to build healthy community life and to live personally with wisdom. Their refusal to listen was the fundamental error from which all other difficulties flowed.

---

[11] Augustine, *City of God* 22.30, cited in Lienhard, p. 204.

[12] Wenham, p. 330.

[13] This conforms to the pattern of other legal treaties of the time.

[14] Noth, p. 197. The correspondence is far from exact.

a. The curse of defeat (26:14–17)

When Israel first refuses to listen to God, he sets in train some disciplinary steps with a view to capturing their attention and rekindling their obedience. His discipline would be seen in their defeat on one or more of three fronts. They would be defeated in the battle for health, as disease of some sort afflicted them, as it had done a number of times during their sojourn in the wilderness (e.g. Num. 16:41–50; 21:4–9; 25:1–9). They would be defeated in the battle for food, as harvests they had grown would be reaped and enjoyed by other nations. They would be defeated in the battle for freedom, as they fought and lost wars against enemy powers and were forced to surrender their liberty and be ruled over by others. Each time, the unhappy events would be limited in duration and designed to turn them back to God.

b. The curse of drought (26:18–20)

If the initial step of corrective discipline did not have the desired effect, God would increase the severity of his discipline.[15] The statement that he would punish them *seven times over* is not intended to lead people to calculate the harshness of the punishment mathematically, but is symbolic of a significant increase in severity, 'a definite number for an indefinite increase in the severity of judgment'.[16] By sending a drought and making their fields rock-hard, God ensures that they would not secure a harvest, no matter how much backbreaking effort they put into their farming. Their pride would thus be directly challenged, and it was to be hoped that this would result in their acquiring a new humility before God.

c. The curse of wild beasts (26:21–22)

The first two curses have undone the first blessing. The third curse undoes the second blessing. Having promised them peace in the land, including security from 'wild beasts' (6), if they obeyed, God now, in the face of continuing hostility from his people to his word, withdraws his blessing and permits *wild animals* to roam among them with devastating consequences. Children would be seized by them and dragged off and killed. Domestic animals would be maimed and destroyed. And the nation would be drastically reduced in number. Early in Elisha's ministry, forty-two youths were

---

[15] The Heb. word *yāsar* in vv. 18 and 28, usually translated 'to punish', means 'to discipline'. See Deut. 8:5.
[16] Kaiser, p. 1180.

savaged by bears after they had scorned his prophetic office. This tragic episode illustrates this curse being put into effect (2 Kgs 2:23–25).

d. The curse of devastation (26:23–26)

Further refusal to accept God's correction leads to his more active involvement in the exercise of discipline. To this point the curses may be seen as the outworking of natural circumstances, in that 'the food-producing, life-sustaining infrastructure of creation' had been withdrawn.[17] But now God himself steps in to express personal hostility towards his errant people. The fourth curse describes the people cowering behind the walls of their cities under siege from their enemies. God has withdrawn his protection from them and leaves them to face the consequences of their disobedience. So they experience, without relief, the usual dire effects of living under a prolonged siege; namely, plague and famine. This curse reverses the fourth blessing.

e. The curse of total destruction (26:27–39)

The final curse is the worst of all and is invoked only when the others have failed in their mission of redemptive correction. Its goal is still restoration rather than retribution. But when God's patience finally runs out and his 'rage collides with Israel's stubborn pride',[18] total destruction follows. People would be destroyed, not only by the enemy, but even by their own parents, who are forced to commit cannibalism in order that they themselves might survive (29).[19] Idol shrines would be destroyed. Lifeless bodies would be piled up where once they sold their souls to foreign gods.[20] Civilization would be destroyed as cities and sanctuaries were razed to the ground. The land would be wasted and the people scattered. In this tragic way, the sabbath rest that the people had refused to grant their land in defiance of God's command would at last be achieved *and the land will have the rest it did not have during the sabbaths they lived in it* (35).

A further paragraph (36–39) follows the fortunes of the population after the destruction of their land and quickly pulls the rug out from under the feet of any who see hope in the remnant who survived. The survivors will

---

[17] The phrase and idea are those of Brueggemann, *Theology*, p. 540.

[18] Bellinger, p. 158.

[19] 2 Kgs 6:28–29; Jer. 19:9; Lam. 2:20; 4:10; and Ezek. 5:10 report the fulfilment of these words.

[20] Levine, p. 188, writes: 'This is a deeply ironic statement: The Israelite warriors and citizenry will be slain at the very altars and cult centres where they offended God by their worship of foreign gods and idols.'

be so terrified that *the sound of a wind-blown leaf will put them to flight* (36). They will have no inner resources left to enable them to stand up to any enemy, let alone any military equipment. All they would be capable of doing was running away and hiding. Their demeanour would be the opposite of the 'heads held high' (13) that characterized those who knew the blessing of God. The net result would be that those who survived the demise of their nation would *perish among the nations* and *waste away* in foreign lands (38–39). Because of sin, Israel would be no more.

Herein lies at least part of the answer to those who ask, 'Why does God allow suffering?'[21] God had sent clear warnings that certain behaviour would reap certain consequences. But tragically, Israel heeded neither these warnings nor those of the later prophets. They pushed God into ratcheting up his curse until the time came when, patience exhausted, the ultimate curse of destruction fell and the threat became a reality. Any discipline that had taken place until then had been a light practice run. The actuality was far worse. Jerusalem was destroyed and its temple razed in 587 BC. The land was scorched and its remaining people taken captive in 582 BC. Those who were not deported were scattered, and the nation ceased to exist (2 Chr. 36:15–21). For a generation or more Israel experienced the long, dark night of the exile. God's word (this time his word of judgment rather than of grace) had again proved true.

3. 'If you confess . . .': the possibility of restoration (26:40–46)

But the curse is not God's final word. No matter how disloyal Israel may prove, they are still God's covenant people and he promises them that he will never renege on his covenant. *I will remember my covenant with Jacob and my covenant with Isaac and my covenant with Abraham, and I will remember the land* (42). Exile would give the land its sabbath rest, while exacting payment from Israel for the debt of sin. But beyond the time of exile there lay the hope of restoration, because God is incurably gracious.

Restoration does not come cheaply. The seriousness of the people's sin has to be confessed if restoration is to be experienced. They are called upon to acknowledge that their wrongdoing was 'treachery' (NRSV), because they had committed treason against their sovereign God, and it

---

[21] Knight, p. 164.

had arisen, not as a result of unintended negligence or accidental drift, but from deeply entrenched attitudes of *hostility* towards him (40). The mention of *uncircumcised hearts* (41) invites them to see that their action has, in effect, foolishly put them outside the covenant (the sign of which was circumcision) and made them no different from other nations, who were excluded from its privileges. God's grace longed to restore them, but that did not mean he could wink at sin as if it were of no consequence. The only way back lay through the path of self-humbling, on which they would re-evaluate what they thought of themselves and of God. They had to return to being servants of God rather than expecting God to serve them. They would have to enthrone God again as their sovereign and depose themselves, so they no longer acted as their own sovereign authority. Furthermore, they would accept his discipline as justly deserved rather than seeking to be excused it, realizing that their sin had to be paid for.

But God's covenant word would triumph. He would not go back on his promise and ultimately could not condemn to complete destruction the people whom he had elected to be his own and delivered in awesome power from slavery (44). Mercy would indeed triumph over judgment (Jas 2:13).

God's final word is always a word of promise, grace and hope. In recording the final days of Israel, the Chronicler recounts that 'God gave them all into the hands of Nebuchadnezzar' (2 Chr. 36:17). There we might think the story would end. But God has not finished yet, and the Chronicler, too, ends on a note of hope. His final words were not about Nebuchadnezzar, king of Babylon, who took people into captivity, but about Cyrus, king of Persia, who freed people from captivity and let the people go up to Jerusalem once again to build another temple for the Lord their God, the God of heaven (2 Chr. 36:23). Similarly, Amos, having for eight chapters pronounced the message of God's judgment, ends on a note of hope. The final episode Amos envisages in the story of God's people is not that of the dreadful day of the Lord, when the sun would go down at noon and the earth be darkened in broad daylight (Amos 8:9), but the day when 'David's fallen shelter' would be repaired and its ruins rebuilt and the blessings of abundant harvests restored (Amos 9:11–15). The closing words of the Old Testament follow suit. After condemning Israel for their indifference to God and warning that none would endure the day of his coming (Mal. 3:2), Malachi's final words are words of grace. He looks to the day beyond the day of punishment, when 'the sun of righteousness will rise with healing in its rays' (Mal. 4:2). God is indeed a God of restoration, and therein lies the hope for many a person who has sinned grievously in his or her past life. New beginnings are always possible where there is genuine repentance.

4. 'If my people . . .' today

The table of blessings and curses needs to be applied with care. It neither promises us automatic material blessings in return for our obedience to God, nor gives us a weapon to wield against those who live in disobedience to God's word. It does, however, have some timeless truths to teach.

The central message is that there is blessing in walking in harmony with God, and danger in alienating ourselves from God – a message that remains as true as ever.

The concept that God works in the ordinary affairs of nations to bring about his blessing or to exercise his judgment also remains as true as ever. The measure of peace and prosperity, or of ill fortune and hardship, that a people experiences may be *some* indication of that. He is no distant God, storing up judgment to be dispensed only in the future. Romans 1:18–32 declares that his judgment is already at work in the world.

The blessing of God, Jesus taught, is experienced by the poor in spirit, those who mourn, who are meek, who hunger and thirst for righteousness, who are merciful, who are pure in heart, who are peacemakers and who are persecuted because of righteousness (Matt. 5:3–12). The greatest blessings we experience, as Paul reminds us, are spiritual and are found in the enjoyment of our relationship with him (Eph. 1:3).

The curses of God cannot be experienced by those who are members of the new covenant, because Christ has already borne the curse in his body on the cross, removing it once and for all from those who have faith in him (Gal. 3:10–13).

The discipline of God, however, may still be experienced by his people in real, even tangible, ways. This discipline is a sign, not of his ultimate wrath, or of his indifference, but of his love. It is designed as a corrective measure to bring his people back to the right paths. We are foolish to make light of it or to lose heart when he rebukes us (Heb. 12:4–12). His discipline always calls us to renewed humility and repentance.

The curses of God remain terrifying for those who persistently walk in hostility to God. Among those whom Jesus cursed were people who were rich, well fed, happy and popular in the present age, as a result of their disobedience to God (Luke 6:24–26). He also cursed the zealous, spiritual leaders who were hypocritical blind guides, and who put stumbling blocks in people's way rather than helping them to know their God (Matt. 23:1–39).

The curses of God are real and are actively being played out in our world today in a multitude of ways. Romans 1:18–32 gives us insight into how 'the wrath of God is being revealed from heaven against all the godlessness and wickedness of people, who suppress the truth by their wickedness'.

The curses of God are not for us to inflict, but for him: '"It is mine to avenge; I will repay," says the Lord' (Rom. 12:19, quoting Deut. 32:35).

The heart of God still lies in restoration. In Christ, his final word is still a word of the second chance, a word of new beginnings. He still longs to restore, even those who have fallen woefully and experienced the darkness of a long alienation from him. Just as he brought Israel out of Egypt and later out of exile, so he still sets free people who are oppressed, giving them their own personal experience of the exodus and restoring them to his favour. He longs for his people to walk in his world with their 'heads held high' (13).

The word of God is a covenant word and he will never forget his promises.

F. The manual of dedication: enamoured of God's grace (27:1–34)

Leviticus 27:1–34

23. God's word about consecration

The final chapter of Leviticus comes as something of a surprise. After reaching the moral and spiritual heights of the Holiness Code, we may think this chapter is an anticlimax. It seems about as inspiring as a tax table. The previous chapter appears to bring the whole of Leviticus to a fitting conclusion, so why, we may ask, is this chapter necessary? The language that was characteristic of the Holiness Code is absent here, leading most to believe that this chapter had an independent existence and is not part of the code. All these factors combine to persuade many specialists that this chapter was a later addition to the book.[1]

However, while many speak of it as an appendix,[2] the chapter is not to be devalued, nor is its message to be considered a second-rate afterthought.[3] In fact, the chapter brings the book of Leviticus full circle and returns readers to the place where they started.[4] The book began with a discussion of voluntary offerings: the burnt, grain and peace offerings. Only then did it turn to a discussion of the compulsory offerings. From then on, the book gave attention to those things that were required of Israel, with only the occasional glance at offerings or actions that were not obligatory. But this final chapter returns to a consideration of the

---

[1] Budd, p. 378; Noth, p. 203. See the discussion in Milgrom, *Leviticus 23 – 27*, pp. 2407–2409.

[2] Noth, p. 12; Levine, p. 192.

[3] Hartley, p. 482, and Demarest, p. 278, both see Lev. 27 as the obverse of Lev. 26. In the former chapter the Lord pledges himself to his people, and in the latter his people pledge themselves to him. Clearly there are associations between the two chapters, but the difference in style between them is such that they do not seem to be intended as partners. Explanations that treat Lev. 27 as a conclusion to the whole book seem more natural.

[4] Balentine, p. 212.

property and persons that Israelites might volunteer to the Lord as an expression of faith and gratitude.

Andrew Bonar understood the importance of this as a way of bringing the book to a close. 'The connection of this concluding chapter with all the preceding', he wrote, 'has been considered a difficulty with many. But most obviously the connection is one of *feeling*.'[5] The preceding chapters have expressed God's heart and will for his people. This chapter is about the people expressing their devotion to him, freely and fully, beyond the call of duty or the minutiae of required obedience. Lovers delight in giving gifts, and do not feel constrained to limit them to the predictable occasions of birthdays and anniversaries. Love motivates them to give spontaneously and extravagantly. Since God has set out the good news of his law for Israel, would God's people not want to stand back with adoration and gratitude, and ask, 'What shall I return to the LORD for all his goodness to me?'[6] Nothing less than total consecration gives an adequate reply to that question.

1. The provision God makes (27:1–25)

One expression of consecration was for worshippers to *dedicate* something they owned to the Lord, so that it would be placed at his disposal and used in his service. This done, it might in practice prove more beneficial if a monetary value could be placed on the offering and its redemption price, rather than the offering itself, be given to the priests. The main section of the chapter sets out the provision God makes for redeeming property that has been vowed in this way to God.

a. The dedication of persons (27:2–8)

Hannah's consecration of Samuel is a prime example of such a dedication (1 Sam. 1:1–28). In gratitude for the Lord's hearing her prayer, Hannah made over her son to serve in the temple under Eli's direction. The language used is reminiscent of the language of slavery. By this act, in other words, the dedicated person becomes a slave of God.[7] But, however genuine the intent, it would not always have proved practical for people

---

[5] Bonar, p. 493.

[6] Ps. 116:12; Bonar, p. 494.

[7] Wenham, p. 338.

who had been dedicated to God literally to go and serve alongside the priests – the temple could get overcrowded. So arrangements were made for their value to be calculated and the money presented to the priests instead. The values are shown in Table 3.

Ages 1 month – 5 years
Male   5 shekels[8]
Female   3 shekels

Ages 5 – 20
Male   20 shekels
Female   10 shekels

Ages 20 – 60[9]
Male   50 shekels
Female   30 shekels

Age 60+
Male   15 shekels
Female   10 shekels

In setting out the table in this form, the two factors that affect the calculation of value are immediately apparent: first the person's age and second the person's gender. The first indicates that the value is calculated according to the productive capability of the person who has been dedicated, especially in regard to his or her ability to undertake heavy labour. People who are in that phase of life where they have reached their full working capacity are valued more highly than those who have yet to do so, or those whose strength and energy are on the wane.

The same principle explains the differentiation between genders. The differentiation says nothing about the intrinsic worth of a man in contrast to a woman. It reflects what they are perceived to be able to contribute to a society whose economy is essentially manual.[10] The evidence of this lies in the fact that a woman in the prime of life is priced more highly than a man in any of the other age groups. Rather than denigrating women, the values, which vary between 50% and 66% of the value of men, show that 'they must have been considered an indispensable and powerful element

---

[8] Five shekels is the redemption price for a firstborn male, Num. 18:15–16.

[9] Twenty was the age of conscription in Israel, Num. 1:3.

[10] Budd, p. 381; Levine, p. 193; Wegner, p. 43.

in the Israelite labour force'.[11] This interpretation of the difference also fits with the wider context. In other respects, women were valued just as highly as men, and in one case even more so. A woman could both offer a votive offering and be the subject of one just like a man. And Harris, somewhat lightly, points out that while brides had to be purchased, bridegrooms came free. But this said nothing about the respective value of each.[12]

The valuations given are high. According to Walter Kaiser, the average person would earn only one shekel a month. The cheapest redemption price, therefore, was set at three months' wages, and the dearest at over four years'. The tariff would discourage flippant vows, and perhaps that was its intent.

These high prices also lead to one other feature of this provision that deserves comment. It is a voluntary offering, and so, as with the other voluntary offerings, God is concerned that even people who could not afford *to pay the specified amount* should not be prevented from making it (8). Their attitude of heart proved acceptable even if the size of their bank balance, as it were, did not prove adequate. The priests were therefore charged with negotiating a price that the worshipper could afford. The offerings of the poor were just as welcome as the offerings of the rich, and God devised a way for that message to be conveyed to Israel.

b. The dedication of animals (27:9–13)

If the dedication took the form of an animal, there were several factors to be borne in mind. First (9–10), worshippers were discouraged from vowing in haste and repenting at leisure. They could not vow a perfect specimen and then later, thinking that they had been too rash, decide to offer one of lesser quality. This loophole was easily closed by the simple regulation that those attempting to do so would forfeit both the original animal they had vowed and the substitute they had hoped to fob off on the priest.

Since this is a voluntary offering, an animal that was *ceremonially unclean* was on this occasion acceptable (11). Unclean animals could not be offered in sacrifice,[13] but they could prove useful in other jobs around the tabernacle by, for example, providing transport or hauling goods.

---

[11] Milgrom, *Leviticus 23 – 27*, p. 2372.

[12] Harris, p. 650.

[13] The words *one that is not acceptable as an offering to the LORD* in the NIV should probably be translated 'they may not be offered as a sacrifice' (11), underlining the contrast already implicit between clean and unclean animals. See Milgrom, *Leviticus 23 – 27*, p. 2378.

In many cases, however, the offerer would have intended to contribute the money rather than the beast, and where this was so, the priest would assess its value and the offerer would be required to pay that and add *a fifth . . . to its value* as a redemption price (13). The priests acted as umpires, and there was no appeal against an umpire's decision.

c. The dedication of houses (27:14–15)

Given the Jubilee laws (25:25–34), the reference to houses must relate to the dedication of town houses rather than to ancestral family property. If these were given to the priests, the priests were at liberty to use them as they wished. If the offerer desired at some later time to redeem the house, the same procedures were put in place as for animals: the priest would fix the value, to which 20% would be added as the redemption price.

d. The dedication of land (27:16–25)

Two types of land dedication are envisaged. First there are fields that are inherited as part of the family's land (16–20), and then fields that have been bought in addition to these (22–25). The regulations show an awareness of the Jubilee laws, and it must be assumed that, even where they are not mentioned, the rights and responsibilities spelt out there take precedence over what is said here. Yet it was possible for owners to dedicate their fields to the Lord so that the priests would benefit from their produce. The value of the land is determined by how much seed it takes to sow[14] and by how many years are left before the next Jubilee, unless it was dedicated in the Jubilee year itself, in which case the value was fixed. Should owners wish to take them back and use them for themselves, they were required to pay the price fixed by the priests plus the additional 20%. They were strongly encouraged to do so, because if they had not done so by the next Jubilee the fields would pass permanently from their possession into the hands of the priesthood and become holy land – *like a field devoted to the Lord* (21). These laws were designed to prevent sharp practice by landowners at the expense of the tabernacle.

It was also possible to dedicate land that had been purchased, as opposed to inherited, but in this case the land would revert to the original owner at the Jubilee. If such land was dedicated, it was to be redeemed

---

[14] There is a debate as to whether *the amount of seed required for it* refers to what is sown or to what is harvested from it. See Hartley, pp. 482–483, and Wenham, p. 340.

immediately – *the owner must pay its value on that day* (23) – at the price set by the priests, who would take into consideration the time remaining before the Jubilee; but no surcharge is added.

The values were calculated in sanctuary currency (25). The shekel essentially referred to a unit of weight rather than to minted currency and weighed 11.5 grams (just under half an ounce) of silver.

2. The restrictions God imposes (27:26–34)

A tremor of apprehension about the offering of voluntary gifts to God runs right through this chapter. The currents of religious emotion flow strongly, and it is all too easy to be swept away by them in the midst of a ceremony or celebration, and rashly promise what is later regretted. Genuine emotion can also give way too easily to ostentatious display. In an effort to prove our devotion to God (and perhaps even to convince ourselves of it), we can fall victim to the need for extravagant gestures.[15] Cool reflection may subsequently make us seek a way of delivering on our promises without paying the full costs involved. One route to bargain spirituality is to count a gift twice and give God what already belongs to him, in the pretence that it is really a new, voluntary gift. The second section of Leviticus 27 is designed to prevent such cut-price devotion. Three areas are mentioned where God already has rights.

a. Restrictions concerning the firstborn (27:26–27)

The firstborn of any human or domestic animal already belongs to God. But whereas firstborn sons must be redeemed when they are a month old at the cost of five shekels,[16] the firstborn of the flock or herd may not be redeemed in this way (Num. 18:17–19). They already belong to the Lord as of right, so it would be a sham to pretend they were being given to him as an act of voluntary devotion. The worshipper did not actually own them, and so could not give them. Unclean animals, however, fall into a different category. There is no requirement to present their firstborn to the Lord, and so they could be donated to the tabernacle and then redeemed. Such a gift would be an authentic act of devotion.

---

[15] Not all extravagant gestures are wrong. Some really do grasp the wonder of God's grace, as when the woman who had led a sinful life anointed the feet of Jesus with expensive perfume, Luke 7:36–50.

[16] Num. 18:15–16. See note 8 above.

b. Restrictions concerning devoted things (27:28–29)

The strongest form of vow was 'the devoted or proscribed thing'.[17] If something was proscribed it was either made over for exclusive use in the sanctuary for ever, or utterly destroyed. It could never be redeemed. The practice referred to in verse 29 is clear. There were a number of circumstances in which a person or community was put under 'the ban', such as when they worshipped other gods (Exod. 22:20; Deut. 13:12–18), or were the spoils of war (Josh. 7:1–22). The practice mentioned in verse 28, however, is a little unclear. It probably refers to someone swearing a solemn oath to proscribe property for the Lord's use – a non-Israelite slave is most likely meant.[18] If this is so, the restriction here is saying that such an offerer may not change his or her mind. Once something is 'devoted', it is proscribed and cannot be redeemed in the pretence that it was an additional, voluntary offering. What is proscribed already belongs to the Lord and cannot be counted as a gift twice.

c. Restrictions concerning the tithe (27:30–33)

The same is true of the tithing of grain and animals. The fuller regulations regarding the tithe are set out in Numbers 18:21–29[19] and Deuteronomy 14:22–29. Tithes seem to be mandatory offerings to the Lord, and since they are the Lord's due they could not be presented as if they were also a voluntary offering.

The question of which animals were to be part of the tithe was determined by having the animals pass *under the shepherd's rod*, and every tenth animal, regardless of its condition, was selected and set aside for the Lord. Strict enforcement of the procedure was enjoined so that owners did not fix the results with a view to keeping the best for themselves and giving the most feeble to the Lord. To ensure this did not happen, the same tactic as was mentioned in verses 10–11 was employed. Any farmer who tried to substitute a bad animal for a good one would forfeit both.

The tithe of grain or fruit, however, could be redeemed – presumably, though it is not specified here, at a price determined by the priests. To that price the 20% mark-up was to be added (31).

---

[17] Hartley, p. 484. 'To proscribe' is 'to embargo' or 'to restrict' or 'to place under an interdict'.

[18] See Levine, pp. 198–199.

[19] Num. 18 refers to this tithe being given to the Levites, who, in turn, tithed them to the priests.

3. The dedication God desires

From this final chapter two key issues emerge that are of relevance for God's people of any age.

a. Demonstrating devotion

The Israelites realized that they had much for which to thank God. He had brought them 'from slavery into freedom, from sorrow to joy, from mourning to festivity, from darkness to great light, and from bondage to redemption'.[20] Having done so, he remained their faithful covenant friend, who continued to forgive, guide, protect, provide for, prosper and rule over them and their families. For all this they wanted to express their gratitude. To do so adequately meant they felt the need to go beyond what was required by law and give offerings freely and from the heart. If they felt gratitude, how much more should we, who can see the full wonder of God's love for us in the cross of Jesus Christ? Religion should be a matter not of duty but of love. If we truly understand the cost and meaning of grace, the expression of our devotion will go far above and beyond anything we are told to do and may well involve extravagant gestures of giving. We shall seek, not to scrape by, gaining a mere pass mark in obedience, but to excel in zeal for the Lord. We shall not skimp on our giving, but contribute to the Lord's work generously, even sacrificially.

Yet, in expressing our devotion, we need to be wise. Well-intended vows made with enthusiasm in the heat of the moment during wonderfully intense periods of worship can return to haunt us. But, having made the promise to God, we dare not go back on our word. Qohelet, the teacher, in a passage that could be a commentary on Leviticus 27, warned of the trap into which we can easily fall:

> Guard your steps when you go to the house of God. Go near to listen rather than to offer the sacrifice of fools, who do not know that they do wrong.

> Do not be quick with your mouth,
>   do not be hasty in your heart
>   to utter anything before God.

---

[20] From the Passover liturgy. See Derek Tidball, *The Message of the Cross*, The Bible Speaks Today (Leicester: IVP, 2001), p. 63, for a fuller quotation and context.

God is in heaven
    and you are on earth,
    so let your words be few.
A dream comes when there are many cares,
    and many words mark the speech of a fool.

When you make a vow to God, do not delay to fulfil it. He has no
pleasure in fools; fulfil your vow. It is better not to make a vow than
to make one and not fulfil it. Do not let your mouth lead you into sin.
And do not protest to the temple messenger, 'My vow was a mistake.'
Why should God be angry at what you say and destroy the work of your
hands? Much dreaming and many words are meaningless. Therefore
fear God.
(Eccl. 5:1–7)

Few might have the courage blatantly to renege on their promises to
God. But many resort to more subtle strategies to soften their unpre-
meditated vows and avoid the full cost of their rash pledges. Leviticus 27
is devised to prevent God's people from doing this. Rules for redeeming
property are stated and prices set. Loopholes are closed and no-one is
permitted to save face by pretending to offer God as an extra what is
already his. As he is faithful to his words, so he expects his people to be
faithful to their promises, however costly, ill-considered or inconvenient.

It is perhaps for this reason that, while the custom of making vows is
not unknown in the New Testament, the practice is not advocated, while
the tragic incident of Ananias and Sapphira serves as a continuing
warning not to make promises to God lightly (Acts 5:1–11; see also 18:18;
21:23). What is advocated is, first, that no-one should offer a vow or a tithe
at the expense of observing the weightier matters of justice and compassion (Matt. 23:23–24), and, second, as we have seen before, that Christians
should always speak with unimpeachable integrity.[21] The best way to
express our consecration to the Lord is to commit ourselves to live every
day with compassion, to treat others justly and to walk in integrity.

This final chapter of Leviticus warns us that our devotion to God,
though welcome, must always be genuine. He will hold us to our vows of
consecration.

---

[21] 2 Cor. 1:17–20; Jas 5:12. See p. 60

b. Giving generously

The commitment to the greater values of justice, compassion and integrity does not absolve us from the responsibility of giving financially to the work of God. Leviticus 27 speaks of ways in which the Israelites gave beyond what was required in the compulsory sacrifices and supported the work of the priests through tithes and voluntary financial offerings.

The tithe was obligatory. Its origin is found in the 'tenth of everything' Abram gave to Melchizedek, king of Salem and priest of God Most High, as he returned from rescuing his nephew Lot and his possessions from captivity (Gen. 14:17–20). It was a sign of Abram's gratitude to God for Lot's deliverance, voluntarily, perhaps even spontaneously, given, and it resulted in blessing for Abram. The practice later became enshrined in the law so that, from the time of Moses onwards, people gave a tenth of their crops, their fruit and their animals to the Lord. It was the chief way in which the tabernacle and the work of the priests and the Levites were supported. At the end of the Old Testament era, the prophet Malachi affirmed that there was still a close connection between giving the tithe and receiving God's blessing. The failure to give would result in a failure to receive; the blessing of giving would lead to the blessing of receiving (Mal. 3:8–12).

Nowhere in the New Testament is tithing commanded. But, far from releasing us from the obligation, this only clears the ground for the New Testament to lay before Christians an even greater expectation with regard to giving to God's work.[22] The practice of tithing would have been assumed, at least in Jewish Christian circles. But the principles that inform distinctively Christian giving exceed it handsomely.

The principles are outlined by Paul in 1 Corinthians 16:1–3 and 2 Corinthians 8 and 9. The former makes clear that our giving should be regular ('On the first day of every week'), inclusive ('each one of you'), deliberate ('should set aside a sum of money'), proportional ('in keeping with your income')[23] and responsible ('saving it up'). In the rich teaching of the latter passage the following principles may be selected and briefly stated. Christian giving is not cold charity ('they gave themselves first of all to the Lord', 8:5). Christian giving is a demonstration of grace (the 'grace

---

[22] Gregory the Great (Homily 40) said: 'What is said by the law is less exacting than what is commanded by the Lord. The law prescribed the giving of a tithe, but our Redeemer ordered those who would follow the way of perfection to give up everything.' Quoted in Lienhard, p. 204.

[23] Note also the teaching of Jesus in Mark 12:41–44.

of giving', 8:7). Christian giving is modelled on Jesus ('you know the grace of our Lord Jesus Christ', 8:9). Christian giving takes account of what one has ('the gift is acceptable according to what one has', 8:12). Christian giving aims at meeting needs ('that there might be equality', 8:13). Christian giving requires responsible accountability ('We want to avoid any criticism of the way we administer this liberal gift', 8:20). Christian giving involves generosity ('whoever sows generously will also reap generously', 9:6). Christian giving involves a willing spirit ('not reluctantly or under compulsion, for God loves a cheerful giver', 9:7). Christian giving never leaves the Christian worse off ('You will be enriched in every way', 9:11). Finally, Christian giving results in thanksgiving to God ('your generosity will result in thanksgiving to God', 9:11).

In the light of such teaching, the tithe should probably be regarded as the minimum a Christian should give. With prayerful deliberation, arising from grateful hearts, and in a systematic rather than an erratic, emotionally driven manner, God's people should give over and above that, if they are able, knowing that 'God is able to bless you abundantly, so that in all things at all times, having all that you need, you will abound in every good work' (9:8).

Clearly Israel did not always reach the required standard. But when they understood the grace of God they gave willingly and liberally. Generous giving was often the first step towards the repair of the temple and the revival of true religion among them, as the stories of kings Joash and Josiah demonstrate (2 Chr. 24:8–14; 34:9–11). When God's people give, God blesses. Perhaps the greatest need of the church today is to grasp in fresh ways the wonder of God's grace. Then we too might 'excel in this grace of giving' (2 Cor. 8:7) and the work of God might be revived.

Leviticus cannot be said to end on a down note. In speaking of the consecration of the people to God it shows a people enamoured of his grace. Leviticus ends on a high note, testifying to a faith not of law but of grace, not of duty but of love, not of drudgery but of gratitude. Here was a people that had been set free to be holy.

The Bible Speaks Today:
Old Testament series

The Bible Speaks Today:
New Testament series

The Bible Speaks Today: Bible Themes series

The Message of the Living God
His glory, his people, his world
Peter Lewis

The Message of the Resurrection
Christ is risen!
Paul Beasley-Murray

The Message of the Cross
Wisdom unsearchable, love indestructible
Derek Tidball

The Message of Salvation
By God's grace, for God's glory
Philip Graham Ryken

The Message of Creation
Encountering the Lord of the universe
David Wilkinson

The Message of Heaven and Hell
Grace and destiny
Bruce Milne

The Message of Mission
The glory of Christ in all time and space
Howard Peskett and Vinoth Ramachandra

The Message of Prayer
Approaching the throne of grace
Tim Chester

The Message of the Trinity
Life in God
Brian Edgar

The Message of Evil and Suffering
Light into darkness
Peter Hicks

The Message of the Holy Spirit
The Spirit of encounter
Keith Warrington

The Message of Holiness
Restoring God's masterpiece
Derek Tidball

The Message of Sonship
At home in God's household
Trevor Burke

The Message of the Word of God
The glory of God made known
Tim Meadowcroft

The Message of Women
Creation, grace and gender
Derek and Dianne Tidball

The Message of the Church
Assemble the people before me
Chris Green

The Message of the Person of Christ
The Word made flesh
Robert Letham

The Message of Worship
Celebrating the glory of God in the whole of life
John Risbridger

The Message of Spiritual Warfare
The Lord is a warrior; the Lord is his name
Keith Ferdinando

The Message of Discipleship
Authentic followers of Jesus in today's world
Peter Morden

The Message of Love
The only thing that counts
Patrick Mitchel

The Message of Wisdom
Learning and living the way of the Lord
Daniel J. Estes